MATERIALISM AND
POLITICS

Cultural Inquiry

EDITED BY CHRISTOPH F. E. HOLZHEY
AND MANUELE GRAGNOLATI

The series 'Cultural Inquiry' is dedicated to exploring how diverse cultures can be brought into fruitful rather than pernicious confrontation. Taking culture in a deliberately broad sense that also includes different discourses and disciplines, it aims to open up spaces of inquiry, experimentation, and intervention. Its emphasis lies in critical reflection and in identifying and highlighting contemporary issues and concerns, even in publications with a historical orientation. Following a decidedly cross-disciplinary approach, it seeks to enact and provoke transfers among the humanities, the natural and social sciences, and the arts. The series includes a plurality of methodologies and approaches, binding them through the tension of mutual confrontation and negotiation rather than through homogenization or exclusion.

Christoph F. E. Holzhey is the Founding Director of the ICI Berlin Institute for Cultural Inquiry. Manuele Gragnolati is Professor of Italian Literature at the Sorbonne Université in Paris and Associate Director of the ICI Berlin.

MATERIALISM AND POLITICS

EDITED BY
BERNARDO BIANCHI
EMILIE FILION-DONATO
MARLON MIGUEL
AYŞE YUVA

ici BERLIN PRESS

ISBN (Paperback): 978-3-96558-018-3
ISBN (Hardcover): 978-3-96558-021-3
ISBN (PDF): 978-3-96558-019-0
ISBN (EPUB): 978-3-96558-020-6

Cultural Inquiry, 20
ISSN (Print): 2627-728X
ISSN (Online): 2627-731X

Bibliographical Information of the German National Library
The German National Library lists this publication in the Deutsche Nationalbibliografie
(German National Bibliography); detailed bibliographic information is available online at
http://dnb.d-nb.de.

In Europe, the paperback edition is printed by Lightning Source UK Ltd., Milton Keynes,
UK. See the final page for further details.

The digital edition can be downloaded freely at: https://doi.org/10.37050/ci-20.

This publication was made possible through generous financial support from the Alexander
von Humboldt Foundation.

ICI Berlin Press is an imprint of
ICI gemeinnütziges Institut für Cultural Inquiry Berlin GmbH
Christinenstr. 18/19, Haus 8
D-10119 Berlin
publishing@ici-berlin.org
www.ici-berlin.org

Marco Polo describes a bridge, stone by stone.

'But which is the stone that supports the bridge?' Kublai Khan asks.

'The bridge is not supported by one stone or another', Marco answers, 'but by the line of the arch that they form.'

Kublai Khan remains silent, reflecting. Then he adds: 'Why do you speak to me of the stones? It is only the arch that matters to me.'

Polo answers: 'Without stones there is no arch.'

Italo Calvino, *The Invisible Cities*

Contents

Abbreviations

The following abbreviations will be used in the footnotes for Spinoza's works, which are based on the Spinoza Series (Edinburgh University Press): *Ethics*, followed by the Roman numeral of the part, and Praef. (preface), Def. (definition), Exp. (explanation), Ax. (axiom), App. (appendix), DA # (Definitions of the Affects from part three), or the Arabic numeral of the proposition, and Schol. (scholium), Dem. (demonstration), Cor. (corollary), Lem. (lemma), Post. (postulate); *Theological-Political Treatise: TTP*, followed by the Roman numeral of the chapter and by the Arabic numeral of the paragraph according to Karl Hermann Bruder's edition; *Political Treatise: TP*, followed by the Roman numeral of the chapter and the Arabic numeral of the paragraph; *Letters: Ep.*, followed by the Roman numeral of the corresponding letter and the addressee of the letter between square brackets; *Treatise on the Emendation of the Intellect: TdIE*, followed by the Arabic numeral of the paragraph added by Bruder; *Metaphysical Thoughts: CM*; followed by the Roman numeral of the chapter. In all case, references are to *The Collected Works of Spinoza*, ed. and trans. by Edwin Curley, 2 vols (Princeton, NJ: Princeton University Press, 1985–2016), abbreviated as *CWS* I for volume I (1985) and *CWS* II for volume II (2016), and followed by the Arabic numeral of the page. When relevant, the authors will also refer to the standard critical edition of Spinoza's Latin works — *Spinoza opera*, ed. by Carl Gebhardt, 4 vols (Heidelberg: Winter, 1925) — followed by the Roman numeral of the volume and the Arabic numeral of the page.

For the works of Karl Marx and Friedrich Engels, *MEW* refers to *Marx-Engels-Werke*, 44 vols (Berlin: Dietz, 1956–2018) and *MECW* to *Marx & Engels Collected Works*, 50 vols (London: Lawrence and Wishart, 1975–2004). The *Werke* are for the most part available online at <http://www.mlwerke.de/me/me_mew.htm> [accessed 12 September 2020] and <https://marx-wirklich-studieren.net/marx-engels-werke-als-pdf-zum-download/> [accessed 1 November 2020].

Acknowledgments

We would like to thank the Alexander von Humboldt Foundation for their generous financial support, without which this book would not be possible. We thank the devoted editorial team from the ICI Berlin Press, Christoph Holzhey and Claudia Peppel, as well as our most diligent proofreader Lindsay Parkhowell, who revised all the texts included in this volume. We thank Baptiste Gasset for the translation of Chapter 3, Nicolas Allen for Chapter 4, and Ron Faust for Chapter 17.

We thank the ICI Berlin Institute for Cultural Inquiry, the Centre Marc Bloch (CMB), the Institute for Philosophy at the Free University of Berlin (FU Berlin), the Centre for Interdisciplinary Women's and Gender Studies (ZIFG) of the Technical University of Berlin (TU Berlin) for their institutional support, which allowed us to organize the conference *Materialism and Politics* in April 2019.

Finally, we warmly thank all those who have been with us in the discussions held at our informal colloquium Materialism and Politics in Berlin (2018–2020).

THE EDITORS

From 'Materialism' towards 'Materialities'

THE EDITORS

THE ACTUALITY OF MATERIALISM

What is the relevance of materialism for thinking politics? Throughout modernity, materialism has been associated with fatalism, naturalism, heresy, atheism, and linked to political ideas such as republicanism, democracy, and communism. In the nineteenth century, the field of confrontation in which materialism was engaged shifted beyond the theoretical and political dimensions to encompass the economic and the social as well. Materialism dethroned the conception of an abstract political subject and the centrality of state institutions in favour of a materialist critique centred on the materiality of social relations. However, the development of contemporary capitalism transformed the meaning of such a critique. The policies of neoliberal capitalism have sought to expand control beyond the state to regulate the materiality of social reproduction itself. Through multiple forms of expropriation, neoliberal policies have aimed at controlling the bodies and, more broadly, the materialities underlying the processes of capitalist domination.

This context has led to a reconsideration of the notion of 'matter', which is once more at the heart of the political arena — whether in the form of subject's bodies or of rivers and mountains endowed with legal personality. In this sense, materialism has regained influence at the centre of philosophical debates as the doctrine most suitable to embrace the various and at times dissonant, even contradictory, interpretations of matter and its activity.

Far from representing a unified discourse or trend, materialism has multiple definitions and uses. In the contemporary discursive field we can observe two main currents: on the one hand, what has recently been called 'New Materialism',[1] and on the other a '(post-)Marxist materialism' (or a renewed 'historical materialism', or 'dialectical materialism').[2] Although these two interpretations are not completely op-

---

1   See, in particular, the collective volumes edited by Diana Coole and Samantha Frost, *New Materialisms: Ontology, Agency, and Politics* (Durham, NC: Duke University Press, 2010) as well as by Rick Dolphijn and Iris van der Tuin, *New Materialism: Interviews & Cartographies* (Ann Arbor, MI: Open Humanities Press, 2012). They both offer a genealogy of the expression 'New Materialism', as well as an overview of its authors and internal debates. According to the editors of the latter, the term appeared in the second half of the 1990s and was first used by authors such Manuel DeLanda and Rosi Braidotti, themselves echoing themes developed by Gilles Deleuze and Félix Guattari, Donna Haraway, and Bruno Latour. Among the most prominent and representative publications of this trend, we could also mention Karen Barad's *Meeting the Universe Halfway: Quantum Physics and the Entanglement of Matter and Meaning* (Durham, NC: Duke University Press, 2007) and Jane Bennett's *Vibrant Matter: A Political Ecology of Things* (Durham, NC: Duke University Press, 2010).

2   The renewal of Marxism and Marxist-based materialism is surely an older movement and can be traced back to the end of the 1960s. It is a far less homogenous trend and in fact appears in several different modes. All of them address, however, the limits of traditional Marxism and acknowledge the need to redress it. It is strongly represented in France, for example, by Louis Althusser and his group of students (see *Reading Capital: The Complete Edition* (London: Verso, 2016)). Even if this collective volume has mostly privileged readings from this French tradition, the contemporary return to Marx and the notion of materialism can also be traced back to other trends, such as, first, the Frankfurt School — and the renewal of 'philosophical materialism', 'historical materialism', 'dialectical materialism', or even 'interdisciplinary materialism', through which the early writings by Max Horkheimer have tried to define the Institute for Social Research; second, Ernesto Laclau and Chantal Mouffe's 'discursive materialism' and the revision of 'historical materialism' understood as 'radical relationalism' (cf. Facundo Vega's contribution to this volume); third, Robert Kurz's further development of Marx's 'theory of value' and 'the general truth of the materialist thesis as it pertains to the process of human development as a whole' ('The Crisis of Exchange Value: Science as Productive Force; Productive Labour; and Capitalist Reproduction (1986)', in *Dossier: Marxism and the Critique of Value*, ed. by Neil Larsen, Mathias Nilges, Josh Robinson, and Nicholas Brown (=*Meditations: Journal of the Marxist Literary Group*, 27.1–2 (2013–14) <https://www.mediationsjournal.org/toc/27_1> [accessed: 15 November 2020]); fourth, Antonio Negri's engagement with the notion of materialism and the critique of the 'transcendental foundation of power'. Negri's work goes in the direction of a reappraisal of materialism's classic reductionism (including those of the 'dialectical materialism') towards what he calls a 'materialism of *praxis*' or a 'rigorous materialism' capable of maintaining 'the tension between actual determination and

posed, they do highlight different dimensions of what one understands by materialism and, above all, they employ different argumentative strategies. Proponents of New Materialism tend to return to physics to re-found an ontology that stresses the activity of things, thus expanding political agency far beyond the human realm and criticizing anthropocentric policies. On the other hand, (post-)Marxist proponents tend to revise and renew the Marxist tradition by addressing other forms of domination that were not traditionally taken into account, such as gender, race, colonialism, and ecological exploitation.

The aim of this book is not to propose a reconciliation or a synthesis of these different materialist tendencies, but to portray their great variety and even contradictions *without* excluding the possibility of an encounter between them. As the reader will notice in the organization of our sections, we have chosen some main areas of encounter or common ground among the many possible ones, including the actuality of Baruch Spinoza's materialism, the renewal of theories of the 'milieu', feminist theories on matter, and critical reappraisals of historical materialism.[3] Other encounters, such as the crossroads between materialism and ecology as well as with post- and de-colonial perspectives, are still engaged with, despite not being the main areas of focus of this volume (for example, in the contributions from Frieder Otto Wolf and Alex Demirović).

Regarding Spinoza's materialism, a consideration must be made. Historians of philosophy have clarified the restricted sense in which Spinoza can be said to be a 'materialist'. He never used the term 'materialism' (that was posterior to his work) and more readily writes 'extension' instead of 'matter'. In this sense, they have argued that one can say only that he is a materialist if one understands by materialism a 'principle of intelligibility of reality based on extension' (though extension cannot give a principle of intelligibility for the whole reality).[4] Since

---

constitutive project within the fullness of subjects' (*Time for Revolution* (London: Bloomsbury, 2013), p. 128).

3   Each part has an introduction: Stefan Hagemann for Part I, Marlene Kienberger and Bruno Pace for Part II, Alison Sperling for Part III, and Daniel Liu for Part IV. The starting point of this book is the conference *Materialism and Politics* held at the ICI Berlin and the Centre Marc Bloch in Berlin in April 2019, where each session was introduced by moderators, who agreed to once again introduce a part here.

4   Chantal Jaquet, *Les Expressions de la puissance d'agir chez Spinoza* (Paris: Publications de la Sorbonne, 2005) <https://doi.org/10.4000/books.psorbonne.127>, in particu-

the end of the seventeenth century, Spinoza's association with materialism was especially based on the identification of his philosophy with the critique of religion, in the form of either atheism or pantheism. This identification became central for some of his eminent readers such as Pierre Bayle, Denis Diderot, and Friedrich Heinrich Jacobi, as well as in the whole quarrel of pantheism. It seems that this critique of religion, which was so central, is nowadays relatively secondary amongst scholars in their analysis of Spinoza's materialism. Since Louis Althusser's *Lire le Capital*, from 1965, and Antonio Negri's *Savage Anomaly*, from 1981 — which mobilized Spinoza within Marxist perspectives in order to offer a non-Hegelian reading of Marx —, the interest in Spinozist thought has nonetheless continued, as its adoption by authors such as Étienne Balibar or Frédéric Lordon demonstrates. These uses are far from being able to be unified, but what Althusser and Negri still have in common is that they seek to establish a link between Marxist criticism, in a political perspective, and Spinozist ontology.[5] These uses are still important enough today for us to have dedicated a whole part of this volume to them and for a number of contributions to return, for example, to the importance, from a materialist perspective, of the concepts of 'immanence', 'multitude', and 'transindividual' in Spinoza's philosophy, as we will discuss later in the introduction. Here too, the post-Marxist field does not exhaust the question of the materialist legacy of Spinoza, and renewed references to Spinoza are also to be found in neo-materialist authors such as Jane Bennett,[6] who see in it a possible critique of an overly anthropocentric Marxist materialism through the notion of 'conatus' which applies to all beings and allows us to think of a non-inert matter.

The selective thematic focus of this volume reflects the fact that materialism cannot and should not be reduced to a single definition

---

lar pp. 211–15. See also André Tosel, *Du matérialisme, de Spinoza* (Paris: Kimé, 1994); Dimitris Vardoulakis, *Spinoza, the Epicurean — Authority and Utility in Materialism* (Edinburgh: Edinburgh University Press, 2020). Pascal Sévérac also returns to this point in his contribution to this volume and, more broadly, in his book *Qu'y a-t-il de matérialiste chez Spinoza?* (Paris: H Diffusion, 2020).

5   Florence Hulak analyses the difference between what she calls Althusser's structuralist and Negri's subjective Spinozism (cf. 'Spinoza après Marx, ou le problème de l'ontologie marxienne', *Revue de métaphysique et de morale*, 56.4 (2007), pp. 483–98).

6   Bennett, *Vibrant Matter*, p. x.

and theme. The fact that materialism has often — depending on the relevant period and its dominant schools of thought — been reduced to one thesis such as mechanism, fatalism (as discussed in Ayşe Yuva's contribution), or, in the Marxist variant, economism, is a problem in itself. These variegated reductions alert us to the fact that materialism needs to be approached in a non-reductionist way, or that such reductions must, in the final analysis, be explained in terms of their theoretical reasoning, practical goals, or historical basis. Materialism cannot be reduced to one single factor, scale, or explanatory model, whether it be atoms or the relations of production.[7] Many contributions in this volume (such as those by Chiara Bottici, Marianna Poyares, Émilie Filion-Donato, Christoph Holzhey, and Wolf) acknowledge and develop this necessarily pluralistic perspective.

Therefore, as a collective endeavour, this volume pursues the opening up of materialism towards a critical and non-reductionist form. This is not only a question of saying that there are a plurality of materialisms which are sometimes in competition, as was already the case in the nineteenth century between the scientist and Marxist materialist positions. Rather, the plurality of materialist approaches reflects the diversity of matter itself and of its conceptions, as well as the plurality of the political problems it raises. These problems are just as diverse as they are connected, for example through reflections on women's bodies, labour conditions, or the historical context of a theory. Not wanting to reduce these pluralities to a unity and to stress their historical, geographical and concrete situatedness, we chose to principally use the term 'materialities'.

---

7   Methodologically speaking, Althusser's concept of 'overdetermination' was useful to us. With it, he does not mean the reduction of all planes of reality other than economic reality to a pure phenomenon or reflection: on the contrary, he means to oppose the reduction of the dynamics of reality to a single simple contradiction, as the simplified Hegelianism of certain variants of Marxism might suggest. Cf. Louis Althusser, *For Marx*, trans. by Ben Brewster (London: Verso, 2005), p. 101 and subsequent pages. He therefore opposes the 'mechanist-fatalist temptation in the history of nineteenth-century Marxism' (ibid., p. 105). He refers to Engels on this point and quotes the letter to Josef Bloch of 21 September 1890, to conclude with 'the accumulation of effective determinations [...] on the ultimate determination by the economic' (ibid., p. 113), which is why he adopts the term 'overdetermination'.

AGENCY AND ACTIVITY

Materialism in this volume is fundamentally linked to the idea that matter is not inert but acts upon, and therefore changes, itself and its surroundings. However, the definition of both matter and activity cannot be set once and for all.

For a long time, materialist authors were accused of conceiving of human agency as entirely determined by material causes. According to the opponents of modern materialism, this determinism did not make it possible to fundamentally distinguish human agency from the movements of inanimate bodies, since both would be subjected, according to this paradigm, to the same physical laws. Marx, in turn, added a layer of complexity, stressing the primacy of the relations of production, which eventually gave rise to the accusation of economic fatalism. The question of whether human existence is doomed to determinism or even fatalism plagued materialism throughout history. Cornelia Möser's and Poyares's contributions challenge this classic problem by showing that determinism does not imply fatalism, which is understood as an extreme form of the submission of human activity to necessity, or even to destiny. In this way, it is precisely by pluralizing the modes of determination that materialism counters fatalism. In particular, in recent years, factors other than socioeconomic ones became central to materialist analysis through the understanding of the body. Catherine Perret's contribution to this volume, for example, proposes a way out of this apparent fatalism by suggesting a reconceptualization of social bonds beyond the logic of value. She addresses a certain tradition of critical theory that reifies what it tried to criticize and that as such ended up commodifying social bonds. This tradition, according to her, has overlooked that within the organization of labour, human bodies are not simply 'automatons', but through their techniques, always keep an inventive quality.

This is not the only way out of fatalism proposed in the volume. Stefano Visentin's, Ericka Itokazu's, and Holzhey's contributions reflect on the relationship between freedom, contingency, and necessity at the crossroads of politics and (meta)physics. By stressing the radical determinism of God's power in Spinoza's philosophy, Visentin underscores that it does not preclude political freedom, whereas Itokazu argues that such an argument does not suppress the experience of contingency in human life. Holzhey's contribution, in turn, challenges the distinction between determinism and fatalism. But he does not question the existence of a contingency which, according to him, lies at the point of transition between the realms of physics and action: political action is not founded on any ontology.

The question of fatalism and determinism introduces a reflection on the way human bodies act. This is an eminently political question which several contributions in this volume are engaged with. That is, they take on the task of redefining our understanding of human bodies and of matter in general, challenging our traditional view of them as non-inerts. In other words, bodies are not, according to these contributions, only passive receivers of movement coming from an external cause (which would possibly be spiritual), but have within themselves a principle of movement understood as 'force' or 'energy'. Following this problem, Bottici, who also re-reads Spinoza, proposes that women's bodies cannot be thought of as objects that are given once and for all — a claim which echoes Judith Butler's understanding of matter and the body[8] — and should rather be thought of as processes. She argues that distinct conceptions of gendered bodies can structure the socio-political reality differently.

This idea of 'processuality' and the non-inert nature of bodies leads to a rethinking of individuality, as well as to the very division between activity and passivity. Hence the reference in Filion-Donato's and Bottici's contributions to Gilbert Simondon's concept of 'transindividuality',[9] according to which an individual, in the broad sense, that is, a person, but also an object and a collectivity, does not exist as such outside of its encounters with other individuals. Here, again, this materialist conception is often inspired by Spinoza — Étienne Balibar

---

8   Judith Butler, *Bodies that Matter: On the Discursive Limits of 'Sex'*, Routledge Classics (Abingdon: Routledge, 2011), p. 7: 'In both the Latin and the Greek, matter (*materia* and *hyle*) is neither a simple, brute positivity or referent nor a blank surface or slate awaiting an external signification, but is always in some sense temporalized. This is true for Marx as well, when "matter" is understood as a principle of trans-formation, presuming and inducing a future. The matrix is an originating and formative principle which inaugurates and informs a development of some organism or object. Hence, for Aristotle, "matter is potentiality [*dynameos*], form actuality"'.

9   Gilbert Simondon, *L'Individu et sa genèse physico-biologique* (Paris: PUF, 1964), p. 31.

being one of the most prominent proponents of such an argument.[10] Accordingly, 'transindividual' desires and passions, rather than individuals, are the fundamental methodological elements to understand social relations.[11] In this vein, Mariana Gainza's contribution to this volume formulates a critique of the misuse of Spinoza's theory of the passions[12] and warns against the dangers of aligning Spinozist ethics with neoliberal imperatives and its submission to 'desires'.

However, while this transindividuality goes far beyond the sphere of the human, it highlights, more fundamentally, the political implications of relating human agency to the activity of matter. On this point, one can indeed observe a debate in the volume between the positions presented by the contributions of Möser and Poyares, on the one hand, and Filion-Donato's contribution, on the other.

The conception of social life as intra-active and co-constitutive is elaborated in the New Materialist viewpoints of the kind found in Filion-Donato's contribution. It can be said that while Marx underscored, by means of his materialist conception of history, that nature is active, insofar as it changes and is changed through human action, the New Materialists have insisted, through their focus on 'actants', on a conception of activity independent of human action.[13]

However, this broadening of the concept of 'activity', as Möser puts it, can blur the distinction between human agency and the 'efficiency of things'. As she writes, 'a substance does not choose to impact its environment the way a human can choose to go on strike'. Rethinking the activity of things, of matter, is not enough to challenge the organization of the world where women are dominated. Poyares via Susanne Lettow also warns us against the danger of transferring agency onto 'anonymous, meta-historical forces like matter or life'.[14] She re-

---

10 Étienne Balibar, *Spinoza politique. Le Transindividuel* (Paris: PUF, 2018), p. 199.

11 Following Frédéric Lordon, *Capitalisme, désir et servitude. Marx et Spinoza* (Paris: La Fabrique, 2010), Marx's analysis of domination under a capitalist mode of production can be supplemented with a Spinozist theory of passions, which can prove to be a way out of the economic fatalism alluded to above.

12 Lordon, *Capitalisme, Désir et Servitude*, p. 10.

13 Bruno Latour, *Reassembling the Social: An Introduction to Actor-Network-Theory*, Clarendon Lectures in Management Studies (Oxford: Oxford University Press, 2005).

14 Susanne Lettow, 'Turning the Turn: New Materialism, Historical Materialism and Critical Theory', *Thesis Eleven*, 140.1 (2017), pp. 106–21 (p. 111) <https://doi.org/10.1177/0725513616683853>.

proaches some neo-materialist authors like Rosi Braidotti for assuming 'ontological parity between the vitality of atoms in their exchange of electrons and the vitality of social interactions, equating them under generic descriptions such as "agential assemblages"': for her, this may lead to the assertion that power relations and physical forces are 'ontologically analogous'.

Responding to this objection, Filion-Donato shows that these critiques are not entirely justified. In fact, it would be too hasty to say that New Materialism equates non-humans to humans in terms of agency. Though some New Materialists indeed attempt to widen the notion of the subject, it is essential to remember that not all argue that non-humans acquire subjectivity or agency — which is why they are called 'actants' and not 'agents'.[15] New Materialists would simply invite us to take the potency and effects of matter and objects upon humans seriously.

The notions of 'actants' and 'agents' highlight the existence of multiple scales of action and determination relevant for politics. It is not new that the scale of the state and that of the nation are judged insufficient, even mystifying, for materialist criticism. This can be shown through a broad comparison of different contributions to this volume. For example, Elena Vogman, analysing Nikolai Y. Marr's theory of language, proposes to go beyond the 'national' scale of language in favour of an analysis of social and class strata. In a different fashion, Bottici and Demirović criticize an idea of political action conceived through the sole macro-scale of the state. But, while Bottici suggests not to wait for the state's recognition, Demirović instead proposes not to wait for the state to pursue the common interest or the ability to exercise a common political goal. Facundo Vega, in his contribution, criticizes Ernesto Laclau for not appropriately considering the importance of the action of the 'many' and for (over)emphasizing, instead, the role of the

---

15   Latour writes in *Reassembling the Social* that 'ANT is not the empty claim that objects do things "instead" of human actors: it simply says that no science of the social can even begin if the question of who and what participates in the action is not first of all thoroughly explored, even though it might mean letting elements in which, for lack of a better term, we would call *non-humans*' (p. 72; emphasis in the original). He therefore prefers the term 'actant' to speak of the action or affordances of 'non-humans' and 'actor' when speaking specifically of human actants. Bennett also speaks of actants: 'an actant is a source of action that can be either human or nonhuman' (*Vibrant Matter*, p. 8).

leader's body, which unifies popular will, in the beginning of a process of emancipation. In Vega's view, this would restrain Laclau's previous materialist project.

Finally, this question of the scales of action allows us to grasp, in all its multiplicity and equivocity, the conventional materialist idea of an action of the 'milieu'. Marlon Miguel's contribution addresses the problem of the local scale of action through the politicization of education. He analyses the social re-education work with young delinquents undertaken by the Soviet pedagogue Anton Makarenko. Rather than a directive relationship between master and student, Miguel conceives of pedagogy as a materialist emancipative and local process entirely structured and mediated by a collectively constructed milieu.

NON-REDUCTIONIST MATERIALIST EPISTEMOLOGY AND THE
MULTIPLICITY OF CAUSES

The claim that no scale of activity can be reduced to another brings us to the consideration of a political gesture that is central to the present volume: a non-reductionist definition of materialism. The critique of reductionist materialism takes different forms in this volume, but what they have in common is the affirmation that the intelligibility of social existence and political life cannot be subordinated to an underlying given reality, be it in the form of a more fundamental level of existence or an ultimate purpose.

We find this perspective synthesized in Balibar's recovery of the idea of a 'materialism without matter', introduced in 1993 in his text *Marx's Philosophy*. By borrowing the concept from Friedrich H. Jacobi, Balibar identifies a kind of materialism in Marx that 'has nothing to do with a reference to *matter*'.[16] This expression, which is extensively analysed by Poyares (and referred to by Bernardo Bianchi), is implicitly present throughout the entire volume. In general, we argue

---

16   Étienne Balibar, *The Philosophy of Marx* (London: Verso, 1995), p. 23. His conceptualization is based on Marx's opening thesis on Feuerbach, and, therefore, on the distinction regarding the 'old materialism' from Marx's own attempt to redefine the concept of materialism: 'the chief defect of all previous materialism (that of Feuerbach included) is that things, reality, sensuousness are conceived only in the form of the object, or of contemplation, but not as sensuous human activity, practice, not subjectively'. See Karl Marx, 'Theses on Feuerbach', in *MECW* [*Marx & Engels Collected Works*, see abbreviations], v (1976), pp. 3–5 (p. 3).

that Marx's gesture has been much overlooked in the Marxist and even post-Marxist traditions, which have, in turn, given rise to forms of dogmatism responsible for reintroducing stadialist ideologies and teleology in socio-political analysis.[17] By contrast, Balibar's theoretical insights represent a red thread in this volume uniting analyses concerned with both the broader contemporary renewal of Marxist debate, as well as the reappraisal of the meaning of materialism in this tradition, which is addressed by the contributions from Vittorio Morfino, Poyares, Wolf, and Vega. In addition, the implicit or explicit engagement with the challenge of stadialist conceptions in the Marxist tradition is addressed by Miguel, Perret, Pascal Sévérac, and Vogman. Both dimensions are articulated in Bianchi's contribution, as he proposes to identify the development, in Marx, of a non-reductionist kind of materialism that refuses every form of stadialism, especially in view of the relationship between knowledge and political action.

Through its reference to practice, Marx's materialism entails the refusal of any unidirectional conception regarding the relationship between nature and human existence:[18] here matter is not a 'first

---

17   In our account, stadialist arguments amount to the parallel between the evolution of societies and that of individuals, whereby they progress through identical stages organized according to a linear upward movement, from an original infantile stage of indolence to the 'mature' stage of action and self-determination. In the history of Marxism, stadialist arguments were favoured in the Second International, largely due to Georgi V. Plekhanov, who argued that one must first fight for a bourgeois revolution so that a socialist revolution can take place in a further moment. After the influence of Stalin's *Dialectical and Historical Materialism*, published in 1938, this perspective became a dogma of Marxism-Leninism. In this perspective, all peoples must invariably go through five successive and linearly organized modes of production: primitive communism, slavery, feudalism, capitalism, and socialism. Stadialism has been largely criticized for imposing a model brought from the outside and for overlooking local circumstances, as well as for justifying domination on the basis of the claim of a 'lower', and therefore deficient, stage of evolution. Sévérac's contribution to this volume invites us to criticize, however, the very metaphor at the basis of stadialist arguments: the difference between the child and the adult. In taking precautions against the preconization of childhood as an absolute value, as if rational and emotional development had no value, Sévérac nevertheless proposes a positive interpretation of it, insofar as the child is a being that challenges us to reflect upon the ways their aptitudes can be increased (a task for which adulthood does not offer a model).

18   Ludwig Feuerbach's materialism instead implied a sort of idealism, insofar as it restated a series of dichotomies between passivity and activity, representation and subjectivity, and essence and existence. One can, therefore, understand Gérard Bensussan's argument of describing Feuerbachian philosophy as a 'translational thought'. See Gérard Bensussan, 'Feuerbach et le "Secret" de Spinoza', in *Spinoza au xixe siècle*, ed. by André Tosel, Pierre-François Moreau, and Jean Salem (Paris: Publications de la Sorbonne,

nature' that is employed as an *arche*. Still, it is also not a layer of reality subordinated to external principles — this argument echoes Visentin's usage of the Spinozist expression '*non defuit materia*'. Even though Marx, following Hobbes, states in the *Holy Family* that 'matter is the substratum of all changes going on in the world',[19] this understanding needs to be complemented by his other considerations, such as those expressed in the 'Theses on Feuerbach', stating that matter cannot be reduced to object or to subject; it cannot exist outside of processes in which it is modified and modifies things. For this very reason, Marx's philosophy entails a non-reductionist approach to materialism, which is to be understood as a non-contemplative materialism, leading to a 'materialist conception of history'.

Our understanding of a non-reductionist definition of materialism concerns not only a refusal of unidirectional explanations about the relationship between nature and human existence, but also the rejection of any explanation in terms of linear models of causality. In the sixth thesis *ad* Feuerbach, Marx claims: 'but the essence of man [...] is the *ensemble of the social relations*'.[20] This gesture points to a new direction concerning materialism, whereby the notion of the human is to be defined through practice, among which one can include 'tool-making',[21] as well as all human activity, which should be analysed at the collective scale rather than on the individual one. Both Perret and Vogman highlight this shift in their contributions. According to this view, toolmaking — and, more broadly, all transformation of nature by human action — should not be regarded as the outcome of the emergence of a highly developed brain, just as human activity is not the effect of the emergence of *homo sapiens*, but its cause. Socialized activity in the world is the basis of the process of 'hominization' — a thesis that resonates throughout this volume. In this thesis we can

---

2007), pp. 111–23 (p. 119) <https://doi.org/10.4000/books.psorbonne.158>. By this he meant that Feuerbach always intended to 'turn the predicate into the subject and thus as a subject into object and principle [...] in this way, we have the unconcealed, pure, and untarnished truth'. See Ludwig Feuerbach, 'Preliminary Theses on the Reform of Philosophy', in *The Fiery Brook* (London: Verso, 2012), pp. 153–73 (p. 154). Marx's materialism is not translational just as it is not reductionist.

19   Friedrich Engels and Karl Marx, *The Holy Family, or Critique of Critical Criticism*, in *MECW*, IV (1975), pp. 3–211 (p. 129).

20   Marx, 'Theses on Feuerbach', p. 4; emphasis added.

21   Karl Marx, *Capital*, 3 vols (London: Penguin, 1976), I, trans. by Ben Fowkes, p. 286.

observe yet another strong Spinozist characteristic: just as humanity should not be understood as prior to social action, the mind is not prior to the affects of the body.[22] In Spinoza, the process of singularization is inseparable from a process of composition and decomposition with other bodies, which is the basis of an understanding of history *sub durationis* and not under the perspective of time — an idea developed in Itokazu's contribution to this volume, where, in opposition to the concept of time, she associates 'duration' to singularization, therefore proposing a positive conception of finitude.

Therefore, our political understanding of materialism is inseparable from two features: a theory of causality that underscores the multiplicity of factors, and the refusal of any idea of origin or foundation.[23] While the latter feature is clearly posited by Althusser's writings from the 1980s, he developed the former in the 1960s.[24] In *The Underground Current of the Materialism of the Encounter*, Althusser introduces the concept of 'taking hold' (*prise*), which is a corollary of the concept of 'encounter'. 'Taking hold' here refers to the process of individuation (autonomization): to the mayonnaise that takes hold when it emulsifies or a SARS-CoV-2 which, coming from a different species such as a bat, infects and takes hold in a human body. This critique of the foundation of the late Althusser can be connected to his writings concerning 'structural causality', understood in opposition to linear causality, from

---

22   According to Spinoza, 'the Mind does not know itself, except insofar as it perceives the ideas of the affections of the Body'. See *Ethics* II, 23; *CWS* I, p. 468. This means that the mind is the ensemble of ideas stemming from the fortuitous encounters of one's body with external things, by means of which it is constantly affecting and being affected. See *Ethics* II, 28; *CWS* I, p. 470. The fact that these affections are not accidents external to us, but constitutive of our own bodies (and therefore of ourselves) has led Lorenzo Vinciguerra to the development of the concept of 'field of traceability'. See his *Spinoza et le signe. La Genèse de l'imagination* (Paris: Vrin, 2005), p. 118.

23   As Althusser asserts, 'the whole that results from the "taking hold" of the "encounter" does not precede the "taking-hold" of its elements, but follows it; for this reason, it might not have "taken hold", and, a *fortiori*, "the encounter might not have taken place"'. See Louis Althusser, 'The Underground Current of the Materialism of the Encounter', in *Philosophy of the Encounter: Later Writings, 1978–87*, ed. by François Matheron and Oliver Corpet, trans. by Geoffrey M. Goshgarian (London: Verso, 2006), pp. 163–207 (p. 197).

24   Although complementary, these two moments can be identified with two moments in the work of Althusser, as Morfino discusses in this volume. Morfino nevertheless identifies in the texts of the 1980s an eschatological tendency which is not to be confused with the materialist tendency, as 'it affirms communism as simple *parousia* to-come'.

the 1960s.[25] An effect is not merely assignable to a cause, as existing in itself, but to a cause *insofar as it is intertwined with other relations* that constitute the structure in which it is situated. In the political field, this problem brings Vega to reflect on Laclau's post-foundational definition of politics. According to him, Laclau remains too fascinated by 'the extraordinary', itself based on the Heideggerian ontological concept of 'political difference'. Instead, Vega rejects a theory that would re-new the mythical origins of emancipation and proposes to rethink the ordinary irruption of the 'many' in politics. This conception of the political is no longer conceived as a 'superstructure' but as an 'ontology of the social'. This perspective resonates with Mauricio Rocha's contri-bution. By underscoring the importance of Deleuze's discovery in the late 1960s of 'expression' as a decisive concept in Spinoza's philosophy, Rocha demonstrates how this finding allows Deleuze to develop a non-hierarchical conception of reality, which ultimately leads to the idea of 'plane of immanence' and to the valorization of politics in his work.

All in all, 'materialism without matter' does not mean the refusal of matter. It entails the rejection of a foundational ontology that would inevitably exhaust other ontological levels, including that of the polit-ical, that is, no level of reality can be totally reduced to another. In this vein, 'materialism without matter' implies an anti-reductionist analysis of the political, of the discourses, and even of philosophical activity.

MATERIALISM AND PHILOSOPHICAL DISCOURSE

This volume proposes that materialism should be understood in a broader sense to include discourse which, although incorporeal, relates to matter and acts upon bodies. A number of contributions to the volume (such as those from Bianchi, Demirović, Gainza, Perret, Sévérac, Wolf, and Yuva) address this relationship between materialism and the criticism, even subversion, of 'ideology', which is a concept that must also be problematized.

---

25   See Louis Althusser, 'On Genesis', in *History and Imperialism: Writings, 1963–1986*, ed. and trans. by Geoffrey M. Goshgarian (Cambridge: Polity, 2020), pp. 33–36 (p. 34). As an example, Althusser refers to the physical concept of 'causality of a field', which we propose to think in connection with Vinciguerra's concept of 'field of traceability' (see note number 22 above).

In 1970, Althusser rehabilitated the question of 'ideology' by indicating its centrality to political thought. According to the philosopher, if ideology represents an imaginary relation between individuals it nevertheless has a 'material existence'.[26] Ideology materializes itself in theories, apparatuses, and practices that can and should be the object of analysis. Althusser's gesture to read Marx against Marx and to 'open him up' was taken over by contemporary authors. Balibar, for example, in a text about both Althusser and Marx, characterizes the latter's materialism not as theoretical content or method but through 'the *fact* that Marx inscribed in theory itself the *limits*, and thus the *conditions*, imposed on its historical efficiency by the fact that theory consist of "ideas"'.[27] Balibar points towards the crucial idea of a 'finite theory' as developed in this volume by Wolf's contribution.

According to Michel Foucault, the Althusserian project concerning the question of 'ideology' remained too dematerialized, abstract, and intellectual, too 'state-centred'.[28] But despite his criticisms, it is precisely Foucault who, in a certain sense, developed an analysis of the materialities that constitute and modulate subjectivity. Furthermore, in *The Order of Discourse* he also introduced the idea of an 'incorporeal materialism' in order to rethink the notion of 'event'.[29] Foucault's thesis is that there is a materiality of discourse: while it is certainly a materiality very different from that of bodies and things, he nevertheless claimed that 'discursive events' take effect on the material level. The relation of things and discourses are not to be thought according to a mechanical causality nor an ideal necessity; instead, the philosopher

26 Louis Althusser, 'Ideology and Ideological State Apparatuses (Notes towards an Investigation)', in 'Lenin and Philosophy' and Other Essays (New York: Monthly Review Press, 1971), pp. 127–86.

27 Étienne Balibar, 'Althusser's Object', trans. by Margaret Cohen and Bruce Robbins, Social Text, 39 (Summer 1994), pp. 157–88 (p. 177; emphasis in the original); French original as 'L'Objet Althusser', in Politique et philosophie dans l'œuvre de Louis Althusser, ed. by Sylvain Lazarus (Paris: PUF, 1993), pp. 81–116 (p. 110).

28 Pierre Macherey clearly shows the importance of this critique of Foucault: the 'power', the 'energy' of the ideology is so efficient because 'it is not diffused from a unique centre that would be the State' (Pierre Macherey and Orazio Irrera, 'Michel Foucault et les critiques de l'idéologie. Dialogue avec Pierre Macherey', Methodos. Savoir et textes, 16 (2016) <https://doi.org/10.4000/methodos.4667>.

29 Michel Foucault, 'The Order of Discourse: Inaugural Lecture at the Collège de France, given December 2, 1970', in Untying the Text: A Post-Structuralist Reader, ed. by Robert Young (London, Routledge, 1981), pp. 51–78 (p. 69).

proposes to analyse the 'relation, the coexistence, the dispersion, the overlapping, the accumulation, and the selection of material elements'.[30] Although the discursive order is characterized by hazardous, aleatory, contingent, and discontinuous events, they can all still be retraced and analysed.[31] The idea of 'materialities' in the plural, which is utilized by many contributions to this volume, emphasizes the importance of resisting the temptation of reductionism in all its forms. It shows the necessity of philosophically taking into account 'worlds feelings, of practices, organizations, institutions, and even ideas', as Wolf remarks in his contribution.

In this sense, philosophical analysis should be enriched by materials that come from other disciplines, such as those obtained through ethnographic work. In this way it can enlarge its discursive field, avoiding some risks contained in pure abstraction, while at the same time employing critical tools that can de-naturalize or de-essentialize the immediacy of those same materials.[32] The study of materiality and the materialist approach do not imply giving up on philosophy, but it certainly means broadening the task of philosophy in order to reconsider

---

30 Ibid.

31 The idea of 'incorporeality' is inspired by Foucault's readings of the Stoic philosophers. It is very present also in the nearly contemporaneous book from Deleuze entitled *Logic of Sense*. In *A Thousand Plateaus*, Deleuze (with Guattari) takes over the notion and provides very intelligible examples of it. The enunciative act pronounced by a judge that transforms the accused into the guilty is described as an incorporeal attribute, though decisive for the body of the individual (Gilles Deleuze and Félix Guattari, *A Thousand Plateaus: Capitalism and Schizophrenia*, trans. by Brian Massumi (Minneapolis: University of Minnesota Press, 1987), p. 81). Lorenzo Vinciguerra's re-reading of Spinoza and the problem of the sign also further develops the idea of a semiotic materialism or, in his words, of a 'sémiophysics' (*Spinoza et le signe*, p. 136). Finally, one can also mention the neologism '*matérialisme*' (the materiality of the word), invented some years later, in 1975, by Jacques Lacan ('Conférence à Genève sur le symptôme', texte établi par Jacques-Allain Miller, *La Cause du Désir*, 95 (2017), pp. 7–24 <https://doi.org/10.3917/lcdd.095.0007>.

32 Cf. Althusser, *For Marx*: 'Others, of more scientific bent, proclaimed the "end of philosophy" in the manner of certain positivistic formulations in *The German Ideology*, in which it is no longer the proletariat or revolutionary action which take in charge the realization and thereby the death of philosophy, but science pure and simple: does not Marx call on us to stop philosophizing, that is, stop developing ideological reveries so that we can move on to the study of reality itself?' (p. 28) and '*The German Ideology* sanctions this confusion as it reduces philosophy, as we have noted, to a faint shadow of science, if not to the empty generality of positivism. This practical consequence is one of the keys to the remarkable history of Marxist philosophy, from its origins to the present day' (pp. 33–34).

the historical and, in every sense of the word, the material situatedness of any philosophical problem.

Even though this volume adopts a rather contemporary perspective, it nonetheless begins with a reflection on the return to Spinoza, as well as the return to other past materialist movements — Althusser's work, for example, belongs to a historical moment that is no longer entirely ours. While the understanding of the historical, social moment to which philosophical works belong is a part of the materialist project, their re-actualization is equally important — an approach which is exemplified in Bottici's contribution to this volume and its actualization of an anarchist tradition in feminist theory. This approach supposes a philosophical reading of past texts which, without being teleologically oriented towards our time, actualizes relevant potentialities contained in 'thinking' the present, while helping to reveal radical discontinuities in the ways of posing a problem in contemporary or past terms — as we see, for example, in Miguel's, Vogman's, and Yuva's contributions. While their efforts to analyse the materialisms of the Soviet era, or even older materialisms from the eighteenth and nineteenth centuries, may seem outdated, they offer, in fact, contemporary reflections on how to redefine the role and nature of the 'milieu' in education, of the gesture in human exchange, work, and language, or of ideology in the history of materialism.

What is ultimately at stake is the fact that old theories, whether philosophical or not, should not automatically be considered outdated simply because they do not belong to our historical moment. On the one hand, the historical horizon of some past authors is still, to some extent, ours; on the other hand, the identification of new practical problems leads to the discovery of original theoretical territories which, even if they constitute something 'new', may still nevertheless be located in the past. Materialism, whether it arises from the philosophers who have claimed this label or the kinds of methods we discuss in this volume, does not imply a form of theoretical 'presentism' postulating that only contemporary theories can help us in the urgency of rethinking the present.

The history of materialism is full of controversies which involve both the materialist authors themselves as well as the insufficiently emancipatory dimension of certain so-called materialist theories and their uses. Rather than seeking to provide the final word, this volume aims at giving expression to the tensions and irresolvable polemics of the complex materialist discursive field. As such, we have aimed, above all, to show the multiplicity of paths, tools, and strategies that materialism both in the past and in the present offers to critically rethink political activity.

I. THE ACTUALITY OF SPINOZA'S MATERIALISM

Introduction to Part I

STEFAN HAGEMANN

Thinking about the philosophical foundations of a concept of emancipatory politics leads inevitably to the problem of materialism. According to such a perspective, in order for political practice to be understood as emancipatory, it cannot be conceived as an action that is a priori conditioned by the (moral as well as juridical) freedom of its subjects. On the contrary, political action should be conceived as the process in which the subjects realize their (individual and collective) freedom. Each of the chapters in this part delve into this intricate relation between philosophy, politics, and materialism. They start from the insight that it is necessary to reflect on the material conditions upon which a processual realization of freedom is based. In such a view, the actuality of freedom is inseparable from the process of its realization, and this is why such a realization should not be conceived as a liberation from the material conditions on which it is based, but instead as an immanent process.

The chapters in this part illuminate various aspects of Spinoza's philosophy that are significant for a materialist concept of politics. **Mariana de Gainza**'s contribution, which also provides an overview of the newer interpretations of Spinoza, addresses the relationship between the Spinozian idea of immanence and the concept of dialectical negativity. If, within the discussion on the theoretical foundations of emancipatory political practice, Spinoza's thought was considered to provide the conceptual resources to break with the predominance of Hegelian Marxism and its insistence on negativity as the driving force of political and historical processes, this positioning of Spinozism as an anti-dialectical, immanentist school of thought opposed to dialectical negativity runs the risk of simply affirming the status quo when it does not also offer the theoretical means to draw a line between right and wrong political practice. By discussing the relation between morality and ethics, Gainza now shows that there can be a productive dialogue between the dialectical thought of Critical Theory and Spinoza's immanentist thought.

In order to develop a concept of emancipatory practice, it is decisive to determine the relation between freedom and necessity. Here too, the appeal to Spinoza can provide substantial insights, as **Stefano Visentin** shows in his contribution. Spinoza's denial of free will in favour of a reconciliation between freedom and necessity proves to be productive. Visentin shows that Spinoza's doctrine of the identity of freedom and necessity has an eminently political meaning, both for criticizing deficient forms of government and with regard to the foundations of a true political governance. According to Visentin's reconstruction of Spinoza, political freedom can be conceived as the process of transforming individual freedom into the collective freedom of the multitude. This is the basis of Spinoza's doctrine of the practical predominance of democracy. In this perspective, political practice can finally be conceived as a continuous transformation of historical reality.

However, the very concept of history seems to pose serious problems in the context of Spinozian thought, since with Spinoza's denial of finalism the concept of historical progress could be radically questioned, if not rendered impossible. In her contribution, **Ericka Itokazu** shows that this is by no means the case, but that, on the contrary, a substantial concept of history as a non-teleological process can be gleaned from Spinoza's ontology. The Spinozian concept of duration is at the centre of her argument: In contrast to the negativity of time, duration should be understood as a positive process of individuation in the sense of an immanent causality. From this perspective, the process of history can then be understood as the tension between imaginary

time and the positive duration which is constitutive for human practice.

The two concluding contributions in this part deal with the authors who were responsible for the renewal of Spinoza Studies in the
second half of the twentieth century, namely Gilles Deleuze and Louis
Althusser. **Mauricio Rocha** investigates the importance of Deleuze's
appropriation of Spinoza in the forging of a political Spinozism, which
was neglected in France until the end of the 1960s. Accordingly,
Rocha discusses the central concepts of Deleuze's Spinozist investigations, such as 'expression', 'immanence', and 'power'. Furthermore,
Rocha focuses on the importance of the Sephardi philosopher for
the development of Deleuze's own philosophical system. Meanwhile,
Vittorio Morfino's contribution reconstructs the different tendencies
that can be identified in the work of Althusser. The first of these tendencies is materialist and based on the concept of structural causality,
whereas the second is eschatological and grounded on the idea of a *parousia*. Both tendencies deal with questions that are inevitably related
to Althusser's writings on Spinoza, and which resonate with themes
present in the other contributions, such as the refusal of teleology and
the concept of encounter.

Materialist Variations on Spinoza
Theoretical Alliances and Political Strategies
MARIANA DE GAINZA

MORAL PHILOSOPHY OR ETHICS?

In his 1963 lectures, Theodor Adorno said that it was important not to abandon reflection on the 'good life' in terms of a *moral philosophy* and to resist the temptation of replacing its concepts with those of an *ethics*.[1] In broad strokes, his argument was the following: It is clear that the notion of morality rests on an essential conformism because it presupposes an ideal convergence between individual behaviour and public customs, so that *the good life* amounts to an obedience to community norms and acceptance of its actual forms. What is more, this conformism (a respect for a petrified facade of opinion and society) is redoubled by the affinity between morals and Puritan values: the Puritan subject's rigidity and narrow conventionalism is perfectly suited to a reactive defence against any questioning of the status quo. That is why a preference instead for the notion of *ethics* — as a call to live according to one's own nature — would thus seem admissible. If the definition of the ethical *good life* refers to the capacity to deploy, according to

---

1   Theodor W. Adorno, *Problems of Moral Philosophy* (Stanford, CA: Stanford University Press, 2001).

one's own time and dispositions, each *ethos* or mode of singular being, then it seems to offer a sort of antidote against an externally imposed morality.

However, this call for an *ethics* of the 'good life', while understandable, is just 'pure illusion and ideology'.[2] Beyond the emptiness of the assertion that one must live in harmony with one's own being lies the fact that the contents of one's self-identity, which are thought to be genuinely spontaneous, are in fact provided by the dominant culture. Congruence with one's own constitution or nature is nothing more than a form of compliance with certain cultural values. A naturalist ethics would thus be a kind of 'bad conscience of morality', a 'morality that is ashamed of its own moralizing' that still behaves as morality but no longer wishes to be a 'moralizing morality'.[3]

For these reasons, Adorno prefers to retain the concept of 'morality', which, despite its anachronism and evident limitations, has the advantage of avoiding further adulterations of the true problem: the contradiction between the particular and the general, between freedom and law, or better still, between empirical existence and the good life, which is an unrealizable aim in the context of an oppressive norm.

If we were to accept certain prejudices supposing the incompatibility between critical-dialectical philosophies and Spinozism,[4] then it would follow that Spinoza's *Ethics* can also be subject to the Adornian critique of ethics. Indeed, there is a contemporaneous sort of neo-Spinozism which is perfectly in line with a neoliberal *ethos* that is associated with a pervasive rhetoric revolving around desire and affect. Along with the political and communicative strategies of global right-wing parties and tendencies, these neo-Spinozist perspectives imagine individuals as subjects of an affective self-consciousness that knows how to recognize what it loves and hates, a self-consciousness that defends the freedom to determine what it shall consume. But the items that one 'spontaneously' prefers or chooses (which can be such different things as commercial goods, political ideas, current information, or beliefs) tend to coincide, in point of fact, with a preference that

---

2   Ibid., p. 10.

3   Ibid.

4   Prejudices associated, in particular, to the tradition of readings of Spinozism that comes from Gilles Deleuze and passes through Antonio Negri.

has already been defined in another scene as the most suitable for that given profile. As an ideological mode, contemporary capitalism both reflects and reinforces the demand for accumulation, on the one hand, and the affective dispositions of the subjects, on the other, in a kind of virtuous convergence of differences that intends to uphold the expansion of global financial power.

This convergence is a fitting illustration of precisely what Adorno was concerned with in his critique of ethics. This is why I think it is imperative to assert — against those prejudices that rigidly separate dialectics and immanence — that Spinoza's *Ethics* can and should be approached with the Adornian gesture that denounces the purported identity between particular and universal, and replaces it with *contradiction*, a contradiction that can still be found in moral philosophy today despite its conservative tendencies.

SPINOZA'S MATERIALISM

The approach of combining Adorno and Spinoza that I attempt here is based on a materialist reading of Spinoza, whose articulating axes are worth explaining. The term 'materialism' is a problematic one. It does not help us to form a clearly shaped perspective because it was used to designate very different theories which are, in many cases, mutually incompatible. It is a noun traversed by the echoes of various controversies (between realism and idealism, empiricism and innatism, objectivism and subjectivism) that have been present as tensions within philosophy from the beginning; to put it more precisely, they have been present as tensions ever since Hegelian philosophy retroactively (and controversially) organized the history of philosophy into the confrontation of opposing positions. In any case, I want to cautiously assume this heritage, albeit in the way in which a certain Spinozian Marxism has re-signified it.

To consider how a modern sense of 'materialism' reached Spinoza, it is worth recalling that Robert Boyle (whose experiments on nitro were discussed in Spinoza's *Correspondence*) was the first to introduce the term, in 1674, in his work *The Excellency and Grounds of the Corpuscular or Mechanical Philosophy*. Between theorists and chemists that embraced the postulates of corpuscular-mechanical philosophy, 'materialists' were those that reduced phenomena to a few material components. This sense of the noun was consolidated when Cartesian dualism rewrote the old controversies about matter and form as an assertion of the existence of two substances: extended reality and thinking reality. Since that transformation, three major traditions, separated by their ontological emphasis, can be identified within modern philosophy: one that assigns a privileged reality to the ideal or psychic (spiritualism), to the material or physical (materialism), or to the balanced character of a reality that encompasses both ontological dimensions (monism).

In addition, in terms of Spinozist philosophy it is also relevant to consider the 'ancient materialism' represented by the atomism of Democritus, Epicurus, and Lucretius — a philosophical current that also interested Marx, who wrote his doctoral thesis on 'The Difference between the Democritean and Epicurean Philosophy of Nature'. Spinoza vindicated the ancient materialists in an explicitly controversial way when he wrote against the Platonic-Aristotelian tradition:

> To me the authority of Plato, Aristotle, and Socrates is not worth much. I would have been amazed if you had mentioned Epicurus, Democritus, Lucretius, or any of the Atomists, or defenders of invisible particles. But it's no wonder that the people who invented occult qualities, intentional species, substantial forms, and a thousand other trifles contrived ghosts and spirits, and believed old wives' tales, to lessen the authority of Democritus, whose good reputation they so envied that they had all his books burned, which he had published with such great praise.[5]

Furthermore, in relation to contemporary discourse, let us consider the statement about Spinoza's materialism made by Pierre-François Moreau:

> We can talk about a materialism in Spinoza on the condition that we do not thereby understand a determination of the mind by the body. To those who object that Spinoza [...] maintains the balance between mind and body, [and therefore is] as spiritualist or idealist as he is materialist, we must answer

---

5   *Ep.* LVI [to Hugo Boxel]; *CWS* [*The Collected Works of Spinoza*, see abbreviations], II, p. 423.

that, precisely, tradition does not maintain that balance, and
the simple fact of giving the body as much importance as
the mind already constitutes an enormous effort of materialist
rebalancing.[6]

Let us retain what Moreau calls here a *rebalancing effort*, that is to
say, a kind of compensatory endeavour that uses the same conceptual
elements of a philosophical tradition but adjusts the importance given
to them. When that rebalancing — as in the case of Spinoza — works
by rescuing the body from its traditional subordination to the mind,
such an effort can legitimately be considered materialist. However,
the image of a balance that must be restored, of a compensation or
counterweight that works by levelling out an imbalance, does not fit
Spinozist materialism as I understand it. Such a metaphor supposes
that the elements whose relative weights must be equalized are already
constituted and that it is only necessary to modify the weights in the
balance to stabilize it.

    This model is overly simplistic where a 'materialist rebalancing' is
concerned. The Spinozian valuation of the body, rather than compen-
sating with an undervaluation (giving the body as much importance
as the mind), constitutes a theoretical innovation that transforms the
idea of the body, insofar as thought is capable of doing justice to the irreducible reality it faces. This means that the body can be apprehended
in its own corporeal being when it is understood through the absolute
quality or attribute that explains it — without referring it to a mind.
The effort to understand a particular thing is made on the basis of
the recognition of its irreducibility (without homologating it to other
things or realities).

    With this in mind, the terms of Moreau's statement can be re-
formulated as follows: Spinoza's enormous effort of materialist rebalancing consists of an anti-hierarchical ontological equalization of
essentially unequal realities, an 'adjustment' made through the recognition of an essential imbalance: in this way, he has achieved a
theoretical justice for heterogeneous realities. So this Spinozian effort
is materialist, not because the body is its object (it is clear that we
can elaborate a materialist understanding of the ideas, as it is common

---

6   Pierre-François Moreau, *Problèmes du spinozisme* (Paris: Vrin, 2006), p. 65; my translation.

to find idealist theories of the body), but because it builds the just perspective that takes each reality into account, considering its irreducibility. Therefore, *materialism* is an ontological way of conceiving the power of thought to understand the singular quality of a reality.

TOWARDS A CARTOGRAPHY OF CONTEMPORARY SPINOZISM

With this notion of *materialism* in mind, we can now redirect the discussion back to our initial aim of relocating the question of *ethics* within materialism and in dialogue with critical theory. I will develop a sort of cartography of contemporary Spinozism, taking as a starting point a citation from Pierre Macherey, who said that 'Spinoza obsesses and haunts us as if his work were a theoretical unconscious that conditions and guides a large part of our intellectual choices and effective commitments; and that helps us to reformulate most of the problems that concern us'.[7] Using Macherey's idea, I will assert that a set of contemporary readings of Spinoza can be grouped under the heading 'Spinozism', understood as the response to something condensed in the name 'Spinoza' that both obsesses, haunts, and conditions us: something that orients intellectual alternatives and practical commitments, and that lends a particular contour to certain inquiries, both ethical-political and theoretical.

While determining the Spinozist camp in this way it is possible to distinguish different interpretations. We can reproduce those interpretations and distribute them along an axis, the purpose of which would be to measure how the haunting of Spinoza is acknowledged by his readers, or what kind of relationship is established between a given thought and a Spinozist idea. Firstly, I would like to imagine the pure form wherein a thought considered to be a 'theoretical unconscious' would manifest itself: as an explicit absence, or a merely implicit presence. There thus exists a mode of 'thinking *in* Spinoza', where 'Spinoza', rather than being the object addressed by thought for further examination, instead constitutes a sort of *speculative element*, a terrain or medium in which thinking takes place. This mode of interpretation appears, for example, in Freud's declared affinity for Spinoza,

---

7   Pierre Macherey, *Avec Spinoza. Études sur la doctrine et l'histoire du spinozisme* (Paris: PUF, 1992), p. 7; my translation.

when he writes in a letter: 'I readily admit my dependence on Spinoza's doctrine. There was no reason why I should expressly mention his name, since I conceived my hypotheses from the atmosphere created by him, rather than from the study of his work. Moreover, I did not seek a philosophical legitimation'.[8] Secondly, there are researchers in the history of philosophy who have produced an enormous amount of texts in a field identified as *Spinoza Studies*. In these cases, Spinoza is the explicit object of the inquiry, and the haunting force of his name manifests itself in the rigorous and in-depth efforts of researchers to reconstruct the conceptual framework of his system.

Between these two extremes of interpretation (Spinoza as an explicit object of study, and Spinoza as a speculative element, absent from the actual research) a reading such as Althusser's explicitly asserts the Spinozian perspective as the supporting framework for his own theoretical interventions — yet he does so without elaborating the specific connections that were useful for him. Althusser effectively displays a mode of 'being Spinozist' that consists in taking from Spinoza certain hypothesis that he never proclaimed but did authorize;[9] in fact, these Spinozist coordinates can be seen all throughout Althusser's texts, where they act as a type of channel for his own discourse that then flows — while contained by that immanent structure — onto other vital and urgent matters.

Another famous interpretation of Spinoza, in this case by Deleuze, also responds to the interpellation produced by the name 'Spinoza'. Deleuze became the explicit interlocutor of a philosophical conversation that creates a common discursive groundwork. I would say that the terms of Deleuze's philosophy emerge through a composition with other voices (among which Spinoza's and Nietzsche's voices figure prominently), while they also display an analysis whose plasti-

---

8   Sigmund Freud to Lothar Bickel, 28 June 1931, quoted from Yirmiyahu Yovel, *Spinoza and Other Heretics: The Adventures of Immanence* (Princeton, NJ: Princeton University Press, 1989), p. 139; English translation in H. Z. Winnik, 'A Long-Lost and Recently Recovered Letter of Freud', *Israel Annals of Psychiatry*, 13 (1975), pp. 1–5.

9   'We were guilty of an equally powerful and compromising passion: *we were Spinozists*. In our own way, of course, which was not Brunschvicg's! And by attributing to the author of the *Tractatus Theologico- Politicus* and the *Ethics* a number of theses which he would surely never have acknowledged, though they did not actually contradict him'. Louis Althusser, 'On Spinoza', in *Essays in Self-Criticism*, trans. by Grahame Lock (London: New Left Books, 1976), pp. 132–41 (p. 132).

city seeks to distil the conceptual content of things themselves. And different results arise from the reciprocal contamination of these specific interlocutions: a Deleuzian Spinoza, a Deleuzian Nietzsche, a Spinozian/Nietzschean Deleuze; but also a Nietzschean Spinoza and a Spinozian Nietzsche.

From a different angle, we can observe that while Deleuze's reading is more philosophical than political, a reading such as Antonio Negri's, which draws directly on Deleuze, is more political than philosophical. Negri's interpretation has inspired a whole series of contemporary uses of Spinoza that renew his concepts as a kind of stimulant for political action in the present. Responding to the urgent nature of such multivalent interventions, the name 'Spinoza' is wielded as a kind of ontological guarantee for the emancipation of humanity.

The underlying benefit of understanding these different ways of relating to Spinoza is that they represent different ways of actualizing *immanence*, and this is true whether his philosophy appears as a speculative atmosphere favouring the production of ideas, or as an underlying structure explaining a series of argumentative moves, or as the theoretical-political inspiration for an imagination that trusts in concrete horizons of collective happiness.

To return to the polarity that organizes this argument, I would say that the works in the history of philosophy that address Spinoza as their explicit object of study principally focus upon the immanence of history in his philosophical texts. Spinoza's thought is reconstructed as a situated thought that participates in the life of his time and all the debates that traverse it; and this reading, which extends from the present back to seventeenth-century thought, argues for a universal dimension of certain human dilemmas. Of course, the readings I have located at the opposite side of the spectrum do not suppress history, but they relate *immanence* to the power of the human intellect to produce effects. When Freud admits his dependence on Spinoza's philosophy, he means that *immanence* is connected to the power of the singular and a certain dimension of universal experience. But now immanence refers to an ethics whereby 'knowledge is the most powerful affect'.[10]

---

10   'I am really amazed, really delighted! I have a precursor, and *what* a precursor! I hardly
        knew Spinoza: what brought me to him now was the guidance of instinct. Not only
        is his whole tendency like my own — to make knowledge the most *powerful passion*

Thus, methodological precautions around historical distance are not of any great concern for this type of Spinozism, wherein everything that may emerge from the reader's sensibility and acuity is suitable for *discovering* or *inventing* other realities and concepts.

The range of readings that I have briefly sketched out are distributed according to the nuances resulting from the tension between the presence or absence of Spinoza. This same series of contemporary readings (whose shared affinity, as I have said, can be considered from Macherey's idea of Spinoza as a theoretical unconscious) can be further interrogated by analysing their position in relation to Marxist philosophical and political debates from the 1960s onward. This is especially important because these 'Spinozisms' were essential for this period's response to the hegemony of Hegelian philosophy in critical theory (that is to say, in the theory that was affected, under various modes, by the *theoretical revolution* of Marx). Within this new virtual axis, which intercepts the aforementioned one, the relevant polarity distinguishes two positions vis-à-vis Hegelian dialectics: an open rejection (Deleuze) and a critical revision (Althusser).

It was Deleuze who most decisively responded to the challenge of breaking with dialectical negativity, and instead asserted the central concept of his project as *difference*. According to Deleuze, the concept of contradiction began to reveal its conservative core when compared to the potentialities that came with a politics of difference: he argued that contradiction revealed itself as a constellation of sad passions associated with the interiorization of subjection, a culture dominated by the specular dynamic of resentment, and a logic that ultimately served as an accomplice to the state's quest to capitalize on social conflicts for the accumulation of power. By contrast, Althusser was more cautious in his questioning of dialectics and, in his self-critical writings, ultimately recognized that 'a Marxist cannot make the detour

---

— but also in five main points of his doctrine I find myself; this most abnormal and lonely thinker is closest to me in these points precisely: he denies free will, purposes, the moral world order, the nonegoistical, evil; of course the differences are enormous, but they are differences more of period, culture, field of knowledge. *In summa*: my solitariness which, as on very high mountains, has often, often made me gasp for breath and lose blood, is now at least a solitude for two. Strange!'. Friedrich Nietzsche, 'To Franz Overbeck [Postmarked Sils Engd., July 30, 1881]', in Christopher Middleton, *Selected Letters of Friedrich Nietzsche* (Chicago: University of Chicago Press, 1996), pp. 176–77 (p. 177).

via Spinoza without paying for it. For the adventure is perilous, and whatever you do, you cannot find in Spinoza what Hegel gave to Marx: *contradiction*'.[11] Given Althusser's commitment to the renovation of Marxist thought, he performed an incisive critique of the contemporary versions of Marxism — especially those whose response to the determinist suffocation of the 'laws of history' was a subjectivist voluntarism that placed its faith in the end of oppression — while still never claiming outright that dialectical thought should be abandoned. The complexity of immanent causality was arraigned in order to counteract the simplifying and homogenizing nature of Hegelian dialectics, wherein the object of critique became the *specific structures* of idealist dialectics (that is, the simple negation, the negation of the negation, the identity of contraries, the transformation of quantity into quality, and the logic of the dialectical overcoming). Althusser pursued all this without eliminating the notion of contradiction from the conceptual horizon, which remained necessary for thinking of politics in its constitutively conflictual dimension.

Having offered this sort of cartography of contemporary Spinozist materialism, I must confess my own affinities: in the axis that displays the presence or absence of a direct reference to Spinoza in discourses attempting to address the present conjuncture, my sympathies lie with the Freudian strategy. I think the potency of the Spinozian perspective is at its most uniquely productive when one assumes it as one's own —without accepting the interdictions that come with speaking a 'Spinozist langue'. Along the other axis distributing positions facing dialectics, my sympathies are with the Althusserian strategy: the acceptance that one must be anti-dialectical in order to think on Spinoza's terms not only impoverishes the conceptual universe, but also leads to serious political limitations if it means to renounce incisive moments of twentieth-century emancipatory thought (especially works such as Adorno's, which sought to combat fascism in its several manifestations that included those of Western democracies).

Furthermore, a certain negative dialectics becomes necessary when, as I have suggested, there exists (as there does today) a type of neo-Spinozism that is functional to the neoliberal *ethos*. The management of affects by the global right-wing movements and governments

---

11   Althusser, 'On Spinoza', p. 141.

is evinced in two complementary ways. On the one hand, stoking and channelling social hatred, which in turn becomes the affective infrastructure required to demonize social policies and their beneficiaries and to spread an anti-political attitude among the masses (in Latin America, the right-wing forces have sought, in this way, to delegitimize the politics pursued by progressive governments — who are disqualified as *populists* — over the last decade). On the other hand, cultivating false emotions and banal happiness as the support for *positive thinking* that disposes people to deny pain (their own and that of others) and inhibit their sensitivity to the point that they become numb and are unable to recognize any kind of distress. This form of positive thinking reinforces adaptation to ever more hostile conditions of life and neutralizes any critical reflexivity that would allow for a questioning of the purported inevitability of the neoliberal course of the world. The resulting disposition is one in which people *trust* and *wait* for businessmen and post-fascist leaders to join up with the individual efforts of those who deserve the *good life* (that is, the part of the population that 'puts in the effort' and struggles to survive 'without outside assistance'). Against both tendencies, it would be useful to exercise a certain Adornian dialectical negativity.

Now I will attempt to assimilate the Adorno/Spinoza intersection into this schema that presses for the importance of certain theoretical alliances in the name of a materialist critique of the contemporary world.

SPINOZA AND ADORNO, ALLIES IN CRITICISM

Adorno and Spinoza can be regarded as materialist critics of moral philosophy because both of them depart from the Platonic tradition in a similar way. The model of the *subject* that emerges from Platonic philosophy — as the theoretical response to a practical need to justify the existing social order — is replicated across Western philosophical moralism right up until the present day. When that moralism seeks to justify the social order by relying on the *identity* between particular and general, Adorno responds by emphasizing the falsehood of that identification and re-establishing the legibility of the *contradiction* hidden by the idealist operation.

Spinoza's political anti-moralism, which he asserts as anti-Platonic,[12] goes with his Machiavellianism. His assertion that 'no men are less suitable to guide Public Affairs than Theorists, or Philosophers'[13] is in direct conflict with the Platonic model of the Philosopher King. But against the temptation of a vulgarly pragmatic interpretation of this defence of politics against philosophical idealism, Spinozian ethics is far from any immediate facticity (that is to say, far from the affirmation of the things and men in their existing state) and instead produces something that is explicitly labelled as a 'model': one must 'form an idea of man, a model of human nature which we may look to'. This is then a theoretical-practical necessity that is upheld by straining the system's own postulates: although nature does not work in favour of ends or models, and despite the fact that nothing in it can be regarded as either perfect or imperfect, 'we shall say that men are more perfect or imperfect, insofar as they approach more or less near to this model'.[14]

So, while Spinoza's ethics is anti-moralist on the practical terrain, and anti-Platonic on the philosophical terrain, it nevertheless calls for the need to use *ideal models* (analogous to what moral philosophy conceives of as the 'ought' that guides all behaviour). The counterpoint between reality and model, between the actual functioning of things and the invocation of another, sought-after mode of being, is deployed in order to think of *human types* and *forms of life* capable of condensing the critical energies of the present. And that operation allows for non-conventional modes of conceiving of the meaning of *realism* within philosophical-political discussion.

Therefore, the opposition between reality and model in Spinozian ethics can be schematized in the following manner: if the *image of man* evoking an inexistent human nature corresponds to norms of an existing social order, the *idea of man*, arising from what an actually existing human nature *can do*, would correspond to a non-existent social order, since it would emerge from the transformation of the present.

---

12   See *Ep.* LVI [to Hugo Boxel]; *CWS* II, p. 423.
13   *TP* I, 1; *CWS* II, p. 504.
14   *Ethics* IV, Praef.; *CWS* I, p. 545.

I would argue that this counterpoint coincides precisely with the 'contradiction' that Adorno says we must not abandon: the short-circuit at the heart of reality itself. But if we think this alongside Spinoza, we are able to see that this 'contradiction' does not assume the form of a logical contradiction. Instead, it has the complex structure of a chiasmus, which contrasts a false reality with a true model. Against the *false reality* — where the idealized, non-existent individual (whose free self-determination is based on his desire, will, and understanding) responds to the imperatives of an existing order (which requires the aforementioned falsity for its own reproduction) — a *true model* is invoked, one which connects the power of the collectively existing individual with the possibility of a just, non-existent order.

However, it must be said that this model is not an utopian one: efforts of thought aimed at this transformation are not guided by an image of a future society to be obtained ('a Fantasy, possible only in Utopia'[15]) but rather by the attempt to think the actual given conditions and developments unfolding from a situation in the sense of its subversion.

The idea of a 'model', which serves the role of imagining a reality more perfect than the present reality, constitutes a peculiar type of realism which is far from all pragmatic reproductive possibilism. Thinking rigorously from the conditions of a present conjuncture does not mean, however, that the political response to this concrete situation is conceived of as the *political expression* of those conditions, that is, as a political ratification of facts. Quite the contrary: this political response is motivated by the desire to transform those conditions, a desire which is recognized in an imperative: *suffering must cease.* Such an imperative is clearly not derived from the norms that organize this given order, but rather from the sensibility associated with another ethics or morality.

To conclude, what I am suggesting here is that this anti-Platonic, Spinozian/Machiavellian realism is compatible with the Adornian critique of facticity and administrative utopianism that tries to spiritualize it; and it is compatible with the fragile promise of emancipation that emerges from the determinate negation of this actuality.

---

15   *TP* I, 1; *CWS* II, p. 503.

Non Defuit Materia
Freedom and Necessity in Spinoza's Democratic Theory
STEFANO VISENTIN

INTRODUCTION: ONTOLOGY AND POLITICS IN SPINOZA

One of the most relevant novelties introduced by the studies of the last decades on Baruch Spinoza's political philosophy concerns the emergence in his works of a profound connection between politics and ontology. Just to give an example, in a recent book Antonio Negri wrote: 'The political thought of Spinoza is to be found in his ontology', since 'in Spinoza the political is [...] a potency exceeding all measure, an accumulation not of substantial (individual) segments but of modal (singular) potencies'.[1] It is a statement which can be read within a specific historical context, namely the birth of modern capitalism, which Negri described with the following words:

> When modernity inaugurated the capitalist development, the new productive forces (and above all the living labour) had to be subjected to an ancient, eternal seal of power, to the absoluteness of a command that legitimized the new relations of production. From then on every attempt to break this frame

1   Antonio Negri, *Spinoza for our Time: Politics and Postmodernity*, trans. by William McCuaig (New York: Columbia University Press, 2013), pp. 9–10.

was considered reprehensible and heresiarch [...]. With this it was affirmed that modern metaphysics (and when we say metaphysics, we always mean in some way theology) sharpened its political claim. Since then, in fact, metaphysics has always been political.[2]

Despite the great relevance of this new interpretation, which is a radical innovation in terms of reading Spinoza's two political treatises, this chapter maintains that such a reading can be developed in two further directions: on the one hand, by fostering the dialogue with a more historically contextualized perspective; on the other hand, by theoretically problematizing the implicit (and in some case even explicit) teleologism of this interpretation. In this direction, an important step has been made by Étienne Balibar in his seminal essay on the fear of the masses,[3] but there are still some more issues to take into account.

One of these issues is certainly the political meaning of the identity Spinoza establishes between necessity and freedom. This identity has been studied at length by the scholars of Spinoza's ontology,[4] but it has never received the attention it deserves from scholars of Spinoza's political philosophy. The issue concerning the political relationship between freedom and necessity or, in other words, the relationship between subjective and objective conditions of collective action, is a real 'raw nerve' of modern political theory. This is because it brings into question the very possibility of whether humans can modify their (collective) lives: in a certain way, the meaning of concepts like emancipation, progress, reform, and revolution depends on the resolution of the problem of the complex connection between freedom and necessity.

---

2   Antonio Negri, 'Politiche dell'immanenza, politiche della trascendenza. Saggio popolare', in *Storia politica della moltitudine*, ed. by Filippo Del Lucchese (Rome: DeriveApprodi, 2009), pp. 86–96 (p. 87; my translation). See also Stefano Visentin, 'A ontologia política de Espinosa na leitura de Antonio Negri', *Cadernos Espinosanos*, 38 (2018), pp. 151–70.

3   Étienne Balibar, 'Spinoza, the Anti-Orwell: The Fear of the Masses', *Rethinking Marxism*, 2.3 (1989), pp. 104–39.

4   Jonathan Bennett, *A Study of Spinoza's Ethics* (Cambridge: Cambridge University Press, 1984) is one of the most relevant essays on this subject published in the last decades; but another significant example is also provided by Don Garrett, *Nature and Necessity in Spinoza's Philosophy* (New York: Oxford University Press, 2018).

Compared to the approach taken by the vast majority of modern political philosophers, Spinoza followed quite an original path when attempting to address this problematic, which depends on the peculiarity of his ontology. His provocative perspective can be summarized by the corollary of *Ethics* II, Def. 6: 'By "reality" and "perfection" I understand the same thing':[5] a definition which never ceased to haunt his readers, because, if it is very difficult to accept that the world in which we live is perfect, it is almost unacceptable to consider human actions, both individual and collective, as such, especially when their consequences are negative — not to say catastrophic — for other people, even when they simply diverge from the intention of the agent subject(s). It is a well-known fact that, from the very beginning of the *Ethics*, Spinoza emphasizes the distinction between his conception of freedom and the idea of free will, stating that 'that thing is called free which exists from the necessity of its nature alone, and is determined to act by itself alone';[6] from this perspective, the consequences which this distinction produces on men's collective lives and actions, that is on their history, must be taken into account. Three fundamental issues must be highlighted: Firstly, what are the political effects of the illusory character of free will, i.e. how is such an illusion used politically, and by whom? This issue is taken into account by Spinoza both in *Ethics* I, App., and in *Theological-Political Treatise*, Praef., where it is exposed as the dilemma of voluntary servitude. Secondly, given the ontological identity of reality and perfection, how can a form of government which limits its subjects' freedom be considered a perfect government (this is the case of absolute monarchy or tyranny, which Spinoza deals with in the *Political Treatise*)? Thirdly, as a consequence of this second point, how a free multitude is created is something that must be understood, especially how it differentiates itself from a subjugated one and, even more so, how a subjugated multitude can develop in a free one. This last point plays a fundamental role in the definition and fulfilment of

---

5   'Per perfectionem et realitatem idem intelligo' (*CWS* [*The Collected Works of Spinoza*, see abbreviations], I, p. 447; *Gebhardt* II, 85). It is worth noting that this definition is not enclosed within *Ethics* I, devoted to the discussion of God's nature, but within *Ethics* II, which takes 'The Nature and the Origin of the Mind' (*CWS* I, p. 446) into account; therefore, this identity concerns not only the infinite nature of God, but also the finite nature of his modes.

6   *Ethics* I, Def. 7; *CWS* I, p. 409.

a democratic regime, i.e. of the most absolute and desirable form of political organization[7] (although some scholars, e.g. Alexandre Matheron and Riccardo Caporali, have shown that Spinoza's democracy is far from being perfect).[8] What is at stake here is the new materialist approach to both individual and collective behaviours, which Spinoza tries to elaborate: an approach which, anticipating Marx's reading of Feuerbach,[9] aims to overcome the radical dichotomy between freedom and necessity established by Descartes, thus revealing a new philosophical and political path within the conceptual framework of modernity.[10]

THE POLITICAL CONSEQUENCES OF THE IMAGINARY NATURE OF FREE WILL

In the *Theological-Political Treatise*, Spinoza remarks that

> Now if nature had so constituted men that they desired nothing except what true reason teaches them to desire, then of course a society could exist without laws; in that case it would be completely sufficient to teach men true moral lessons, so that they would do voluntarily, wholeheartedly, and in a manner worthy of a free man, what is really useful.[11]

On the one hand, this statement expresses the idea that a civil and political organization is needed for humans to live in peace, but, on

---

7   See *TP* XI, 1; *CWS* II, p. 601; *Gebhardt* III, p. 358: 'I come, finally, to the third and completely absolute state [*omnino absolutum imperium*], which we call Democratic'.

8   Alexandre Matheron, 'Women and Servants in Spinozist Democracy', in his *Politics, Ontology and Knowledge in Spinoza* (Edinburgh: Edinburgh University Press, 2020), pp. 260–79; Riccardo Caporali, 'La moltitudine e gli esclusi', in *Spinoza: individuo e moltitudine*, ed. by Riccardo Caporali, Vittorio Morfino, and Stefano Visentin (Cesena: Il Ponte Vecchio, 2007), pp. 93–104.

9   See Karl Marx, 'Thesen über Feuerbach', in *MEW* [*Marx-Engels-Werke*, see abbreviations], III (1958), pp. 5–7. Spinoza's heritage in the thought of Marx has been extensively debated in the last decades: see Karl Ritter, *Prozesse der Befreiung. Marx, Spinoza und die Bedingungen eines freien Gemeinwesens* (Münster: Westfälisches Dampfboot, 2011); Frédéric Lordon, *Willing Slaves of Capital: Spinoza and Marx on Desire* (London: Verso Books, 2014); Franck Fischbach, *La Production des hommes. Marx avec Spinoza* (Paris: Vrin, 2014).

10   The idea of 'another' modernity, different if not opposed to the mainstream one developed by Descartes, Hobbes, Rousseau, and Hegel, is very present in Negri's thought; see, e.g. Michael Hardt and Antonio Negri, *Commonwealth* (Cambridge, MA: Harvard University Press, 2009).

11   *TTP* V, 20; *CWS* II, p. 144.

the other hand, it also emphasizes the many risks threatening the construction and duration of the same, especially the very difficult task to transform the choices of irrational individuals into rational ones. Humans are not born rational and free, as the seventeenth century doctrine of natural law — especially Hugo Grotius's — used to claim; instead, they are naturally subjugated by affects, as the title of *Ethics* IV asserts.[12] This enslavement coincides with human beings' impotence to moderate their passions and with their constant exposure to the power of external phenomena they cannot govern.[13] Nevertheless, humans imagine they possess natural freedom according to which they believe that they consciously want what they desire and what they try to achieve: '[humans] think themselves free, because they are conscious of their volitions and their appetite, and do not think, even in their dreams, of the causes by which they are disposed to wanting and willing, because they are ignorant of [those causes]'.[14]

Imagination is a constitutive element of human impotence, as it promotes the transformation of the human 'internal' subjugation to passive affects (i.e. passions) into an 'external' enslavement to those who are able to take advantage of such passivity and use it to establish political authority based upon ignorance and superstition (above all the clergy and the monarchs). Spinoza remarks upon this in *Ethics* I, App.: 'For they [the priests] know that if ignorance is taken away, then foolish wonder, the only means they have of arguing and defending their authority is also taken away'.[15] It could be said that the more humans imagine they are endowed with free will, the more they are enslaved or at risk of being enslaved. The alliance between priests and kings instrumentally manipulates the natural illusion of freedom, which affects all human beings, and establishes, in Spinoza's own words, 'the greatest secret of monarchic rule'.[16] This manipulation

---

12 *Ethics* IV; *CWS* I, p. 543; *Gebhardt* II, p. 205: 'On Human Bondage, or the Power of the Affects' (*De servitute humana seu de affectuum viribus*).

13 Ibid.

14 *Ethics* I, App.; *CWS* I, p. 440.

15 Ibid.; *CWS* I, pp. 443–44.

16 *TTP* Praef.; *CWS* II, p. 68; *Gebhardt* III, p. 7: 'The greatest secret of monarchic rule [*regiminis Monarchici summum arcanum*], and its main interest, is to keep men deceived, and to cloak in the specious name of Religion the fear by which they must be checked, so that they will fight for slavery as they would for their survival'.

induces humans to fight for their servitude as if they 'freely' accepted a single individual's dominion who then goes on to become the one and only reference point for all their hopes and desires. Moreover, the passivity of such an imagination reinforces the idea (or better, the image) of a God promoted by the theological-political apparatus, as *Ethics* II, 3, Schol. confirms in an extraordinary analysis which combines anthropology, psychology, and theology:

> By 'God's power' ordinary people understand God's free will and his right over all things which are, things which on that account are commonly considered to be contingent. For they say that God has the power of destroying all things and reducing them to nothing. Further, they often compare God's power with the power of kings. But we have refuted this [...]. Again, if it were agreeable to pursue these matters further, I could also show here that the power which ordinary people fictitiously ascribe to God is not only human (which shows that ordinary people conceive God as a man, or as like a man), but also involves lack of power.[17]

Spinoza's criticism of free will involves a radical calling into question of God's 'vulgar' image — here the term *vulgus*, i.e. the common people or plebs, does not refer to a determinate social group, but rather to all those who are subject to the hallucinatory power of imagination — and especially of the view that God is considered to possess an absolutely undetermined will, the 'power of destroying all things'. This alleged power over life and death leads to the attribution of a divine origin for monarchs, such that their freedom reveals itself in the right to condemn their subjects to death. However, according to Spinoza, God's freedom has nothing to do with such a nihilist representation. Spinoza's God is an infinite power (*potentia*, not *potestas*) strictly determined in every action, a productive force which actually realizes *every single potentiality*, since it '*non defuit materia* [did not lack material]', that is, in the words of *Ethics* I, App., God has the capacity 'to create all things, from the highest degree of perfection to the lowest'. To be even more precise, Spinoza's God is an infinite power '[b]ecause the laws of his nature have been so ample that they sufficed for producing all things that can be conceived by an infinite intellect'.[18] This is also

---

17   *Ethics* II, 3 Schol.; *CWS* I, p. 449.
18   *Ethics* I, App.; *CWS* I, p. 446; *Gebhardt* II, p. 83.

why one of the most relevant aspects of Spinoza's republicanism can be found in his criticism of the superstitious and alienating structure of monarchy. *Non defuit materia* can thus be read as the motto of Spinozist materialism, since it means that the infinite power of God is far from being circumscribed by the finite power of the human mind, which can only understand it, so to say, 'intensively' but not in its entire extension; moreover, *non defuit materia* also implies that this power is materialist and continuously produces concrete transformations of reality, including human reality, by means of an internal intervention into the structure of the body (again, including collective bodies).

TYRANNY AS A 'PERFECT' POLITICAL REGIME

In *Ethics* III, Praef., Spinoza states that humans cannot be considered 'a dominion within a dominion [*veluti imperium in imperio*]',[19] or as those who must not follow the laws of nature as if they were part of a different realm. This assertion is not only true for common people but also for kings, who, as the *Political Treatise* points out, 'are not gods, but men, who are often captivated by the Sirens' song'.[20] In Spinoza's view, kingdoms are founded on subjects' weaknesses rather than on king's strengths, since 'a whole multitude would never transfer its right to one or a few people, if its members could agree among themselves and not go from the kind of controversy generally aroused in large Councils to a rebellion'.[21] Thus, the existence of monarchical governments does not depend on the qualities of a single exceptional person but rather on the passivity of popular imaginations and affects, which expresses the (relative) impotence of a multitude which is unable to create a more developed and rational regime. In other words, a kings' authority is produced by the fear the multitude incites in itself much more than by the fear incited by kings over the populace. This reflexive fear[22] comes from the natural (that is: necessary) complexion of human im-

---

19   Ibid., *CWS* I, p. 491; *Gebhardt* II, p. 137.
20   *TP* VII, 1; *CWS* II, p. 544.
21   *TP* VII, 5; *CWS* II, p. 547.
22   See Stefano Visentin, 'Paura delle masse e desiderio dell'uno. Considerazioni sull'ambivalenza della *potentia multitudinis*', in *Storia politica della moltitudine*, ed. by Del Lucchese, pp. 181–98.

agination, which prevents the multitude from peacefully resolving the inevitable disputes and conflicts that arise internally. For this reason, Spinoza emphasizes that 'a multitude freely transfers to the king only what it cannot have absolutely in its power, i.e., an end to controversies and speed in making decisions',[23] in order to avoid the threat of uninterrupted sedition within the citizenry; this is also the reason why 'a Commonwealth is always put at greater risk on account of its citizens than on account of its enemies'.[24]

Because the conferral of absolute power upon the monarch derives from a collective hallucination, it follows that the 'perfection' of monarchies and even tyrannies originates from very natural and necessary causes that define the history of these regimes, including their birth, developments, and crises. Moreover, this identification between reality and perfection plays a fundamental political role because it rejects any moralistic justification of monarchy that would consider the monarch's power as the result of an ethical superiority of one man over the masses, or of tyrants' authority as God's punishment for citizens' sins. On the contrary, Spinoza removes the monarch-tyrant from the centre of the stage and integrates them into a wider causal configuration in terms of a collective subject (the multitude), which then appears as the main political actor, even within the historical circumstances where this collective subject appears to be at the lowest level of its capacity. The *imperium* (that is, the articulated structure of power relationships within an organized collectivity)[25] is thus always 'defined by the power of a multitude (*potentia multitudinis*)',[26] even when this power appears to be a sort of impotence or incapacity to give birth to free and democratic regimes.[27] However, this impotence is necessary, and this necessity frees politics of any moralistic or voluntaristic overdetermin-

---

23   *TP* vii, 5; *CWS* ii, p. 547.

24   *TP* vi, 6; *CWS* ii, p. 534.

25   The Latin term is hereby maintained because translating the Spinozist meaning of *imperium* with a single English word is very difficult, if not impossible, since neither sovereignty (as in Curley's translation), nor 'State', nor 'dominion', nor 'government' are fit to express the complexity of a political structure which is composed by laws and institutions, but also by (collective) imagination and affects.

26   *TP* ii, 17; *CWS* ii, p. 514.

27   In his *Imperium. Structures et affects des corps politiques* (Paris: La fabrique, 2015), Frédéric Lordon points out that 'there is no tribunal for the peoples' merit or fault, there is only the entirely positive measure of their power' (p. 157; my translation).

ation: there is neither a God to reward or punish humans, nor a devil to deceive them, nor original sin to cloud their free willingness to do good; there is only the natural constitution of a finite mode — or a composition of finite modes — which expresses the divine power in a dynamic and continuously transforming historical reality. It is not a coincidence that, in *Ethics* IV, Praef., Spinoza once again takes into account the meaning of perfection in a different context from the quotation already given in *Ethics* II, Def. 6. The emergence of this new definition of perfection is preceded by several references in *Ethics* III to a gradation of perfection in terms of it being lesser or greater, as in the following example: 'We see, then, that the mind can undergo great changes, and pass now to a greater, now to a lesser perfection.'[28] Therefore, the concrete existence of minds (and bodies) can modify their reality — that is, their perfection — insofar as they affect and are affected by other minds (and bodies), and this is true so long as minds and bodies are seen as equally enmeshed in this process:

> Perfection and imperfection therefore are only modes of think-ing, i.e. notions we are accustomed to feign [*fingere*] because we compare individuals of the same species or genus to another. But the main thing to note is that when I say that someone passes from a lesser to a greater perfection, and the opposite, I do not understand that he is changed from one essence, or form to another [...]. Rather, we consider that his power of acting [*agendi potentiam*], insofar as it is understood from his nature, is increased or diminished.[29]

With this meaning, the word 'perfection' expresses the measure of the power of an individual (or a collective) to act in a specific moment of their lives, therefore it indicates the intersection between reality as the essence of a God's finite mode and the same reality as the indefinite perseverance in existence, that is, as a continuous and necessary transformation.

---

28 *Ethics* III, 11 Schol.; *CWS* I, p. 500. See also *Ethics* III, DA 2 and 3; *CWS* I, p. 531; *Gebhardt* II, p. 191: '2. Joy [*Laetitia*] is a man's passage from a lesser to a greater perfection. 3. Sadness [*Tristitia*] is a man's passage from a greater to a lesser perfection.'

29 *Ethics* IV, Praef.; *CWS* I, pp. 545–46; *Gebhardt* II, pp. 206–08.

THE NECESSARY FREEDOM OF THE MULTITUDE

The third and last point concerns the meaning of political freedom in Spinoza's thought, and the conditions by which a multitude can concretely realize it. In a fascinating essay, François Zourabichvili has called this issue 'the enigma of the free multitude'.[30] To face this issue (from a different but complementary perspective to Zourabichvili's), a brief summary of Spinoza's conception of natural law must be taken into account, in order to highlight the original and profound connection between freedom and necessity it contains. In the *Theological-Political Treatise*, Spinoza writes that every individual is 'naturally determined to existing and having effects in a certain way' by his natural right, therefore this right is the expression of a 'determinate power' (*determinata potentia*),[31] which defines a real and effective space of action, legitimately included (to maintain a juridical lexicon) within the infinite effects and connections caused by divine power. From this perspective, as André Tosel once noted in a fundamental essay,[32] the mode's finitude is a positive one, since it expresses an operative part of an infinite power to act. The ethical problem *par excellence* is thus, to use Tosel's words, 'to become active on the foundation of an irremovable passivity',[33] since every human, just as every finite mode, is 'both a product and a producer of transitive indefinite operations, which at the same time express themselves as intrinsic determinations'.[34] To put it in a slightly different manner, the issue becomes how to relate to other humans who affect us from a perspective which, although unable to entirely overcome this otherness, nevertheless tries to build connections on the basis of what is common by promoting both the internalization of positive affections and the externalization of what affects others in a positive way. Obviously, such positivity is far from being absolute, because it is delimited by the power of other modes,

---

30   François Zourabichvili, 'L'Énigme de la multitude libre', in *La Multitude libre. Nouvelles lectures du 'Traité Politique'*, ed. by Chantal Jaquet, Pascal Sévérac, and Ariel Suhamy (Paris: Amsterdam, 2008), pp. 69–80.

31   *TTP* XVI; *CWS* I, p. 282; Gebhardt III, p. 189.

32   André Tosel, 'La Finitude positive', in his *Spinoza ou l'autre (in)finitude* (Paris: L'Harmattan, 2008), pp. 157–72.

33   Ibid., p. 163; my translation.

34   Ibid., pp. 165–66; my translation.

and, as far as humans are concerned, by the ambivalent character of affects and imagination; nevertheless, since every individual occupies a specific place within the spatio-temporal continuum, they also develop the capacity (in Spinoza's words, the *aptitudo*)[35] to compose their bodies and ideas — including their imagination and affects — strategically (to recuperate the military metaphor used by Laurent Bove).[36] They do this in order to resist the external forces which try to break up their cohesion and which would therefore weaken the common power they want to build. Consequently, the ability to be active (that is, to be an adequate cause of one's own actions), and thus to be free, depends on the permanent confrontation and collision with the external world, driven by the striving to modify the relationships towards it (and in particular towards other humans), to increase our power, and to resist the power of others according to our capacity. Hence, everyone's determinate *potentia* materializes within an existential and indeterminate framework in a continuous variation of its increments and reductions. Nonetheless, as *Ethics* II, 45 Schol. states, 'even if each thing is determined by another singular thing to exist in a certain way, still the force by which each one persists in existing follows from the eternal necessity of God's nature'.[37] As Christopher Skeaff recently noted in his book *Becoming Political*, this persistence cannot be interpreted as a 'norm' in the legal sense, that is, as the conformity to a predetermined rule, but rather as 'the power to transform the conditions of one's activity'.[38] Here the 'extrinsic [and extensive] finitude' of a mode's power coincides with its 'intrinsic [and intensive] infinitude', producing an indefinite striving to persevere — that is, to increase one's power — in existence.

---

35   In *TP* IV, 4; *CWS* II, p. 526; *Gebhardt* III, p. 293, 'capacity' (*aptitudo*) is defined with the following words: 'When we say each person can decide whatever he wishes concerning a thing of which he is the master, this power must be defined not only by the power of the agent [*non sola agendi potentia*], but also by the capacity of what he's acting on [*ipsius patientis aptitudine*]'.

36   Laurent Bove, *Affirmation and Resistance in Spinoza: Strategy of the Conatus* (Edinburgh: Edinburgh University Press, 2020).

37   *CWS* I, p. 482.

38   Christopher Skeaff, *Becoming Political: Spinoza's Vital Republicanism and the Democratic Power of Judgment* (Chicago: University of Chicago Press, 2018), p. 84.

The same existential indefinite nature of a mode's finite power, which Spinoza calls 'vacillation of mind [*fluctuatio animi*]',[39] is traceable in the life of a mode's aggregate, since, as Spinoza states in *Ethics* II, Def. 7: 'if a number of individuals so concur in one action that together they are all the cause of one effect, I consider them all, as to that extent, as one singular thing'.[40] The political existence of a multitude develops as a transition from a degree of power to a different degree of power; therefore, the different political regimes analysed by the *Political Treatise* cannot be understood as rigid and monolithic realities, but rather as the effects of a continuous variation of the *potentia multitudinis*, which produces what could be called a *fluctuatio imperii*, that is, the uninterrupted transformation of a political regime into another.[41] In this perspective, the relationship between the power (*potentia*) of the multitude and the *imperium*, as defined in the *Political Treatise* II, 17, can assume two different configurations: on the one side, it can be represented as an internal determination — so that the *potentia multitudinis* coincides with the *imperium*'s laws and commands; but, on the other side, in specific circumstances, this determination emerges from the 'outside', so that the action of the multitude on the *imperium* assumes the shape of a form of resistance to its laws and commands.

Two examples of this second relationship can be found in the *Political Treatise*: the first one concerns the aristocratic regime, the second one the political consequences of the affect of indignation. Regarding his analysis of aristocracy, Spinoza points out that this kind of *imperium* is based upon the clear distinction between the patricians and the rest of the multitude who are excluded from institutions and even from the rights of citizenship.[42] Therefore, the only instrument the multitude possesses to obtain political visibility is that of instilling fear in the rulers: 'The only reason its [aristocratic] rule is not in practice absolute is that the multitude is terrifying to its rulers. If it [the multitude] doesn't claim that freedom for itself by an explicit law, it still

---

39   *Ethics* III, 17 Schol.; *CWS* I, p. 504; *Gebhardt* II, p. 153: 'This constitution of the Mind which arises from two contrary affects is called "vacillation of mind".'

40   *CWS* I, p. 447.

41   Skeaff defines this movement as a 'scalar, as opposed to dichotomous, understanding of freedom and power that finite individuals [and finite ensemble of individuals as well] are capable of achieving' (Skeaff, *Becoming Political*, p. 86).

42   See *TP* VIII, 3; *CWS* II, p. 566.

claims it tacitly and maintains it.'[43] The *potentia multitudinis* applies an affective 'pressure' on the institutional framework, determining it from the outside, and thus constituting an apparent otherness which cannot be integrated unless it is through the transformation of the institutions themselves. The second example concerns the emergence of a collective aversion to the ruler(s), due to their behaviours which strongly collide with citizens' imaginative constitution:

> So for the Commonwealth to be its own master, it is bound to maintain the causes of fear and respect. Otherwise it ceases to be a Commonwealth [...]. To slaughter and rob his subjects, to rape their young women, and actions of that kind, turn fear into indignation, and hence turn the civil order into a state of hostility.[44]

The transformation of the multitude's fear into indignation (which is defined as 'hate toward someone who has done evil to another' in the *Ethics*)[45] produces a radical change in the political order of the *imperium* and creates the conditions for the emergence of a 'state of hostility' (*status hostilitatis*), which resembles the Hobbesian state of nature/state of war, with the relevant difference that the conflict is now polarized between those who were formerly ruled and the former rulers in a sort of reinterpretation of the Machiavellian theory of humours.[46]

In these two examples, the multitude expresses its power through an affective dynamic which is not integrated into political institutions but rather obeys a very natural law that can be summarized in the

---

43 TP VIII, 4; CWS II, p. 567. See also Stefano Visentin, 'La parzialità dell'universale. La moltitudine nell'imperium aristocraticum', in *Spinoza: individuo e moltitudine*, ed. by Riccardo Caporali, Vittorio Morfino, and Stefano Visentin (Cesena: Il Ponte Vecchio, 2007), pp. 373–90.

44 TP IV, 4; CWS II, p. 527. But see also TP III, 9; CWS II, p. 521: 'Because the Commonwealth's Right is defined by the common power of a multitude, it's certain that its power and Right are diminished to the extent that it provides many people with reasons to conspire against it.'

45 *Ethics* III, DA 20; CWS I, p. 535.

46 Niccolò Machiavelli, *The Prince* [1513], ed. by William J. Connell (Boston, MA: Bedford, 2005): 'For in every city these two different humours are found, whence it arises that the people desire to be neither commanded nor oppressed by the great, and the great desire both to command and to oppress the people'. And this situation arises because the people do not want to be dominated or oppressed by the nobles, and the nobles want to dominate and oppress the people' (ch. 9).

statement: 'being frightening in order not to be afraid' (the reversal of
the famous Tacitan saying: *terret vulgus, nisi metuat*).[47] Nevertheless,
the externality of this power to the *imperium* does not only involve negative consequences for the existence of a political subject, which could
appear to be the case at first sight, since the power itself expresses the
relentless and necessary (that is, it stems from the multitude's nature)
movement of the collective imagination and passions. The institutional
framework must continuously adapt itself to these passions, producing
a collection of different institutions that replace one another without,
however, denying the very essence of the political body. In fact, in the
Political Treatise, Spinoza reminds us:

> When disagreements and rebellions are stirred up in a Com-
> monwealth — as they often are — the result is never that
> the citizens dissolve the Commonwealth — though this of-
> ten happens in other kinds of society. Instead, if they can't
> settle their disagreements while preserving the form of the
> Commonwealth, they change its form to another. So when I
> speak of the means required to preserve the state, I understand
> the means necessary to preserve its form without any notable
> change.[48]

An important consequence of this statement is that every transition is
caused by an increase or decrease in the multitude's power, and every
political regime can be seen as a determinate (both ontologically and
historically) expression of the democratic natural structure of a political organization. Thus, democracy takes on a dual meaning: it reveals
the political regime which expresses the highest degree of collective
power (although it is known that even within a democratic regime
some transitions of *potentia* are still present), but it also exhibits the
immanent movement of this power within every form of government.

In a similar way, freedom is never a 'natural' property of human
beings but rather a process of liberation: being free in an absolute

---

47   *TP* vii, 27; *CWS* ii, pp. 558–59: 'What we've written may be ridiculed by those who
      think the vices common to all mortals belong only to the plebeians — those who
      think "that there's no moderation in the common people; that they're terrifying, unless
      they themselves are cowed by fear"; or that "the plebeians either serve humbly or rule
      proudly, like despots", and that "there's neither truth nor judgment in [the plebeian
      class]", etc. But everyone shares a common nature, we're just deceived by power and
      refinement.'

48   *TP* vi, 2; *CWS* ii, p. 562.

sense means to be able to use one's own power, principally reason but also affects and imagination, insofar as they help to unify every individual's strength. That is why freedom and necessity coincide, since everyone's natural power derives from a necessary causal chain which involves a basically infinite network of relations and mutual transformations. However, another definition of freedom can be found, in which Spinoza expresses the (imaginary) discordance between the essential determination of the mode's power and the existential indefinite nature of the same power, and at the same time the attempt to overcome it both individually and collectively. Given this situation, how can the multitude escape the threat of an infinite conflict among humans while promoting the transitions which increase power and cooperation to the detriment of those which produce impotence and divisions? How can the multitude become free? In the *Theological-Political Treatise*, Spinoza states that 'we've never reached the point where a state is not in more danger from its own citizens than from its enemies, and where the rulers don't fear their citizens more than their enemies'.[49] Therefore, a political process aiming at collective emancipation should begin with unmasking the phantasmagorical nature of the regimes which disempower the multitude's affects and imagination — that is, all regimes, such as monarchy, tyranny, and oligarchy, which are founded on negative passions, primarily on fear (fear which rulers and the ruled inspire in each other, but also an overall fear which the multitude inspire in themselves). The second step (only logically, not chronologically) should consist in implementing common spaces (spaces of rights, communication, exchanges, even of conflicts, provided that they are regulated by laws),[50] so that positive affects can find a way to develop into a rational form (since rationality always derives from a collective development). In the *Theological-Political Treatise*, Spinoza calls a 'republic' the process of gradual transformation of individual liberty into a 'general freedom [*communis libertas*]'.[51]

---

49   *TTP* xvii, 17; *CWS* ii, p. 299.

50   See Filippo Del Lucchese, *Conflict, Power, and Multitude in Machiavelli and Spinoza: Tumult and Indignation* (London: Continuum, 2009); Stefano Visentin, 'From Security to Peace and Concord: The Building of a Free Commonwealth in Spinoza's Political Treatise', *Theoria*, 66.2 (2019), pp. 71–90.

51   *TTP* Praef., 10; *CWS* ii, p. 69; *Gebhardt* iii, p. 7: 'For it is completely contrary to the general freedom to fill the free judgment of each man with prejudices, or to restrain it in any way.'

The republic's aim is 'to free each person from fear':[52] not simply to guarantee a supposed natural freedom to everyone, but rather to foster the shift from an imaginary independency of the will — which is always at risk of being turned into voluntary servitude — to a network of powerful relationships among individuals who are able to free them from their fears and illusions, or at least to prevent these fears and illusions from being dominant. Freedom can thus reveal itself as both the quest for security and the organization of popular surveillance; as both the freedom of judging, as well as the resistance of the many to the oppression of the few.

To conclude, freedom, especially political freedom, can acquire different meanings in Spinoza's philosophy, but it is always deeply connected to the necessity of the causal process generating the body, the imagination, and the affects of the multitude. Such a dynamic identity of necessity and freedom causes both the practical predominance of democracy (which is meant as the immanent movement of the multitude) and the theoretical superiority of a democratic political science, which is based upon the refusal of any transcendent legitimacy of authority or individualistic perspectives. This is an ontological and materialist conception of democracy. For this reason, Spinoza states that '[a] man who is guided by reason is more free in a state, where he lives according to a common decision, than in solitude, where he obeys only himself':[53] in fact, obeying oneself, within the solitude of an abstract individualism, generates an imaginary and thus unstable freedom, which must be replaced by a progressive freedom, engaging all citizens in a common process of emancipation from their fear and passivity.

---

52   *TTP* xx, 11; *CWS* ii, p. 346; *Gebhardt* iii, pp. 240–41: 'From the foundations of the Republic explained above it follows most clearly that its ultimate end is not to dominate, restraining men by fear, and making them subject to another's control, but on the contrary to free each person from fear, so that he can live securely, as far as possible, i.e., so that he retains to the utmost his natural right to exist and operate without harm to himself or anyone else.'

53   *Ethics* iv, 73; *CWS* i, p. 587.

Temporality and History in Spinoza
The Refusal of Teleological Thought

ERICKA MARIE ITOKAZU

INTRODUCTION: SPINOZIST ISSUES BETWEEN MATERIALISM AND IDEALISM

Some remarkable studies have shown Baruch Spinoza's influence on various materialist traditions and even on idealist philosophies.[1] Wherever he is quoted there seems to be some sort of dispute over the recognition of Spinoza as a predecessor of that particular tradition. However, there is a general consensus of the idea that Spinozism implies the refusal of any transcendent entity and the assertion of a radical immanence inextricably linked to the denial of final causality and teleology.

> All the prejudices I here undertake to expose depend on this one: that men commonly suppose that all natural things act, as men do, on account of an end; indeed, they maintain as

---

1 Vittorio Morfino, *Genealogia di un pregiudizio. L'immagine di Spinoza in Germania da Leibniz a Marx* (Hildesheim: Olms, 2016); *The New Spinoza*, ed. by Warren Montag and Ted Stolze (Minneapolis: University of Minnesota Press, 1997); Yirmiyahu Yovel, *Spinoza and Other Heretics: The Adventures of Immanence* (Princeton, NJ: Princeton University Press, 1989); André Tosel, *Du matérialisme, de Spinoza* (Paris: Kimé, 1994).

certain that God himself directs all things to some certain end,
for they say that God made all things for man, and man that
he might worship God. [...] Thus this prejudice was changed
into superstition, and struck deep roots in their minds. This was
why each of them strove with great diligence to understand and
explain the final causes of all things.[2]

Given this striking statement from the *Ethics*' Appendix, Spinoza's rejection of finalism is almost undisputed. The foundation of the New
Science as a modern project seems to depend on taking finalism out
of the laws of nature (*Philosophia naturalis*). This teleology was preserved, however, by René Descartes in regard to God's will and human
free will (*Prima philosophia*) — in which cases freedom determines the
possible and the contingent.

The refusal of the teleological explanations for both *Prima philosophia* and *Philosophia naturalis* could be the key to understanding
why Spinoza's philosophy is of interest to so few scholars of history.[3]
After all, by refusing to give any ontological status to the categories of
possibility and contingency, his philosophy seems to reduce human
actions to fatalism, especially if understood in terms of the rigid law
of *Philosophia naturalis*. By a mistaken understanding of the efficient
cause, the laws of nature are reduced to a restrictive form of necessary
causality, thus making human freedom almost impossible to conceive.
Moreover, the idealist tradition of Spinozism has often rejected his
Prima philosophia precisely because there is no place for free will and
a fundamental notion of the theories of history, i.e. time.[4] On the

---

2   *Ethics* I, App.; *CWS* [*The Collected Works of Spinoza*, see abbreviations], I, pp. 440–41.

3   For example, Yovel recognizes that Spinoza's radical immanence and the refusal of all
     transcendent entities influenced Ludwig Feuerbach's concept of self-alienation as man
     projecting his essence outward into a separate, divine world, from which this essence
     then confronts him as external and oppressive (see Yovel, *Spinoza and Other Heretics*,
     pp. 73–74); nevertheless, Yovel also writes: 'meanwhile, we should address the broader
     question of teleology, which prompted our discussion of Marx in first place. Based
     upon the foregoing analysis of man-in-nature, how does Marx's philosophy of imman-
     ence — lacking an inherent teleology while maintaining a historical perspective —
     trace its own way between Hegel and Spinoza'? (ibid., p. 93).

4   As Vittorio Morfino notes in *Plural Temporality: Transindividuality and the Aleatory
     between Spinoza and Althusser* (Leiden: Brill, 2014), 'The powerful acosmic interpret-
     ation of Spinoza [is] magnificently expressed in the following lines by Bloch' (p. 14):
     '*The world stands here as a crystal, with the sun at its peak, so that nothing casts a shadow.
     [...]* Time is missing, history is missing, development is missing and especially any
     concrete multiplicity in the one ocean of substance. [...] Spinozism stands there as if

one hand, under the rigid laws of nature and necessary causality, we have a materialist fatalism (and the impossibility of freedom); on the other hand, by refusing free will and the notion of time, we have the impossibility of temporality in human history.

This chapter's proposal is to rethink Spinoza's rejection of finalism, and to relate the question of time to the problem of the final cause. I ask whether our understanding of Spinoza's critique of time as a refusal of teleological thought is successful or not, and whether thinking history as a non-teleological process could be possible. Furthermore, I clarify whether or not this can be done without the central notion of time.

To avoid creating any anachronisms, I shall only propose a hypothetical outline as to what the Spinozist critique of a historico-teleological thinking *could* be. After all, the theory of history is not a seventeenth-century problem. However, it is precisely that century that may provide the only philosophy actually capable of countering the kind of finalism which theories of history rely upon.[5] This is the case insofar as one considers all historico-teleological thinking to depend upon the following four conditions:

1. the linearity of time;

2. a temporality that is progressively determined towards the future;

3. a continuity of time established by means of a relation between successive instants external to each other (in order to get rid of fatalism). That is, the connection between past, present, and future should not be determined by necessary causality but by free causality;

4. as a result, and in order to be able to conceive of *praxis*, human actions must be determinable, by themselves or accidentally, because they are *possible* actions. They are determinable by free

---

there was eternal noon in the necessity of the world, in the determinism of its geometry and of its both carefree and situationless crystal — *sub specie aeternitatis*' (Ernst Bloch, *The Principle of Hope*, trans. by Neville Plaice, Stephen Plaice, and Paul Knight, 3 vols (Cambridge, MA: MIT Press, 1986), ii, pp. 852–53).

5   The following arguments are a tentative attempt to reproduce, with a Spinozist lexicon, the thesis that 'democracy is a historical question' made by Marilena Chaui, 'A questão democrática', in her *Cultura e democracia: o discurso competente e outras falas* (São Paulo: Cortez, 2006), pp. 144–69 (p. 145).

will, but they are not necessary actions, that is, they are not already determined by nature. If these actions carry out their final goal, such an outcome would therefore be unpredictable and have to be explained in contingent terms.

This being said, I'd like to highlight the most important arguments of *Ethics* I. In this section, Spinoza demonstrates that the infinitely infinite, the one unique substance, is the cause of itself and operates by immanent, necessary, and efficient causality over the whole of nature (be it the *Natura Naturans* or the *Natura Naturata*). Extension and Thought are thus no longer independent substances, but attributes of the same unique and absolutely infinite substance. In other words, this viewpoint eliminates contingency, possibility, and finalistic causality.

In the famous Appendix, such categories (the contingent, the possible, and the final cause) appear as substitutes accomplished by human (imaginary) projections in two ways: firstly, the understanding of necessity is replaced by the imagination of the accomplishment of final causality; secondly, the inexorable interiority of immanent causality is imaginarily replaced by the impregnable exteriority of transitive causality. I argue here that these projections and replacements are made from a single instrument of imagination: time.

THE PROBLEM OF TEMPORALITY IN SPINOZA: THE NEGATIVITY OF TIME

The most important texts to analyse Spinoza's definitions of time are his early writings. In the *Metaphysical Thoughts*, Spinoza's own position seems to be nothing but an account of Descartes's philosophy, who defined time as a being of reason (*ens rationis*) or a mode of thought that serves to measure duration in the same way as number measures motion. According to Descartes's *Meditations*, if one exists, one is a possible existence, and one's duration therefore will need a continuous creation to actualize its possible existence. That is why an external force, or in Descartes's terms, God as an external and transcendent causality, is required to maintain these created things in existence.

> For a lifespan can be divided into countless parts, each completely independent of the others, so that it does not follow

> from the fact that I existed a little while ago that I must exist
> now, unless there is some cause which as it were creates me
> afresh at this moment — that is, which preserves me. For it is
> quite clear to anyone who attentively considers the nature of
> time that the same power and action are needed to preserve
> anything at each individual moment of its duration as would
> be required to create that thing anew if it were not yet in exist-
> ence. Hence the distinction between preservation and creation
> is only a conceptual one.[6]

Hence, duration consists of a linear, homogeneous, continuously and punctually recreated existence. The same action and force is indeed required at any instant, no matter how short this instant might be, to recreate such an existence again and again, making all instants independent from each other and thus detaching the present instant from that which immediately preceded it. Moreover, because duration is composed of parts and is divisible, it becomes measurable in the same way that geometric space is measurable. That is, it becomes a geometrized duration measured by geometric time.

In Spinoza's early writings, therefore, time, number, and measure seem to be legitimate beings of reason. This is why one finds a certain transitivity between duration and that which measures it. Time and duration, like Siamese twins, thus become neutral, homogeneous, and perfect doubles of Extension as presented by Descartes's *Principles of Philosophy* in the section dedicated to physics.

Despite making use of Cartesian terminology, however, Spinoza's argument does not allow us to speak properly of an essence of time, for it is neither an objective essence (i.e., an idea inside of us) nor a formal essence (i.e., a condition of things outside of us). Although Spinoza calls it a 'being of reason', he adds to this nomenclature the proviso that, in spite of this choice of words, time cannot properly be called a 'being'.[7] According to Spinoza, time has no formal reality. That is, it has no existence outside of us. Furthermore, time has no objective reality: it does not possess the status of an idea, be it true, false, or fictitious. Time is not an essence inside of us, while outside of us it

---

6   René Descartes, *Meditations on First Philosophy*, in *The Philosophical Writings of Descartes*, trans. by John Cottingham, Robert Stoothoot, and Dugald Murdoch, 3 vols (New York: Cambridge University Press, 1984–91), II (1985), pp. 1–62 (p. 33).

7   *CM* I; *CWS* I, pp. 299–310.

has no existence. That is, it has *no ontological density* of any kind. To summarize this idea, we can say that for Spinoza *time is on the verge of non-being.*[8]

However, in 1663, Spinoza changed his position on this topic. Duration, henceforth conceived as indivisible, resists the measures that time would apply to it.[9] After Spinoza's Letter xɪɪ,[10] it becomes clear that those who explain duration through time fail to conceive of it properly, for time is but a mere abstraction. Time loses its epistemological value and ceases to be a legitimate being of reason to become, on a path of no return, one of the 'aids of the imagination' (*auxilia imaginationis*). In the following section, we will see what changed in Spinoza's concept of duration.

THE POSITIVITY OF DURATION

Following the demonstrations of the *Ethics*, we understand that there is no transcendent God above all 'created things', for they are now called 'finite things' or just finite modes (or affections) of the infinite substance, that is, God or Nature (*Deus sive Natura*). In the definitions of the *Ethics*, Spinoza argues that eternity and the duration of finite modes are indivisible. This is the main difference with his earlier writings.

To understand what it is to be a finite mode requires apprehending how, in this philosophy of immanence, Spinoza abandons the relation of *transcendent causality* between the infinite substance and its finite modes. The necessity of the substance's efficient cause is now determined by *immanent causality*, which displays the inner relation of substance's power to the power of the substance's finite modes,[11] that is, the inner force of *conatus*: 'each thing, as far as it can by its own

---

8   See Ericka Itokazu, 'Au-delà du temps mesure. La question du temps chez Spinoza', in *Ontologia e temporalità. Spinoza e i suoi lettori moderni*, ed. by Giuseppe D'Anna and Vittorio Morfino (Milano: Mimesis, 2012), pp. 387–98.

9   The displacement of the role of time in Spinoza's philosophy is admirably explored in the works of Chantal Jaquet (see especially her *Sub specie æternitatis. Études des concepts de temps, durée et éternité chez Spinoza* (Paris: Kimé, 1997).

10 *Ep.* xɪɪ [Lodewijk Meyer]; *CWS* ɪ, p. 200.

11 On this subject, I recommend the work of Nicolas Israël, *Spinoza. Le temps de la vigilance* (Paris: Payot, 2001).

power, strives to persevere in its being' and 'the striving by which each thing strives to persevere in its being is nothing but the actual essence of the thing'.[12]

Duration, therefore, is no longer understood as a succession whose continuity is homogeneously neutral and which is characterized by an existential linearity restored instant after instant through continued creation. Instead, duration is understood as continuous, no longer as homogeneous or uniform, and certainly not as measurable by means of the operations of time. On the contrary, duration itself is the expression of diverse, multiple, and heterogeneous movements, insofar as the *conatus* — the constitutive inner power of duration — is also its *actual essence*. Indeed, every variation of power — every simultaneous affection of the body and of the mind — of this essence implies the diverse, multiple, and heterogeneous passages of this very body and this very mind. This is why, as is the case with the substance, duration is not divisible. Because it is the very characteristic of finite modes, duration can only be conceived of as a whole from which no parts can be divided.

In fact, after Spinoza's Letter XII, it is perfectly clear that duration can no longer be related to time. Not only is immanent causality the very core of Spinoza's thought, but it also constitutes a profound shift away from Cartesian philosophy. In Spinoza, one no longer has to cope with the complex problem of a divisible duration conceived as a succession of instants external to each other, precisely because this succession of instants requires the action of an external cause without which we simply could not understand how we continue to exist. Hence, with Spinoza, finite modes are no longer understood as instantaneous possible existences, and duration ceases to be dependent on God's continued creation (contra Descartes). The relation between the infinite and the finite is no longer that of an opposition between the eternal and the instantaneous, nor is it an external relation. Rather, the relation between the infinite and the finite is an internal or, better yet, an immanent relation.

---

12   *Ethics* II, 6 and 7; *CWS* I, p. 499.

In such a philosophy, a finite thing is defined as that which 'can be limited by another of the same nature'.[13] Using this definition — certainly one of the finest in the history of philosophy — Spinoza explains finitude as simply the fact of being among and in relationship with other finite beings. Thus, finitude is no longer characterized by ephemerality or mortality, and instead thought of as the fact that all existences are always interconnected. To be a finite thing means simply to *co-exist*, to exist with other singular things: finitude is precisely the reciprocal determining factor of the existence of finite things.

The co-existence of this *conatus* with and among other finite modes is shaped and characterized by multiple movements of body compositions, re-compositions, and decompositions, interwoven through many encounters and disagreements, and through the immeasurable production of desires (*conatus-cupiditas*), joys, and sorrows of affective life, be they individual or collective.

If duration is no longer understood as succession, if it cannot be reduced to a mere linear continuation — i.e. to a continuity whose ability to be measured comes from its being emptied of any of the movements that are proper to its existence — then how should one understand Spinoza's definition of duration as 'an indefinite continuation of existing'?[14] To be clear, here, the term 'indefinite' does not mean indeterminate. Spinoza uses this adjective ('indefinite') to define duration because a finite existence is not determined by its actual essence. That is, the limitation of a finite existence is not determined by its inner efficient cause (derived from the immanence of the substance within the *conatus'* essence) that makes it exist and, in itself, could never make it cease to exist.[15]

Here we can apply some lessons we have learned from Letter XII to the *Ethics*, for in that letter Spinoza presented various definitions of the 'infinite': there are things we call 'infinite, or if you prefer, indefinite',[16] he says, 'because they cannot be equated with any number' and we might say, to no measure of time, 'though they can be conceived to be greater or lesser' as in the case of *conatus*. Or, to quote the definition

---

13   *Ethics* I, Def. 2; *CWS* I, p. 408.
14   *Ethics* II, Def. 5; *CWS* I, p. 447.
15   'The striving by which each thing strives to persevere in its being involves no finite time, but an indefinite time' (*Ethics* III, 8; *CWS* I, p. 499).
16   *Ep.* XII [Lodewijk Meyer]; *CWS* I, p. 205.

given in *Ethics* III, 4 Dem.: 'For the definition of any thing affirms, and does not deny, the thing's essence, *or* it posits the thing's essence, and does not take it away'.[17] Therefore the term from the *Ethics*, 'indefinite duration', is derived from the absence of inner boundaries in the *conatus*. Now, to assert the absence of an internal limit is precisely to acknowledge and to affirm the internal positivity of the *conatus* and to posit the absence of any inner negativity. In other words, to be 'indefinite' is our finite way of being infinite.

Duration is, so to speak, positively undefined. Its definition actually occurs through the unfolding of its power within the existential field among many other finite modes. In the end, this dynamic definition results from the composition of experience as a mosaic of multiple affects, affections, and desires. Duration (or 'the indefinite continuation of existing'), therefore, far from indicating a negation or a lack of determination, points to its opposite, that is, an immeasurable field of dynamic determinations, interwoven through the relations of one's internal power to exist and act with the external powers of many others. In other words, existence is defined through one's various relationships with the world, with living beings, with people, etc. When seen in this way, duration is inseparable from the *conatus* which guarantees its dynamic breadth and exceptional ontological density.[18]

It is impossible for us to strive for a complete definition of that dynamic force within such ontological density. Duration is not only indivisible but should also be understood as inapprehensible. Defining the continuation of existence is precisely not to understand it as a process, that is, as the movement of the *conatus* in its various internal determinations and external limitations. To seek to define duration is not to conceive of it but to confuse it with time. Or, to put it clearly, to seek to intellectually define duration is to imagine it, rather than to conceive of it; and as per Letter XII's warning, to imagine duration is to separate it from the substance, that is, *to imagine efficient and immanent causality in the shape of transcendent and external causality.*

---

17   *CWS* I, p. 498.
18   The argument about the positivity of duration and the negativity of time is a part of a major section from my doctoral dissertation: Ericka Marie Itokazu, 'Tempo, duração e eternidade na filosofia de Espinosa' (Universidade de São Paulo (USP), 2008) <https://www.teses.usp.br/teses/disponiveis/8/8133/tde-18032009-110714/pt-br.php> [accessed 02 July 2020].

For this reason, Spinoza affirms that we are bound to have only an
extremely inadequate knowledge of our duration or of the duration of
the singular things outside us,[19] since we are bound to imagine efficient
causality in the shape of transitive causality. The interesting thing is
that the same restriction that impedes adequate knowledge and any
satisfactory definition of duration now seems to open up a wide range
of determinations and movements of our power in the unfolding (*sub
duratione*) of existing and acting.

Sub duratione, the non-definition of duration, is the corollary of
our existence among other existences which is identical to the process
of singular things in the intertwining of simultaneous encounters of
composition or decomposition — a contrariety or complementarity of
images and relations — but also in the union or opposition of forces.
In other words, *sub duratione* is the very nature of the modal condition
of finite things in continuous and multiple sets of relations to other
existences, but above all it is a continuous process of power (*potentia*),
that is, the perseverance in one's own being.

It should be noted that there are two distinct processes which
are not equivalent even though they may seem similar. As per *Ethics*
II, we know that a body cannot be conceived of as an isolated unit
amongst other bodies, since to be a singular thing is to be an individual
composed of many others, each of which is also composed by many
other individuals, etc.[20] From the concept of body, Spinoza characterizes a continuous process of composition and decomposition with
other bodies, as though self-regeneration[21] were occurring thanks to
the relations with other internal and external individuals within what
we can call a multiple and continuous process of *singularization* occurs.
However, in *Ethics* III and IV, after the demonstrations concerning
the *conatus*, Spinoza highlights another process which is relevant here:
these singular things can then constitute, in their actual essence, a com-
positional or oppositional power in relationship with other external

---

19   *Ethics* II, 30 and 31; *CWS* I, pp. 471–72.
20   'By singular things I understand things that are finite and have determinate existence.
      And if a number of individuals so concur in an action that together they are all the
      cause of one effect, I consider them all, to that extent, as one singular thing' (*Ethics* II,
      Def. 7; *CWS* I, p. 447).
21   *Ethics* II, 13; *CWS* I, pp. 457–62.

forces that have the possibility of not only diminishing this *conatus* but also of destroying it.

In Spinoza's political writings, our natural right is defined by our power as a political expression of the *conatus*. Thus, a singular thing is determined by the multiple relations of an individual *conatus* or a collective one (as the *multitudinis potentia*) against external forces (*potestas*) within which it strives to persevere in its own existence. The duration of singular things is also inapprehensible in the political process of this individual and collective *conatus*. Thus, they establish relations with other forces that simultaneously determine their inner ethical power to freedom or slavery, and their political power within the various internal relations of a political body or against external relations with a political *potestas*.

The central dynamics of composing or opposing ourselves (as individuals and as a collectivity) rests in both processes, in a continuous definition of our existence: we are immersed in the world that we are also comprised of, and we persist and endure as a singular and collective *conatus* in and with this world as beings capable of producing common affects and actions. One understands how, in this dual movement of singularization and perseverance, which is also within the continuously in-definition of ethical and political existence, duration is as dense and thick from the ontological viewpoint as it is dynamic and indomitable from the historical viewpoint.

THE POSITIVITY OF DURATION OR THE NEGATIVITY OF TIME?

From what we have just seen, it should be easy to understand why Spinoza affirms that we may only have an *extremely inadequate knowledge* of duration. The in-apprehensibility of duration makes it impossible to conceive of it intellectually as a complete definition, which forces us to (only) imagine it. This being said, the problem of time and its relation to duration becomes harder and more complex at another level. Indeed, imagination is not the source of error, as Spinoza demonstrates; rather, the error consists precisely in taking imagination for intellection, that is, taking a misconception for a concept.[22] There are

---

22   *Ethics* II, 17 Dem.; *CWS* I, pp. 465–66.

things one can only conceive of and never imagine, such as eternity; on the other hand, there are things one can only imagine and never conceive of, such as one's duration and the duration of external things.

The consequence is inexorable: seeking to understand duration necessarily involves imagining it through time. And this is exactly what, as Spinoza wrote in Letter XII, separates us from the substance. I would like to summarize the triple mechanism operated by time as follows:

a) First mechanism: we are inclined, by a natural impulse, to confuse time with duration.[23] We begin to divide the total and indivisible inner force of duration into parts. We are inclined to imagine our immanent force (our *conatus*) by means of the image of transitive causality introduced by the negativity of time.

The continuity of our existence becomes the experience of its own fragmentation, since time does not bind one moment to another. On the contrary, time itself is the division that splits the indivisible inner force of duration into a before and an after, transforming the continuity of a life into a contiguity of isolated moments. As a result, we get used to smudging the ground on which the power of our existence unfolds, so that we feel deeply alienated (*ab aliio*), that is, separated from ourselves. To confuse duration with time is to be forced to deal with the argument presented in Letter XII: 'For composing Duration of moments is the same as composing Number merely by adding noughts'.[24] Transitive causality replaces desire's immanent determination (our *conatus-cupiditas*) for the emptiness of free will (its misconception). The emergence of time reveals the eclipse of the *conatus*, transforming the power of a life into a non-power to live.

b) Second mechanism: although neither number, nor measure, nor time have any reality of their own, many 'have confused these three [aids of the imagination] with things themselves'.[25] Thus, to confuse time with duration produces a concrete effect, that

---

23   *Ep.* XII [Lodewijk Meyer]; *CWS* I, p. 202.
24   Ibid., 204.
25   Ibid.

is, the imaginary construction of the reality of time outside of us.

This argument has a mirroring relation to the preceding argument. Given that duration is perceived as extremely fragmented, and living is perceived as various split instants that do not support their own continuity, we endeavour to imagine the consistency of our existence maintained by an exterior and continuous support. As an imaginary replica of Descartes's continued creation, we will imagine an endless and external time, an eternity which is the sole imaginary entity capable of colligating the split instants within oneself. Time becomes an external reality outside of us, and its mechanism and action are independent of all human actions. Since time is external, unrelated to anything, and devoid of a beginning as well as of an end, it becomes the symbol of the infinite beyond us. Our internal relation to the substance, established by immanent causality, will therefore be imagined as the transcendent causality of the absolute above us.

However, because it is an imaginary construction, its very nature is to present itself in various figures. It does not matter whether these figures are linear or cyclical ones, eschatological or soteriological, for they shall always be the metamorphic face of a Time *edax rerum*. One cannot escape the order of nature. There, life is perceived as a strange experience in which a single operator not only fragments the course of life, but also merges the instants it has split, reversing the constitutive power of the *conatus* from the inside out, and subsuming it under an imaginary external power (*potestas*) of an infinite Time that devours everything.

c) Third and final mechanism: of all aids of the imagination, only time is able to fragment duration and to introduce, in a philosophy of the necessary, the experience of contingency. As long as one exists, one's *conatus*, the striving inner force to persevere in existence, is also one's actual essence. Even though essence and existence are inalienable pairs, in this paradoxical and imaginary experience, time (and time only) is capable of clandestinely alienating the inalienable.

This is why the operation of time introduces contingency and possibility, notions that Spinoza defines as the misconception of the necessary bond between essence and existence.[26] The ontological density of the *conatus'* inner process in singular things, necessarily determined by their intertwined co-existence, is now dissolved by the fiction that all things are individually isolated, for they are now separated from the substance and turned into *particular* things whose existence is corruptible by the contingency of the world.

> For each singular thing [...] must be determined by another singular thing to exist and produce effects in a certain and determinate way, and this again by another, and so to infinity. But since we have demonstrated from this common property of singular things that we have only a very inadequate knowledge of duration of our body, *we shall have to draw the same conclusion concerning duration of singular things.* [...] From this it follows that *all particular things are contingent and corruptible.* For we can have no adequate knowledge of their duration, and that is what we must understand by contingency of things and the possibility of their corruption. For *beyond that there is no contingency.*[27]

These three mechanisms are the source of the multiple variations of desire (*conatus-cupiditas*) that are related to *Ethics* IV and its demonstrations of Human Bondage (De servitute humana). The Powers of the Affects (*Affectuum viribus*), or their intensity, is connected with temporal operations which determine hope, fear, despair, security, and *flutuatio animi*, all of which are temporal affects and fundamental political passions. The 'future contingents', the possible existence and corruption of the world, *Fors Fortunae,* and servitude: all of these images contribute to an internal superstition which is based on a passion forged by time, just like fear that simultaneously requires hope about the image of an external entity upon which we are dependent and which reinforces all theologico-political power. This could include the image of the impossible union with the infinite of an eternal and

---

26   Cf. *Ethics* IV, Def. 3; *CWS* I, p. 546: 'I call singular things contingent insofar as we find *nothing*, while we attend *only to their essence*, which necessarily *posits their existence* or which necessarily *excludes it*'. See also *Ethics* IV, Def. 4; *CWS* I, p. 546: 'I call *the same singular things* possible, insofar as, we *do not know* whether those causes are determined to produce them'; my emphasis.

27   *Ethics* III, 31 Dem. and Corol.; *CWS* I, p. 472.

transcendent God, or the secular image of the end of history, or the image of a final emancipation of humanity in which we overcome our endless and miserable present. The soteriological or the eschatological expectations are both temporal projections of finalist thought that instil fear and hope in the heart of one's affective life.

Spinoza defines fear as an inconstant sadness and hope as an inconstant joy, and writes that they are both 'born from the idea of a future or a past thing whose outcome we to some extent doubt'.[28] Fear and hope, however, are so inconstant that they take the shape of existential doubt, and in this case we might understand that to doubt is *not to affirm* the power of our existence. On the contrary, doubt suspends our ability to act, that is to say, it suspends the action of our *conatus*. That is why Spinoza explains that there is no fear without hope, and there is no hope without fear. The inability to act is introduced by the negativity of time; the soul's *vacillation* of mind is the passion that most makes us politically and existentially powerless. Vacillation is like being a prisoner of permanent doubt floating between fear and hope. It is an affective experience of impotence, of lacking power to act, as if we were all merely possible existences in a contingent world.

Removing doubt about the 'uncertainty of the future' is the same as requiring that the *conatus* gets rid of the impossible image of the same future being simultaneously fearsome and hopeful, even though this amounts to cultivating the fiction of an 'uncertain present' that brings the promise of our 'possibility to act'. Through such an inversion of images, it is 'the present' that would become 'uncertain'. It becomes open to the imaginary possibility of human actions as a decision towards a better future, that is, the false image of free will and the very definition of finalist thought. To avoid the powerless effort of a suspended existence due to the vacillation of mind and in order not to expect the impossible disclosure of future times in the present (the verge of despair), some effort to build a resistance to doubt is required. The introduction of an action is required, even if it is the image of free will seeking the good: the closest affective image of some certainty, a fragile and necessary pulse of the *conatus* from within passional life.

---

28   See *Ethics* III, DA 12 and 13; *CWS* I, p. 534.

How can we understand that same process outside of finalist thought and within the operation of the efficient cause?

First, by paying attention to the fact that these teleological operations reveal another important concept in Spinoza: *utilitas*. As he defines it: 'By good I shall understand what we certainly know to be useful to us',[29] and 'by the end for the sake of which we do something I understand appetite'.[30] These definitions are clearly reinverting what has already been inverted by our imaginary misconception. Thus, Spinoza uses the lexicon of teleological thought, a corollary of servile imagination, precisely to escape servitude. This is why, in *Ethics* IV, he explains that one must differentiate the 'contingent' from the 'possible'. The distinction between these images determines the intensity of distinct passions which are more or less subservient to fortune.[31] Further, they determine different interrelations of human actions within the political body that produce different dynamics inside of it — transforming fear and hope into either security (certainty of a future joy), or into despair (certainty of a future sadness) — and explain the social dynamics of a political body, generating a higher or lesser propensity to either freedom or servitude.

Our appetite (our efficient cause), based on its imagination as a final causality and on its imagined quest for what is good (*utilitas*), in fact proposes a determination in order to rid itself of the doubt and uncertainty brought forth by our fears and hopes. For this, it is required that the *conatus* push aside the fearsome image of contingent futures, even though this amounts to fostering *the imaginary construction of an uncertain present*. The confrontation of the *conatus'* determinations with the contingent future, even if it is through imagined free will and finalism, thus produces an individual action, or a cooperation of individuals in action, which, in turn, develops into a renewed effort (isolated or in common) to transform the image of the *contingent* future into another *possible* future. That is *actually and precisely the appropriation of the present time*. The same mechanism can also simultaneously explain,

---

29   *Ethics* IV, Def. 1; *CWS* I, p. 546.
30   *Ethics* IV, Def. 7; *CWS* I, p. 547.
31   'An affect toward a thing which we know does not exist in the present, and which we imagine as possible, is more intense, other things being equal, than one towards a contingent thing' (*Ethics* IV, 12; *CWS* I, p. 552).

in terms of passional processes, the corporal imaginary constructions that survive through the actions of time (be it an individual or political body). The traces of memory (*vestigia corporis*) and social memories,[32] as well as the corporal striving to maintain the image of its own existence, is what is expressed by the internal dynamic of resisting, or renewing,[33] the culture, language, customs, habits, rites, and ceremonies.

CONCLUSION: SPINOZA AND HISTORY

We can now see how both the denial of time's ontological status and the positive density of the *conatus* is likely to change one's views on Spinozism. *Tempus* is not an essence, existence, *res*, *idea*, or epistemological value for knowledge or the sciences. This is perhaps so because time is precisely this innate negativity, or the only instrument capable of introducing the fissures of contradiction within the intense and plain positivity of duration. This is precisely what we were looking for: the connection between the positivity of duration and the negativity of time seems, little by little, to reveal itself as the dynamic composition of the existential human realm (be it individual or collective) of striving in existence with all its consequences within the realms of imagination, ethics, and, above all, politics.

To conclude, one might ask how to understand the historical process implied by these remarks. The question about the relationship between history and time can be renewed. To seek a theory of history with the notion of time turns out to be an idealized abstraction that surrenders to the temptations of finalist thought, and an error that confounds knowledge with imagination, a concept with a misconception, and a science with an ideology.

In contrast, to understand history *sub duratione* amounts to rethinking the challenges of a materialist conception of history. Given the in-apprehensibility of duration and its ontological positivity, the

---

32   See Laurent Bove, *La Stratégie du conatus. Affirmation et résistance chez Spinoza* (Paris: Vrin, 1996) and Lorenzo Vinciguerra, *Spinoza et le signe. La Genèse de l'imagination* (Paris: Vrin, 2005).

33   'An affect whose cause we imagine to be with us in the present moment is stronger than if we did not imagine it to be with us' (*Ethics* IV, 9; *CWS* I, p. 551).

historical process maintains in itself an overture to immeasurable and indomitable determinations for multiple images and operations of time, which contain passions and actions of reciprocal relations between *conatus*. The *affectuum viribus* is now determined by the opposition of affects: 'By opposite affects I shall understand, in what follows, those which pull a man differently, although they are of the same *genus* — such as gluttony and greed, which are species of love, and are opposite not by nature, but accidentally'.[34] The accidental is entirely different from the contingent and the possible, and not related to time. Spinoza designates the accidental as that which constantly modifies the inner force of our *conatus* through the relations between things of the same *genus* in a multitude of affections and affects, which are multiple interconnections of various and diverse durations constantly composing and de-composing the complex thread of a dynamic tissue of the maintenance of their own existence, in other words, their own historicity.

If one thinks of the movement of history as a non-teleological process, and if one thinks about the relation between materialism and history in Spinoza's philosophy, perhaps the answer can simply be this: human actions do not occur according to a succeeding temporal framework (characterized by transitive and final causality), whether it is pursuing a linear, cyclic, progressive, or regressive time, since human history does not move through time. On the contrary, it is the imagination of time experiencing accidental causes (through the multiple efficient and partial causalities intertwining and presenting in our own power) that mobilizes us into history.

TRANSLATED BY BAPTISTE GRASSET

---

34   *Ethics* IV, Def. 5; *CWS* I, p. 546.

Spinozist Moments in Deleuze
Materialism as Immanence

MAURICIO ROCHA

INTRODUCTION

Gilles Deleuze's interpretation of Baruch Spinoza in the late 1960s was of seminal importance in the creation of a political Spinozism. His reading of Spinoza likewise had a great impact on debates ranging across (post)structuralism, psychoanalysis, and Marxism. In fact, subsequent currents of thought, with little direct connection to Deleuze's 1968 book *Expressionism in Philosophy: Spinoza*, have discovered elements there that have proven fruitful for further elaboration.[1] Deleuze's thought, it should be pointed out, is guided by a relation of strict fidelity to Spinoza — an author that accompanied the inflections

---

1   Gilles Deleuze, *Expressionism in Philosophy: Spinoza*, trans. by Martin Joughin (New York: Zone Books, 1992). Interviewed by Pierre-François Moreau and Laurent Bove, Alexandre Matheron claimed that Deleuze exerted more influence on Spinoza Studies in France through his *Difference and Repetition* than through his *Expressionism in Philosophy* (see Alexandre Matheron, 'À propos de Spinoza', *Multitudes*, 1.3 (2000), pp. 169–200). It should be stressed that in Brazil, Marilena Chaui had already analysed the political topics that would become of interest to Spinoza's European readers in the mid-1980s (Antonio Negri, Étienne Balibar, André Tosel, Moreau, Bove, Vittorio Morfino, etc.). See her *Política em Espinosa* (São Paulo: Companhia das Letras, 2003), with texts ranging from 1979 to 1995.

in Deleuze's trajectory and in his treatment, alongside Félix Guattari, of numerous contemporary political issues.[2] To name a few of those topics: the relation between economic processes, structures of social power and the state (all examined from a geo-economic and geopolitical point of view), interpreted through a political-economy perspective carefully attuned to the libidinal economy, and vice-versa.

Listing the available works about Spinoza in late 1960s France, Pierre Macherey pointed to the near complete absence of any commentary about the political dimension of Spinoza's thought — a *terra incognita*.[3] Martial Gueroult's and Deleuze's 1968 publications were thus all the more earth-shaking: both were decidedly undiplomatic, breaking with established certainties and shedding new light on a thinker that had himself defied established orthodoxies. Deleuze's book was part of a series of renewed interpretations of the Sephardic philosopher that included works by Gueroult, Alexandre Matheron, and Bernard Rousset.[4] But it was through Deleuze's reading that Spinoza was transformed into the privileged figure in which philosophy and social dynamics could be reunited.[5] His study of Spinoza was wholly original, involving the development of different philosophical problems, such as 'image of thought',[6] the 'surface meaning', and the 'logic of paradoxes',[7] as well as his recovery of the medieval

2   According to Deleuze's secondary school students, in the 1950s, he often spent months discussing the opening of Spinoza's *Ethics* (cf. François Dosse, *Gilles Deleuze and Félix Guattari: Intersecting Lives*, trans. by Deborah Glassman (New York: Columbia University Press, 2010), p. 103). A survey of references to Spinoza in the work of Deleuze can be found in Éric Alliez (see his 'Appendix I: Deleuze's Virtual Philosophy', in *The Signature of the World, Or, What Is Deleuze and Guattari's Philosophy?*, trans. by Eliot Ross Albert and Alberto Toscano (New York: Continuum, 2004), pp. 85–103).

3   Among the works mentioned by Macherey, it's worth recalling those from the early twentieth century (Léon Brunschvicg, Victor Delbos, Albert Rivaud, Alain [Émile Chartier]), the 1940s (André Darbon) and the early 1960s (Sylvain Zac), as well as Ferdinand Alquié's courses and the *quasi* confidential texts of Madeleine Francès (1937), Marianne Schaub (1978), and the work of Paul Vernière (1954).

4   Martial Gueroult, *Spinoza*, 2 vols (Paris: Aubier-Montaigne, 1968), I: *Dieu (Éthique, 1)*; Bernard Rousset, *La Perspective finale de l'Éthique* (Paris: Vrin, 1968); Alexandre Matheron, *Individu et communauté chez Spinoza* (Paris: Minuit, 1969).

5   Pierre Macherey, 'Spinoza 1968: Guéroult et/ou Deleuze', in *Le Moment philosophique des années 1960 en France*, ed. by Patrice Maniglier (Paris: PUF, 2011), pp. 293–313.

6   See Gilles Deleuze, *Difference and Repetition*, trans. by Paul Patton (London: Athlone, 1994).

7   See Gilles Deleuze, *The Logic of Sense*, trans. by Mark Lester and Charles Stivale (London: Athlone, 1990).

concern for the 'univocity of being' (present in all his three works of that period). The result of their encounter was that both Spinoza and Deleuze were refashioned. Their philosophical alliance produced startling, unexpected mutations within Deleuze's work.

For Deleuze, the history of philosophy is the determination of the conditions and implications of a generative problem. That problem, in turn, is what confers sense on philosophy's concepts; this is what Deleuze means when he writes of 'milieu' and its double connotation in French: taking things 'in the middle' and seeking 'to grasp the (conceptual) milieu'. Milieu is then opposed to a doctrinal description of an exhaustive and static content, following the speculative path of that which has already been thought.[8] It has been said that Deleuze's pedagogy consisted in insisting (methodologically and deontologically) on the role that 'problems' play. The problem-question relation has nothing to do with ignorance or scepticism, be it learned or vulgar: what allows one to connect and discriminate among propositions is a problematic that allows those very propositions to have sense, opening a horizon of meaning and conceptual production. Without the determination of the problematic, the enunciative act lacks any immediate sense, since the argumentation in any case is subordinated to the act of 'posing a problem'.[9] A philosophy is thus the development of a problem that never depends on a voluntary choice of a philosopher: the philosopher is affected by an external restraint, a regime of signs that forces her or his thought — since thinking is not the voluntary exercise of a faculty. This lends itself to a certain humorous misreading of one of Deleuze's most famous phrases: 'it was on Spinoza that I worked the most seriously according to the norms of the history of philosophy'.[10] Rather than repeating what Spinoza said, it was as if Deleuze preceded him: he intervened in Spinoza's thought at the same time that he commented it — all while opening himself up to the thought upon which he was intervening.[11]

---

8   Cf. Manola Antonioli, *Deleuze et l'histoire de la philosophie* (Paris: Kimé, 1999).

9   François Zourabichvili, *Le Vocabulaire de Deleuze* (Paris: Ellipses, 2003), p. 66.

10   Gilles Deleuze and Claire Parnet, *Dialogues*, trans. by Hugh Tomlinson and Barbara Habberjam (New York: Columbia University Press, 1987), p. 15.

11   Pierre Macherey, *Avec Spinoza. Études sur la doctrine et l'histoire du spinozisme* (Paris: PUF, 1992), p. 237.

We should regard with suspicion the chronology (or *doxa*) that identifies *Anti-Oedipus*, published in 1972, as a turning point in Deleuze's work and as a point of departure from *Expressionism in Philosophy*.[12] In fact, his writings from the late 1970's abandoned the problematics of the *Anti-Oedipus*. Those later works, which fed into his and Guattari's *Thousand Plateaus*, actually saw the conceptual influence of Spinoza grow more prominent:[13] 'plane of immanence', 'war machine', 'nomadism', 'apparatus of capture', 'assemblage', 'minority', 'lines', etc. Several texts from the 1970s, contemporary with Deleuze's political engagements, serve to document that mutation. This turn towards politics was for its part connected with Deleuze's startling and dramatic rejection of structuralism in the late 1960s. It also marked his crowning achievement: to think the simultaneity of sense and event in the interpretation of Spinoza's absolute immanence.[14] Deleuze recognized that in phenomenology and structuralism there was a transcendence of sense, an *invariant* that neutralizes production and becoming.[15] In opposition to it, Deleuze's treatment of Spinoza via the problem of expression led him to address the question in terms of logic; that is, Deleuze's approach thus highlighted the critical force of a philosophy based on the reciprocity between matter and thought.[16]

A constant in Deleuze's texts from the 1960s is his critique of representation. One way of understanding this stance was the philosopher's persistent unease with institutions. It was Spinoza, here, who

12   Rafael Becker, 'Natureza e direito em Deleuze' (doctoral thesis, Pontifícia Universidade Católica do Rio de Janeiro, PUC-Rio, 2018), p. 188. See also François Zourabichvili, *Deleuze, une philosophie de l'événement* (Paris: PUF, 1994).

13   Gilles Deleuze, *Kafka: Pour une littérature mineure* (Paris: Minuit, 1975), Deleuze and Guattari, *Rhizome: Introduction* (Paris: Minuit, 1976), and Deleuze, 'Spinoza and Us' (1978), in his *Spinoza: Practical Philosophy*, trans. by Robert Hurley (San Francisco: City Lights Books, 1988), pp. 122–30. See also Zourabichvili, *Deleuze*.

14   François Zourabichvili, 'Deleuze et Spinoza', in *Spinoza au XXᵉ siècle*, ed. by Olivier Bloch (Paris: PUF, 1993), pp. 237–46 (p. 239).

15   In that respect, David Lapoujade wrote: 'Logical doesn't mean rational. We could even say that for Deleuze a movement is all the more logical the more it escapes rationality. The more irrational, the more aberrant, and yet the more logical'. See his *Aberrant Movements: The Philosophy of Gilles Deleuze*, trans. by Joshua David Jordan (Cambridge, MA: MIT Press, 2017), p. 27.

16   See Anne Sauvagnarques, *Deleuze, l'empirisme transcendental* (Paris: PUF, 2009), pp. 150–55.

allowed Deleuze to examine the issue from the perspective of production, relating forms of institutional representation and the passivity of social formations to institutional norms and conduct.[17] This
about-face suggests that Deleuze was no longer seeking to revert Platonism and its underlying 'image of thought', but rather to imbue
philosophy with immanence and 'to install oneself on this [plane of
immanence]'.[18] The concept of 'plane of immanence', which appears
for the first time in his *Kafka*, reappears in his article 'Spinoza and Us'.
There, Deleuze could be found radicalizing the immanentist procedure by subtracting the markers of power from within philosophy and
thought.[19] Deleuze's Spinozism grew even more political after joining
with Guattari: the concept of 'expression' is related to an *affirmative
logic*; that of 'power' to a reconceptualization of both *politics* and *law*;
that of 'common notions' to a renewed understanding of the *composition of powers (potentiae).*[20]

EXPRESSIONISM IN PHILOSOPHY

Marilena Chaui stresses that Deleuze's *Expressionism in Philosophy*
was a revolutionary work for its discovery of expression as a central
concept in Spinoza's philosophy. The concept of 'expression' was vital
for grasping Being as absolutely complex, internally differentiated, its
distinctions revealing the qualitative difference of expressive essences.
From there followed Deleuze's refutation of an emanative and subjectivist interpretation of attributes, in favour of a logic of expression:
substantial attributes are qualities (intrinsic divisions, by degree of
power) and infinite quantities (extrinsic division in extensive parts),
always univocally the same and differentiated or expressed in inten-

---

17 Guillaume Sibertin-Blanc introduced the first effort to connect philosophy, politics,
    ethics (or critique and clinic) in Deleuze and Guatarri. Cf. his 'Politique et clinique,
    recherche sur la philosophie pratique de Deleuze' (doctoral thesis, Charles de Gaulle
    University – Lille III, 2006).

18 Deleuze, 'Spinoza and Us', p. 122.

19 See Ovídio Abreu, 'O procedimento da imanência em Deleuze', *Alceu*, 5.9 (2004), pp.
    87–104.

20 Vincent Jacques, 'De Différence et répétition à Mille plateaux, métamorphose du
    système à l'aune de deux lectures de Spinoza', in *Spinoza-Deleuze: Lectures croisés*, ed.
    by Pascal Sévérac and Anne Sauvagnargues (Lyon: ENS Éditions, 2016), pp. 29–44 (p.
    30)

sive degrees that do not break their unity — that is, in 'modes'. It was here that Deleuze forged a political Spinozism: by thinking the relation between mind and body according to a logic of isonomy and isomorphism; by concerning himself with the connections between things and ideas; and by grasping the central place of the body and the *conatus* conceived as intensity and power (or *potentia*).[21]

Deleuze approaches the medieval problem of the univocity of Being in order to inject politics into metaphysics. In this debate, both logical and ontological, God differs from his effects by the degree of power in realizing a single and unitary being. Thus, forms, functions, species, and genres are secondary — there can be more differences between two individuals of a single species than between individuals of supposedly difference species. Differences between beings do not stem from generic forms and specific differences, as if Being were enunciated differently in various senses, as in the peripatetic adagio. In the univocal Being — which, according to Deleuze, 'is said in one and the same "sense" of everything about which it is said'[22] — the only conceivable difference concerns the degree of power. At issue then is knowing what assemblages a being can form — each degree of power corresponds to the power to affect and be affected. Power is no longer distinguished from action; that is, the power to be affected is necessarily fulfilled by virtue of the assemblages it can form, where a certain, determinate degree of power is always necessarily carried out. The power of the individual thus varies according to their encounters. Hence the formula: 'philosophy merges with ontology, but ontology merges with the univocity of Being'.[23] The One will thereafter be thought of as the *differentiator* of differences, the internal difference or immediate (disjunctive) synthesis of the multiple and its transversal, hierarchy-less communication between beings that merely differ.

In *A Thousand Plateaus* too we read: 'pluralism = monism'.[24] What is at stake in that formulation is thinking internal difference and the ex-

---

21   Marilena Chaui, 'Intensivo e extensivo na Ética de Espinosa: a interpretação dos modos finitos por Deleuze', in *Deleuze Hoje*, ed. by Sandro K. Fornazari (São Paulo: Fap-Unifesp, 2014), pp. 21–40 (p. 22).

22   Deleuze, *The Logic of Sense*, p. 179.

23   Ibid.

24   Gilles Deleuze and Félix Guattari, *A Thousand Plateaus: Capitalism and Schizophrenia*, trans. by Brian Massumi (Minneapolis: University of Minnesota Press, 1987), p. 20.

teriority of relations: 'The univocity of Being does not mean that there is one and the same Being; on the contrary, beings are multiple and different, they are always produced by a disjunctive synthesis, and they themselves are disjointed and divergent, *membra disjuncta*.'[25] Chaui identifies the effects of this mutation, and its logic, with Deleuze's encounter with Guattari:

> What could be more Spinozist than conceiving of multiplicities, without referring to a subject, as *haecceities*? Or to conceive of the individual as a component or element of the multiplicities under the form of singularities whose duration are mobile or nomads, made and unmade according to their encounters or relations? Or even to conceive of the mode of realizing multiplicities not according to the model of the tree's hierarchical transcendence, but as the immanent horizontality of the rhizome, with its plateau-like plane of composition, understood as degrees of intensity?[26]

THE PHILOSOPHY OF SPINOZA IS A LOGIC

Deleuze's interpretation seeks to re-establish Spinoza's logic of expression — of speculative affirmation and practical joy — on three levels. Firstly, as a theory of substance, which explains how the substance is expressed univocally in infinite forms of being. That is, substance is conceived in infinite attributes, formally distinct and diverse, but not opposed nor separate from each other; attributes do not bear a relation of eminence, analogy, or equivocity with each other. This signals the end of all privileges in ontology. Secondly, the logic of expression is a theory of the idea, explaining how thought is adequately expressed through its own determinations — signalling a *via regia* towards materialism, as per Louis Althusser.[27] On this reading thought does not have to be measured against an external reality. This in turn implies a methodological programme — a theory of common notions. Thirdly,

---

25   Deleuze, *The Logic of Sense*, p. 179. See also Deleuze, *Difference and Repetition*, p. 39.

26   Chaui, 'Intensivo e extensivo', p. 22; trans. by Nicolas Allen. The commentary refers to the preface to the 1987 Italian edition of *Thousand Plateaus*.

27   Louis Althusser, 'The Only Materialist Tradition, Part I: Spinoza', in *The New Spinoza*, ed. by Warren Montag and Ted Stolze (Minneapolis: University of Minnesota Press, 1997), pp. 3–19.

the logic of expression would be a theory of finite modes, explaining how the expression of the substance through its attributes gives way to the expression of the latter in modes. Expression is real when the relation between that which is expressed and that which expresses is modal — when the things themselves are expressive. Furthermore, a theory of finite modes institutes the conditions for a self-regulation that communicates the organization of affects. This in turn implies the question of individuation,[28] wherein the notion of 'problem' acquires an ethical-political content and leads to the question of prudence in experimentation.[29]

Chapter VIII from *Expressionism in Philosophy* describes how Spinoza destabilized seventeenth-century rationalism: from within rather than as a departure from Cartesian thought. The implications of that subversion, writes Deleuze, is that thought is conceived as independent from the constitution of a subject — what Spinoza calls the 'spiritual automaton'.[30] Concerning the intelligence of causes, the same method leading to the knowledge of Nature also leads to the knowledge of the forms produced by the mind: ideas have causes and are themselves causes, in the same manner as things do. Rather than being the function of a psychological consciousness, or a sovereign subject of knowledge, ideas are what explains the things in thought and the thoughts we have about them — which are adequate, when we are the cause, and inadequate when we are only partial causes of them. True ideas thus need to express their own causes, their own regime of production. The Spinozist formula *'verum index sui'*[31] means that the criteria for validating a true idea are not extrinsic to it, and do not require an external sign confirming it. On the contrary, it means that its criteria are immanent to its own plane of expression. This way of thinking breaks with the paradigms of 'analogy' or 'eminence', which establish between thought and that which is thought an external relation of agreement or conformity.[32] This is one way of understanding

---

28   Cf. Macherey, 'Spinoza 1968: Guéroult et/ou Deleuze'.

29   Cf. Jacques, 'De *Différence et répétition* à *Mille Plateaux*'.

30   *TdIE* 85; CWS [*The Collected Works of Spinoza*, see abbreviations] I, p. 37.

31   See *Ethics* II, 43 Schol. 2; CWS I, p. 479; and *Ep.* LXXVI [to Albert Burgh]; CWS II, p. 475.

32   In the seventeenth century, the form of representation of truth in terms of adequacy establishes such an external relation.

the *Ethics' ordine geometrico demonstrata*: geometry is not a formalism that assures access to the truth, but rather a form of expression that allows for the unfolding of discursive figures where the very structure of the real, in its constitution, is expressed. The logic of expression is thus a logic of immanence — a logic whose vantage point allows the thing to be thought as it is. After all, the act in which the thing is thought is indistinguishable from the act through which the thing is produced.[33] Expression has nothing to do with a designation or a representation: that which is expressed cannot be dissociated from the act of expression; expression is not the act of deploying a set of similar, silent images.[34] To speak in terms of a logic means that this way of thinking corresponds to a form of distributing and relating ideas according to a ternary (or triadic) schema. This schema interposes, between the expressed and that which expresses, the act of expressing or the expression as such; it dynamically posits the conditions of what they are in themselves, and simultaneously establishes the conditions of their relation, which is not indicative or representative, as would be the case in a relation of two terms.[35]

POWER OR RIGHT

In *Expressionism in Philosophy*, Deleuze examines rights from the point of view of power relations as the immanent content of the political field. He does so based on the description of a historic shift in the very concept of natural right,[36] wherein Spinoza's concept of *potentia*

---

33   See the passage on the idea of the circle in Spinoza's *Treatise on the Emendation of the Intellect* (*TdIE* 33; *CWS* I, p. 17).

34   The allusion here is to 'mute pictures on a panel', with reference to Spinoza's criticism of René Descartes (*Ethics* II, 49 Schol.; *CWS* I, p. 486).

35   'We everywhere confront the necessity of distinguishing three terms: substance which expresses itself, the attribute which expresses, and the essence which is expressed. It is through attributes that essence is distinguished from substance, but through essence that substance is itself distinguished from attributes: a triad each of whose terms serves as a middle term relating the two others, in three syllogisms. | Expression is inherent in substance, insofar as substance is absolutely infinite; in its attributes, insofar as they constitute an infinity; in essence, insofar as each essence in an attribute is infinite' (Deleuze, *Expressionism in Philosophy*, pp. 27–28).

36   This was a recurring problematic in Deleuze's monographic works up until the late 1960s. See his book on Hume from 1953, which discusses the notion of the contract; the text *Instincts and Institutions* from 1955, which offers a programme for the study

is decisive. In his treatment, the idea of a 'theoretical' right, as a moral faculty and voluntary disposition that could either receive recognition or go unrecognized amounts to a form of mystification — as the effect of an expected increase of power, or the sadness issued by the lack of power. Spinoza struggles against the idea of rights as connected to a prior legal order — be that of institutions, eminent or divine justice, be it an objective law, authorizing or prohibiting certain actions, or the idea of subjective rights. Instead, he proposes to understand the equality of rights as a right itself (or power) that goes beyond a mere formalism: institutions and collective practices depend on the common interest, as well as on inter-individual relations; they are not derived from pre-existing duties, but rather from the constitution, involving the 'many', of the right (or power) — hence Spinoza's formula: *jus sive potentia.*

As Étienne Balibar observes,

> In the *TTP*, Spinoza had defined the notion of 'right' in the form of a thesis — 'the right of the individual is co-extensive with its determinate power' (TTP, 237). In the TP, he goes on to develop all the consequences of this definition and, in the process, to demonstrate his originality as a theorist. Taken literally, this thesis means that the notion of 'right' has no *priority*, for that priority belongs to the notion of 'power'. One might say that the word *right (Jus)* is used to express the originary reality of power (*potentia*) in the language of politics. But by doing so we have not introduced a separation between right and power, since the word *originary* does not imply *proceeding from* or *grounded in* (which is why, in particular, any interpretation of Spinoza's definition as a variant on the idea of 'might is right' is clearly mistaken). Spinoza's purpose here is not to justify the notion of right, but to form an adequate idea of its determinations, of the way in which it works. In this sense, his formula can be glossed as meaning that *the individual's right includes all that he is effectively able to do and to think in a given set of conditions.*[37]

---

of sociality; and his course on Jean-Jacques Rousseau from 1959, which intervenes in the debate on the state of nature by contrasting antiquity's concept (from Plato to Cicero) with that of Hobbes — the same strategy he would apply in *Expressionism in Philosophy*, in the Vincennes courses on Spinoza, which are contemporary with the publication of *A Thousand Plateaus*, and in the courses on Foucault from the mid-1980s. The source Deleuze cites is Leo Strauss' *Natural Right and History* from 1954 — Strauss reappears in Deleuze and Guattari's 1991 meditation on tyranny in *What is Philosophy?* (New York: Columbia University Press, 1994).

37   Étienne Balibar, *Spinoza and Politics* (London: Verso, 1998), p. 59.

Power is an object of admiration, less for its visible effects than for its invisible operations, its effect-producing properties. This admiration affects superstition, turning power into something unfathomable — hence the relation between power and the passions, whereby psychic life manifests itself in the image of an arbitrary and capricious will with no cause (and as something to be dominated by reason). However, if particular things are defined by their power, this means that none of them possess efficacy all on their own.[38] Spinoza scholars diverge on the uses of the terms *potentia* and *potestas* in Spinoza — both translated as 'power' in English —, and Latin classics tend to add confusion to that vocabulary by using *potentia* to name an absolutely tyrannical power, whereas *potestas* refers to a power authorized by law. Spinoza combines their uses with particular variations, sometimes using the term *potestas* to determine the *potentia*, and yet refusing to found *potentia* in *potestas*. On the contrary, it is *potentia* that founds power — to act and to understand, to affect and to be affected.

Beyond the etymological controversy, the problem is metaphysical: for Spinoza, *potentia* is always actual; it is not potentiality, such as the Aristotelian *dunamis* (δύναμις), of which *potentia* is the Latin translation. *Dunamis* and *energeia* (ενέργεια), actuality, are thus fused in the term *potentia*. Galilean physics played a decisive role in this operation. The (physical) phenomenon is the result of a temporal point of view, the manifestation of a state, of the process leading to that result. That process, leading to the event properly speaking, and to the relation — called 'eternal' by Spinoza — is the same process through which all differentiation becomes possible and which corresponds to the necessary correlation between variables. What is therefore at stake is to grasp the differences in themselves, as variations correlating with other variations. This serves as a corrective to the habit of fixating on an image of difference.[39] Deposing that transcendental principle, it becomes necessary to recognize the universal dependence of things. Hence, the concept of *conatus*, drawn from the vocabulary of seventeenth-century

---

38 See *Ethics* III, Praef.; *CWS* I, p. 491: 'Indeed they seem to conceive man in nature as a dominion within a dominion'.

39 Cf. Françoise Barbaras, 'Le Concept de puissance dans l'héritage de la science cartésienne', *Archives de Philosophie*, 64.4 (2001), pp. 721–39; Mogens Lærke, 'Immanence et extériorité absolue. Sur la théorie de la causalité et l'ontologie de la puissance de Spinoza', *Revue philosophique de la France et de l'étranger*, 134.2 (2009), pp. 169–90.

physics, means the individuated expression of *potentia*, as the striving each thing does to persevere without any finality. With the *conatus*, Spinoza denies all hierarchy among natural beings.[40] By rejecting finalism, he introduces a 'near-plebeian democratic egalitarianism in the ontology',[41] in keeping with the logic of univocity. This is what allows one to think of right in terms of power: as a degree of physical intensity that expresses itself in a relation of composition between an actually existing body (an extensive part) and a mind (which is the idea of that body). Different from Hobbes, who reduces *conatus* to a question of kinetics,[42] Spinoza thinks of *conatus* dynamically as a force and intensity, a continuous clash and conflict, not just among external bodies (as in Hobbes), but also, and especially, internal to each of them.[43]

The right of every being is always a part of the power of the whole of Nature: that which allows one to act on all other parts. For that reason, the measure of right is that of individuality, which in turn undergoes variations according to encounters with higher and lower powers, producing more or less effects. The extension of natural right is, therefore, defined by the composition of the natural laws of the individual with the laws of all Nature. This composition produces greater or lesser variations in a being's free power depending on whether that power is impeded or aided by external causes. All power depends on the *relation* that it produces according to the laws of *its nature* along with the other laws of Nature that impede or aid that production. This is a right that is immanent to the circumstances of an existing thing: 'as much right as power'.[44] The reality or unity of the right is nothing more than the complex of relations into which individuals enter, summarized in Spinoza's phrase: what can a body do?[45] Deleuze very often repeated this question and he took it up as both a legal and an ethical model:

---

40   See *Ethics* II, Def. 6; *CWS* I, p. 447: 'By reality and perfection I understand the same thing'.

41   André Tosel, *Du matérialisme, de Spinoza* (Paris: Kimé, 1994), p. 140; trans by the editors.

42   That is, of inertia and velocity, hence the continuous conflict of bodies external to one another in the state of nature.

43   Cf. Chaui, *Política em Espinosa*, pp. 289–314.

44   See *TP* II, 3; *CWS* II, p. 507: '[…] each natural thing has as much right by nature as it has power to exist and have effects'.

45   See *Ethics* III, 2 Schol.; *CWS* I, pp. 494–97.

All a body can do (its power) is also its 'natural right.' If we manage to pose the problem of rights at the level of bodies, we thereby transform the whole philosophy of rights in relation to souls themselves. [...] The theory of natural rights implies a double identification of power with its exercise, and of such an exercise of power with a right. 'The rights of an individual extend to the utmost limits of his power as it has been conditioned.' This is the very meaning of the word *law*: the law of nature is never a rule of duty, but the norm of a power, the unity of right, power and its exercise. There is in this respect no difference between wise man and fool, reasonable and demented men, strong man and weak. They do of course differ in the kind of affections that determine their effort to persevere in existence. But each tries equally to preserve himself, and has as much right as he has power, given the affections that actually exercise his capacity to be affected. The fool is himself a part of Nature, and in no way disturbs its order.[46]

Power will always extend as far as it can — it lacks nothing and is always actual — and operates between determinate thresholds — varying by quantity/intensity — since for each existing thing there always exists another more powerful thing in Nature.[47] And because power is no longer distinguished from action, the power to be affected is necessarily related to its actual assemblages. Furthermore, a certain, determinate degree of power is always necessarily performed, making the power of the individual affected vary more (through joy) or less (through sadness), according to their encounters.

This concept of power interconnects physics with ethics and politics. For Spinoza, men only become free when they take control of their power to act and think, that is, when the *conatus* is determined by adequate ideas from which active affects are derived, and which in turn are explained by their own activity and by that which constitutes their nature. The institution of the political body corresponds precisely to the moment when the presumed solitude of individuals leads to the formation of a higher individual. The constitution of life in common under a form of political power (*imperium*) takes place in order to concretize the natural right of each one and of all, since collective natural right is conserved in that form of association.

---

46   Deleuze, *Expressionism in Philosophy*, pp. 257–58.

47   See *Ethics* IV, Ax. 1; *CWS* I, p. 547.

Seventeenth century metaphysics cannot but be political. In a context where absolute monarchy thrived, the image of a Creator endowed with free will serves as a mirror for sovereignty — and vice versa. The logical battles taking place in Part 1 of the *Ethics*, concerning the doctrines and lexicons inherited from the Middle Ages, capture the transposition of religious superstitions in the realm of civic life as a process of mystification. Spinoza's work thus reverts a long-standing history of transcendentalism in history. In Deleuze's review of Gueroult's book on Spinoza, he stresses the rigorous interrelation of power and 'necessary productivity'. He relates this interrelation to Spinoza's rejection of the providential figure of a Creator that acts by free will, through an understanding that decides between possible alternatives.[48]

From there follows the defence of Spinoza's conception of the 'materiality of the sign': the sign is a perceived sign, independent of the consciousness that perceives it and that remains passive. This 'encounter' is not of a signifier with a pre-existing and given meaning to be interpreted. There is no recognition: the sense is physical, ethological, a variation of power, not the reserve or principle of a pre-existing given with an establishing meaning, origin or end. To give the sign an irrational meaning presupposes the ignorance of divine activity; to think of it as the vehicle for a different, hidden, eminent, allegorical meaning would be theoretically mindless and a mystification, but also implies political submission and a dependency on hermeneutical translators of the 'divine message' expressed through compulsory commandments.

This materialist conception of the sign leads to a semiotics of the passions of the social body, as developed in the *TTP*. There, Spinoza shows how the constitution of the political body depends on a system of imaginative signs whose function is to stabilize the affective dynamic of the multitude. With this, one can read in Spinoza the materialist philosophemes that are found throughout his philosophy: the rejection of divine transcendence and finalism; the equality of attributes and the materialist vindication of the body, as a celebration of its productive force that does not break with causal determination and with

---

48   Gilles Deleuze, 'Gueroult's General Method for Spinoza', in *Desert Islands and Other Texts. 1953–1974*, ed. by David Lapoujade, trans. by Michael Taormina (Cambridge, MA: MIT Press, 2004), pp. 146–55 (p. 146).

the fact of belonging to Nature; the concept of power, the physical world as natural order with no external principle; the identification of reality with perfection and of the degree of reality with the degree of perfection or power. In the last instance, this entails a rejection of any hierarchy among natural beings according to spirituality and morality — founded on sin, merit, and punishment.[49]

COMMON NOTIONS AND THE COMPOSITION OF POWERS

Deleuze considers common notions to be a theoretical driving operator that favours experimentation, furnishing the condition for that process in the face of the constitutive conflicts of society (conceived according the logic of power). These notions reflect the demand to think the multiplicity of Nature from a rigorously immanent point of view. This is also its most distinctively materialist feature in Spinoza: reason not as transcendence, but as that which radicalizes cooperation and communication.[50] But while Spinoza's *Ethics* rejects any normativity founded on transcendence, it does not abolish the normativity proper to life — to psychic and collective individuation.[51]

> The common notions form a mathematics of the real or the concrete which rids the geometric method of the fictions and abstractions that limited its exercise.
>
> The common notions are generalities in the sense that they are only concerned with the existing modes, without constituting any part of the latter's singular essence (II, 37). But they are not at all fictitious or abstract; they represent the composition of real relations between existing modes or individuals. Whereas geometry only captured relations *in abstracto*, the common notions enable us to apprehend them as

---

49 Tosel, *Du matérialisme*, p. 136.

50 Ibid., p. 147.

51 The last three chapter of *Expressionism in Philosophy* deal with common notions: the entire seventeenth century, part of the eighteenth century, and the twentieth century all presuppose them. The emphasis falls on the distinction between an 'order of formation' and an 'order of application', in the character of general, although not abstract, ideas and in the aspects of the concept of reason that derives therein. This is accompanied by a set of questions: how do we manage to experience a maximum of joyful passions? How do we manage to experience active affections? How do we manage to form adequate ideas? Chapter V of *Spinoza: Practical Philosophy* (pp. 110–21), dealing with Spinoza's unfinished *Treatise on the Emendation of the Intellect*, takes up chapter XVIII of *Expressionism in Philosophy* (pp. 289–301).

they are, that is, as they are necessarily embodied in living beings, with the variable and concrete terms between which they
are established. In this sense, the common notions are more
biological than mathematical forming a natural geometry that
allows us to comprehend the unity of composition of all Nature
and the modes of variations of that unity.[52]

Deleuze claimed that Spinoza placed empiricism in the service of rationalism,[53] and that the study of the relations of composition among
things would demand a programme of physical-chemical and biological experimentation, since we have no prior knowledge of those relations of composition. In fact, common notions suggest a transition in
Spinoza's philosophy that would impact the connections between the
imagination, rationality, and affective dynamism. Common notions
suppose a practice (a process of experimentation) and the conditions
of that process, since the process itself does not exist prior to the formation of common notions. Through them, the 'common' articulates
the relation under which two modes, at least, come into agreement
and compose a new relation. Consequently, forming a common notion
is a function of the joyful passions, as the increase in the power to
act and to think; sadness, born from the encounter with a body that
does not agree with ours, does not lead to the formation of common
notions. The common notion is the first adequate idea, derived from a
long experimentation (hence its complexity, since it is simultaneously
practical and speculative).

For Spinoza, reason is realized by the action of bodies on
other bodies.[54] Reason takes root in affections and the common
properties of bodies, starting with imaginative perceptions. This
explains Spinoza's rejection of the antagonism between imagination
and reason, body and soul, desire and will. Given that human beings
are not born rational but rather experience rationality, reason is, in
the first instance, an effort to select and organize good encounters
that compose with us and inspire in us joyful passions. That is, it
consists in striving to select affections (states of the affected body)
that correspond to affects (variations) that agree with reason. The

---

52   Deleuze, *Spinoza*, pp. 56–57.
53   Deleuze, *Expressionism in Philosophy*, p. 149.
54   Guéroult, *Spinoza*, II: *L'âme (Éthique, II)*, p. 341.

guarantee of the constitution of knowledge and rationality, in its varied forms, is nothing more than that assemblage and that composition of bodies and minds.

Common notions are not fictions, they do not substitute a thing for its image nor do they classify by species, genre, number, or by some sort of transcendentality. They are ideas in general; they do not lead us to know a singular essence, but rather are constitutive of relations. Above all, they represent something in common among bodies (properties): be they common to all (motion and rest) or certain bodies (two, at least, mine and that of another). When the corresponding relations of two bodies are composed, they constitute a new relation — a new form — of a higher power. The common notion is a representation of that composition among two or more existing bodies.[55] All bodies, even where they do not agree, have something in common, like motion and rest. At a certain point, the common notions make it possible to understand at what level differences and oppositions are formed. But since they do not allow us to know the essence of things,[56] we can still fall into abstractions, should we forget their inessential and relational character. Only the third kind of knowledge has this character of grasping things in their singularity.

In the entry concerning the common notions in *Spinoza: Practical Philosophy*,[57] Deleuze seems to mimic the movement that he was pursuing throughout the 1970s. Then, he favoured a theory that would establish a plane of immanence that is both theoretic-practical and vital — an epistemology involving a determinate relation between life and thought. Being that the composition of powers is based on multiplicity, it became possible for Deleuze via Spinoza to formulate the problem

---

55   Pierre-François Moreau points out this experimental character in the formation of common notions. See his *Spinoza. L'expérience et l'éternité* (Paris: PUF, 1994), p. 279. Pascal Sévérac notes the use of the noun *convenientia* in the ontological sense in Spinoza's *Ethics* (*Ethics* II, 29 Schol.; *CWS* I, p. 476), just as in his *Treatise on the Emendation of the Intellect* (*TdIE* 25; *CWS* I, p. 15). See his *Le Devenir actif chez Spinoza* (Paris: Honoré Champion, 2005), p. 110. Both analyses deal with inadequate perception, which isolates that which is perceived from that without which it cannot be understood. On the other hand, adequate perception is born from the contemplation of various things at the same time, with those things being grasped in their real relations, according to that which agrees, differs, or is opposed. Cf. chapter XVII of Deleuze's *Expressionism in Philosophy*, pp. 273–89.

56   See *Ethics* II, 37, 38, 40 and 44; *CWS* I, pp. 475–78 and 480–81.

57   See Deleuze, *Spinoza*, pp. 54–58.

of sociability and institutional creation as an activity of assessment and experimentation. In the last instance, Spinoza's ethics is now placed in the service of a *practical problem*, which concerns the understanding of groups: are they subjects or subjected (*assujetis*)? This reformulation, in turn, was the clinical and political problem of analysis and experimentation in the social field, which Deleuze explored alongside Guattari.[58] And it was along that line of inquiry that they sought to understand the ways in which society is constituted and instituted, according to the Spinozist perspective suggested by Deleuze. It was also an invitation to follow the 'lines of differentiation'[59] in which Spinoza appears to be offering a theory of productive desire (in *Anti-Oedipus*) — in the ethological inspiration over and against morality; in the concept of *assemblage* determined by the logic of powers, or in the logic of coessential positivities and coexisting affirmations that orchestrate the 'Plateaus' on the state, politics and law.[60] Their project, in the last instance, involved what one might call a 'machinic historical materialism', and whose properly philosophical thesis defines the problem of thought not according to the subject/object relation, but rather by scrutinizing (and tracing the cartography of) the relations among land and the territories, in consideration of the true movement of becoming and the production of the real.[61]

TRANSLATED BY NICOLAS ALLEN

---

58   Sibertin-Blanc, 'Politique et clinique', p. 48.
59   A formula created by Luiz Orlandi, 'Linhas de ação da diferença', in *Gilles Deleuze: Uma vida filosófica*, ed. by Éric Alliez (São Paulo: Editora 34, 2000), pp. 49–63 (p. 58).
60   Deleuze, *Spinoza*, p. 95.
61   Guillaume Sibertin-Blanc, *Politique et état chez Deleuze et Guattari. Essai sur le matérialisme historico-machinique*, Actuel Marx confrontation (Paris: PUF, 2013), pp. 39, 42, and 99.

Are there One or Two Aleatory Materialisms?

VITTORIO MORFINO

A LITTLE EXCURSUS CONCERNING MY PREVIOUS INTERPRETATION

To answer the question of whether there are one or two aleatory materialisms I will introduce and then analyse a series of texts that I have written over the last twenty years concerning Louis Althusser's writings from the eighties.

In primis, I will take into consideration the 'Introduction' that I wrote with Luca Pinzolo for the Italian translation of some of Althusser's writings from the eighties, which was published under the title *Sul materialismo aleatorio* (On aleatory materialism): the collected texts included 'On Marxist Thought', 'The Underground Current of the Materialism of the Encounter', the two texts that appeared in the journal *Lignes* on Machiavelli and Spinoza, and the 'Portrait of a Materialist Philosopher'.[1] The book was published in 2000.[2] In the second edition of 2006,[3] we added the translation of the text 'On Aleatory Materialism', which had meanwhile been published in the Journal *Multitudes*.[4]

Our thesis as outlined in the introduction to this volume can be briefly summarized as the continuity between the Althusser of the sixties and the eighties. The implicit polemical objective, although we did not quote him, was undoubtedly an article by Antonio Negri published in a special issue of *Futur antérieur* (*Sur Althusser, Passages*) entitled 'Pour Althusser. Notes sur l'évolutions de la pensée du dernier Althusser' (For Althusser: Notes on the Evolution of the Thought of the Last Althusser),[5] in which he identified a *Kehre*, or turn, in the thought of the 'last' Althusser.

By contrast, Luca Pinzolo and I argued that 'in the writings of the 80s [...] Althusser takes up some of the crucial themes [...] of the great works of the 60s, *Reading Capital* and *For Marx*: those of temporality, contradiction, and complexity'.[6] To illustrate this statement, we quoted strategic passages from Althusser's works, such as the 'Outline of the Concept of Historical Time' (1965), 'Contradiction and Overdetermination' (1962), and 'On the Materialist Dialectic' (1963), and again the distinction between whole and totality from 'Is It Simple to Be a Marxist in Philosophy?'(1976).

---

1   Louis Althusser, 'Sur la pensée marxiste', in Althusser and others, *Sur Althusser. Passages* (Paris : L'Harmattan,1993), pp. 11–29; 'Le Courant souterrain du matérialisme de la rencontre', in *Écrits philosophiques et politiques*, ed. by François Matheron, 2 vols (Paris: Stock/IMEC, 1994–95), I (1994), pp. 539–79, in English as 'The Underground Current of the Materialism of the Encounter', in Louis Althusser, *Philosophy of the Encounter: Later Writings, 1978–87*, ed. by François Matheron and Oliver Corpet, trans. and intro. by Geoffrey M. Goshgarian (London: Verso, 2006), pp. 163–207; 'L'unique tradition matérialiste', ed. by Oliver Corpet, *Lignes*, 18 (1993), pp. 71–119; 'Portrait d'un philosophe matérialiste', in *Écrits philosophiques et politiques*, I, pp. 581–82, in English as 'Portrait of the Materialist Philosopher', in Althusser, *Philosophy of the Encounter*, pp. 290–91.

2   Louis Althusser, *Sul materialism aleatorio*, ed. by Vittorio Morfino and Luca Pinzolo (Milan: Unicopli, 2000).

3   Althusser, *Sul materialism aleatorio*, ed. by Morfino and Pinzolo, 2nd edn (Milan: Mimesis, 2006).

4   Louis Althusser, 'Du matérialisme aléatoire',*Multitude*, 21.2 (2005), pp. 179–94 (p. 189).

5   Antonio Negri, 'Pour Althusser. Notes sur l'évolutions de la pensée du dernier Althusser', in Althusser and others, *Sur Althusser*, pp. 73–96 (p. 83).

6   Vittorio Morfino and Luca Pinzolo, 'Introduzione', in Althusser, *Sul materialism aleatorio*, pp. 7–12 (p. 8; my translation).

In addition, we gave particular importance to a passage from 'Contradiction and Overdetermination' in which Althusser criticizes the Marxist theory of revolution as the effect of a simple contradiction between forces of production and relations of production. Concerning the Russian Revolution ('a result of the intense overdetermination of the basic class contradiction'), Althusser writes: 'we should perhaps ask what is *exceptional* in this "exceptional *situation*", and whether, like all exceptions, this one does not also clarify its rule — is not, unbeknownst to the rule, the *rule itself*. After all, *are we not always in exceptional situations?*'.[7]

The conclusion of our introduction insisted precisely on this last point: the writings of the eighties take into consideration the complexity of the structure (which was at the centre of Althusser's investigations in the sixties) from the point of view of the 'beginnings and genesis of such complexity'. Given this focus, the distinction between conjuncture and conjunction emerges as important, as does (and especially so) the Epicurean model of the parallel fall of atoms and their encounter made possible by the *clinamen*. It is important to emphasize that this theme has nothing to do with the revival of a causality by freedom in the Kantian sense, which moreover was always a privileged object of Althusser's criticism. Instead, it concerns the resumption of the theme of complexity as always-already-given, not in the perspective of its revolutionary dissolution but rather of its own aleatory constitution. In this sense, contingency is not opposed to necessity but to teleology. The void and Epicurean atoms are not foundations for freedom but instead the guarantee of the absence of a plan that precedes their encounter. Nothing except the factual circumstances of the encounter has prepared the encounter. This is the meaning of the Althusserian insistence on void and on nothing: not a mystical discourse that renders the void another name for God, but the nothing of all which is not pure facticity.[8]

The second text that I take into consideration is 'Il materialismo della pioggia di Louis Althusser. Un Lessico' (Louis Althusser's Materialism of the Rain: A Lexicon), which I published in *Quaderni*

---

7   Louis Althusser, *For Marx*, trans. by Ben Brewster (London: Verso, 2005), p. 104; emphasis in the original.

8   Morfino and Pinzolo, 'Introduzione', pp. 10–11.

materialisti,[9] in the hope of revealing the systematic structure that can be retraced within the fragmentary nature of the writings of the eighties. As to the question of continuity / discontinuity, I suggested that in these writings it was possible to identify some of the most important themes and problems of the writings of the sixties, even if, undoubtedly, they were contained within a totally different style:

> The later texts are above all impressionistic, at times autobiographical, at other times anecdotal. [...] Moreover, all of the texts cited in these essays are recalled from memory, resulting in frequent distortions of the original sources, if not outright inventions. These texts in no way demonstrate the systematicity characteristic of Althusser's two masterpieces from the 1960s, *Reading Capital* and *For Marx*, where an entirely new conceptuality was produced through an incisive, close reading of Marx's texts; here, Althusser often transforms his references at will.[10]

Apart from this marked difference in style, I identified the most interesting theoretical element by bringing to the fore 'certain aspects of the texts from the 1960s that have until now remained at the margins (most importantly, the theme of the necessity of contingency)':

> This reclamation of earlier marginal moments in Althusser's text is possible due in large part to the insistent deployment of a new constellation of terms [...]:
>
> 1. void/nothing;
> 2. encounter;
> 3. fact/Faktum/factual/facticity;
> 4. conjuncture/conjunction;
> 5. necessity/contingency.[11]

Insisting on the interpretative line of the 'Introduction' I have maintained a close correlation between the concept of void or nothing and the concept of encounter 'such that considering one in isolation will result in altering the nature of both'.[12]

---

9   Vittorio Morfino, 'Il materialismo della pioggia di Louis Althusser. Un Lessico', *Quaderni materialisti*, 1 (2002), pp. 85–108, in English as 'An Althusserian Lexicon', trans. by Jason Smith, *Borderlands*, 4.2 (2005) <http://www.borderlands.net.au/vol4no2_2005/morfino_lexicon.htm>.

10   Ibid.

11   Ibid.

12   Ibid.

It is precisely from this point that I reopened my reading of the 'last' Althusser, in particular of 'The Underground Current of the Materialism of the Encounter', in an intervention ('Il primato dell'incontro sulla forma') I gave at a conference that took place in Venice in 2004.

The two fundamental gestures I made in this intervention were the affirmation of the rhetorical function of the void and the latent centrality of Charles Darwin. On the void, I said:

> I would like to maintain that the emphasis on the concepts of 'nothing,' the 'null' and the 'void' has a purely rhetorical function; that contingency and the aleatory are the effect of an encounter and not of the nothing or the void. If this rhetorical function is transformed into a theoretical proposition, it risks transforming the theory of the encounter into a theory of the event or of freedom.[13]

On Darwin:

> What I would like to argue is that Althusser's position is dia-metrically opposed to Aristotle's, and that the thesis that is never written *apertis verbis* in 'The Underground Current' is in fact its fundamental theoretical centre: the primacy of the encounter over form. [...] [This] can be read in a totally new light when we juxtapose it with an author that Althusser refers to only once: Charles Darwin.[14]

I have argued for the centrality of Darwin's role based on the fact that the only time his name was mentioned was in relation to a confer-ence organized in Paris by Dominique Lecourt and Yvette Conry, in which Lecourt presented an intervention entitled 'Marx au crible de Darwin.'[15] In this lecture he placed the English naturalist at the highest point of a philosophy of the encounter which would also include Epi-curus and Machiavelli, an intervention that seemed to me at the very least in dialogue with Althusser if not directly inspired by him.

After this little excursus, I am finally able to return to the question posed by my title, namely whether there are 'One or Two Aleatory

---

13   Vittorio Morfino, *Plural Temporality: Transindividuality and the Aleatory between Spinoza and Althusser* (Leiden: Brill, 2014), p. 97.

14   Ibid., p. 104.

15   Dominique Lecourt, 'Marx au crible de Darwin', in *De Darwin au darwinisme: science et idéologie*, ed. by Yvette Conry(Paris: Vrin, 1983), pp. 227–49.

Materialisms'. Of course, this question resonates with —and polemically opposes — an article published by François Matheron and Yoshihiko Ichida entitled 'Un, deux, trois, quatre, dix mille Althusser. Considérations aléatoires sur le matérialisme aléatoire'.[16] Through the developments outlined in my introduction and the two essays I have quoted, my answer to this question was that there was only one aleatory materialism in continuity with the Althusserian thought of the sixties. And not only! When I found in some unpublished texts from the sixties, that Althusser had used certain categories like 'conjunction', 'encounter', and 'take hold', I ended up backdating aleatory materialism to the sixties. Now, however, I'm asking myself whether this was the right way to think the problem, and whether it is not necessary to first take into consideration the role of these categories in the theoretical context of the sixties and then confront them with the thought of the eighties.

INSTEAD OF GENESIS

Let us first take into consideration the context in which these categories emerge in the texts from the sixties. They seem to shed light on the question of the disjunction established in *Reading Capital* between genesis and structure: in other words, the disjunction between the theory of the body, of the actual structure of society (to be even more precise, of the mechanism that produces what Althusser calls the 'society-effect'), and the theory of bourgeois society as a historical result.

It seems to me that Althusser introduced the concepts of encounter and conjunction to solve two problems in his theory that may have a common origin. Firstly, his insistence on the Marxian term *Verbindung*, which is translated as 'combination' but thought of as 'combinatory', did not allow him to think of the constitutive nature of relations and, secondly and concurrently, did not allow him to clearly conceptualize an alternative to the concept of 'genesis', which he, how-

---

16   François Matheron and Yoshihiko Ichida, 'Un, deux, trois, quatre, dix mille Althusser. Considérations aléatoires sur le matérialisme aléatoire', *Multitude*, 21.2 (2005), pp. 167–78.

ever, openly refused. I would like to address these two problems in turn in the following paragraphs.

Firstly, in 'The Object of Capital', in particular in the chapter dedicated to Marx's critique of political economy, Althusser stresses Marx's use of the term *Verbindung* to think the relations of production beyond any model of intersubjectivity.[17] A *Verbindung*, or, to return to the terms of the 1857 Introduction, a distribution, is 'a certain attribution of the means of production to the agents of production, in a certain regular proportion fixed between, on one hand, the means of production and, on the other, the agents of production'.[18] Althusser notes that there are even more distinctions to be found in Marx: on the side of the means of production, there is a distinction between the object and the instruments of production, and on the side of the agents, there is one between the immediate agents of production and the owners of the means of production. Althusser then concludes:

> By combining or *inter-relating* these different elements — labour-power, direct workers, masters who are not direct workers, object of production, instruments of production, etc. — we reach a definition of the different *modes of production* which have existed and can exist in human history.[19]

Here Althusser adds an important remark: this *Verbindung* of the pre-existing determinate elements 'would sincerely and truly constitute a combinatory'.[20]

In the second edition from 1968, Althusser fine-tunes his analysis, affirming that this operation 'might make us think of a combinatory' but that the specific nature of the relations put into play from these different combinations define and strictly limit the field:

> To obtain the different modes of production these different elements do have to be combined, but by using *specific modes*

---

17   Louis Althusser, 'L'objet du *Capital*', in *Lire le Capital* (Paris: PUF, 1996), pp. 245–418 (p. 385), in English as 'The Object of *Capital*', trans by Ben Brewster, in *Reading Capital: The Complete Edition* (London: Verso, 2015), pp. 215–355 (p. 329).

18   Ibid., p. 386, eng. tr., p. 329.

19   Ibid., p. 388, eng. tr., p. 330.

20   Althusser and others, 'Variantes de la première édition', in *Lire le Capital* (Paris: PUF, 1996), pp. 635–61 (p. 645).

> *of combination* or '*Verbindungen*' which are only meaningful in
> the peculiar nature of the *result* of the combinatory.[21]

Why did Althusser make this correction? We can suppose that the
translation of the term *Verbindung* with combination and Althusser's
further reading of this in terms of a 'combinatory of elements' could
make one think of a pre-existence of the elements, which then enter
into different relations in different modes of production. The correction Althusser introduces in the second edition of *Reading Capital*
seems to aim at avoiding the risk of thinking of invariable elements
combined in different ways in different modes of production.

Regarding the second problem, we can list a series of texts, including the little note 'On Genesis', the letters to René Diaktine, and the
'The Humanist Controversy'. In these texts, the reason for the absence
of the concept of 'genesis' appears in full light. In a letter to Diaktine
dated 22 August 1966, Althusser insists at length on the question:

> Whoever says genesis says the reconstitution of the process
> through which a phenomenon A has actually been *engendered*.
> That reconstitution is itself a process of knowledge: it has
> meaning (as knowledge) only if it *reproduces* (reconstitutes)
> the real process that *engendered* phenomenon A. You will see
> immediately that whoever says genesis says from the outset
> that the process of *knowledge* is *identical* in all its parts and in
> their order of succession to the actual process of engendering.
> [...] That means, to speak in less abstract terms, that who-
> ever elaborates the genesis of a phenomenon A can *follow the
> tracks*, in all its phases, *from the origin* of the actual process
> of engendering without any interruption, that is, without any
> discontinuity, lacuna, or break (the words hardly matter). This
> *immediate* and total overlap [...] *implies* the idea [...] that the
> subject of the real or actual process is a single and same *subject,
> identifiable* from the origin of the process to the end.[22]

The 'genesis' paradigm therefore implies a kind of organic unity
between the concepts of 'process of generation', 'origin of the process',
'goal or end of the process', 'identity of the subject of the process of

21   Althusser, 'L'objet du *Capital*', p. 388, eng. tr., p. 331.
22   Althusser to Diaktine, 22 August 1966, in Louis Althusser, *Écrits sur la psychanalyse*
      (Paris: Stock/IMEC, 1993), pp. 83–110 (pp. 83–84), in English as *Writings on Psycho-
      analysis: Freud and Lacan*, trans. by Jeffrey Mehlman (New York: Columbia University
      Press, 1996), p. 55.

generation', unity impregnated by the reference to an experience, the experience of generation, 'be it that of the child who becomes an adult or that of the seed that becomes a vegetal or living being'. In the genetic model, the individual we find at the end of the process, which we are confronted with, is already present in the seed. According to Althusser, this makes the structure of each 'genesis' teleological:

> Every genetic thought is literally obsessed by the search for a 'birth', with all that is entailed by the ambiguity of that word, which presupposes [...] the [...] idea that what is to be observed in its very birth *already bears its name*, already possesses its identity, [...] already exists in some manner *before its own birth* in order to be born![23]

Althusser adds that the concept of 'genesis' — as with any ideological concept — 'recognizes misunderstanding, that is to say, designates a reality by covering it with a false knowledge, an illusion'. The reality that the concept of genesis misunderstands is 'the emergence of the phenomenon A, radically new compared to all that precedes its own emergence':

> Whence the imperative of a *logic* different from that of *genesis*, but precisely to *think* that reality and not to *dispense* with thinking that reality. I have for a long time now been insisting on the necessity of constituting that new logic, which amounts to the same thing as defining the specific forms of a materialist dialectic.[24]

In a short note written exactly one month later on 22 September 1966, entitled 'On Genesis', Althusser gave a name to this new logic which he meant to replace the logic built around the 'ideological (religious) category of Genesis'. He called it the 'theory of the encounter' or 'theory of the conjunction'. A privileged example, as in the letter to Diaktine, is the logic of the constitution of the capitalist mode of production:

---

23   Ibid., p. 86, eng. tr., p. 57.
24   Ibid., p. 89, eng. tr., p. 59.

1. the elements defined by Marx 'combine'. I prefer to say (in order to translate the term *Verbindung*) that they 'conjoin' by 'taking hold' in a new structure. This structure cannot be thought, in its irruption, as the effect of a filiation; it must be thought as the effect of a *conjunction*. This new Logic has nothing to do with the linear causality of filiation or with Hegelian 'dialectical' causality [...]

2. Yet *each* of the elements that come to be combined in the conjunction of the new structure (in this case to hand, accumulated money-capital; 'free' labour-power, that is, labour-power divested of its work tools; and technological inventions) is itself, as such, a *product*, an *effect*.

What is important in Marx's demonstration is that the three elements are not *contemporaneous* products of one and the same situation. In other words, it is not the feudal mode of production which, by itself, thanks to a providential finality, simultaneously engenders *the three elements* required for the new structure to 'take hold'. Each of these elements has its own 'history', or *genealogy* (to borrow a concept from Nietzsche's that Balibar has used felicitously in this connection): the three genealogies are relatively *independent*. [...]

Thus the genealogies of the three elements are independent of each other, and independent (in their co-existence, in the co-existence of their respective results) of the existing structure (the feudal mode of production). This excludes all possibility of a resurgence of the myth of genesis.[25]

The plurality of genealogies in this passage indicates precisely the opposite of genesis, that is, it indicates the emergence of a plurality of elements that coexist but which are not contemporary effects of the same situation.

We can find a similar critique of the concept of genesis in the 'The Humanist Controversy', picking up on the debate raised in the Marxist field by what Althusser calls 'the recent discoveries of human palaeontology'.[26] Here, the reference is to André Leroi-Gourhan and

---

25   Louis Althusser, 'Sur la genèse', in *Écrits sur l'histoire* (Paris: PUF, 2018), pp. 81–86 (pp. 81–82), in English as 'On Genesis', in *History and Imperialism: Writings, 1963–1986*, trans. by Geoffrey M. Goshgarian (Cambridge: Polity, 2020), pp. 33–36 (pp. 33–34).

26   Louis Althusser, 'La querelle de l'humanisme', in *Écrits philosophiques et politiques*, II (1995), pp. 433–532 (p. 504), in English as 'The Humanist Controversy', in his *The*

his theory that 'the "ancestor" of the human line'[27] is a being that, while only having a modestly developed brain, has the distinctive particularity of an upright position and free hands for making instruments under conditions which are social and not individual. These discoveries would seem to fill in the gap separating current human societies from the animal origins of the human species, because from its origins onwards the human species would be constituted by beings who lived together and produced rudimentary instruments. In this regard, Althusser cites Jean Suret-Canale who, on the basis of Leroi-Gourhan's theory, claimed that social labour is the original cause of humanization.[28] Criticizing this position on the question of anthropogenesis, Althusser focused on the spontaneous persistence of a conception that cannot resist associating materialism and genesis.[29]

Genesis signifies filiation — it signifies that we are dealing with one individual whose transformations we can follow in the spontaneous form of an empiricism that weaves a continuous thread. Just as it seems to break with a genetic scheme, the genesis of man from ape introduces another genetic scheme within the human kingdom which identifies the originary individual. Althusser writes:

> The Originary Individual; he has been identified, he makes 'tools' of some unspecified sort, he lives in groups: *he's the one, all right.*[30]

Althusser opposes a theory of the encounter against this schema of the 'originary', the privileged example of which is the capitalist mode of production as the result of a process that does not have the form of a genesis. Remaining within the metaphor of filiation, Althusser writes:

> We must go much further, and say that the Sons who count in the historical process *have no father,* because they need several, and these fathers are in their turn the sons not *of a single father* [...], but of several.[31]

Humanist Controversy and Other Writings (1966–67), trans. by Geoffrey M. Goshgarian (London: Verso, 2003), pp. 221–305 (p. 284).

27   Ibid., p. 505, eng. tr., p. 284.
28   Ibid., p. 508, eng. tr., p. 286.
29   Ibid., p. 515, tr. eng., pp. 292–93.
30   Ibid., p. 517, tr. eng., p. 294.
31   Ibid., p. 520, eng. tr., p. 296.

As we have seen, the critique of the concept of genesis is constantly accompanied by the historical example of primitive accumulation.[32] The other example found in Althusser's texts is that of the unconscious. In the letter to Diaktine from 22 August 1966, Althusser writes:

> When one wants to think through the 'genesis' of the un-conscious, [...] one starts with the result within knowledge, namely, the existence of that identified 'individual' called the unconscious, and elaborating the genesis of the unconscious consists in moving back to its birth, to the point at which one witnesses its birth, but one manages only with difficulty to rid oneself of the idea that in a certain way, to elaborate the genesis of the unconscious means to seek out, even before its birth, all that already *prefigures and announces* it, already contains it in person, even in the form of a draft, but that resembles it and *that is already it*, that already bears its name, that is already *identifiable* [...]. One has the greatest difficulty conceiving that prior to the unconscious absolutely *nothing* exists that resembles the unconscious; one always tends to recognize it in germ, as a promise, draft, element, prefiguration, etc., *before its own birth* precisely because one conceives its *irruption* in the form of a *birth*.[33]

Althusser thus rejects the concepts of genesis and birth in favour of concepts such as 'encounter', 'taking hold', 'conjunction'. We can take as an example this passage from the *Three Notes on Discourse Theory*:

> We can [...] *set out the elements* which are present and 'preside' over the conjunction that 'takes hold' in the form of the uncon-scious. [...] The elements involved exist in the characters of the familial theatre, the familial situation: an ideological 'situation' in which are produced, as constitutive of this 'situation', the effects of the articulation of the mother's and father's uncon-scious with and in the structure of this ideological situation. Unconsciouses articulated with the ideological, unconsciouses articulated with each other by way of (in) their articulation with the ideological: this is what constitutes the 'situation' that presides over the establishment of the unconscious in the child.[34]

---

32   Cf. Althusser's 22 August 1966 letter to René Diaktine, p. 61.

33   Althusser to Diaktine, 22 August 1966, p. 87, eng. tr. p. 58.

34   Louis Althusser, 'Trois notes sur la théorie du discours', in *Écrits sur la psychanalyse*, pp. 111–70 (pp. 146–47), in English as 'Three Notes on the Theory of Discourses', in *The Humanist Controversy and Other Writings*, pp. 33–84 (p. 62; emphasis in the original).

It is interesting to remark that the concept of the 'void' also has a role between the set of concepts used to substitute the scheme of the genesis, but in very precise way, as a 'determinate absence':

> I believe you will agree with the very general principle that *absence* possesses a certain efficacy on the condition, to be sure, that it be not absence in general, nothingness or any other Heideggerian 'openness' but a *determinate* absence playing a role in the space of its absence.[35]

One might perhaps advance the hypothesis that this 'theory of the encounter' intervenes in these texts of the sixties as a rectification of a formalist theory of structural causality, or at least the potential risk of such a theory. In other words, it seems to me that the functioning of the theory of structural causality is secured by three theses: 1) the thesis of the constitutiveness of relations; 2) the thesis of the primacy of the encounter over the form; 3) and the thesis of plural or differential temporality. Now, these three theses must be thought in an intertwined fashion. In fact, T1 without T2 produces the reversibility of genesis and structure or the impossibility of thinking the becoming of the structure, T2 without T3 leads to think the encounter as a discontinuous event in a unique time-line, and T3 without T1 ends up thinking a multiplicity of unrelated times.

THE TEXTS OF THE EIGHTIES

Finally, we can address the content of the writings from the eighties, where a series of concepts persists: the 'encounter', 'taking hold', 'constitutive relations'. This persistence may make us think that we are dealing with the same materialism of the sixties, and the privileged example of primitive accumulation also returns, even if the reference to psychoanalysis and the unconscious disappear completely. I would argue that this conceptual constellation constitutes one of the two tendencies present in these writings, namely what I have called here the materialist tendency; indeed, besides these concepts, we find others whose history of appearance in Althusserian thought remains to be written, for example the Deleuzian concept of 'rhizome', the Marxian

---

35   Althusser to Diaktine, 22 August 1966, p. 90, eng. tr., pp. 60–61.

concept of interstice or the pair margin-centre. Allow me to quote a passage on the *Theses of June* on the rhizome and interstice:

> The world is now an unpredictable flow. If we want to give an image, we must go back to Heraclitus (we do not bathe twice in the same river), or Epicurus (primacy of void on the atomic corpuscles). If we want to give a closer image, following in this Deleuze [...] we must not represent the world according to Descartes as a hierarchical tree, but rather as a rhizome. For me, I would prefer another image, that of Marx. Marx said: the gods exist in the interstices of the world of Epicurus. He added: in the same way, commercial relations existed in the interstices of the slave world. I would say the same thing: communist relations (communism is the end of the relations of economic exploitation, the end of state domination and the end of ideological mystifications) exist in the interstices of the imperialist world.[36]

And here a passage on the pair margin-centre:

> Marx said: the proletariat camps on the margins of bourgeois society. And he put it in the centre, at the heart of the class struggle of bourgeois society. What was Marx doing? He made of the margin the centre. The problem today is formally the same. You have to make the margin the centre.[37]

Of course, the use of these concepts, although rare and episodic, sketches a different tendency than the one we have designated as the materialist one — which is rooted in the sixties' problematic — and which we could define as eschatological to the extent that it, on the one hand, rejects the hierarchical structure of the whole (which means, at the same time, the temporal complexity of the conjuncture) and, on the other, and as a consequence of this, affirms communism as simple *parousia* to come.

In this sense, the illuminating concept of the conflicting presence of these two tendencies in the texts of the eighties is precisely that of void: it is an expression of the materialist tendency if thought in a triangulation with the concepts of *clinamen* and atomic elements (we could say that void, *clinamen,* and atoms are the conceptual tools that

---

36   Louis Althusser, *Thèse de juin*, IMEC, ALT2. A29.60.04, p. 9.
37   Ibid., p. 12.

render a theory of encounter or of conjunction thinkable), and within this conceptual relationship it expresses the simple rejection of the anteriority of the logos, of the genesis; nevertheless, when it is thought in connection with the concept of world it became an expression of the eschatological tendency (of course there are some passages in which the two tendencies intersect each other). Here is an example:

> I simply want to say that this world, empty of any assured and stable structure, empty of theory, depoliticized to the extreme [...] I simply want to say that this world offers itself and that it is to take. I studied the theme of 'fortune' (the good occasion) in Machiavelli, and I came to the conclusion that fortune in its higher form is the void: the absence of obstacles.[38]

If we try to lend systematicity to this set of concepts (forcing them, perhaps) it seems to me that they shape the second tendency present in the writings on aleatory materialism (a tendency which predominates in the writings of 1985–86), an eschatological tendency in which the void must become full, the margins centre, the interstices worlds, where absence does not have a determinate character but is rather the expectation of a full *parousia*, which the theory of structural causality of the sixties had considered as both impossible and imaginary:

> What reigns in silence is a big wait![39]

CONCLUSION

To conclude, I propose the following interpretative schema. If we take the writings of the eighties as a whole (something that Luca Pinzolo and I did by publishing them with the title *On Aleatory Materialism*) we can find the re-elaboration of the material deposits in two different temporal streams, the first one which comes from the years 1966–67 (I would call it the materialist tendency), the second from the years 1976–78[40] (the eschatological tendency). One can perhaps ascribe to

---

38   Ibid., p. 10.

39   Louis Althusser, 'Sur le matérialisme aléatoire', p. 189.

40   I am thinking particularly of some passages on communism in Louis Althusser, *Les Vaches noires. Interview imaginaire* (Paris: PUF, 2016), pp. 251–67 or on the margins in *Être marxiste en philosophie* (Paris: PUF, 2015), pp. 212–16.

the first tendency the new elaboration of the materials leavened by a second stream, coming from the beginning of the seventies with the courses on Rousseau and Machiavelli and the text on Imperialism.[41] Of course the two tendencies produce a tension which traverses the writings and the concepts of these years, a tension that can perhaps explain the different, if not opposing, interpretations the writings of these years have produced.

However, perhaps it is possible to take a step further and risk an hypothesis that could only be proven with precise and rigorous work on these texts, a part of which has not yet been published:[42] one could try a more precise periodization of these writings by saying that in the writings of 1982 there is a dominance of the materialist tendency, whereas in the writings of 1985–86 there is a dominance of the eschatological tendency.

---

41   Louis Althusser, *Machiavelli et nous*, in *Ecrits philosophiques et politiques*, ɪɪ, pp. 39–167; Louis Althusser, *Cours sur Rousseau*, ed. by Yves Vargas (Paris: Les temps de Cerises, 2012); Louis Althusser, 'Sur l'impérialisme', in *Écrits sur l'histoire*, pp. 103–260. In any case an important reconstruction of this stream of thought can be found in Stefano Pippa, *Althusser and Contingency* (Milan: Mimesis International, 2018).

42   I'm referring to the group of text that are listed in the Althusser archive as ALT2.029 (*Textes divers, 1982–1986*).

II. THE MATERIALITY OF THE MILIEU AND THE MATERIALIST EDUCATION

Introduction to Part II
MARLENE KIENBERGER AND BRUNO PACE

In a dialectical dance between the reproduction of an established order and a counter-acting resistance, what survives over time? This part of the volume has assembled what we could regard as 'materialisms of transmission', that is to say, a milieu-mediated connection between evolution and education. The texts in this part approach these questions from different angles and consider them in their diversity: three (Pascal Sévérac, Marlon Miguel, Bernardo Bianchi) investigate what a materialist approach to education could look like; the other two (Elena Vogman, Catherine Perret) present a transdisciplinary perspective on the evolution of languages, gestures, movements, and social norms in relation to tools, labour, and economic organization. All of the authors show an interest in unconventional paths in the history of philosophy, pedagogy, linguistics, or anthropology.

Vogman dives into multiple aspects of Nikolai Marr's theory of language. Marr developed a paleontological and archaeological view on history as a non-linear process, and Vogman shows that his views were pretty much aligned with Walter Benjamin's critique of historicism as teleological and a-processual. Marr, whose theories were banned by Stalin himself in the 1950s, sought the origin of languages in a materialist foundation — namely, in the gesture, which he connected to the use of tools and economic organization. He depicts different gestures in different societies that survive throughout time as remnants of the past, and thereby proposes the anachronistic coexistence of material traces from different historical stages and temporalities.

Against the backdrop of rising nationalisms, Marr insisted on a materialist constitution of languages — perceiving them as a class phenomenon and a fundamental element of class struggle — and his theory negates any reconstruction of linguistic families that is based on race. Vogman shows that Marr's paleontological linguistics, which in his time was condemned for being fictional and unscientific, can nowadays be read as a political genealogy of languages as well as a fruitful contribution to linguistics, which he accused of disregarding the languages of oppressed people. Vogman depicts Marr as a multidisciplinary intellectual and the inventor of his own syncretic version of historical materialism.

Perret analyses the multiple relationships between tools, hands, the mouth, gestures, and speech, as well as their roles in human evolution. Tools are considered as extensions of our bodies, whereas hands are seen as the intersection between gesture and speech. The human technical milieu and its constitutive gestures survive over time and is mediated by producing bodies. Perret, who draws upon Marcel Mauss and André Leroi-Gourhan, emphasizes that a few collective human characteristics, e.g. social norms, were able to become emancipated from the biological and started undergoing an evolutionary process in their own right. At the same time, they are inscribed into biological bodies and ultimately shape emotions, movements, and bodily rhythms. Using the foundations of Leroi-Gourhan's anthropology, she re-evaluates the critique of contemporary capitalism, which continuously forces us to reduce our understanding of social bonds to the 'hallucinatory power of value'. By identifying the materialities of social bonds which are not reducible to the logic of value, she resists the 'gregarization' — meaning the turning into a herd behaviour — of society that is induced by the exploitation of the technical in favour of economic interests.

Perret's kinaesthetic materiality of social bonds — which can be described as the sensitivity towards movements and gestures that are needed for cooperative production — is not too far from the materiality of the 'social glue' needed to build a collective which is presented by **Miguel**. Miguel discusses the situation of Anton Semyonovich Makarenko, the well-known Soviet educator who formulated an anti-theory of education based on one sole guiding principle: 'the creation of a real collectivity'. In the Gorky colony where he lived and collectively organized a society with delinquent children in miserable conditions, Makarenko focused on the formation of a sensibility that goes beyond the individual perspective. He believed that the educator must immanently learn from the situation, take the unique circumstances into account, and rearrange them so that the collective educates itself. In theoretical terms, Miguel shows the connection between Makarenko's educational practice and Karl Marx's 'Theses on Feuerbach': Humans are, at the same time, products and producers of their own circumstances.

This recursive loop can also be found in **Bianchi**'s text about emancipation and the question of a materialist education. He argues that education should not be conceived as an activity that seeks to explain the human reality from the outside. In this way, Bianchi dissolves the traditional subject-object dichotomy as well as stadialist and hierarchical conceptions of the relationship between knowledge and politics. His materialist gesture, therefore, consists in neutralizing the principle of the ignorance of the masses by redefining the relationship between politics, knowledge, and education. By drawing on Étienne Balibar's 'materialism without matter' and his theory of transindividuality, Bianchi proposes the idea of a recursive loop between individuation and individualization, as well as between knowledge (and education) and political agency.

While Bianchi's analysis of a materialist education centres on Marx and Balibar, **Sévérac** focuses on a Spinozist education based on reason and knowledge that aims at a transformation of the affective sensibility of the body. In his text, he delineates a Spinozist 'physics of thought' as it is applied to a moral education. He emphasizes the transformation that takes place in the child's body that is being educated. Sévérac sketches out an education which is opposed to the traditional, moral education, and highlights how it must cultivate an ability to 'speak out', a 'moral force' and 'love for freedom', which can enable the educated to resist any tyrannical abuse of power.

The texts in this part raise and seek to answer important questions at the intersection of materialism, education, evolution, and politics.

How difficult is it to question what seems unquestionable because of established traditions? How can a thinker resist a tradition and thereby transform its body of knowledge? To what extent does the scope of materialist thought undergo a transformation when an author redefines what the questions and foundations could be and when they elaborate new ways of considering different materialities? What survives when the necessity of these questions and foundations are challenged, and an author suggests that they are contingent on the circumstances they are inscribed within?

May the following texts continue raising questions that transmit and transform the materialist trends.

Language Follows Labour
Nikolai Marr's Materialist Palaeontology of Speech
ELENA VOGMAN

Today the Soviet archaeologist, palaeontologist of speech, and inventor of the theory of 'linear' or 'gestural speech', Nikolai Marr (1864–1934), seems to be almost forgotten. The Georgian-born author is mostly known for his 'New Theory of Language', otherwise called the Japhetic theory, yet Marr's work on the disciplinary margins, his incessant invention of new fields of knowledge, and his 'archaeological' vision of history is comparable to such lateral thinkers as Aby Warburg or Carl Einstein. In contrast to these authors, however, Marr practiced archaeology, which led him to some crucial discoveries in the Caucasus and a vast materialist theory of culture, which he understood as evolving by 'strata'[1] and conditioned by historical and economic relations. Regarding the impact of labour on the development of culture, Marr's 'palaeontology of speech' emphasized the role of the gesture as genuine component of language and thought. At the same time, Marr's Marxist disposition did not prevent him from publishing the first Russian translation of Lucien Lévy-Bruhl's *Méntalité Primitive*, accompanied with a special foreword by the author. Shortly after the publication, Lévy-Bruhl was decried as one of the 'bourgeois' and 'idealist' philosophers along with Marcel Proust and Sigmund Freud.

---

1   A geological layer of rock, soil, or other material.

Marr's theory of language, which is also known as Japhetology (*iafetologia*), implied the existence of a 'Japhetic' family, which the languages of the Caucasus, the Near East, and some non-Indo-European languages of Eurasia and Africa were supposed to belong to. After the Russian Revolution, Marr founded the Japhetic Institute in Saint Petersburg, which was part of the State Academy of History of Material Culture, where in the 1920s several poets and artists attended lectures, including Sergei Eisenstein. Marr ventured to produce alternative models of temporality, which involved a new perspective on the history of culture, and at the same time questioned the epistemic ground on which such a history had been written and perceived until that point. This epistemic shift went hand in hand with a critical opening of the inherited disciplinary boundaries provoking Marr to create new fields of knowledge, disquieting and sometimes disturbing other fields, which became the reason why his critical attempts remained underacknowledged or were even forgotten.

On the one hand, Marr's materialism operated in close proximity to the materiality of culture — its archaeological objects, its traces and linguistic manifestations — and, on the other hand, it operated in a more speculative anthropological dimension by addressing language's origins. This dimension challenged the orthodox model of historical materialism and introduced a series of ingenious and apocryphal claims. In this non-linear, 'fossilized' time Marr discovered a crucial form of life, a 'survival', which served as the basis for his materialist palaeontology of speech. It was this model of time that transformed Marr's theory of language into a critical instrument aimed at both the racist linguistic theories of his time and the dominant Indo-European linguistics that was based on the arbitrariness of the sign.

In order to better seize the drifting trajectory that led Marr to a paleontological model of history and language, my text will first draw upon his archaeological expeditions to the Caucasus by examining a number of photographic documents which are preserved at the Institute of History of Material Culture in Saint Petersburg. These materials symptomatically reveal the impact that archaeological practice and palaeontology had on Marr's linguistic theory, or 'Japhetology', with particular regard for its implied temporality. Secondly, I will briefly trace Marr's language theory, especially his late text 'On the Origin of language'. Japhetology became the object of different waves of critique formulated from both philological and linguistic perspectives follow-ing the official ban of Marr's theory, which was pronounced by Stalin personally in the 1950s. An analysis of manifold parallels between Marr's approach and the poetico-theoretical methods of his contem-poraries, in particular the poets Andrei Bely and Velimir Khlebnikov, remains still to be written, insofar as they tempted to reconfigure teleo-logical temporalities in order to lay bare the vertiginous complexity of historical events. A different model of history would appear once Marr's linguistic approach is located in a constellation with these other authors' approaches. The rhythmical occurrences and re-occurrences of historical events which Khlebnikov and Bely observed in their in-vestigations reveal history's entanglements with psychic and poetic economy rather than with the irreversible course of history.

MARR'S ARCHAEOLOGICAL EXPEDITIONS

Marr studied every discipline offered at the faculty of Oriental Studies in Saint Petersburg. He specialized in the Armenian, Georgian, and Iranian languages, and swiftly became one of the leading orientalists of his time. In 1892 — aged only 27 years old — Marr undertook his first archaeological expedition to Ani, the ruined medieval Armenian city situated on the territory of the Russian Empire, in today's Turkey alongside the closed border with Armenia. In the following decades Marr undertook foundational archaeological work in Sinai, Palestine, and the ancient sites of Armenia, such as Dvin, Garni, Ani, and the lake Van. Marr's research into the buried culture, architecture, and language of the city of Ani (the first traces of which date back to the fifth century) was pioneering in its approach and still remains an important point of reference. His book *Ani, a Written History of the City and the Excavations*, published many years later in 1934, included materials from eleven expeditions between 1892 and 1917.[2]

Marr's study of the excavated monuments of Ani opens with a folded leaflet: a map of the ancient city. The author marks different sites

2   Nikolai Marr, *Ani, knizhnaia istoria goroda i raskopki na meste* [Ani, a Written History of the City and the Excavations] (Moscow: OGIZ, 1934).

and multiple discoveries are depicted in his text, such as the Church of the Holy Redeemer, the wall of Ashot, King Gagik I's church of Saint Gregory or 131 fragments of an Armenian Inscription, etc. Already in 1905, Marr had critically qualified the title as the 'written history of Ani', that is, 'the history of the Armenian Bagratid Kingship based on literary evidence, such as the traditional history of Armenia in general', as 'limited and legendary'. Without an account of its silent material traces, its surviving remnants, the past appears as 'poor and dead'.[3] Marr opposes such traditional literary history to the astonishing 'life' of Ani's excavated ruins: archaeological landscapes that offer an insight into history's 'concrete materiality'. The evidence of a vanished culture that Marr obtained from his excavations reverses, in his view, the certitude of a 'nationally constituted Christian cultural history', which is anachronistically claimed as 'Armenian'. Opposing such assertions of literary history, Marr assembles a series of syncretic elements, of Chalcedonian influences alongside Georgian ones, which he analyses in his text.[4]

One quality of Marr's text seems remarkable: while deciphering fragments from Ani's lost culture he emphasizes the destructive forces of history, which attest, in each recovered monument, to an irreversible loss. One can identify in this leitmotiv of destruction, which traverses Marr's archaeological gaze, a dialectical attention to the vanished layers of culture and memory. This dialectics of residues returns in his future research in the palaeontology of language: Marr will try to recover the history of language— especially the history of oral languages — from ephemeral contemporary vernaculars. In his work history appears not as a homogeneous and teleological flow but rather as an archaeological layering inhabited by survival and coexistence.

Another important element of Marr's early archaeological work, one that marks his entire oeuvre, is his attention to material culture. 'Material culture', which he sometimes writes as a compound noun, appears at decisive junctures in Marr's texts, expanding the semantic field of this conceptual constellation. While in his early archaeological investigations it describes the methodological focus he uses for the

---

3   Nikolai Marr, *O raskopkah i rabotah v Ani leta 1906* [On the Excavations and Works in Ani in Summer 1906] (Saint Petersburg: Imp. akad. nauk, 1907), p. 2.

4   Ibid.

Figure 1. Nikolai Marr, The palace of Paron, Ani, ca. 1898. Archive of the
Institute of History of Material Culture, Saint Petersburg, inventory
number Q 756-76.

objects of the Institute of History of Material Culture — excavated
monuments and concrete material evidence from Ani, for example —
in his theory of language 'material culture' refers to the conditions
in which linguistic material is produced and studied in the field of
the palaeontology of language: It describes the method of reading
the history of thought in its relation to the origins of language and
Marxist theory. He writes, 'the problem of thought is one of the most
relevant if not the most relevant theoretical issue in the world, precisely
because its roots lie not in itself and not in nature, but in the material
basis, described in the framework of dialectical materialism.'[5] In this
passage written shortly before his death in 1934, Marr takes the stance
of historical materialism; but far from abandoning an anthropological
perspective on the history of culture, an archaeological vision of time,

5   Nikolai Marr, 'Iazyk i myshlenie' [Language and Thought], in *Izbrannye raboty* [Se-
     lected Works], 5 vols (Leningrad: Gosudarstvennaia akademia istorii material'noi
     kul'tury (GAIMK), 1933–37), III (1936), pp. 90–121 (p. 104).

and a highly syncretic and speculative method of research, Marr's 'materialism' embraced different stages of his scientific investigations beginning with his early archaeological work.

This early focus on 'material culture' — its concrete objects and traces — is symptomatic of his early work with images. While preparing for his first archaeological expedition to Ani in 1891 Marr took a three-month-course in photography, and insisted that the Imperial Academy of Science provide him with expensive equipment and a camera.[6] Marr's travel diaries bear witness to his emphasis on documentation and to the transmission of his archaeological experience. He even refused to continue his trip without a camera, which should have been sent to him a week after his departure for Ani's archaeological site. We read in his diary: 'I am deeply concerned while waiting for the camera, the site can be damaged by unforeseen events.' Weeks later, after the camera finally arrived, Marr's entries became very laconic: 'I'm exclusively occupied with taking images (documenting excavated fragments of paintings) and developing them.'[7]

Photographs constitute a considerable part of Marr's surviving archive, which today numbers approximately 10,000 pieces from different archaeological expeditions and his later study of 'gestural' or 'linear speech'.[8] These materials helped Marr to establish a research instrument for the Institute of History of Material Culture, which became part of the Historical-Archaeological section of the St. Petersburg University. Marr also made use of these documents in his research and lectures, an approach which was prescient for understanding images as arguments in their own right. For several reasons, this visual archive and its use value in Marr's theoretical work have remained neglected. Furthermore, a major part of his archive was destroyed during the 1917 revolution, as the train which Marr used to send his collection to the Caucasian Historical Institute in order to establish the first museum of Ani was destroyed during its journey. Surprisingly, this traumatic loss

---

6   Archive of the Institute of History of Material Culture, Saint Petersburg, fonds 1, inventory 61/1893, pp. 94–95.

7   Nikolai Marr, Diary from 23 May and 9 June 1892, Archive of the Institute of History of Material Culture, Saint Petersburg, fonds 1, inventory 33/1892, pp. 41 and 173.

8   See also T. M. Devel and T. B. Tomes, 'Sobranie N. Ia. Marra v fotoarchive LOIA AN SSR' [N. Ia. Marr's Collection in the Archive of the Institute for History of Material Culture], Istoriko-filologicheski zhurnal, 3 (1971), pp. 289–95.

Figure 2. Nikolai Marr, The side pylon of a church, Garni, 1909–10.
Archive of the Institute of History of Material Culture, Saint Petersburg,
inventory number Q 77-18.

of the archive coincides with Marr's shift from archaeology to language
theory, leading him to more speculative, anthropological, and paleontological perspectives.

LANGUAGE'S ORIGINS

Marr's groundwork for the 'New Theory of Language' dates back to his talk at the Academy of Sciences on 21 November 1923, when he formulated a double hypothesis. On the one hand, he refused a prevalent racial genealogy of language by stating that there is no Indo-European language family based on race. On the other hand, he claimed that 'there is no primal unitary language, but a multitude of tribal languages'. In this way he disqualified the theory of the *Ursprache* as 'an instrumentalized ideological fiction'. In contrast to such a fiction, Marr constructed a materialist perspective that regards language in Marxist terms as a class phenomenon: 'There is no language which is not class language, hence there is no thought which is not class thought.'[9] Yet, despite this radical claim, Marr was far from merely adapting any dogmatic stance of historical materialism. In his theory of 'material culture' he proposed that language is a tool that evolves in relation to labour and, as a consequence, that it is a fundamental element of the class struggle. At the same time, he considered labour as being part of a complex cultural process which required a meticulous study of its objects, traces, and 'survivals' — a crucial concept in Marr's palaeontology of language. In this way, Marr's highly productive period of linguistic palaeontology, which dates from 1923 to 1934, was marked not only by a remarkable transposition of his archaeological experience to the level of language theory and culture, but also by an invention of his own syncretic version of historical materialism evolving alongside a constant reformulation of his own positions.[10]

The dialectical doubt present in Marr's thought, which can be described as 'perpetually drifting' because it is perpetually seduced by new linguistic cases — which Marr conceived of as new 'material' bases as well as a 'formal and ideological' frameworks for his analysis — was inspiring for many contemporary artistic practices, especially those of poets. At the same time, Marr's critics, such as the linguist and founder of Eurasianism Nikolai Trubetskoi, dismissed his linguistic approach

9   Marr, 'Iazyk i myshlenie', p. 91.
10   Nikolai Marr, 'Novyi povorot v rabote iafeticheskoi teorii' [New Turn in the Work of Japhetic Theory], in *Izbrannye raboty*, I (1933), pp. 312–46; 'Aktual'nye problemy i ocherednye zadachi iafeticheskoi teorii' [Current Problems and Imminent Tasks of the Japhetic Theory], in *Izbrannye raboty*, III, pp. 61–77.

as well as his anti-colonial positions as those of a 'half-mad graphoma-
niac', and advised his works to be reviewed by a psychiatrist more than
a linguist.[11] Such criticisms followed the formula, 'First the conclusion
comes, and only afterwards the analysis of the material',[12] which was a
way of alluding to Marr's seemingly biased method and consequently
of ignoring his archaeological and materialist investigations. Beginning
with Stalin's personal ban of Marr's theory in the 1950s, his Institute
was closed, and his theories regarded as an obscure perversion of science and a linguistic aberration. To a large extent, Marr's critics have
accused him of being non-systematic; at the same time, it must be said
that Marr's genealogical approach, which takes places at the margins
of different disciplines, as well as his syncretic reading of the history of
culture cannot be understood from within a narrow historicist perspective. This is why critics considered Marr a pseudo-scientist who sought
to 'prove the unknown by the unknown',[13] and principally referred to
Marr's lack of a properly 'linguistic education' and 'a concrete method
of comparative historical research in linguistics' in order to discredit
him.[14] Ultimately, his 'new theory of language' has been characterized
as 'a highly attractive myth', even in recent scholarship.[15]

In his text from 1925 entitled 'On the Origin of Language', which
was quickly also published in a German translation, Marr recalled the
central theses of Japhetic theory. In this text he claims that Western Indo-European linguistics were merely oriented 'to the data of

---

11   Trubetskoi to Jakobson, 6 November 1924, in *N. S. Trubetzkoy's Letters and Notes*, ed.
      by Roman Jakobson (The Hague: Mouton, 1975), p. 74. See also Stefanos Geroulanos
      and Jamie Phillips, 'Eurasianism versus IndoGermanism: Linguistics and Mythology
      in the 1930s' Controversies over European Prehistory', *History of Science*, 56.3 (2018),
      pp. 343–78 (p. 363).

12   Such was the formula against Marr's theory articulated by V. V. Gornung in the
      beginning of the 1950s, quoted after Vladimir Alpatov, *Istoria odnogo mifa: Marr i
      marrism* [The History of One Myth: Marr and Marrism] (Moscow: Ed. URSS, 2004),
      p. 15.

13   Ibid., p. 42.

14   Ibid., p. 11.

15   Ibid., p. 33. Alpatov questions the attractiveness of Marr's theory of language far
      beyond the ideological instrumentalization through the official Soviet dogma and the
      pre-revolutionary tendencies of universal regard. 'The popularity of Marr's ideas [...]
      was already considerable in the beginning of the 1920s and grew further with the
      formulation of "the new theory of language"'. Alpatov quotes a recent publication
      of Olga Freydenberg, who is one of the most prominent scholars of Marr. Alpatov
      characterizes the attraction of Marr's theory as the 'attraction of a [scientific] myth'.

dead and traditional written languages' and largely proceeded on a philological basis. Similar to the example of Ani, where Marr opposed the living materiality of the ruins to the dead literary historiography, his palaeontology of speech critically discredits contemporary Indo-European linguistics based on racial theory. In opposition to such idealist tendencies in philology, as well as to the reconstruction of ethnic identities, Marr sought to uncover a hidden link to social relations surviving in homonymic affinities between different linguistic clusters. In this regard he countered the Proto-Indo-European theories — such as Otto Schrader's *Sprachforschung und Urgeschichte* — with his own socio-biological approach and paleontological research method. He states: 'Indo-European linguistics cannot deny that it is a science about language from historical epochs. However, regarding the issue of its genesis leading to the prehistory of human speech, it is helpless, it doesn't say anything meaningful.'[16] In this way Marr not only refused an ethnic perspective on language but also introduced a historical temporality into the very notion of 'prehistory', which up until that point was regarded as a homogeneous space-time where nature prevailed over culture and biological life prevailed over social processes.[17]

> Our approach is socioeconomical. Even tribal society is economico-tribal, not zoologico-tribal. And when a tribe is constituted according to its active being and not its native descent, this tribe is a class formation. As such, it is in struggle with other equal class-tribal formations — in a struggle for materials and the subject-matter of production, or for sale of its production, and for this reason we can't exclude the prehistoric tribes from the class society.[18]

Following this argument Marr aimed to reconsider the relation between language and thought: he saw language not merely as means of communication but rather as an instrument (Russian: *instrument*)

---

16   Nikolai Marr, 'Ob iafeticheskoi teorii' [On Japhetic Theory], in *Izbrannye raboty*, III, pp. 1–34 (p. 33).

17   On the 'invention of prehistory' in the second half of the nineteenth century as well as on the discovery of the deep time of the earth, see the excellent study by Maria Stavrinaki, *Saisis par la préhistoire. Enquête sur l'art et le temps des modernes* (Dijon: Les presses du réel, 2019).

18   Nikolai Marr, 'Sredstva peredvizhenia, orudia samozazhity i proizvodstva v doistorii' [Means of Transportation, Instruments of Self-protection and Production in Prehistory], in *Izbrannye raboty*, III, pp. 123–51 (p. 141).

closely tied to the labour process. For this reason, he recognized language in the first bodily tool: the gesture. Marr conceptualized such communication, which he saw as conditioned by economic and social relations, 'kinetic' or 'linear speech'. In this way the theoretical foundation for the genesis of language concerned the origin of vocalization or auditory language from motoric language.

Marr's methodological approach examined 'the picture of the transformation of language in the various eras of language creation by way of comparison', which he called 'diachronic comparative grammar'.[19] By reconstructing, from contemporary linguistic forms, the surviving archaic 'residues', this procedure was said to reveal the historical 'stages' of linguistic development. According to Marr, the primary phonetic speech consisted of four phonetic elements: *SAL, BER, ION,* and *ROSH*. He derived these from tribal names of people from the Mediterranean area. According to the Japhetic theory, all human languages were formed from these four elements, which survived in them and provided the ground for Marr's linguistic palaeontology.

Conceiving of the hand as an evolutionary primal linguistic tool, Marr wrote:

> Primeval man, who did not possess any articulated language, was happy if he pointed to or drew attention to an object, and to do so, he had a particularly well-adapted tool (instrument), the hand, which distinguishes man so sharply from the rest of the animal kingdom [...] The hand or hands were a person's tongue. Hand movements, facial expressions, and in some cases body movements as well, were the only available means (sredstva) of linguistic creation.[20]

From such an irreducible phenomenality of the hand, Marr derived the primal language as being the 'fundamental quality of *japhetic* language'. This is how, following Lévy-Bruhl's '*loi de participation*' and Hamilton Cushing's 'Manual Concepts',[21] he stated that concepts were not connected by means of logical relations but instead by means of sensuous and expressive elements. Cushing described how in Zuni language

19   Nikolai Marr, 'O proischozhdenii iazyka' [On the Origin of Language], in *Izbrannye raboty*, III (1936), pp. 180–215 (p. 182).

20   Ibid., p. 201.

21   Ibid., pp. 202–06.

particular hand gestures and intonations, which accompanied speech, could radically modify its signification. According to Cushing these gestures or intonation nuances preserved aspects of the designated object or acted as a trace pointing at its concrete meaning. On the one hand, this anthropological foundation allowed Marr to formulate the most speculative and provocative thesis in which he identified the hand as the primal operator of language. On the other hand, Marr grounded this anthropology of the hand within a new materialist framework: he replaced the 'mystical' elements of Lévy-Bruhl's concept of '*participation mystique*' with constructive ones, speculating on the social and economic organization of life. Lévy-Bruhl conceived of 'mystical participation' as a mode of perception in indigenous cultures where 'objects, beings, and phenomena can be, though in some way incomprehensible to us, something other than themselves [...] that they give forth and receive mystical powers, virtues, qualities, and influences which make themselves felt outside without ceasing to remain what they are.'[22] Although Lévy-Bruhl never intended to characterize the 'mystical' or 'pre-logical' mode of thinking as a failure of logic or an inability to think rationally, he admitted that there was a nuance of obscurity which accompanied his concept, leading to its inadequacy. 'However', he wrote, apparently confused by his own idea, 'in default of a wholly satisfactory formula, we can make an attempt to approximate it.'[23] For Marr, Lévy-Bruhl's actual confusion could only have arisen from an absence of a materialist standpoint, namely the obscuration of the fundamental relation between thinking and labour, between language and the conditions of cultural production. Marr, who agreed with the radical alterity and singularity of the phenomenon of 'mystical participation', also sought to demystify this concept by tracing its historical dimension.

He argued that 'it is entirely inconceivable that the hand could have been replaced as the producer of a mental value-language, before it was replaced by tools as the producer of material goods, or that an articulated language of sounds could have taken the place of a hand language at that time'. Rather, the foundation for the creation

---

22   Lucien Lévy-Bruhl, *How Natives Think* (1910), trans. by Lilian A. Clare (New York: Washington Square Press, 1966), p. 61.

23   Ibid.

of an auditory language must have been laid 'by some process of productive work'.[24] The origin of an auditory language gained not only a fundamental processual dimension, but it is also inseparably linked to the economic and ergonomic organization of society. In consequence, Marr argued that an articulated language 'could not have emerged before mankind's transition to productive work with the aid of artificially fashioned tools'.[25]

SURVIVING GESTURES

Marr's attempt to introduce a materialist ground into the history of language radically differs from the teleological framework of orthodox historical materialism. Marr understood history not as a linear progression of time but as a multi-layered and polydimensional process closely related to matter, itself conceived as a concrete material involved in the production of time. His notion of 'survival' paradigmatically crystallizes this epistemic shift. However, *survival* would not survive without a history in which its latency, its transformations, and its possible reoccurrence is inscribed. Marr therefore carefully distinguished historical phases or strata which mark the evolution of language — understood in its complex historicity and not as a mere evolution.

> Language [*yazyk*] has nothing to do with a mere sound, but with a phoneme, an articulated sound produced by mankind and accompanied by the labour of the brain apparatus which previously effected the hand with the same ends. Language has to do with a sound directed by thought in the same way as thought directs the hand, the gesture, and the facial expression of linear speech. Ant movements, for instance, do not dispose of any particular technically adapted tool. The entire body moves here. Animal sound language can be the origin of the latest human artistic production in the sphere of sounds, singing and music, while the vibration of the body can be the

---

24   In this article, 'auditory language' refers to a language composed of sounds, and it differs from vocalizations or sounds which Marr saw as a complement to gestural language. He regarded written language as a historically more advanced stage of these forms of communication.

25   Marr, 'O proischozhdenii iazyka', pp. 202–08.

foundation of the linear artistic creation, of dancing etc. But neither the one nor the other led to the human language.[26]

For Marr the caesura which separates linear or gestural speech from articulated language lies within the cultural and economic shift: literary understood as the physical impact of the new conditions of production emerging with the use of the tools. But what does it mean when Marr speaks of surviving gestures as elements of linear speech?

It comes as no surprise that the archival materials show Marr's palaeontology of language documenting and interpreting cases of 'surviving' linear speech. A series of images from Marr's photographic archive, captioned as 'the Gestural language of a Georgian Woman', are preserved at the Institute for the History of Material Culture in St. Petersburg. In a text from 1932 entitled 'Language and Thought', Marr criticized Western linguistics which he saw as indifferent to genealogical problems of thought and to marginal linguistic phenomena, such as gestures, argot, and vernaculars. Paying great attention to women's gestures within patriarchal societies, Marr observed and interpreted kinetic speech as a 'survival', in Russian: *perezhitok*. As a consequence of Stalin's progressive dictum of the first five-year plan, which postulated to 'overcome the survivals [*perezhitki*]' of the past, the concept of *perezhitok* could henceforth only be used in a pejorative sense. Nonetheless, after Stalin's ban, Marr's texts shift from the discredited concept of *perezhitok* to an intimately related one: *perezhivanie*, a neologism in the framework of his language theory. This word, which is based on the same root *zhit'*, 'to live', also denotes an emotionally charged 'experience' in the Russian language. The use value of this silent shift of meaning, in which Marr's concept itself *survives* despite negative political impositions and associations, in the context of Marr's Japhetic theory seems significant.

To return now to the images of Georgian women, what does '*perezhivanie*' mean when manifested in their hand gestures? According to the author, the surviving element of 'linear speech' could only survive because 'its use' relates 'to the everyday life' and to its 'normative pressure'.[27]

---

26   Ibid., p. 200.
27   Marr, 'Iazyk i myshlenie', p. 108.

Such bodily manifestations led Marr to reject Western anthropology's perspective on the 'primitive mentality' as an evolutionary stage
of society in favour of a more complex political and social argument.
Marr gave examples of colonial countries, such as Australia or South
America, where the expression of women's grief, especially that of
widows, traditionally manifested itself through a ban on speech. The
resulting silence was accompanied by gesticulation: for Marr, these
examples were of the 'survival' [*perezhivanie*] of linear speech *par excellence.*[28] He observed similar gestures as a part of a different type of
patriarchal society: following their marriage, women in the Caucasus
were only allowed to speak silently, in gestures. In such a female 'linear
speech' he envisioned a survival of a conflict, a 'women's language'
which was used in the 'struggle of women's matriarchal organization'.[29]
Marr's hypothesis also took into account the dissemination of hand
language in highly heterogeneous geographical and cultural regions
and formations. Through his analysis of the gestures which women
performed in two different photographs, one signifying the sun and
the other the full moon, Marr pointed to the structural similarity of
the two different expressions. In both cases hands were raised to form
a half-circle of the 'orans posture'.[30] However, while the expression of
the sun was emphasized through a light smile, this facial expression is
absent in the case of the moon. Marr's archive also preserves studies of
collective expressions of manual speech, although they do not feature
references or further interpretation.

Such cases open up a double perspective within Marr's thought:
on the one side, there is what he calls the 'manifold semantic eman-
ations' of the 'hand', meaning that one word unfolds a multitude of
potential meanings.[31] Such a polysemic quality proves the hypothesis
of a phonetic speech that originated out of a handful of primal elements
or particular *Urworte*. Alongside words like 'sky', 'cosmos', and 'man',
Marr identified the word 'hand' as a significant part of these primary
linguistic elements. Regarding the question of the primacy of the sky
or the hand, Marr answered from the standpoint of Japhetic theory:

---

28   Ibid.
29   Ibid., p. 107.
30   Ibid., p. 108.
31   Marr, 'O proishozhdenii iazyka', p. 209.

Figure 3. Nikolai Marr [image ordered in 1931], 'Georgian women's gestures: the hands are brought together expressing "the sun"', Tiflis ca. 1931. Archive of the Institute of History of Material Culture, Saint Petersburg, inventory number Q 347-27.

'Guided by the palaeontology of language, it points from the "sky" to the "hand" as to the *Urwort*: the hand of the working man, the creator of the entire material culture, including language.'[32] Hence, the etymology of the word not only implies the gesture, but also provides a knowledge of gestures, which operates by means of its expressive a-mimetic potential (Marr further derives verbs like *giving, taking,* and *offering* from the word *hand*). On the other side, Marr's analysis of the gesture genealogically locates language within the gesture, which then becomes not only a proto-word but an operative prototype of linguistic instruments.

---

32   Ibid. See also the excellent study by Susanne Strätling, *Hand am Werk: Poetik der Poiesis in der russischen Avantgarde* (Paderborn: Fink, 2018), pp. 69–84.

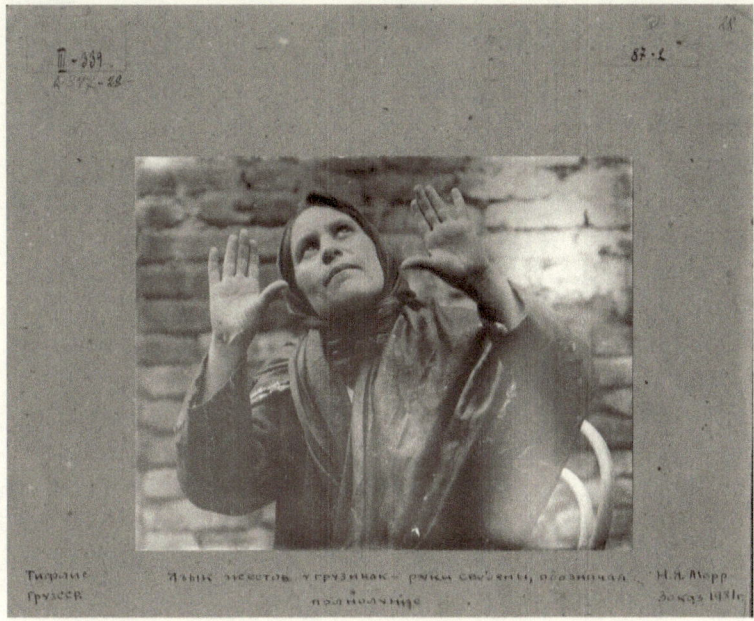

Figure 4. Nikolai Marr [image ordered in 1931], 'Georgian women's
gestures: the hands are brought together expressing "the full moon"',
Tiflis ca. 1931. Archive of the Institute of History of Material Culture,
Saint Petersburg, inventory number Q 347-28.

However, without providing any readymade answer to the problem of the origin of language, Marr dialectically claims: 'Without an
interest in the origin of language, no linguistics is possible. Every theory of language supposes a positive relation to this question.'[33] For
Marr, language is a 'belt in the sphere of the superstructure of society';
it originated in different cultures simultaneously and independently
from one another. But the creative function of labour that effects the
transition between different cultural formations, 'is unitary regarding
its origins, and all its manifold manifestations result from a unitary
creative process affecting the different stages of its development.'[34]

---

33   Marr, 'O proishozhdenii iazyka', p. 183.
34   Ibid., p. 189.

WALTER BENJAMIN AND MARR

This paradoxical figure of thought, which both supposes a loss of origin and the necessity of researching the origin's 'traces and "becomings"' strongly echoes Walter Benjamin's understanding of history. Benjamin, who used a quote from Karl Kraus's *Words in Verse* as an epigraph for one of his theses on history, 'Origin is the goal', composed a virulent critique of history regarded as a linear progression of time. Instead, for Benjamin '[h]istory is the subject of a construction whose site is not homogenous, empty time, but time filled full by now-time [*Jetztzeit*]'.[35]

When the origin is conceived as an *Urphänomen*, one can understand why Benjamin attentively read the German translation of Marr's text 'Über die Entstehung der Sprache' and discussed Marr's theory in his own text from 1935 entitled 'Problems in the Sociology of Language: An Overview'. Despite this interest, Benjamin's reading of Marr is marked by a particular reluctance provoked by the scope of Marr's thought: 'Marr has attempted in his writings to introduce a number of new and generally rather strange ideas into language studies', Benjamin states, helplessly characterizing Marr's ideas as 'too important to be ignored yet too controversial to be adequately discussed here'.[36] The epistemic doubt contained within Benjamin's assessment could derive from the speculative character of Marr's approach and not only from the vast field of his work which was unknown to the German author. But despite this critical hesitation, Benjamin referred to three major points in Marr's theory. The first — Marr's materialist foundation of language in gesture — echoes Benjamin's own concept of 'Stimmgebärde', or voice gesture. The second, intimately related to the first, is Marr's derivation of language from labour: 'This can be linked dir-

---

35   Walter Benjamin, 'On the Concept of History', in *Selected Writings*, 4 vols (Cambridge, MA: Harvard University Press, 1996–2003), IV: *1938–1940*, ed. by Howard Eiland and Michael W. Jennings, trans. by Edmund Jephcott, Howard Eiland, and others (2003), pp. 389–400 (p. 395): 'The concept of mankind's historical progress cannot be sundered from the concept of its progression through a homogeneous, empty time. A critique of the concept of such a progression must underlie any criticism of the concept of progress itself.'

36   Walter Benjamin, 'Problems in the Sociology of Language: An Overview', in *Selected Writings*, III: *1935–1938*, ed. by Howard Eiland and Michael W. Jennings, trans. by Edmund Jephcott, Howard Eiland, and others (2002), pp. 68–93 (p. 74).

ectly to Marr's theory, according to which the manipulation of tools must have preceded that of language. But since the former activity is impossible without thought, there must have been a kind of thought which antedated speech.'[37] The third point, which is highly important for Benjamin's political position at that time, is Marr's critique of the racial foundations of language in the idea of a unitary national language. Highlighting this argument, Benjamin quotes a passage from Marr's 'On the Origin of Language':

> In a word, it would be unscientific and lacking in any real foundation to approach this or that language of a so-called national culture as the native language of the whole population, used by the mass of the people. For the present, the national language as a phenomenon independent of social strata and classes is a fiction.[38]

Marr even went so far as to oppose class affiliation to such national unity of language. In this way Marr could even suppose that in cases of similar social structures different national languages would show more typological class affinities — as affinities between the same classes — than relations between languages of different classes within the same national language. Benjamin could not be indifferent to this idea in the framework of his inquiry into the 'sociology of language', in particular regarding his attention towards minor languages and slang, when he claims:

> Current linguistics, the author constantly reiterates, has little inclination to seek out the sociological problems concealed in the languages of oppressed strata of populations. Indeed, it is remarkable how seldom linguistics, including the most recent linguistics, has concerned itself with argot, except from a purely philological point of view.[39]

The diachronic connection between hand language and auditory language, which forms the methodological core of Marr's palaeontology of language, also provided a crucial aspiration for a materialist approach to the history of culture by politicizing it without reducing

---

37   Ibid., p. 81.
38   Ibid., p. 75.
39   Ibid.

its speculative dimension. On the one hand, there was the possibility, in *living* Japhetic languages, of tracing the archaic structures — anachronistic residues travelling through time — that *live on* in contemporary vernaculars and gestures. In this way, Marr's palaeontology of speech aimed at reconstructing the erstwhile whole from the 'part' represented by the 'fossil remains'.[40] On the other hand, the idea that human culture and language developed in stages, changing step by step in the context of political, social, and economic conditions, suggests the image of a co-presence and co-existence of different societal and socio-historical formations. In conclusion, Marr not only provides evidence of the continued fossil existence of gestural, expressive and sound-language remains in modern languages through analysing their semantic and morphogenetic relationships, but he also reveals their active influence in cultural and religious practices. Important scholars of Marr's work, such as the philologist Olga Freudenberg, have devoted great attention to this last. Thus, Marr refers to the continuing 'magic' effect of the repetition of sound complexes, which he saw in pagan and Christian prayers, in cuneiform inscriptions and in architecture, in Abkhazian 'songs without words', and in Georgian refrains. This anthropological scope of Marr's theoretical preoccupations broadened, from the outset, the narrow perspective of linguistics as a single discipline. Furthermore, it denied any dogmatic or rigid version of historical materialism by privileging the analysis of material culture in its most marginal and temporally remote dimensions (prehistory, vernaculars etc.). This is how materialism paved the way for Marr's linguistic method, which emphasized the importance of gestures and bodily expressions. Against the backdrop of rising nationalisms, Marr insisted on a materialist constitution of language that originated beyond land and race in social relations between labour, culture, and thought. In this way Marr's materialist explorations of the origin of language — an origin that is also forever lost — involves a processual and a-teleological understanding of history and culture.

---

40   Marr, 'O proishozhdenii iazyka', p. 202.

Materialism and Capitalism Today
Zoo-aesthetics and a Critique of the Social Bond after Marcel Mauss and André Leroi-Gourhan

CATHERINE PERRET

INTRODUCTION

The question posed by the editors of this collective volume is one of the most pertinent questions of today: 'What is the relevance of materialism for thinking the political?' In spite of the scientific, philosophical, and cultural corpus at our disposal today, which should be able to reorient the catastrophic process set out by post-industrial capitalism (the tragedy of migration, the ecological disaster, growing inequalities, the rise of populisms, and the return to authoritarian politics), our efforts to renew modern criticism seem destined to remain helpless. Materialism, which I define as the analysis of the determination of social relations by the relations of production, has been largely incorporated and exploited by the contemporary capitalist rationale.

This rationale has extended the reign of the commodity to knowledge on the one hand, and to *psychè* on the other. Today we witness the production and commodification of new subjectivities stemming from consumer practices: the design of identities, the marketing of new forms of experience, and the development of what I call the *genetic paradigm*[1] that has brought the reproduction of the species back into the realm of the normative. These new forms of production transform social bonds into goods, and goods into social bonds. Current capitalism has succeeded at what nineteenth-century determinism did not dare to imagine.

Faced with this situation, it seems necessary to re-evaluate the criticism addressed to the analysis of value, i.e. how this value is embodied.[2] This critical position argues, on the one hand, that social subjects are defined both by their production and by their alienation from this production, and, on the other hand, that the bonds between subjects are realized through the exchange of values. Critical theories of value, which begin with the concepts of fetishism and alienation, are ultimately based on psychology, and have the goal of explaining the paradoxical materiality of goods, i.e. their uncanny 'spirituality'. These theories are consistent with the presuppositions of so-called 'neoliberalism' whether they are based on behaviourism or psychoanalysis.[3] By this I mean that, because critical theories of value think that social bonds are found in the exchange that takes place between subjects, they are easily subordinated to the neo-liberal, capitalistic idea that subjects are qualified as such by what they produce. The main issue with these theories comes from the fact that they function as mirrors of the status quo, and hence they lack potency.

For this reason, I think it is useful to return to the attempts made in the middle of the twentieth century to identify a materiality of social bonds that is not reducible to the logic of value or to what has been called 'the symbolic exchange'.[4] These alternative theories come

---

1   In French, I call this *'le tout-génétique'*.

2   See Jean Baudrillard, *Le Système des objets* (Paris: Gallimard, 1978); *Simulacres et Simulation* (Paris: Gallimard, 1981); as well as Jean-Joseph Goux, *Frivolité de la valeur* (Paris: Blusson, 2000).

3   The term 'neoliberal' has many flaws, including suggesting that capitalism has changed in nature by changing its form. However, it has the advantage of making it clear that it is becoming impossible to discern the implications of accumulation and those of the individual's subjection to the norms supposed to guarantee his or her autonomy.

4   We need to reassess the form of critique that has been dominant until now, which is concerned with the analysis of value and the phenomena of its embodiment. Based upon the analyses of the Frankfurt School since the 1930s as well as the theories of libidinal economy and even most of today's criticisms of neo-capitalism, this critique builds upon the concepts of alienation of the subject and commodity fetishism which are inherited from Marx and Freud. One should also note that in Marx and Freud

from anthropology. They focus on the notion of 'milieu' in order to disconnect this notion from the determinism that inspired it in the last decades of the nineteenth century.[5]

By combining the definition of the *human milieu* as a technical milieu with the distinction between individuation and subjectivation, I would like to propose a reflection on the materialities of the social bond. This bond is effectively embodied because it is symbolic, and because it indicates how alterity is a 'part' of everyone by dividing them. It takes bodily shape. For example, it takes shape in regimes of perception that condition the individual's ability to sense the governing norms of the society they belong to, and to bring them into play, for themselves and towards others, as rhythmical and formal values, in other words, as emotions and as living spaces. Then and only then does the individual experience social reality, and not as a constituent of that reality who is subjected to social order, but rather as an individual who feels, acts, and thinks, and who thus contributes to the renewal of the norms and codes that characterize the social bond.

I develop this argument alongside the work of Marcel Mauss and Leroi-Gourhan. It is indeed impossible to think of this question without one or the other, even if Leroi-Gourhan largely erased the traces of his doctoral advisor in his writings.

MARCEL MAUSS'S 'TECHNIQUES OF THE BODY': BODY-AS-MEDIUM AND THE TECHNICAL MILIEU

I am less interested, for the purposes of this chapter, in Mauss's famous essay on the gift than in his later text on the techniques of the body.[6]

---

the concepts of 'alienation' and 'fetishism' were heuristic and critical. Parasitized and disabled since that time by the dominant positivistic philosophies, they have become explanatory tools used to 'describe (a supposed) reality', as if the subjects were qualified as such, as subjects, by their identification with the objects they produce and exchange, so that effectively the social bond is reduced to what Jean Baudrillard, under the term 'symbolic exchange', likened to death (cf. Jean Baudrillard, *Symbolic Exchange and Death* (Thousand Oaks, CA: Sage Publications, 1993)).

5   The notion of 'milieu' thus appears in opposition to the notion of 'environment'. This distinction has its origin in the works of ethologist Jakob von Uexküll.

6   Marcel Mauss, 'Essai sur le don. Forme et raison de l'échange dans les sociétés archaïques', *L'Année sociologique, nouvelle série*, 1 (1923–24), pp. 30–186; in English as 'Essay on the Gift: The Form and Sense of Exchange in Archaic Societies', in his *The Gift*, expanded edition (Chicago: University of Chicago Press, 2016). Marcel Mauss,

In this text, Mauss produces a theory of the close connection in the human species between 'doing' (or 'making something') and 'forging bonds' (or making social connections). He starts from the analysis of the corporal practices involved in industrial production, which were already dominant in 1936 through Taylorism. Mauss, who was a supporter of cooperative socialism, uses his essay to highlight the relationship between production and cooperation. He points out something that is generally neglected by capitalist reasoning, namely, what exceeds the object produced during the process of technical production: the creation and maintenance of a technical milieu which conditions its production. Mauss develops the thesis of Alfred Espinas,[7] who was the founder of the biology of technology, and conceptualises that *the human milieu is a technical milieu.*

However, Mauss extends the meaning of this proposition in two directions. On the one hand, humans, unlike other animals, do not adapt to their environment. They build it using techniques that '*prosthetize*' their natural faculties and produce new bodies. In this sense, the human milieu is the technical milieu which uses the body as an instrument. On the other hand, because modern production techniques are divided and distributed between individuals, they require a different mode of transmission for procedures that train the body in order to be effective. This transmission both divides and assembles the bodies into an experience and a common practice — modern production techniques 'assemble' a common body from the various bodies at work which passes directly through the sensations of the individual bodies.[8]

Beyond the cliché of automating bodies at work, Mauss shows that modern technical production reveals another body than the body-as-instrument or 'object-body', something he calls a 'body-as-medium'

'Les Techniques du corps', *Journal de psychologie normale et pathologique*, 32 (1935), pp. 271–93; in English as 'Techniques of the Body', *Economy and Society*, 2.1 (1973), pp. 70–88.

7　Alfred Espinas, *Les Origines de la technologie*, Étude Sociologique (Paris: Alcan, 1897); English excerpts as 'The Origins of Technology [excerpts]', trans. by Catherine Schnoor, in *The Roots of Praxiology: French Action Theory from Bourdeau and Espinas to Present Days*, ed. by Victor Alexandre in coop. with Wojciech W. Gasparski (London: Routledge, 1999), pp. 45–91.

8　Workers have to incorporate the entire process of the chain. They have to share the same rhythms to be able to co-ordinate their movements, and, at the same time, to feel each change in this shared rhythm. This co-operation between bodies, and between bodies and machines, requires very specialized techniques of the body.

— or body as 'technical means'.[9] This body-as-medium transforms the material conditions of production into a living circuit of transmission, or technical milieu. It develops an autonomous life of its own that takes shape in bodies that 'act together' and communicate through shared sensations. Mauss thus proposes that the producing body, in the act of producing, is not only a quantifiable work force, but a living mediation that contributes to the survival of this technical human milieu.

I have drawn two hypotheses from Mauss's 'Techniques of the Body'. The first is that the social dimension of the production of value, which is housed in the subject, and the milieu's dimension, which is found in the techniques of the body, are not identical. They coexist, yet are embodied differently. The first dimension is embodied in norms, and the second dimension is embodied in the forms of 'affordances'[10] or 'agentivities' constituted by rhythms, gestures, common practices, or forms which enable cooperation. The body's sensation at work — which is an idea I will develop further in the next paragraph — contributes to its productivity but it does not depend on this productivity.

The second hypothesis is that this sensation of the body at work conditions the possibility of working 'together'. Sensation, Mauss writes, is a 'cog-wheel'.[11] It is a binding agent. The materiality of these social bonds consists in the power of the sensation of constructing action in time by recording it as a rhythm, and of distributing action in space by inscribing it as a gesture. Sensation thus simultaneously establishes the individuation of each body as well as their capacity to cooperate.

As a result of these insights, it is possible to conceive of cooperation which, just like commodification, is a verification of the social bond, as not only dependent on the regulatory ideals shared by the producing subjects, i.e. on the process of subjectivation, but as also dependent on the individuation of this medium-body — this *body-as-means* — which, through its activity, continuously recreates the technical milieu.

---

9   Mauss, 'Techniques of the Body', p. 75.

10   For the use of the term in a practical sense, see the works of Hubert Godard, as well as Carla Bottiglieri, 'Soigner l'imaginaire du geste: pratiques somatiques du toucher et du mouvement', *Chimères*, 78 (2012/13), pp. 113–28 <https://doi.org/10.3917/chime.078.0113>.

11   Mauss, 'Techniques of the Body', p. 85.

The originality of Mauss's thesis is to detach the body from its subjective existence and to consider the body as a direct product of its milieu. Thanks to this reversal of perspective, Mauss makes sensation the a-subjective interface between the biological and social realms, or between an individual's belonging to her milieu and her belonging to society. Mauss thus invites us to think about what remains — even in symbolic exchange — of the order of a kinaesthetic materiality, which is independent of the processes of subjectivation and the logic of value.[12]

GESTURE AND SPEECH AFTER ANDRÉ LEROI-GOURHAN: RETHINKING EVOLUTION

Following in Mauss's footsteps, Leroi-Gourhan sought to think of social bonding in terms of the interplay between 'milieu' and 'society'. Leroi-Gourhan, who was a prehistoric anthropologist in contrast to Mauss's background in sociology, translated the problematic of the 'milieu versus society' in terms of the differences between a species and an ethnic group. Like Mauss, he viewed the principle of individuation in the framework of sensation and its relation to perception. In his opinion, the power of human societies to continue to create their living milieu depends on this process of individuation.

Let us very briefly recall some basic principles of Leroi-Gourhan's thought. In the first place, he posits the thesis that the human species, contrary to what the vulgar evolutionist schema asserts, belongs to a different evolutionary process than primates. The development of humanity, Leroi-Gourhan explains, comes from the increase of their technical genius, which depends on their upright position and the way

---

12 The editors of this volume have pointed out that Mauss's redefinitions and objections towards a more traditional Marxian conception of value are centrally important for the notion of materialism. Though I agree, discussing Mauss's complex relationship to Marxism is beyond the scope of this chapter. One must note, however, that Mauss was interested in the bodies of workers in action, and looked (thanks, in particular, to cinema) at the 'physio-socio-psychological assemblies' that production lines are. Indeed, Mauss does not, as most observers of his time did, see the effect of a giant mechanism spreading throughout society, but rather points out the tiny cogs of individual sensations that link the physiological, sociological, and psychological aspects of such systems. What fascinates him is the way in which each body in its own plurality matches the plurality of the others, each of which is a unique cog within the whole of the mobilized bodies.

in which this restructures the relation between the hand and the brain: orthostasis frees the hand from the locomotive function and the mouth from the feeding function. It hence releases the hand for gesture and the mouth for word/speech.

Leroi-Gourhan's second essential thesis is the distinction he makes regarding the exteriorization of the species-specific individual body through its techniques. On the one hand, the specific individual body is externalized through its techniques, which includes techniques of production and memorization. On the other hand, this specific individual body is externalized into the 'social body' that groups individuals together in ethnic groups, introduces the development of these ethnic groups, and provides these individuals with the memory they lack through education and learning. Leroi-Gourhan calls this second plane of evolution and externalization 'ethnic', and he notes that education ensures the reproduction of the social order by institutionalizing this reproductive order and the power structures that guarantee its legitimacy.

Therefore, there are distinct planes of evolution that have their own logic instead of a single evolutionary process. This includes, firstly, the species-specific evolution, which concerns the individual body and which depends on the relation between hand and brain. This is further concretized in the development of techniques; and secondly, the ethnic evolution that concerns human societies. This evolution is embodied in the modes which individuals, institutions, and norms are grouped under.[13] These planes of evolution are autonomous, which means that they can diverge; this possible divergence of the species-specific and the ethnic is one of the major questions discussed in *Le Geste et la Parole*.[14]

---

13   The editors of this volume have asked if norms take on different planes for Mauss and for Leroi-Gourhan and if the ethical plane of Leroi-Gourhan is approximately the same as the social plane of Mauss. Though I find these questions interesting, again, a thorough elaboration would necessitate a whole article. What I can say here is that Leroi-Gourhan tried to eclipse the Maussian heritage in his work, even though the connections between them cannot be adequately deduced from their texts. I propose such a connection through a restitution of the link between their work, and it, therefore, is my own hypothesis.

14   André Leroi-Gourhan, *Le Geste et la Parole*, 2 vols (Paris: Albin Michel, 1964–65), I: *Technique et Langage* (1964); II: *La mémoire et les Rythmes* (1965); in English as *Gesture and Speech*, trans. by Anna Bostock Berger (Cambridge, MA: MIT Press, 1993).

In fact, the techno-economic evolution takes place between these two planes.[15] As capitalism develops, technical development is put at the service of the economic development of societies, i.e. of the for-profit economy. This third historical factor leads to the exploitation of technologies in favour of a normative rationality that homogenizes societies, globalizes cultural issues, and creates a kind of undifferentiated mega-ethnicity in which the need for individuation is forgotten.

For Leroi-Gourhan, the acceleration of techno-economic evolution in modern societies provokes the divergence between specific evolution and ethnic evolution, or the individual body and the social body. By producing new forms of experience and new identities, the techno-economic evolution makes us forget that the technical genius of humanity rests within the species-specific body of the individual. This is the body of one who, for the last 40,000 years, has 'thought' with her hand and who has developed her cognitive and symbolic faculties through the use of (1) her body, (2) her physical skills, and (3) the lived relation of this body to space and time. Throughout this time, the body has not changed: the hand, as the intersection between gesture and speech, remains the organ upon which the individuation of individuals depends. The hand is also the source of the capacity of the social body to adapt to the transformations of its environment and to create new milieus.

According to Leroi-Gourhan, the exploitation of the technical apparatus developed by homo sapiens' specific body in favour of the interests of the economic organization of its social body runs the risk of a *gregarization* — a turning into a 'herd behaviour' — of the human species. With this risk there is not only the added risk of a technical loss of creativity, but, more broadly, also a loss of social inventiveness, as well as a decline in the power of humanity to emancipate itself by producing its own forms of life.[16]

15　The term 'techno-economy' is an attempt to answer the question of the connection between capitalism and these two planes.

16　'The great problem of the world as it already exists calls for a solution: How shall this archaic mammal, with its archaic needs that have been the driving force of its ascent, continue to push its rock up the hillside if one day it is left with only the image of its reality? At no time in its development has this species yet had to break away from itself since the days of the *Australanthrope*. Homo sapiens lived his interminable adventure concretely; today the human is on the point of exhausting the resources of the planet,

When seen from this perspective, the criticism of neo-capitalism reaches another level, because it advances beyond a question of the human in society and the subject that produces values and towards the question of the human in its environment. Here it is not enough to denounce the exploitation of the worker's labour force, because it is necessary to think of the nature of the body at work: the body-as-medium of Mauss and the specific body of Leroi-Gourhan. The body must be thought of as existing in a milieu, and as a body involved as much in the production of material goods, raw materials, equipment, and objects as in the production of intangible goods, knowledge, know-how, and services. We need a new way of thinking about the body.

CONCLUSION: TOWARDS A ZOO-AESTHETICS

Yet, according to Leroi-Gourhan, a lock can maintain the development of humanity on the horizon of its species-specific body. This lock is a third plane of evolution that Leroi-Gourhan calls the aesthetic plane. This third evolutionary plane re-inscribes ethnic evolution in the body of specific humans. This plane is based on perception and on the power of human perception to re-incorporate the norms and values of the society of which the individual is a member. It is based on her power to reshape or relive these norms and values as incarnated emotions and as lived spaces, as rhythmic, sensitive, and formal values. This power of perception, which, for Leroi-Gourhan, reinstates humanity in its species condition, meaning its animal condition, ensures the plasticity of social connections and their transformation through the transformation of rhythms, gestures, and figures. Leroi-Gourhan thus develops a 'zoo-aesthetics', which I will, to conclude, discuss in order to show how we can critically enquire into alienation beyond the traditional theory of value.

Leroi-Gourhan writes:

> Can we see the perception and creation of rhythmic symbols as something deeply rooted in the animal world which — on

---

and already the myth of human transplantation into space has sprung up. But there can be no going back over the ground already covered. We can dream that when arriving on a distant star, the human will encounter Pithecanthropus and the southern elephant but will not revert to flint knapping' (Leroi-Gourhan, *Gesture and Speech*, p. 407).

emergence at the human level — displays the same characteristics as technics and language? To put it differently, since the
technical function in human beings exteriorizes itself in port-
able tools and since the perceived object too is exteriorized in
a verbal symbol, can we assume that movement in all its forms
— visual, auditive, and motor — was also 'freed' and entered
upon the same evolutionary cycle?[17]

This quotation lays the foundation of Leroi-Gourhan's thesis: perception, far from anticipating the act of cognition as the philosophical
tradition suggests, comes from the same specific plane as 'technique'
and 'language'. Perception is not the elaboration of sensation in a
representation, but rather, for Leroi-Gourhan, it remains fundamentally animal. This is why perception can be said to 'intervene': It blocks
the natural, imposed rhythms, just as it blocks the *phantasmata* emerging from sensation, and readdresses them to the body of the sender.
It reincorporates images springing from these imposed rhythms (the
external images coming from the world and the internal ones from
the organism itself) and interprets them (in the performative sense
of 'acting') in the form of new, individuated rhythms. It constructs
a 'corporeity' that, while not to be equated with the physical body,
animates that body and interprets it through figures and gestures by
attaching it to a dynamic that is literally emotional.[18]

   Leroi-Gourhan did not formulate this 'theory of perception' any
further because he had different concerns. However, I have introduced the baselines of this theory to gain an understanding of the
way in which artistic practices reiterate the question of the body in
its milieu today. Among the elements provided by Leroi-Gourhan's
anthropology, the most surprising is the idea that perception, far from
anticipating the act of cognition as the philosophical tradition has presumed, belongs to the same specific plane as technique and language.
Accordingly, as I have pointed out, perception should not be conceived
as an elaboration, i.e. an overtaking of sensation into a higher form
of cognitive representation, but it remains visceral and fundamentally
animal. In other words, even in humans, perception is a kind of activity that cannot be detached from sensation; it functions as an engine

---

17   Leroi-Gourhan, *Gesture and Speech*, p. 274.
18   On 'corporeity', see Michel Bernard, *Le Corps*, second 2nd and revised edition (Paris:
      Editions Universitaires, 1976).

brake that prevents sensation from losing its constructive power and from dissolving into taste by being imagined and intellectualized. It is a regressive faculty that anchors a sensation back into the specific body and that assures the intimate connection between the mechanisms of symbolization and the body. Thus, perception ensures the perennial knot of speech and gesture.

Concurrently with the displacement of the energy of the motor mechanisms towards the mechanisms of symbolization, the palae-ontologist thus imbues an inverse power of investment of the visceral 'depths' of the sensation in the individual through the processes of intellection. Through this bias, he further evokes the recharging power of sensitivity through symbolic activity. For Leroi-Gourhan, human perception is a question of the 'spilling over' or 'transferring' of the ideation mechanisms into technical operations. It guarantees the autonomy of individuation processes in the face of processes of subjectivation. This autonomy takes the a-subjective form of rhythms, gestures, and figures that belong to no one and express nothing, but which are the channel of the re-individuation of values and the basis of their reinvention. It is through the materiality of these rhythms, gestures, and forms that the social body remains connected to the specific body and that the social bonds resist their 'massification'.

The remarkable point here is how the individual creativity that underlies the vitality of the social bonds is not anchored in a subjective, autonomous, or 'symbolic' faculty of creation as tradition dictates, but rather in a regressive movement. This brings the process of symbolization back to the sensory apparatus, or, to use Leroi-Gourhan's terms, it brings the social back to the zoological. This is where we find what already was present in Mauss, namely the inscription of the social bonds in a logic of incorporation supported by sensation. Mauss and Leroi-Gourhan thus provide a framework to understand social bonds in different ways than through the hallucinatory power of value.

Both thinkers anchor the processes of subjection of the social subject in the material logic of the body's individuation in the environment. They are particularly interested in distinguishing the development of techniques as a kind of activity in this logical framework. Yet Leroi-Gourhan, in developing his thought in the field of aesthetics and his conception of this material force of individuation and social bonding as an aesthetic capacity that is realized in rhythms, gestures, and figures, grants it a greater power of actualization than Mauss, who limited it to the sphere of work. Leroi-Gourhan's materialism extends the sphere of politics to aesthetics, which is not only understood as a field of taste, but also as something beyond the sensory faculties of the aesthetic subject, or 'reflecting subject', as one of the essential registers of the specific individual's life. He thus gives us the means to understand why the splitting force of taste, or its power of 'distinction' to borrow a term from Pierre Bourdieu, does not summarize the entirety of aesthetic experience. He also helps us to understand why it remains possible for social subjects to make a living experience of the body in its milieu, through this body that bonds with other bodies using sensation, as well as the work of singularization which we understand as the process of individuation.

Both Mauss and Leroi-Gourhan understand the individuation of the body in the milieu as a material power that is a part of the processes of subjectivation through its ability to form strong connections. Their materialism thus enlarges the sphere of politics beyond the sensitive faculties of the aesthetic subject to all the manifestations of living-speaking bodies. In this sense, it constitutes the basis of a formidable criticism of a theory of value that is only based on the exchange between alienated social subjects.

The Product of Circumstances
Towards a Materialist and Situated Pedagogy
MARLON MIGUEL

INTRODUCTION

In this chapter, I would like to address what could be called a *materialist education*. In order to do that, I first need to briefly remind the reader of some of the main principles of this form of education according to Karl Marx and Friedrich Engels. While these two authors did not write extensively on the question of education, they did open up interesting new paths of thought concerning the relationship between a materialist education and the notion of 'milieu', which were later developed in more detail by other thinkers and practitioners. After this, I will focus on the work of the Soviet educator Anton Semyonovich Makarenko (1888–1939). The similarities between Marxist principles — in particular those of the young Marx concerning the shaping of the human through the transformation of its material conditions of existence — and Makarenko's ideas and practice are too pronounced to be accidental and indeed, as the reader will see, they formed an important

* I acknowledge the financial support of FCT, 'Fundação para a Ciência e a Tecnologia, I.P.' (Stimulus of Scientific Employment, Individual Support CEECIND/02352/2017/CP1387/CT0006).

basis for the Soviet pedagogue's writings. One can argue that these Marxist principles constituted the atmosphere in which Makarenko's thought could emerge.

I am particularly interested in the connection between education and the notions of 'milieu', 'circumstance', and 'situation' which are employed by the materialist educator. Makarenko argued that education should be conceived as a constructed and collective milieu instead of a directive relationship between master and student. He thought that the pedagogical process is mediated by this milieu and, furthermore, that it also allows for a materialist critique of fatalism in education, which should be understood as the idea that students are fated to be a certain way and cannot change. In this way, he worked towards an emancipation from the idea of pre-determined fates — much in vogue at the time — attributable to subjects based on their social background and conditions as well as their personal histories and trajectories.

MARX AND ENGELS ON EDUCATION

Interestingly, Marx's third thesis on Feuerbach connects education or upbringing (*Erziehung*), revolutionary practice, and the notion of 'circumstances' (*Umstände*). This well-known fragment will work as a kind of leitmotif for my argument in this chapter. Marx, along with Engels, who revised and rewrote this text in 1888, claim that:

> The materialist doctrine that men [humans, *Menschen*] are products of circumstances and upbringing, and that, therefore, changed men are products of other circumstances and changed upbringing, forgets that it is men who change circumstances and that the educator must himself be educated. Hence, this doctrine is bound to divide society into two parts, one of which is superior to society (in Robert Owen, for example).
>
> The coincidence of the changing of circumstances and of human activity can be conceived and rationally understood only as revolutionising practice.[1]

---

1   Karl Marx, 'Theses on Feuerbach', ed. by Friedrich Engels, in *MECW* [*Marx & Engels Collected Works*, see abbreviations], v (1976), pp. 6–8 (p. 7).

Even if Marx did not extensively discuss education, the term appears several times in his work, particularly in his collaboration with Engels. According to them, education constitutes a central problem concerning the overcoming of capitalism and of bourgeois values. Interestingly, education often appears as an indirect procedure or force over individual subjects (those who are to be educated) instead of a direct one. That is why it is frequently related to the question of the environment and of the material conditions, in sum, of the circumstances as outlined by the third thesis: if humans are the product of circumstances, then education must imply the transformation of circumstances and of the educators themselves. Marx and Engels present in this thesis a conceptualization of materialism and address a crucial problem: how the forces and relations of a society's mode of production constitute the material conditions that shape the human and that need to be transformed?[2]

The question of education is evoked three times in the *Manifesto of the Communist Party*, in particular to highlight the importance of a social and free education for all children. Furthermore, Marx and Engels emphasize — and again this echoes the *Third Thesis*, however this time accentuating 'economic relations' — that human beings' ideas, views, and conceptions can only change if the conditions of their material existence are also transformed.[3] In spite of the well-known 'epistemological breaks' taking place in Marx's work around 1845–46 where he places a larger emphasis on economy, the question concerning the transformation of the conditions of material existence can already be traced back to *The Holy Family*. In this text the authors claim that 'materialism is connected with communism and socialism'[4] and that

---

2   In 'Principles of Communism', the draft for the *Manifesto*, Engels claims that 'the common management of production by the whole of society and the resulting new development of production require and also produce radically different humans [*ganz andere Menschen*]' (Friedrich Engels, 'Principles of Communism', in *MECW*, vi (1976), pp. 341–57 (p. 353); 'Grundsätze des Kommunismus', in *MEW* [*Marx-Engels-Werke*, see abbreviations], iv (1977), pp. 361–80 (p. 376)).

3   'Does it require deep intuition to comprehend that man's ideas, views, and conceptions, in one word, man's consciousness, changes with every change in the conditions of his material existence, in his social relations and in his social life?' (Karl Marx and Friedrich Engels, 'Manifesto of the Communist Party', in *MECW*, vi (1976), pp. 477–519 (p. 503)).

4   Karl Marx, *The Holy Family, or Critique of Critical Criticism*, in *MECW*, iv (1975), pp. 3–211 (p. 130).

only a *re-arrangement* of the empirical world (*die empirische Welt ein-zurichten*) will bring about the humanization of human beings: 'If man is shaped by his environment [or surroundings, *Umgebung*], his environment must be made human'. Later on, Engels, in his book *Socialism: Utopian and Scientific* (a part of his *Anti-Dühring*, published separately), pursues this problem of the relation between humanization and environment, again returning to Robert Owen[5] and connecting the environment to education:

> Robert Owen had adopted the teaching of the materialistic philosophers: that man's [*Menschen*] character is the product, on the one hand, of heredity, on the other, of the environment of the individual during his lifetime, and especially during his period of development.[6]

All in all, the materialist approach to education stressed by Marx and Engels must take into account the alteration of the milieu – in the German version of the text quoted above, Engels introduces the interesting term '*umgebenden Umstände*',[7] something as the 'surrounding

---

5   Owen's theory, based on his experiences managing cotton mills at New Lanark, emphasizes the notions of 'environment' and 'circumstances' connecting them to the formation of an individual's character. In his *A New View of Society* (1813), one can read how social suffering is born out of 'the inattention of mankind to the circumstances which incessantly surround them' (Robert Owen, 'Essay One: Any general character may be given to any community by the application of proper means', in *A New View of Society or, Essays on the Principle of the Formation of the Human Character, and the Application of the Principle to Practice* (London: Cadell & Davies, 1813) <https://www.marxists.org/reference/subject/economics/owen/index.htm>) [accessed 12 September 2020]. The problem of the relation between circumstances and the formation of character seems to have indeed been in vogue at that time. Stuart Mill, for example, using what he calls an 'ethology', also insists on the correlation of these terms, but in order to redress the concept of 'necessity' and to emphasize how a free individual can mould his character: 'His character is formed by his circumstances [...] but his own desire to mould it in a particular way, is one of those circumstances, and by no means one of the least influential' (John Stuart Mill, *A System of Logic, Ratiocinative and Inductive* (New York: Harper, 1882), p. 1022 <https://www.gutenberg.org/files/27942/27942-pdf.pdf> [accessed 12 September 2020]; see also Terence Ball, 'The Formation of Character: Mill's "Ethology" Reconsidered', *Polity*, 33.1 (2000), pp. 25–48 <https://doi.org/10.2307/3235459>). However, the differences between both thinkers are very important. Whereas Stuart Mill insists on the individual decision over circumstances, Robert Owen emphasises the determinative power of circumstances, the importance of education, and the notion of 'co-operation'.

6   Friedrich Engels, *Socialism: Utopian and Scientific*, in *MECW*, XXIV (1989), pp. 281–325 (p. 294); *Anti-Dühring*, in *MECW*, XXV (1987), pp. 1–309 (p. 249).

7   Friedrich Engels, 'Die Entwicklung des Sozialismus von der Utopie zur Wissenschaft', in *MEW*, IXX (1987), pp. 189–228 (p. 198).

circumstances' — in order to act upon the subjects and to aim at a real transformation. If heredity — or more broadly, we could add, genetic inheritance — constitutes an element of the composition of character, it remains only one factor of the subject's development. In this sense, Engels anticipates and avoids a certain danger concerning the naturalization of character.

The third thesis on Feuerbach underlines the transformation of circumstances related to 'rational understanding', whereas other texts emphasize how a rearrangement of the surroundings, empirical sensibility, and habits are the real key to transformation. Indeed, a materialist education seems to me to indicate the necessity of transforming the body and sensibility of the subject of education, and even their desires and needs. This is precisely what Marx notes in the *Grundrisse* (the chapter on Capital), in a section that addresses the 'circuits' of capital — that is, he notes that the critique of capitalism must go through the fact that this system shapes one's needs and constantly produces new needs that ensure new commodities are vital to one's existence.[8] Therefore, education must not only address this problem critically and intellectually, but also sensibly, by learning how to re-shape desire (or the 'needs') in order to modify capitalism's functioning or 'circuits'.

As a consequence of this focus, some of Marx and Engel's texts seem to open a stimulating space inside a very Germanic tradition where education, emancipation, and formation always appear either as a direct and formative action over subjects (*Erziehung*) or as the development of an internal image (*Bild*) corresponding to their intellectual and rational progress (*Bildung*). In the text for the First International in 1864, Marx claimed that he saw three aspects within the term 'education': the 'mental education', the 'bodily education', and 'technological training'. He also introduced a theme that would establish a new and

---

8   'This necessity is itself subject to change, in that needs are produced just as much as products and the various craft skills. [...] The more the needs which are themselves historically produced, the needs produced by production itself, the social needs which are themselves the OFFSPRING of SOCIAL PRODUCTION and INTERCOURSE — the more these needs are posited as *necessary*, the higher the development of real wealth. Considered as *physical matter*, wealth consists merely in the multiplicity of needs' (Karl Marx, *Outlines of the Critique of Political Economy*, in *MECW*, XXVIII (1986), pp. 49–537 (p. 451; emphasis in the original)). On this subject, see also Glenn Rikowski, 'Marx and the Education of the Future', *Policy Futures in Education*, 2.3–4 (2004) <https://doi.org/10.2304/pfie.2004.2.3.10>.

important tradition in pedagogical theories and would go on to have a long history of its own: the theme of 'polytechnic training.'[9] Although the first aspect listed by Marx is 'mental education', it is important to emphasize the breach opened up by his work through the recognition that to educate is more than only forming the mind (*der Geist*). His ideas were to play a crucial role in the elaboration of theories and practices concerning education, particularly in the Soviet Union.

MAKARENKO AND *THE PEDAGOGICAL POEM*

The role played by circumstances in education, which is explicitly evoked in the third thesis, had strong repercussions in the history of pedagogical practices and was taken over by important educators, psychologists, and thinkers as a basis for their practices.

In this essay I will focus on one such pedagogue: Anton Semyonovich Makarenko.[10] Because of his connection to Stalinism he was, it should be said, quite a polemical author. Furthermore, his educational practice was often dismissed as being simply associated with military and disciplinary methods. However, one should note that in

---

9   'By education we understand three things. Firstly: Mental education. Secondly: Bodily education, such as is given in schools of gymnastics, and by military exercise. Thirdly: Technological training, which imparts the general principles of all processes of production, and, simultaneously initiates the child and young person in the practical use and handling of the elementary instruments of all trades. A gradual and progressive course of mental, gymnastic, and technological training ought to correspond to the classification of the juvenile labourers. The costs of the technological schools ought to be partly met by the sale of their products. The combination of paid productive labour, mental education, bodily exercise and polytechnic training, will raise the working class far above the level of the higher and middle classes' (Karl Marx, 'Instructions for the Delegates of the Provisional General Council', in *MECW*, xx (1985), pp. 185–94 (p. 189)).

10   I used the following translations of *The Pedagogical Poem* to write this essay: *The Road to Life (An Epic of Education) in Three Parts*, 3 vols (Moscow: Foreign Languages Publishing House 1955); *Poème Pédagogique. En Trois Parties*, 3 vols (Moscou, Éditions en Langues Étrangères, 1953); *O Poema Pedagógico* (São Paulo: Editora 34, 2012); *Poema Pedagógico* (Spain: Omegalfa/Biblioteca Libre, n.d.) <https://www.omegalfa. es/downloadfile.php?file=libros/poema-pedagogico.pdf> [accessed 12 September 2020]. Not reading Russian, my access to the original sources and to the Russian critical literature on his work is very restricted. I would like to thank the help of Elena Vogman with the comparison of passages of the original text, which can be found here: <http://makarenko-museum.ru/Classics/Makarenko/Makarenko_ A_Pedagogic_Poem/Makarenko_Ped_poema_full_text.pdf> [accessed 12 September 2020].

his work there is an interesting and ambiguous transition from a more experimental moment to a more authoritarian one which takes places between his two major works — *The Pedagogical Poem* (1935) and *Flags on the Battlements* (1938).

With these observations in mind, I have turned my focus to the consequences and possibilities derived from his 'theory', as well as the ways it was renewed, in particular in the French post-war context, by important figures surrounding the French Communist Party[11] or in the work of the Brazilian educator Paulo Freire and the Latin American context.[12] I would also like to mention that what I call his 'theory' is in fact an *anti-theory* and it appears, at first, as a refusal of the available pedagogical principles of his time.

Poem and (Anti)theory: Circumstances and Materialism

I would like to begin by outlining the context in which Makarenko worked. At the end of 1920, he was invited to head a juvenile colony

---

11   I have in mind the reception of his work by, among others, authors such as Henri Wallon, Louis Le Guillant, Irène Lézine, and Fernand Deligny. These names are part of an important constellation around a social network with maladjusted young people created in 1948 in France and called La Grande Cordée. Irène Lézine, psychologist, translator, and activist of the French Communist Party (PCF), was responsible for the introduction in France of authors such as Lev Vygotsky and Makarenko. At some point, the PCF wanted to turn Deligny into a sort of 'French Makarenko'. Besides their own books and articles, they all took part in *Enfance*, a journal created in 1947 which was initially directed by Wallon. The journal synthesized the current debates around childhood and once again actualized problems such as that of 'character'. All of these thinkers mobilize the notion of 'circumstances' in a particular way. For Deligny, the educator is a 'creator of circumstances' (Fernand Deligny, 'Les Vagabonds Efficaces' (1947), in his *Œuvres* (Paris: L'Arachnéen, 2017), pp. 161–221 (p. 212), available at the platform *Encontro Deligny*: <https://deligny.jur.puc-rio.br/index.php/livros-e-publicacoes/> [accessed 12 September 2020]). Wallon developed a materialist psychology that emphasizes the influences of situation and of milieu on the development of the subject (Henri Wallon, *De l'Acte à la Pensée* (Paris: Flammarion, 1942)). All of them are interested in de-naturalizing the notion of 'maladjustment' (*inadapdation*), showing that diagnoses should never isolate individuals from the social circumstances where their cases evolve. For a development of these questions, I refer to Marlon Miguel, *À la marge et hors-champ: L'humain dans la pensée de Fernand Deligny* (Université Paris 8, 2016) <https://www.theses.fr/2016PA080020/document>; Marlon Miguel, 'Pour une pédagogie de la révolte: Fernand Deligny, de la solidarité avec les marginaux au perspectivisme', *Cahiers du GRM*, 14 (2019) <https://doi.org/10.4000/grm.1696>.

12   See René Capriles, *Makarenko: o Nascimento da Pedagogia Socialista* (São Paulo: Scipione, 1989).

by the Public Education Department in Ukraine, which was called the Gorky Colony.[13] Situated six kilometres from Poltava, the colony was to receive children and adolescents — many of them orphans — for social re-education. The context was tough: the revolution had taken place and the civil war had just finished in the region, leaving people in very miserable conditions. The Public Education Department conceived of Makarenko's task not only as the re-education of these 'young offenders' but also as an experiment to educate the 'new man' in new ways. The young people sent to the colony were more or less dangerous, often very violent people who had committed infractions such as theft, robbery, and organized crime. The first pages of *The Pedagogical Poem* describe the complete distress of Makarenko before the student body. They were resistant to any pedagogical process and, in addition, the material conditions were hardly favourable: the colony simply possessed an unheated, abandoned hangar, which was falling apart. They had neither clothes nor shoes for the kids, nor enough food to feed everyone.

In this wretched state Makarenko was helpless, and he felt that the 'pedagogical science' he acquired reading books (Pestalozzi, Rousseau, Natorp, Blonsky, etc.) offered 'no method, no means, no logic — nothing'[14] to help him deal with the context. In this situation, he decided not to follow any pre-conceived theory, dogma, or received ideas, and

---

13   The name was given only sometime after its creation and was inspired by the readings of Maxim Gorky that took place in the Colony. When the kids discovered that the life of Gorky had been similar to theirs, they took him as a sort of model for their own lives: 'They were stunned by the story, suddenly struck by the idea: "So Gorky was like us! I say, that's fine!" This idea moved them profoundly and joyfully. Maxim Gorky's life seemed to become part of our life. Various episodes in it provided us with examples for comparison, a fund of nicknames, a background for debate, and a scale for the measurement of human values' (Makarenko, *The Road to Life*, I, pp. 135–56). Here Makarenko is not so far from a principle that was fundamental for Paulo Freire's pedagogy: to associate the *conquering of words* with *the conquering of the world* — i.e. the re-appropriation of one's own history and the transformation of the world goes through an acquisition of a certain language. In practical terms, for Freire, in order to learn a word, one must learn its historical, cultural, and political dimensions. Freire associated the educational process with the construction of a political consciousness that would help the pupil to free themselves from oppression and become agents of their own history: 'There is no true word that is not at the same time a praxis. Thus, to speak a true word is to transform the world [...]. To exist, humanly, is to name the world, to change it' (Paulo Freire, *Pedagogy of the Oppressed* (New York: Continuum, 2005), pp. 87–88).

14   Makarenko, *The Road to Life*, I, p. 179.

instead to take what I would call a *materialist stance*, that is, he learnt from daily practices to build his store of hands-on experience, and invented solutions according to what the circumstances gave, presented to him, or demanded.

Indeed, the recurrence of the word 'circumstance' (Обстоятель- ство) in *The Pedagogical Poem* is very striking. Makarenko claimed that every important invention concerning the Colony came from the observation of a certain set of circumstances. His usage of the word — just like with Marx and Engels — certainly mirrored the historical, economic, and social conditions; however, in contrast to their thought, Makarenko referred to a far smaller scale, namely to the singular conditions of the Colony or the kids' trajectories, in sum, the actual *situation* he found himself in. Hence, Makarenko's use of the word referred to a singular position in time and space; it was meant to be attentive, present, and alert to what was happening — to reflect his stance right there, right in the middle of the experience, at each moment. Interestingly, the word employed by the author, Обстоятельство, is built in exactly the same way as the German word used by Marx: *Umstand*. 'Об' is for 'Um', 'Circum' (accusative form of circus, 'circle', 'ring', 'around'), as стояте for 'stand'/'*stehen*', 'stance', 'standing', coming undoubtedly from the Latin *stantia*.[15] And this etymology precisely reflects the attitude that the educator, following Makarenko's opinions, should have: to stand in the middle of the situation and to learn, immanently, what to do from it. Finally, if we remain on the grounds of etymology and follow the sequence of metaphors emanating from this word, we may remark upon the interesting way Makarenko found to work on the transmission of his thought, that is, through the form of *stanzas*. He prefers to write not a doctrine, a theory, a manual, or a kind of reproducible knowledge, but rather a description of his experiences in an immanent literary form — *The Pedagogical Poem*, written between 1925 and 1935, and describing his thirteen years of work at the Gorky Colony, is precisely a literary work, a prose poetry.

The Pedagogical Poem can be read as a kind of anti-theory. However, Makarenko nevertheless presents a horizon or a guiding principle

---

15   It seems, indeed, that the Russian word was 'fabricated': it is a loan translation, a *calque*, deriving from the German and French words.

on top of which the whole experience can be built: the creation of what he calls a 'real collectivity'. This means that the educator must be attentive to the 'embryos' or the 'sprouts' of the collectivity, which are often unpredictable, but may appear all of a sudden and should be saved, 'cherished at all costs' — these embryos constitute the most 'important circumstances' that have to be taken into consideration and analysed during the pedagogical process.[16]

Collectivity and Social Glue

The collectivity is the target of a doubly circular movement. On the one hand, it is the task of the educator to educate the children and adolescents so that they learn to act collectively. This learning is not so much that of reason, but rather the learning of a (new) model of sensibility, of a certain *sense* of the collective. This sensibility refers to the perception and observation of the surroundings, of the 'milieu' (среда, another important word in Makarenko's work), and also relates to the series of prefixes 'um'/'Об'/'circum'.

> This capacity to perceive what is around you, this capacity to perceive what cannot be seen, what is made in the other rooms, to perceive the tonality of life, this capacity of orientation. [...]
> The real Soviet citizen must be able to sense what happens around him with all his nerves, almost unconsciously.[17]

In this extract one can also perceive an echo of Marx and Engel's insistence in *The Holy Family*, which I outlined earlier, on the 'world of senses' and the necessity of rearranging the empirical world so that humans' become aware of themselves. Makarenko, however, gives an even greater insistence on the development of the subject's sensibility and perception, and on their capacity to perceive beyond the limits of their individual space.

On the other hand, and this is the second crucial point, it is not so much the educator who is responsible for educating but rather the juvenile collectivity itself that will (re)educate the children:

---

16   Cf. Makarenko, *The Road to Life*, 1, Chap. 8, a chapter named precisely 'Character and Culture'.

17   Anton Semyonovich Makarenko *apud* Irène Lézine, *A. S. Makarenko, Pédagogue Soviétique (1888–1939)* (Paris: PUF, 1954), p. 39, my translation.

The task of the educator is not at all to educate. It is repug-
nant to good sense to think that a dozen cultivated individuals
gathered by chance at the Gorky colony would be able to educate one hundred and thirty delinquents. [...] It is not the
educator who educates, but the milieu.[18]

The collectivity is thus the product of a long process which is based
on this double progressive movement: Firstly, the formation of a type
of sensibility (and thus of habits, customs, rituals, and traditions) that
goes beyond one's individual perspective and that allows for the progressive production of the *social glue* tying these individuals together.
Secondly, thanks to the daily collective activities, there is an improvement of this same sensibility and the capacity of the individuals to
relate to each other. To claim that it is the milieu that educates means
that the real process through which one is educated is correlated to the
tensions inside the collective activities and the way they are resolved.
That is why Makarenko was often accused of placing the collectivity
at the centre of his pedagogy and not the (individual) child, of not
following the 'reign of psychology' but rather that of work.

Makarenko's main antagonist throughout *The Pedagogical Poem* is
the Public Education Department and its abstract pedagogical science.
What he wants to emphasize is that there should be no knowledge
or moral principle that precedes the solution of the problems emerging from the pedagogical situation. That is why he strategically makes
use of different methods without transforming them into pedagogical
axioms. For example, sometimes Makarenko describes the use of military strategies and even of disciplinary methods (such as the organization of the children in lines and 'detachments', or the practice of
gymnastics); at other times, to the reader's surprise, he may even beat a
child and become very authoritarian. However, and this constitutes the
crucial point, he does not defend any of these attitudes as principles;
on the contrary, he even claims that violence should be avoided at all
costs, as it is, in the end, not really useful to create a collective culture.
If he describes these moments, it is to show that they may appear
as reactions to certain circumstances and show the incapacity of the

18   Anton Semyonovich Makarenko, 'La Colonie de Poltava dite Colonel Gorki (1925)', in
      L'Éducation dans les Collectivités d'Enfants (Paris: CEMEA, Les Éditions du Scarabée,
      1956), p. 57, my translation.

educator — in this case, himself — to deal with the pupils. Indeed, the absolute non-moralistic tone of *The Pedagogical Poem* is very striking, as its narrative follows the flow of human affects and expresses the perseverance to understand and try to deal with them.

To Sunder the Covenants of Fate: The Critique of Characterology

This non-moralistic tone is constantly present in Makarenko's text, which also demands, in turn, a non-moralistic reading. His tone is deeply connected to his refusal of a psychological, behavioural, and characterological approach to educating children. In the colony, common phrases such as 'delinquent' and 'morally handicapped' were, for example, banned from the everyday vocabulary — instead, they used the plural noun 'colonists'. This does not mean, however, that these terms disappeared in his *text*; on the contrary, he made use of them to subvert or satirize them.

Furthermore, he applies the idea of an *active forgetting* of the children's past: 'I considered that the principal method for the re-education of delinquents should be based upon a complete ignoring of the past, especially past crimes'.[19] Makarenko, going against the ideology of his time, de-naturalized delinquency and detached it from a medical status that had the tendency to essentialize and classify children according to an innate character or personality. He further radicalized this position — fighting, as he claimed, against his 'own instincts' — by choosing not to even read the children's records as they were sent to the Colony. To correlate an act (stealing, fighting, drinking, betting) to a character fault would mean not taking into consideration the hard and miserable *circumstances* in which these kids and adolescents grew up. That is why Makarenko minimized these acts so much and instead emphasized that the Colony would be precisely the place to create another set of habits. In this same sense, Makar-

---

19   Makarenko, *The Road to Life*, 1, p. 383. Some lines later, the text follows: 'The usual pedagogical logic at that time aped medicine, adopting the sage adage: "In order to cure a disease, it must first be known." This logic sometimes seduced even me, not to mention my colleagues and the Department of Public Education [...]. As far back as 1922 I had asked the Commission not to send me any more personal records. We quite sincerely ceased to interest ourselves in the past offences of our charges, and with such success that the latter soon began to forget them themselves' (ibid., pp. 383–84).

enko's text rarely describes what the intimate and internal personality of his pupils was supposed to be; he prefers to describe, their abilities, techniques, physical aspects, tones of voice, style, the pace of their walk and speech rhythms, etc. This does not mean that Makarenko does not create descriptive categories in the Colony, but that they are operational and mobile ones that are used to describe the situation in which individuals find themselves and not to essentialize them.

This question of forgetting the past, which was so active in the Colony, is reminiscent of an Althusserian phrase that could very well be a definition of materialism: *ne plus se raconter d'histoires*.[20] This definition was inspired by Althusser's readings of Lucretius and a new pact of the nature capable of 'sundering the covenants of fate'.[21] With it, Althusser pointed to the impossibility of giving a closed, definitive, essential, and determined meaning to things, bodies, and individuals. To put it even more strongly, he highlighted the impossibility of locking an individual into their past determinations. This does not entail a total freedom of things or a refusal of necessity — quite the contrary, in fact — but it does emphasize the ever-possible reconfiguration of things through *encounters*.[22]

Whether one speaks of *encounters* or *circumstances*, what is at stake in this excellent case study is the need to free the miserable kids from the inevitable fate that was determined for them by tribunals, social re-education centres, and prison, where they were repeatedly labelled 'young offenders', 'delinquents', 'morally handicapped', and 'hereditary bums'.[23] Certainly, there is a rhetorical aspect to Makarenko 'forgetting of the past' — for it is less a question of a denial of the past than an attempt to fight against the prescribed fate assigned by the medical

---

20 'Never to tell myself stories, which is the only "definition" of materialism I have ever subscribed to' (Louis Althusser, *The Future Lasts Forever: A memoire* (New York: New Press, 1993), p. 169).

21 Lucretius, *On the Nature of Things*, trans. by William Ellery Leonard (New York: Dover, 2008), I, p. 18.

22 Cf. Louis Althusser, 'Le courant souterrain du matérialisme de la rencontre', in his *Écrits Philosophiques et Politiques*, ed. by François Matheron, 2 vols (Paris: Stock/IMEC, 1994–95), I (1994), pp. 539–79.

23 Once again, Makarenko struggles with the pseudo-scientific literature that tried to create a systematic characterological classification. 'Several efforts have been made in learned works to draw up a satisfactory system for the classification of human characteristics [character], and the greatest pains taken to allot an "amoral" and "defective" place for the waifs' (Makarenko, *The Road to Life*, III, p. 105).

and socio-juridical apparatuses. Indeed, part of the pedagogical process was to *reconnect* past memories and experiences with something new. In this sense, it is interesting to see, for example, how Makarenko acknowledges the kids' dexterity, what skills they learned in the streets (theft, for example), which could then be translated and used productively in the Colony. This translation became possible through new circumstances, activities, and work.[24] As we are going to see, the theatre, which became an important activity of the Colony, was also a place where the kids, playing with life and death both joyfully and with hatred, reconnected to and re-translated their past memories.

The Organization of the Collectivity

This leads to the question of the organization of the Colony which I will briefly present before moving on to my conclusion. First of all, there was an emphatic steering away from the practices of other juvenile re-education centres of the time in which Makarenko insisted on the importance of the Colony's contact with the external world. The colony was meant to be a more or less open space without enclosures or violent surveillance. This led to two important consequences: if they wanted to, the colonists could leave the colony, but in this case they needed to assume responsibility for going back to their past lives of thievery, street life, etc.; furthermore, instead of removing the youths from society, the contact with the external world — such as villages, cities, and farms in the vicinity as well as local commerce and workshops — was a crucial, common dimension of the re-education process. Not only did the colonists regularly deal with the external world in matters concerning the Colony, but people from the outside could also come to the public events taking place at the Colony such as festivities and weekly theatre presentations.

---

24   Here the forgetting of the past meets another element, which is the praise of the movement and of the constant change of circumstances seen as fundamental to the collectivity: 'I thought of the strength of the colonists' collective, and suddenly I realized what was wrong. Why, of course — how could I have taken so long to discover it? It had all come about because we were at a standstill. A standstill can never be allowed in the life of a collective. [...] The universal law of general development was only just beginning to show its true strength. The forms ruling the existence of a free human collective implied progress [or *movement* forward]. The forms ruling death — a standstill' (ibid., II, p. 278).

Secondly, Makarenko, echoing Marx's polytechnic education, proposed a combination of work and education. This was not only a principle *per se* but an essential need for survival. With almost no financial
support and miserable beginnings, the colony was forced to develop
its own economy. Its first main activity, therefore, was agriculture to
produce what to eat. Later on, however, they held many workshops
(engine workshops, for example), music and particularly theatre activities, etc. The Dzerzhinsky Commune, which Makarenko would also
run, and which is described in the third part of *The Pedagogical Poem*,
became famous for its massive production of FED cameras, which
were similar to the Leica ones.

Thirdly, the different activities were organized according to 'detachments',[25] that is, a certain number of kids (girls and boys mixed)
were allocated a certain function (planting beetroots, searching for
firewood in the forest, cleaning spaces, the staging of theatre plays,
etc.). Each detachment had a 'commander', who was someone without
privileges but who was very skilled in a specific function and therefore
responsible for the discipline of the group, the tools they used, and
for the quality of the service they provided. Besides these detachments
with a definitive role, there were also 'mixed detachments', which were
temporary and included people from other detachments for a provisional and precise task. A detachment always had a commander even if
it only had two people in it. Finally, there was a 'soviet of commanders'
that would take and discuss the decisions concerning important affairs
of the Colony, as well as the election and renewal of the commanders.
These elections were accompanied by long discussions and debates.
The soviet of commanders was guided by the aspiration that each col-
onist should be a commander of a mixed detachment at least once.

With this system of detachments, Makarenko aimed at creating an
'extremely intricate chain of subordination in the colony, in which it
was impossible for individual members to become unduly conspicu-
ous, or to predominate in the collective'.[26] The development of the

---

25   The word is associated rather with self-management and guerrilla than with verticalized
      and militarized principles. 'The word "detachment" was an expression used in that
      period when the waves of revolution had not as yet been diverted into the orderly ranks
      of regiments and divisions. Guerrilla warfare, especially in the Ukraine, where it was
      so long-drawn-out, was carried on exclusively by detachments' (ibid., I, p. 348).

26   Ibid., p. 357.

detachment system points towards the structuring of the collectivity according to organizational self-management and polytechnic principles. Besides the system of detachments, a collective popular tribunal was also created to judge problems in the Colony such as theft.

Among the many inventions described by Makarenko, I find the theatre practice developed at the Colony especially interesting. After around the third year of its existence, theatre became a central activity, with the staging of around forty plays per winter in a hangar transformed into a stage and an auditorium for six hundred people that included the local population living near the Colony. There were several mixed detachments that saw to different functions such as acting, wardrobe requirements, heating, scenery, lighting-, sound-, and stage-effects, cleaning, operating the stage curtains, etc. The kids performed all these different activities and Makarenko played the role of the director and prompter. Since they usually had one week to prepare a play of sometimes four or five acts, it was impossible to learn all the text by heart. Thus, the emphasis was on directing how to move oneself in the space, which gestures to use, etc. Makarenko writes that he 'attributed great importance to the theatre, since through its agency the colonists' way of speaking was greatly improved, and their horizons broadened'.[27]

Indeed, the theatre appears to have offered a perfect set of circumstances in which the juvenile collective had to find solutions to staging complex plays in a very short time. The tensions that emerged and the object of the debates inside the collective constituted a crucial part of the pedagogical process. Moreover, it provided an opportunity of practicing the different tasks of subordination, command, and the development of techniques, without which the final result (i.e. the play) would have been impossible. Finally, the theatre process also educated the sensibility related to the perception of space, the movement of bodies and the coordination of gestures — essential elements in the creation of the collectivity.[28]

---

27 Ibid., II, p. 82.

28 Here I should mention another experiment of this period concerning theatre, which seems even more radical: Asja Lācis and the infantine proletarian theatre. In 1918, Lācis started to work with war orphans in Orel and thought that theatre could be a way to 'awaken' them. She divided the group of children into several sections (painting and drawing, music, technical construction (of props, buildings, figures, animals, etc.), rhythm and gymnastics, diction, and improvisation). According to Lācis, whereas

CONCLUSION

Makarenko's work is not straightforward, especially given the fact that he wrote a literary rather than a theoretical account of it. At the same time, it is precisely for this reason that his work is so interesting and remains of importance today. Writing a poem and not a doctrine was the way he found to describe the struggles of an exceptional situation in an immanent and hence also materialist way. In the light of this case study one can ponder if every pedagogical situation, dealing as it does with singular and unique living creatures, will not inevitably prove to be exceptional. In a way, a literary work is able to open up paths of communication, to encourage others to experiment and to invent, instead of confining experience to a set of rules that dictate how to proceed as a manual would do.

Among the paths opened by Makarenko, one of the most important is how he struggles to de-naturalize and de-essentialize individuals, and to emphasize how individuals are always *the products of circumstances*[29] rather than the products of models prescribing what they

---

bourgeois education is geared toward individual development and the final product (the play itself), communist education aims at a 'collective aesthetic form', it insists on the process and the situation as the main pedagogical tools and on the development of the collective rather than of each individual. Finally, the pedagogical process should emphasize the observation and the learning both of the educator and the pupils. 'Our starting point for both educators and those who were to be educated was observation. The children observed objects, the relations of objects and people to one another, and their changeability. The educators watched the children to see what they accomplished and how far they could productively apply their skills. Observation was not only practiced and developed through drawing, painting, and music inside the studio but also outside of it. Early in the morning, and again in the evening, we went outside with the children and made them aware of how colours changed through distance and time of day, how different the sounds and noises were in the morning and evening, and how silence can sing' (Asja Lācis, 'A Memoir', *South as State of Mind*, 9 [Documenta 14#4] ([2017]) <https://www.documenta14.de/en/south/> [accessed 12 September 2020]).

29   In 1999, the French choreographer Xavier Leroy created a very striking performance-lecture hybrid called *Product of Circumstances*, where he combined his double trajectory as researcher in both molecular biology and choreography. After his PhD, he finally abandoned biology in favour of dance, precisely because of the naturalization of a model body and the way academic work seemed so sterile to him. However, in the more traditional dance scene he also found a very crystallised notion of the body. The expression 'product of circumstances' puts into relation both the elements constituting his biographical path that transformed him into a very particular dancer/choreographer and the critique of a unified, biologized, modelled and essentialized conception of body.

should be or become. A characteristic of a materialist education, or even of materialism *tout court*, is precisely to start from the actual and singular situation, to refuse a 'modelled' conception of the human and to take into account the circumstances, whether historical and macro or individual and micro, before proceeding to analyse and judge.

Re-reading Makarenko also affords us an opportunity to rethink how to build a collective, how to think about the materiality of what he likes to call *social glue*, and how to fabricate it. It is a question of building a common horizon at however small a scale — in Makarenko's case, that of the Colony —, one which should be able to help transform society at large. Indeed, the misery of the traditional bourgeois educational system is to have forgotten the importance of the collective construction.

> Perhaps the main distinction between our educational system and the bourgeois one lies precisely in the fact that with us a children's collective is bound to develop and prosper, to visualize a better tomorrow, and to aspire to it in joyful, common efforts, in gay, steadfast visions. Perhaps therein lies the true pedagogical dialectics.[30]

---

30   Makarenko, *The Road to Life*, II, p. 302.

In the Labyrinth of Emancipation
An Inquiry into the Relationship between Knowledge and Politics
BERNARDO BIANCHI

> Étrange parti pris cependant qui valorise aveuglément la profondeur aux dépens de la superficie et qui veut que 'superficiel' signifie non pas 'de vaste dimension', mais de 'peu de profondeur', tandis que 'profond' signifie au contraire 'de grande profondeur' et non pas 'de faible superficie'
>
> Michel Tournier, *Vendredi ou les limbes du Pacifique*

INTRODUCTION

In the Marxist tradition, emancipation is often described as the opposite of either alienation[1] or domination.[2] However, during its politiciz-

---

* This chapter is based on three different strands of my research and aims to demonstrate their interconnection. Firstly, it marks the closure of my research as a fellow at the Alexander von Humboldt Stiftung and the Coordination for the Improvement of Higher Education Personnel of the Brazilian Government (CAPES). Secondly, it engages with the research that has recently resulted in another co-edited volume published by Routledge entitled *Democracy and Brazil: Collapse and Regression*. Thirdly, it aims to bring together these two projects with the debates I have been engaged in with Émilie Filion-Donato, Marlon Miguel, Ayşe Yuva, and many other dear friends from the project 'Materialism and Politics'.

1 See Gérard Bensussan, 'Émancipation', in *Dictionnaire critique du marxisme*, ed. by Gérard Bensussan and Georges Labica (Paris: PUF, 1999), pp. 382–84.

2 See Ulrich Weiss, 'Emanzipation', ed. by Wolfgang Fritz Haug, *Historisch-Kritisches Wörterbuch des Marxismus*, 15 vols (Hamburg: Argument, 1983–), III (1997), pp. 272–89.

ation in the eighteenth century and the first decades of the nineteenth century in the *Vormärz*, it is not so much the alternative between both dimensions, but rather their intertwinement, which becomes evident. In this chapter, I analyse what I consider to be the classical form of the concept of emancipation. This classical form is rooted in two fundamental features. On the one hand, it is based on a dichotomy between passivity and activity, or heteronomy and autonomy. At the same time, the concept is impregnated with the ideal of a process of maturation, which takes the form of a process of intellectual development along the lines of an organic growth.[3]

I analyse, on this basis, how the classical form of the concept of emancipation developed according to a particular philosophical anthropology of autonomy. This, in turn, gave rise to civil law as the common reference for how to conceive political autonomy. My purpose, as I develop in the section 'Tutelage and the Labyrinth of Emancipation', is to demonstrate how this has been done and how this conception has led, however well intended, to a hierarchical understanding of the relationship between knowledge and political action. The latter trait is inseparable from what I define in a homonymous section as 'epistemocracy'.

According to the classical concept of emancipation, those who lack judgment, since they are 'incomplete' individuals, are *alieni juris*, and, consequently, cannot take part in the political life of their community — 'before one can be a free citizen in the state, one must feel free in the bosom of nature'.[4] To emancipate oneself was the great task of that time period as defined by Heinrich Heine,[5] and it became a requirement for the individual to engage in the political realm. Accordingly, emancipation forges an ideal of a fully-fledged individuality in association with epistemic aptitude as the true basis for political autonomy.

---

3   These two features have been partially identified by Ernesto Laclau in a provocative text, which was originally published in 1992. In opposition to Laclau, however, I don't agree that these two dimensions lead to an undecidability between the 'dichotomic dimension' and the 'dimension of ground'. See his *Emancipation(s)* (London: Verso, 1996), p. 1.

4   Elme-Marie Caro, *Problèmes de morale sociale* (Paris: Hachette, 1887), p. 190.

5   Heinrich Heine, 'Reise von München nach Genua', in *Heinrich-Heine-Säkularausgabe*, 27 vols (Berlin: de Gruyter, 1970–), VI: *Reisebilder II (1828–1831)* (1986), pp. 7–72 (p. 61).

The Latin *emancipatio*, derived from the verb *emancipare*, from the expression *ex manus capere*, indeed literally means 'to take off hands'.[6] In Roman law, this referred to the figure of the slave, but, primarily, to the *infant* under the rule of the *pater familias* — the *infant* being the one who does not speak (in + *fāns*). In the German language, the fact of being unable to speak for oneself is at the basis of the noun *Unmündigkeit* and the adjective *unmündig*, which can be literally translated as 'non-mouthed'. *Unmündigkeit* is also a legal concept that corresponds to the English word 'minority', and goes hand in hand with the notion of legal incapacity.[7] In the thought of Immanuel Kant, minority became associated with a problem concerning the attainment of autonomy, a problem directly linked to that of emancipation.[8] Accordingly, it can be said that to emancipate oneself, to become autonomous, means to have a voice, to be able to speak — both in one's private affairs in the form of legal capacity, as well as in the political realm in the form of political rights.

In the section 'Materialism and Emancipation', I outline a very intriguing formula employed by Étienne Balibar: materialism without matter.[9] Following Balibar's usage of the expression and its connection to Karl Marx's 'Theses on Feuerbach', this conception of materialism

---

6   Reinhardt Koselleck and Karl Martin Grass, 'Emanzipation', in *Geschichtliche Grundbegriffe: Historisches Lexikon*, ed. by Reinhardt Koselleck, Otto Brunner, and Werner Conze, 7 vols (Stuttgart: Klett-Cotta, 1972–97), II (1975), pp. 153–97.

7   I am referring to minority in reference to its meaning in terms of age. In English, as in French and Spanish, the term minority (*minorité* in French and *minoría* in Spanish) combines two different meanings: (i) the situation of a group that is smaller in number, and (ii) the period before the attainment of majority. This is not the case in German (nor in Italian and in Portuguese), which distinguishes between *Minderheit*, minority in terms of number, and *Unmündigkeit* (or *Minderjährigkeit*), minority in terms of age.

8   See Immanuel Kant, 'An Answer to the Question: What is Enlightenment?' [1784], in *Practical Philosophy*, trans. by Mary J. Gregor, The Cambridge Edition of the Works of Immanuel Kant (Cambridge: Cambridge University Press, 1996), pp. 15–22 (p. 17). In the current chapter, I have chosen to translate *Unmündigkeit* in the work of Kant as 'minority' and rejected other options such as 'immaturity', following the choice made by Gregor in the Cambridge edition. I believe this choice is well justified for two reasons. Firstly, it is the best option considering how Kant employs the concept throughout his entire work, especially in the *Doctrine of Right* (first section of *The Metaphysics of Morals*, which was also translated by Gregor in the Cambridge edition of the works of Kant). Secondly, 'minority', differently from 'immaturity', is a legal concept and, therefore, is more in line with *Unmündigkeit*.

9   Étienne Balibar, *La Philosophie de Marx* (Paris: La Découverte, 2014), p. 61. I also refer the reader to Marianna Poyares's contribution to this volume.

posits the reciprocal constitution between activity (*Tätigkeit*) and subjectivity, which means that the emergence and development of human beings are inseparable from their practice. On this basis, I argue in favour of what I consider to be a materialist concept of emancipation, a topic further developed in this volume by Marlon Miguel and Pascal Sévérac. This conception is fundamentally distinct from the classical concept in so far as it rejects, from the outset, the premises of the philosophical anthropology of autonomy, which are based on the concept of minority (*Unmündigkeit*) and lead to epistemocracy. Therefore, I argue that a materialist concept of emancipation is rooted in the dismissal of the concept of minority. This means, ultimately, the rejection of hierarchical ways of articulating the relationship between epistemic competence and political agency, which opens up different approaches to education. However, instead of reversing the 'principle of the ignorance of the people'[10] into the 'principle of the wisdom of the people', the question seems rather to lie in conceiving a form of education akin to the democratic principle of self-organization, leading to a process of reciprocal constitution of knowledge and political agency.[11]

TUTELAGE AND THE LABYRINTH OF EMANCIPATION

On the eve of the French revolution, the Marquis de Condorcet, in his *Essay on the Constitution and Functions of the Provincial Assemblies*, distinguished between those who are entitled to the right of citizenship (*droit de cité*) and those who are *naturally excluded* from it: 'the exclusion of minors, monks, servants, men convicted of crimes, all those who may be presumed not to have an enlightened will [*volonté éclairée*], or a will of their own [*volonté propre*]; those who may legitimately be suspected of a corrupt will'.[12] A year later, Emmanuel-Joseph de Sieyès laid the foundation of a fundamental distinction in constitutional the-

---

10   See Catherine Colliot-Thélène, 'L'Ignorance du peuple', in *L'Ignorance du peuple: Essais sur la démocratie*, ed. by Gérard Duprat (Paris: PUF, 1998), pp. 17–40.

11   I argue, furthermore, that a materialist education should not be conceived as the activity of explaining human reality, as if this were composed of circumstances separated from our own practice.

12   Marquis de Condorcet, *Essai sur la constitution et les fonctions des assemblées provinciales*, in *Œuvres de Condorcet*, ed. by Arthur Condorcet O'Connor and François Arago, 12 vols (Paris: Firmin Didot Frères, 1847), VIII, pp. 115–662 (p. 130; my translation).

ory between active and passive citizenship which was enshrined in the French law of 22 December 1789:[13] 'all can enjoy the advantages afforded by society; but only those who contribute to the public establishment are [...] true, active citizens, the true members of this association'.[14]

The principle of autonomy, which is connected to the idea of an independent and enlightened will, was a central trope of political rhetoric in the late eighteenth century. In fact, autonomy is what enabled Condorcet to differentiate between natural and political individuals — a distinction that could have no place in the *ancien régime* which, being an organic society of corporate bodies, assigned political power not to the individuals themselves but to *status*, that is, to the belonging of an individual or group of individuals to specific sectors of the society. In this sense, the 'minors' did not constitute a group like other groups who were excluded from political life. After all, they were not a determinate social category such as monks, servants, etc. In Condorcet, as in the writings of Sieyès, autonomy is the only thing that can legitimize legally binding obligations in either the political or private sphere. Therefore, legal capacity and political autonomy go hand in hand.[15]

In the same way, in Kant's *Metaphysics of Morals*, autonomy is forged along the lines of the legal capacity:

---

13   This distinction was enshrined in the third article, section i, of the above-mentioned law.

14   Emmanuel-Joseph Sieyès, *Reconnoissance et exposition raisonnée des droits de l'homme et du citoyen* (Paris: Chez Baudouin, 1789), p. 21; my translation.

15   For this reason, Pierre Rosanvallon states that the foundations of the modern tradition of civil law and those of political theory overlap (*Le Sacre du citoyen. Histoire du suffrage universel en France* (Paris: Gallimard, 1992), p. 100). In fact, in French civil law, the usage of the word 'emancipation' was widely connected to the legal capacity (*capacité juridique*). At the end of the seventeenth century, Antoine Furetière defined emancipation in his dictionary and encyclopaedia as the freedom 'to act in one's affairs and to govern one's income without the assistance of a tutor' ('Émancipation', in *Dictionnaire Universel*, 3 vols (The Hague and Rotterdam: Arnoud et Reinier Leers, 1701), ii, pp. 33–34 (pp. 33; my translation). In the Napoleonic Civil Code of 1804, it is stipulated that emancipation can be both tacit, as in the case of marriage (art. 476 et seq.), or explicit, when a *minor* is prematurely released from parental authority. These conceptions reverberate in Antoine-Gaspard Boucher d'Argis's spirit when he writes, in 1755, the article 'emancipation' for the *Encyclopédie* of Denis Diderot and Jean le Rond d'Alembert: emancipation is 'an act that places certain persons outside the power of another' ('Émancipation', in *Encyclopédie ou Dictionnaire raisonné des Sciences, des arts et des métiers*, ed. by Jean Le Rond d'Alembert and Denis Diderot, 17 vols (Paris, 1755), v, pp. 546–49 (p. 546; my translation).

The only qualification for being a citizen is being fit to vote. But being fit to vote presupposes the independence of someone who, as one of the people, wants to be not just a part of the commonwealth but also a member of it, that is, a part of the commonwealth acting from his own choice in community with others. This quality of being independent, however, requires a distinction between *active* and *passive* citizens, though the concept of a passive citizen seems to contradict the concept of a citizen as such. — The following examples can serve to remove this difficulty: an apprentice in the service of a merchant or artisan; a domestic servant (as distinguished from a civil servant); a minor (*naturaliter vel civiliter*); all women and, in general, anyone whose preservation in existence (his being fed and protected) depends not on his management of his own business but on arrangements made by another (except the state). All these people lack civil personality and their existence is, as it were, only inherence.[16]

By drawing on civil law, Kant takes 'civil personality' as the measure of citizenship. Nevertheless, the reference to civil law as a repository for reflecting on political theory is obviously not specific to Kant. In Thomas Hobbes, this reference appears, for example, in Chapter XVI in *Leviathan*, where he develops his theory of representation.[17] Hobbes was adamant that in the absence of purposive actions assignable to a personal identity, only a tutor could give final consent for any transaction in which the minor had a part. That is, because 'children, fools, and madmen [...] have no use of reason', they lack authority, that is, 'the right of doing any action'.[18] Furthermore, because unrepresented minors are not legal persons, their tutelage is nothing more than a form of 'representation by fiction'.[19] Tutelage was different to the authority of the parents over their offspring (*patria potestas*) which arose solely

---

16 Immanuel Kant, *The Metaphysics of Morals* [1797], in *Practical Philosophy*, trans. by Mary J. Gregor, The Cambridge Edition of the Works of Immanuel Kant (Cambridge: Cambridge University Press, 1996), pp. 353–603 (p. 458).

17 For the indebtedness of Hobbes's theory to civil law, see Mónica Brito Vieira, *The Elements of Representation in Hobbes: Aesthetics, Theatre, Law, and Theology in the Construction of Hobbes's Theory of the State* (Leiden; Boston: Brill, 2009), p. 156.

18 Thomas Hobbes, *Leviathan or the Matter, Form, and Power of a Commonwealth Ecclesiastical and Civil*, ed. by William Molesworth, in *The English Works of Thomas Hobbes*, 11 vols (London: Bohn, 1839), III, pp. 150 and 148.

19 Ibid., p. 149. See also David Runciman, *Pluralism and the Personality of the State* (Cambridge: Cambridge University Press, 1997), p. 21.

from natural right.[20] Instead, it was understood as the corollary of a de facto situation concerning the lack of individuality of the minor. It had no normative anchorage: tutelage did not aim at creating individuals or producing autonomy.[21]

John Locke radically changed this position, as he connected the authority of the parents to the duty of educating their offspring. The power of parents over their children derived from their educative duty, that is, their obligation to 'inform the mind, and govern the actions of their yet ignorant nonage [...]'.[22] Therefore, even though children were to look upon their parents as 'absolute governors',[23] their parents were not to behave only as sovereigns but also as educators. This meant that parental authority was not only conceived of in terms of sovereignty, as in Hobbes, but also in connection to education.

We find this precise idea in Kant as well, not exactly in the text of 1797, but in *An Answer to the Question: 'What is Enlightenment [Aufklärung]?'*, which was published in 1784, where the idea of minority as preparation for autonomy is clearly posited.

> *Enlightenment is the human being's emergence from his self-incurred minority. Minority* is inability to make use of one's own understanding without direction from another. This minority is *self-incurred* when its cause lies not in lack of understanding but in lack of resolution and courage to use it without direction from another. *Sapere aude!*[24]

Here, a *second form of minority* emerges, which is different from the kind of minority that is mentioned in *The Metaphysics of Morals*. In this text, Kant connects minority to the Enlightenment as its opposite and, at the same time, its final objective, its *raison d'être*. Kant states that this condition of being *alieni juris* occurs even in the condition

---

20   In Hobbes, tutelage is the form of *patria potestas* which is specific to civil society.

21   In this respect, tutors are analogous to sovereign.

22   John Locke, *The Second Treatise of Government*, in *Locke: Two Treatises of Government* (Cambridge: Cambridge University Press, 2003), pp. 265–428 (p. 306). It's worth recalling that the term 'nonage' was also used to translate Kant's *Unmündigkeit* into English, as it was done by Mary Campbell Smith <http://www.columbia.edu/acis/ets/CCREAD/etscc/kant.html> [accessed 30 June 2020].

23   John Locke, *Some Thoughts Concerning Education*, in *The Educational Writings of John Locke*, ed. by John William Adamson (Cambridge: Cambridge University Press, 2011), pp. 21–180 (p. 33).

24   Kant, 'What is Enlightenment?', p. 17.

of natural majority or maturity.[25] At the same time, he is obviously not simply dealing with a *minority resulting from the law* (*civiliter*), as he refers to in *The Metaphysics of Morals*, which is related to all those who, despite having reached the age of maturity, remain minors before the law, as was the case for all those still under tutelage. According to Kant, the minority in this case is not a mere product of nature, but rather fundamentally a problem concerning the habit of dependence, of letting others decide — a form of voluntary tutelage. Moreover, Kant's text from 1784 introduces the idea of minority as *preparation for autonomy* and not simply its opposite. In contrast to his other writings, Kant's *What is Enlightenment* is more in line with the old problem of voluntary servitude,[26] which implicitly points in the direction of Étienne de la Boétie.

The connection between Kant's thought and La Boétie's *Discourse on Voluntary Servitude*, originally published in 1574, was definitively consolidated by Johann Benjamin Erhard who, in 1793, translated it into German and had it published in *Der neue teutsche Merkur*, which was an important journal of dissemination for the *Aufklärung* at that time. Unlike the Monarchomachs,[27] La Boétie's text sheds light on how subjects voluntarily adhere to a despotic government — not simply out of fear or sheer violence — so that they become accustomed to tyranny. For Erhard, the minority cannot simply be described in terms of a relation of domination by force or by law, since self-incurred minority (which is an expression he borrowed from Kant) corresponds to a 'degree of formation of the spirit'.[28] In Erhard's eyes, Kant offered

---

25   On this specific occasion, one could write 'natural maturity', because in this case Kant is referring to ripeness, or the biological condition of maturation.

26   Even though this formulation does not entirely match what could be described as minority in light of Kant's *Critique of Judgement*, since, in the latter text, Enlightenment is identified as the 'liberation from superstition' (*Befreiung vom Aberglauben*), both texts suggest an idea of minority as preparation for autonomy.

27   It is worth recalling, in this regard, the work *Vindiciae Contra Tyrannos*, originally published in 1579, and possibly written by Philippe de Mornay, considered to be one of the most celebrated *Monarchomach* treatises of that time period. This book formulated, for the first time, a theory of the sovereignty of the people as the origin of the king's power (Hubert Languet, *Vindiciae Contra tyrannos, or, Concerning the Legitimate Power of a Prince over the People, and of the People over a Prince* (Cambridge: Cambridge University Press, 1994).

28   Johann Benjamin Erhard, *Über das Recht des Volks zu einer Revolution* (Berlin: Syndikat, 1970), p. 82; my translation.

an answer to the problem of voluntary servitude posited by La Boétie, in which he proposed that through the propagation of the lights, that is, the diffusion of knowledge, it becomes conceivable to foresee an exit from the state of minority. However, if kept against their will in a state of minority, the people have the right to revolution: 'as long as the ruling class does not prevent the people from the Enlightenment and as long as it maintains its primacy based on the predominance of its own Enlightenment, there will be no revolution of the people'.[29]

It is only when minority becomes a dogma for the people that they have the right to abolish the state that oppresses them. As a result, revolution becomes an act of resistance and not an act of creation. In Erhard's view, it is the dogma of minority in terms of the repression of human progress that causes revolutions, and although he does not use the term emancipation (like Kant), he clearly addresses the concept by tapping into the development of a self-incurred minority towards a majority, or from voluntary servitude to becoming a people who know their rights. Nevertheless, this progress takes the form of a process of intellectual development along the lines of an organic growth. However, as Hans Blumenberg has shown, the limits of the metaphor of organic growth do not only concern the unjustifiable belief in 'a continuous progress of rationality',[30] but instead the fact that the hour of 'political majority' only tolls after a process of intellectual development. By considering Hobbes, Locke, Kant, and Erhard together, one can argue that the attainment of 'the use of reason' coalesces with the 'propagation of the lights', and gives way, paradoxically, to the idea of benevolent forms of tutelage justified by the de facto minority of the people. Under such a worldview the transition from minority towards 'complete knowledge of human rights' becomes ultimately impossible, and tutelage becomes a labyrinth from which emancipation can never emerge.

---

29 Erhard, *Über das Recht*, p. 95; my translation.
30 Hans Blumenberg, *Die Legitimität der Neuzeit* (Frankfurt a.M.: Suhrkamp, 1999), p. 440.

EPISTEMOCRACY

In the period of time known as the *Vormärz*, or 'pre-March', preceding the 1848 Revolutions in the states of the German confederation, Heine took up the argument concerning the connection between emancipation and minority. He wrote that a true transformation must assume the form of a transformation of mentalities, which also justified, in his view, the superiority of German philosophy vis-à-vis the French political transformations of the time. While the transformative energy in France was, in his opinion, directed against feudal privileges, in Germany it was directed instead towards abolishing intellectual obstacles and privileges.[31] By drawing a comparison between Kant and Maximilien Robespierre, Heine underscored the importance of the intellectual transformations that had taken place in Germany, thus highlighting how they were more radical and more mature than the French revolutionary efforts.[32] In Germany, the most important revolutionary task was not seen as being directly political but rather 'spiritual' (*geistig*) or, to put it in contemporary terms, as a matter of consciousness. Heine explicitly praises the Germans, in contrast to the French, whom he characterizes as infantilized, shallow, immature, and prone to unpremeditated action.

A similar argument is to be found in a text by Ludwig Feuerbach from 1842 in which he identifies sensualism and materialism with revolution (and France), while metaphysics and idealism are associated with reformism (and Germany):[33] 'The *heart* — the feminine principle, the sense of the sensible, the seat of materialism — is French-minded; the *head* — the masculine principle, the seat of idealism — is German. The heart makes revolutions; the head, reforms. The head brings things to a *state*; the heart, to *motion*.'[34] When placed in connection with Heine's thoughts, Feuerbach's analysis reveals an argument according to which the French mentality (and its materialism) entails a sort of transformation that is inferior to German philosophy (and its

---

31   See Heinrich Heine, *Zur Geschichte der Religion und Philosophie in Deutschland*, in *Heinrich-Heine-Säkularausgabe*, in *Heinrich-Heine-Säkularausgabe*, VIII: *Über Deutschland, 1833–1836. Aufsätze über Kunst und Philosophie*, pp. 125–230 (p. 191).

32   Ibid., pp. 194–95.

33   Ludwig Feuerbach, 'Vorläufige Thesen zur Reformation der Philosophie', in *Gesammelte Werke*, 14 vols (Berlin: Akademie, 1970), IX, pp. 243–63 (pp. 254–55).

34   Ibid., p. 255; my translation.

idealism) because the latter philosophical culture is not limited to the surface of things. This perspective offers a view that displaces politics by postulating the existence of a field of determination from which politics emerges as a product, or secondary reality, of a core that is located beyond it. This shows how Heine and Feuerbach prepared the argument — which was later much associated with Marx — according to which French materialism (and the politics that stem from it) is ideological.[35]

These arguments implying the separation between depth and surface, or essential and secondary phenomena, are inseparable from stadialist arguments based on the hierarchization of the relationship between intellectual development and political emancipation.[36] Stadialist arguments are also quite common in the discussions surrounding the emancipation of subaltern groups, such as Jews, Blacks, women, the working class, etc.[37] Between 1842 and 1843, Bruno Bauer wrote two interventions on the emancipation of the German Jews: *The Jewish Question* and *The Capacity of Present-day Jews and Christians to Become Free*.[38] In these texts, which were starkly criticized by Marx, Bauer argued that in order to achieve political emancipation Jews needed to be freed from their prior prejudices.[39] According to Bauer, they needed to overcome their state of minority in order to become citizens. Here, again, we can identify the philosophical idea, very prevalent in Germany at the time, that a reform of consciousness must precede political emancipation.

---

35 In this sense, one could rightfully identify Heine's and Feuerbach's writings with Jacques Rancière's category of meta-politics. See Jacques Rancière, *Disagreement: Politics and Philosophy* (Minneapolis: University of Minnesota Press, 2004), pp. 81–82.

36 I refer the reader to the definition of 'stadialism' in the Introduction (p. 11, n. 17). Anti-stadialism here should not be misunderstood as rejection of the idea of stages. It refers instead to the idea of a linear and hierarchical evolution that entails a separation, in the form of a progression, between the moment of formation, on the one hand, and that of political autonomy and activity, on the other.

37 In this case, we could say that the meaning of minority in terms of age (*Unmündigkeit*) encounters its meaning in terms of number (*Minderheit*).

38 See Bruno Bauer, *Die Judenfrage*, first published in 1842 by the *Deutsche Jahrbücher für Wissenschaft und Kunst* and *Die Fähigkeit der heutigen Juden und Christen, frei zu werden*, first published in 1843 by the *Einundzwanzig Bogen aus der Schweiz*.

39 The core of Bauer's argument can be found in the opening pages of 'The Jewish Question', in *The Young Hegelians, an Anthology* (Cambridge: Cambridge University Press, 1983), pp. 187–97 (pp. 187–88).

In 1850, Hermann Scheidler was confronted by the same question and contrasted two fundamental forms of emancipation: inner emancipation (*innere*) and outer emancipation (*äußere*). While the first chiefly concerned superstition and the passions, the second concerned political autonomy.[40] Based on this idea, Scheidler defended the importance of a public pedagogical project (*Volks-* and *Staatspädagogik*) in order to bridge the two forms of emancipation — we are once again faced with the problem of education, which, as we have seen, justified parental authority in Locke's work. This argument leads us to the paradoxical, yet deeply ingrained, relation between domination and education. This concerns not only the fact that education was often employed as a means to dominate, but also the idea that domination prepares for self-rule (educates) those who were deemed still unfit for it. For example, in the context of slavery in the Americas the subjugation and domination of Blacks and Native Americans was often justified 'as a way to prepare them for eventual participation in society as full citizens.'[41]

PRELIMINARY CONCLUSIONS

Even though Sieyès's invention of the distinction between passive and active citizenship was mainly connected to pecuniary hindrances upon the right to vote, entailing a system of censitary suffrage, it was also inserted, as we have seen, into a broader discussion about autonomy and minority. After the revolution of 1848, the Second French Republic abolished the last economic obstacles to exercising the right to vote, and instituted universal adult male suffrage, a trend that later spread throughout the continent. In the same time period, however, another form of exclusion was consolidated: exclusion through illiteracy. However, in Europe, exclusions based on illiteracy have never had the same importance as they had in the Americas.[42] In the United States the propagation of literacy tests, which were administered to voters, spread

---

40   Hermann Scheidler, 'Judenemancipation', in *Allgemeine Encyclopädie der Wissenschaften und Künste*, ed. by Johann Samuel Ersch and Johann Gottfried Gruber, 167 vols (Leipzig: Johann Friedrich Gleditsch, 1850), xxvii, pp. 253–315 (p. 266).

41   Yuko Miki, *Frontiers of Citizenship: A Black and Indigenous History of Postcolonial Brazil* (Cambridge: Cambridge University Press, 2018), p. 55.

42   See Jairo Nicolau, *História do Voto no Brasil* (Rio de Janeiro: Zahar, 2002).

in the mid-nineteenth century and lasted until the second half of the twentieth century. In Brazil, the exclusion of the illiterate became a constitutional norm with the first republican constitution of 1891, which eliminated the censitary suffrage created by the imperial constitution of 1824.[43] As these examples show, in the context of profoundly racialized societies, knowledge became a way of cloaking unequal access to citizenship.

In view of these forms of political exclusion, I want to coin a term, *epistemocracy*,[44] which refers to all forms of discourse according to which political action is dependent on the possession of knowledge and competence by an individual or a group of individuals. Epistemocracy allows for a modern form of tutelage, according to which those individuals and groups of individuals that find themselves in a state of minority (*Unmündigkeit*) should be completely governed as long as their minority persists. In this paradigm even though the *minors* are to be regarded as citizens, they are also denied a say in political life so long as they are deemed minors. Therefore, *epistemocracy* allows for forms of tutelage on the ground of 'epistemic incompetence'. It separates active (*mündige*) citizens from passive (*unmündige*) citizens, or those whose voice should be heard from those whose voice should be ignored. The legitimacy of epistemocracy is different from open domination in that it is built upon the potential reversibility of the situation affecting those deprived of their political rights based on the proviso that, so long as they become epistemically competent, they can leave their minority status and take part in political life. Regarding this view, it must be said that minority is not something *per se*, it is not a natural state resulting from ignorance and backwardness, and nor does it arise from nature. Quite to the contrary: it is the result of ideological constructions by means of which the individuals in a given

---

43   For a discussion about the introduction of the 'literacy census' in Brazil, see Sérgio Buarque de Holanda, *História Geral da Civilização Brasileira*, 11 vols (São Paulo: Bertrand Brasil, 2005), VII, p. 234. The exclusion of illiterate people from their right to vote lasted until 1985 in Brazil, the final year of the military dictatorship.

44   My usage of the concept of epistemocracy must be distinguished from David Estlund's concept of 'epistocracy'. See his *Democratic Authority: A Philosophical Framework* (Princeton, NJ: Princeton University Press, 2007). In opposition to epistocracy, epistemocracy is not limited to the rule of experts, as it does not just concern political rule or governance, but, more importantly, political agency and political participation.

society are endowed with different functions. Consequently, instead of the concept of minority, one should prefer the idea of *minorization*, which underscores the fact that minority is not something that exists by itself, but the result of practices and choices entailing the political distinction between those whose voice is heard and taken into account and those who are deemed to be incomplete individuals — and who, therefore, need to be under tutelage.[45] In this sense, minorization is inseparable from epistemocracy, which ultimately re-enacts different forms of domination, especially those connected to class, gender, and race, under the appearance of differences in competence and knowledge.

MATERIALISM AND EMANCIPATION

As I have outlined in the previous sections, the classical concept of emancipation is inseparable from a political anthropology of autonomy. One of the clearest arguments against epistemocracy corresponds to 'the insurrectional moment of citizenship'[46] as it was theorized by Jacques Rancière in his book *Disagreement*. Furthermore, the relationship of this conception of citizenship (or emancipation) to the question of education was clearly articulated in Rancière's *The Ignorant Schoolmaster*. In this work, emancipation acquires special contours insofar as it is associated with Jacques Jacotot's revolutionary pedagogy; an (anti-)pedagogy which, in the first decades of the nineteenth century, rejected the hierarchy of intellectual capacity and instead asserted that all people were equally competent.[47] For

---

45   I am using the term of minorization in a sense that is not identical to Gilles Deleuze's and Félix Guattari's 'becoming-minor' — or the term 'minoritization' which is derived from it. 'Becoming-minor' and 'minoritization' are built on the basis of the 'minority' as the smaller in number, a meaning that Deleuze extrapolates by saying that it corresponds to a 'state of rule, that is to say, the situation of a group that, whatever its size, is excluded from the majority, or even included, but as a subordinate fraction in relation to the standard of measure that regulates the law and establishes the majority' (Gilles Deleuze, 'One Less Manifesto', in *Mimesis, Masochism, & Mime: The Politics of Theatricality in Contemporary French Thought*, ed. by Timothy Murray (Ann Arbor: University of Michigan Press, 1997), pp. 239–58 (p. 255)).

46   Étienne Balibar, *Equaliberty: Political Essays*, trans. by James Ingram (Durham, NC: Duke University Press, 2013), p. 10.

47   This equality is explained by the following: 'every common person might conceive his human dignity, take the measure of his intellectual capacity, and decide how to

this reason, Jacotot proposed that each person would be able to become a master for the others and to support them in their own intellectual development. Based on Jacotot's perspective, Rancière method 'consists not merely in aiming for future equality, but in directly producing its effects, precisely by positing it as an "axiom" in the first place'.[48] Without equality, the people would become stultified by the superstition of their lack of intelligence.[49]

Through his complete rejection of minorization, Rancière's axiomatic presupposition of emancipation leads us to overlook the problem of education. The title of this section 'materialism and emancipation' points, however, in the direction of what could be regarded as a contradiction; after all, emancipation and materialism are concepts that stem from different traditions. This means that the operation of reconciling both concepts will ultimately imply their transformation into something else. I believe, however, that this reconciliation brings about a form of emancipation that neutralizes epistemocracy, avoiding, nevertheless, the form of an insurrectional moment it takes in Rancière. It also brings about a form of materialist education which is fundamentally anti-stadialist.

As Ayşe Yuva argues in her contribution to this volume, materialism cannot be reduced to a debate regarding the primacy of matter over spirit. Friedrich A. Lange, who was not willing to assign the origin of materialism to a specific time period, stated in 1865 that this tradition was as old as philosophy itself and corresponded to the specific struggle against religious thought, which is also why materialism has so often been associated with impiety.[50] However, Marx and Friedrich Engels instituted a controversy by analysing the origin of the materialist tradition in early modernity. Marx's reception of materialism is complex and even problematic, since his account of the modern his-

---

use it' (Rancière, *The Ignorant Schoolmaster: Five Lessons in Intellectual Emancipation* (Stanford, CA: Stanford University Press, 1991), p. 17).

48   Katia Genel, 'Jacques Rancière and Axel Honneth: Two Critical Approaches to the Political', in *Recognition or Disagreement: A Critical Encounter on the Politics of Freedom, Equality and Identity*, ed. by Katia Genel and Jean-Philippe Deranty (New York: Columbia University Press), pp. 3–32 (p. 29).

49   Ibid, p. 39.

50   Friedrich Albert Lange, *The History of Materialism and Criticism of its Present Importance*, 3 parts (London: Kegan Paul, Trench, Trubner, 1925), I, p. 5.

tory of materialism in *The Holy Family* was fundamentally copied from
Charles Renouvier's 1842 *Handbook of Modern Philosophy* — not the
best source to study the theme.[51] Nevertheless, Marx still achieved a
theoretical breakthrough by proposing a new materialism, at the earli-
est in his 'Theses on Feuerbach' in 1845.[52]

According to Marx's ninth and tenth theses *ad* Feuerbach, materialism is characterized by the reciprocal constitution between activity
(*Tätigkeit*) and subjectivity, which leads to the concept of practice.[53]
This reciprocal constitution takes the form of a 'recursive loop [...]
where the products and the effects are at the same time causes and
producers of what produces them'.[54] Even though Marx had already
proposed the reciprocal constitution between activity and subjectivity
in his *Economic and Philosophic Manuscripts*, in 1844, it was only with
the 'Theses on Feuerbach', from 1845, that he could start to theorize
this recursive loop concretely in terms of social relations, and not abstractly in terms of human essence. This shift represents a radical break
with previous writings, such as his *Contribution to the Critique of Hegel's
Philosophy of Right*.

In 1993, using an expression that he borrowed from Friedrich H.
Jacobi,[55] Balibar proposed that this perspective be named 'materialism
without matter', claiming that 'Marx's materialism has nothing to do
with a reference to *matter*'.[56] The concept of materialism without matter is inseparable from Balibar's further research in terms of transindividuality, which affirms the reciprocity between processes of individu-

51   Which has been meticulously demonstrated by Olivier Bloch, *Matière à Histoires*
      (Paris: Vrin, 1997), pp. 384–441.
52   See the contribution by Frieder Otto Wolf and his discussion around the notion of
      'materialism of materialities'.
53   See Karl Marx, 'Thesen über Feuerbach', in *MEW* [*Marx-Engels-Werke*, see abbrevi-
      ations], III (1958), pp. 5–7 (p. 5). I follow Frank Fischbach's preference for translating
      the term with *practice* — avoiding, therefore, writing the word as *Praxis/praxis*. To
      keep it in the German original represents an undue proliferation of concepts. See
      Franck Fischbach, *Philosophies de Marx* (Paris: Vrin, 2015), p. 27.
54   See Edgar Morin, *On Complexity* (Cresskill, NJ: Hampton Press, 2008), p. 49.
55   See Friedrich Heinrich Jacobi, 'Letter from Jacobi to Fichte', in *The Main Philosophical
      Writings and the Novel Allwill*, ed. by George di Giovanni (Montreal: McGill-Queen's
      University Press, 1994), pp. 497–536 (p. 502). However, Balibar's usage of the expres-
      sion must be distinguished from Jacobi's, since the latter has used it to describe Johann
      G. Fichte's *Doctrine of Science* as an inverted Spinozism.
56   Balibar, *La Philosophie de Marx*, p. 60; my translation. I also refer the reader to
      Marianna Poyares's contribution to this volume.

ation (autonomization) and of individualization (singularization).[57] In his 'Theses on Feuerbach', Marx argues that old materialism is idealist like idealism itself because it assumes reality as a given fact based on the exteriority between subject and object — and not in the form of what I call, based on Edgar Morin, a recursive loop. Because philosophers have neglected the reciprocal constitution between activity and subjectivity underlying human practice, they have historically preferred education, even the 'edification of the masses', to the detriment of revolution[58] — the interpretation of the world, rather than its transformation.[59] Precisely for this reason, Marx says in the third thesis on Feuerbach that 'the educators must be educated themselves'[60] — a problem extensively analysed by Miguel in his contribution to this volume.

I would like to propose a historical example that can address the problems concerning the relationship between emancipation and education that I have outlined in the previous two sections. After the introduction of universal adult male suffrage in France, notably in view of the election of Napoleon III, a preoccupation with educating the people in order to adjust them to political participation led to the fashion known as *démopédie*.[61] This concept, which was analysed by Rosanvallon, involved the art of educating or instructing the people (*demos* + *paideia*). It is an idea that weds together the right to vote and instruction, as if true political agency can only be attained through a previous process of edification of the masses, or, as discussed throughout this text, the kind of epistemocracy that is similar to the examples concerning the exclusion from the right to vote in Brazil and in the United States.

Rather than postulating the axiomatic neutralization of epistemocracy, as Rancière does, I believe a solution against stadialist and

57   See Étienne Balibar, *Spinoza politique. Le Transindividuel* (Paris: PUF, 2018), p. 306. See also Jason Read, *The Politics of Transindividuality* (Leiden: Brill, 2015).

58   Balibar, *La Philosophie de Marx*, p. 61.

59   Marx, 'Thesen über Feuerbach', p. 7.

60   Ibid., pp. 5–6. This question reappears much later, in 1875, in Marx's *Critique of the Gotha Programme*.

61   The term is used following Pierre-Joseph Proudhon's sentence 'democracy is démopédia', quoted by Pierre Rosanvallon, *Le peuple introuvable: histoire de la représentation démocratique en France* (Paris: Gallimard, 1998), p. 127.

hierarchical conceptions regarding the relationship between knowledge and political action is to be found in the idea of a materialist
education. A materialist education cannot be regarded as the transmission of knowledge; instead it must be conceived as intrinsically
political. However, this does not mean that it is political in the sense of
political philosophy. On the contrary, as Balibar recalls: political philosophy has always taught that the multitude is intrinsically violent, and,
therefore, that it is in need of education — which means that it needs to
have knowledge transmitted to it, as if knowledge could be transmitted
from the outside. But autonomy is not the corollary of education. The
ideal of a fully-fledged individuality as the condition for autonomy
was, as we saw, the very basis of the philosophical anthropology of
autonomy, leading to the labyrinth of emancipation. As illustrated in
the case of *démopédie*, such a view leads to the vicious circle of elitism
and tutelage. In opposition to this perspective, materialism can play
a role in redefining the relationship between knowledge and political
action in an anti-stadialist fashion. Accordingly, education becomes
intrinsically political as long as it is regarded in the form of a recursive
loop between the process of learning and the process of acting and
transforming reality. Paraphrasing Marx, one could say: autonomy is
not the reward of education but is, instead, education itself.[62]

---

62   The original sentence is as follows: 'Blessedness is not the reward of virtue but is virtue
     itself' (Karl Marx, 'Hefte zur epikureischen, stoischen und skeptischen Philosophie',
     in *MEW*, XL, pp. 13–258 (p. 155)). Marx quotes Baruch Spinoza's *Ethics* V, 42; *CWS*
     [*The Collected Works of Spinoza*, see abbreviations], I, p. 616.

A Materialist Education
Thinking with Spinoza
PASCAL SÉVÉRAC

THREE MEANINGS OF MATERIALISM

I would like to lay the foundations for what can be called, from Spinoza onwards, a 'materialist education'. Let me clarify from the outset three different meanings of 'materialism' which we can use to understand a 'materialist education':

First, in the empirical or immediate sense, that is, in the sense that a person, a behaviour, or an ideology is said to be materialistic when what is valued is material goods. Therefore, 'to be materialistic' is less a label that is claimed than a label that is applied, often to depreciate what is deemed to be materialistic. This definition of 'materialistic' implies a way of living and thinking that values money, carnal pleasures, and material comfort — in short, a way of life that is probably considered too selfish or individualistic, and that would seem to detract from higher values such as generosity or solidarity, or spiritual values that are more concerned with the salvation of souls than with the enjoyment of bodies. I do not wish to discard this meaning of 'materialism', because being materialistic has something to do with being a materialist, i.e.

*   Author affiliation: Univ Paris Est Creteil, LIS, F-94010 Creteil, France

a follower of materialism (especially since in some languages, such as French, there is only one word: '*matérialiste*').

Secondly, 'materialism' can be understood ontologically, that is, in the sense of a reduction of reality to matter alone: this 'materialist' conception of the world considers consciousness as a function of the body, the mind as an emanation of the brain, and thought as a production of matter. As Félix Ravaisson said, when attributing this definition to Auguste Comte, materialism is the 'doctrine that explains the superior by the inferior':[1] of course, this is a definition proposed by a spiritualist who devalued materialist philosophies. But why should consciousness be superior to the body or mind superior to the brain? Such an idea presupposes a common measure between these two kinds of reality, a presumption that Spinozism had already begun to challenge.

Thirdly and finally, it is possible to identify a 'methodological' materialism that does not itself pronounce on the nature of reality by trying to answer questions such as whether there is a difference in nature between thought and matter or a possible reduction of thought to matter; instead, it studies psychic or mental phenomena in the same way as it would study material or bodily phenomena, that is to say, by taking them as the object of a causal, deterministic explanation, or, as we say today, by 'naturalizing' them. In fact, methodological materialism is based on the idea that the reality of thought or of the psyche (ideas, affects) obeys natural necessity in the same way that the reality of matter or of the organism (the movements of the body) does.

So, from what point of view should a materialist education be understood? I will immediately exclude the second meaning of ontological materialism: Spinoza does not conceive of thought as something reducible to matter. If we can derive a materialist education from his philosophy, it is not in the sense that it adopts such a position on the nature of reality, and therefore on the nature of the first object of education — the child. The child, just like any human being, has a mind, comprised of a psychological or cognitive system, which follows its own laws, and which cannot be reduced to bodily, physiological,

---

1   Félix Ravaisson, *La Philosophie en France au xixe siècle* (1867) (Paris: Vrin Reprise, 1983), p. 189: 'Selon l'excellente définition d'Auguste Comte [...], le matérialisme est la doctrine qui explique le supérieur par l'inférieur'.

and especially cerebral or neural laws. Educating a child is therefore not just about impacting a brain.

Spinoza can be described as 'materialist' in the third sense that we have identified, that is, in the methodological sense: this is a non-reductionist materialism, which considers the mind a natural thing that can be studied as bodies are studied. At the end of the preface to the third part of *Ethics*, Spinoza explicitly declares that he intends to study psychic phenomena as if they were 'lines, planes, and bodies':[2] he intends to geometrize the psyche in the same way that science geometrizes an organism, and to use this method to study the properties and causal laws of bodies, in particular of human bodies. The foundations of a physics of thought are laid on the same model as the physics of matter. However, it should be noted in passing that this methodological materialism is itself based on a certain ontological conception of reality: it is because both thought and matter are in fact the same reality conceived under a different kind of being that it is methodologically necessary to study psychic phenomena as we study material phenomena — or to study material phenomena as we should study psychic phenomena, that is, as phenomena of a single and unique Nature that is regulated by precisely determined laws.[3]

From the point of view of education, this non-reductionist, methodological materialism means two things:

First, that such education consists in impacting on both the psyche and the organism; education in this sense is a way of guiding human behaviour, a way of directing human conduct, the purpose of which is not to allow the child's 'free will' to be exercised. Indeed, from the point of view of a materialist, that is, deterministic education, such free will does not exist; on the contrary, belief in free will is an illusion which the moral system of judgment is based upon. In other words, a materialist education does not have as its ultimate purpose the conferral of self-responsibility, but rather self-knowledge; it is not meant to teach obedience to moral rules but knowledge of procedural

---

2   *Ethics* III, Praef.; *CWS* [*The Collected Works of Spinoza*, see abbreviations], I, p. 492.

3   See *Ethics*, III, Praef.: 'nature is always the same, and its virtue and power of acting are everywhere one and the same, that is, the laws and rules of nature, according to which all things happen, and change from one form to another, are always and everywhere the same. So the way of understanding the nature of anything, of whatever kind, must also be the same, namely, through the universal laws and rules of nature' (ibid.).

rules (knowledge of the procedures that regulate behaviour, self, and other).

Secondly, another meaning of a non-reductionist, materialist education is that the mind is considered an automaton that is regulated in a determined way, just as the body is regulated as a physical automaton. This does not mean that consciousness does not matter: the mind may be a 'spiritual automaton' determined by laws, but it still feels what it is thinking.[4] The child's materialist education is not a behavioural education, or rather, it is a behavioural education insofar as it involves an education of consciousness, which is experience as it is lived in the first person. The way a child experiences things does, of course, have an effect on his behaviour, and this is why an education of behaviour must be an education of the way things are lived, felt, and understood.

Nevertheless, the education that can be derived from Spinoza's thought is perhaps also a materialist education in the first sense that we have given to this term: namely, the empirical meaning of a very particular care given to the body and also, in a sense, to the enjoyment of its power. Let me explain. We have seen that Spinoza's materialism is not a reductionist materialism, which would lose interest in psychological interiority and focus only on external behaviour. Nevertheless, it must also be seen that, from a Spinozist point of view, the mind is the idea of a body existing in action: consciousness is consciousness of a living, affected, and affecting body. The mind is all the more powerful because it is the idea of a body that is itself more developed, more active: 'in proportion as a body is more capable than others of doing many things at once, or being acted on in many ways at once, so its mind is more capable than others of perceiving many at once', says the Scholium of proposition 12 of Ethics III.

It is the strength of the capacity to affect or to be affected — what Spinoza calls the 'capacity of doing things or of being acted on' — that makes up the cognitive strength of the mind: a highly sensitive body, highly capable of being affected and of affecting, is a body whose mind is capable of perceiving many things at once, and, by doing so, is also

---

4   See *Treatise on Emendation of the Intellect* (*TdIE*) 85; *CWS* I, p. 37: 'This is the same as what the ancients said, i.e., that true knowledge proceeds from cause to effect — except that so far as I know they never conceived the soul (as we do here) as acting according to certain laws, like a spiritual automaton'.

capable of rationally understanding the relationships between things (see the Scholium of Proposition 29 of Ethics II).

MATERIALIST EDUCATION AND THE AFFECTIVE SENSIBILITY OF THE BODY

Therefore, the challenge facing a materialist education — an education that, as we have seen, is education in knowledge rather than obedience — is to develop the affective sensibility of the body in order to increase the cognitive sensitivity of the mind, which means to increase its power to act in thought, that is, its power to understand. However, to do this it is necessary to change the body, to transform it even, in the sense that education gives the body another form, another higher nature. The originality of a Spinozist, materialist education lies in exactly this transformation.

In one of the last Scholiums of the *Ethics*, we read:

> In this life, then, we strive especially that the infant's body may change (as much as its nature allows and assists) into another, capable of a great many things and related to a mind very much conscious of itself, of God, and of things. We strive, that is, that whatever is related to its memory or imagination is of hardly any moment in relation to the intellect.[5]

As François Zourabichvili noted in his masterly work on childhood, the subject of the striving in question here is a 'we': *conamur*, we strive.[6] This is important because, as Spinoza explains several times, the *conatus* is a striving to persevere in one's being and not to change into another: it therefore requires the action of another — the 'we' in this case — so that the child's body is changed into another. But who is this 'we'? It is, first and foremost, the collective striving of educators of all kinds, parents, nurses, nannies, childcare workers, paediatricians, teachers, etc. but it can also be the striving of institutions, starting with schools, that contributes to the change in the child's body. It is also the striving of collective practices, care practices, sports education, physical activities, and bodily awareness, all of which contribute to

---

5   *Ethics* v, 39 Schol.; *CWS* I, p. 614.
6   François Zourabichvili, *Le Conservatisme paradoxal de Spinoza. Enfance et royauté* (Paris: PUF, 2002).

increasing the abilities of the child's body. This educational striving is essential — we strive to it '*apprime*', 'first', says the Scholium, and it is, therefore, a major social striving, and it is (perhaps even more so in Spinoza's time than ours) a matter of life and death. Since death is a threat to childhood, especially early childhood, we must help children to quickly overcome this stage of fragility or physiological weakness; we must help children to build another body, stronger, more resistant, more 'capable'.

At the same time, another important clarification is given in this Scholium: the social body strives to change the body of childhood, *quantum ejus natura patitur eique conducit*, or 'as much as its nature allows' (*patitur*: as much as it is acted on), and as much as it assists in it (*ei conducit*). This expression '*quantum ejus natura patitur eique conducit*' is decisive because it adroitly summarizes the terms in which the problem of a materialist education of childhood are played out — namely, the problem of the transformation of the child's sensitive body. This expression also includes a certain ambiguity, as it can be interpreted as a restriction that prevents us from viewing the change effected by education as a real transformation. In this interpretation, the education would change the body as much as it preserves its nature, or to put it another way, it would result in a change 'in' its nature and not 'of' its nature. This latter change is what Spinoza also refers to as a 'death'. However, with reference to the Scholium of proposition 39 of *Ethics* IV, we interpret this change not as a change that simply happens 'to' the body, but a change 'of' its very nature and therefore as a real transformation. Let us read the relevant Scholium:

> [...] But here it should be noted that I understand the body to die [mortem obire] when its parts are so disposed that they acquire [obtineant] a different proportion of motion and rest to one another. For I dare not deny that — even though the circulation of the blood is maintained [retenta], as well as the other [signs] on account of which the body is thought to be alive — the human body can nevertheless be changed into another nature entirely different from its own [in aliam naturam a sua prorsus diversam mutari]. For no reason compels me to maintain that the body does not die unless it is changed into a corpse [mutetur in cadaver].
>
> And, indeed, experience seems to urge a different conclusion. Sometimes a man undergoes such changes [tales patiatur

mutationes] that I should hardly have said he was the same man. I have heard stories, for example, of a Spanish poet who suffered an illness; though he recovered, he was left so oblivious to his past life that he did not believe the tales and tragedies he had written were his own. He could surely have been taken for a grown-up infant [pro infante adulto] if he had also forgotten his native language.

If it seems incredible [incredibile videtur], what shall we say of infants? A man of advanced years believes [credit] their nature to be so different from its own [a sua tam diversam] that he could not be persuaded that he was ever an infant, if he did not make this conjecture concerning himself from (NS: the example of) others. But rather than provide the superstitious with material for raising new questions, I prefer to leave this discussion unfinished.[7]

Beyond the rhetorical precautions given in this Scholium, Spinoza also puts forward a very interesting idea, which despite not being fully founded in reason is stated with sufficient clarity to be identified: namely, that death is not the same as becoming a corpse. Spinozism thus leaves room to think of other forms of death than mere organic death. To illustrate this idea of a non-organic death, Spinoza relies on two examples: firstly, the Spanish poet's amnesia, and secondly the development of the baby, as if the passage from *infantia* to *provecta aetas*, from infancy to adulthood, were a form of death.

THE TRANSFORMATION OF THE BODY

Spinoza certainly advances cautiously on this delicate subject and does not claim that amnesia and adulthood are equivalent to the final death. As so often occurs in Spinoza's discourse, experience is summoned to disturb a habitual conviction: in this example, he means to uproot the identification between death and becoming a corpse. The first experience concerns the amnesia of a certain Spanish poet, who has become forgetful of his own literary creations and is no longer able to recognize what should be most intimate to him or see himself in his works — here amnesia is treated as a certain type of transformation of the body, namely a body defined by its ability to remember. The

---

7   *Ethics* IV, 39 Schol.; CWS I, pp. 569–70.

second experience concerns becoming an adult and is called upon to reinforce this idea of a possible non-cadaveric transformation of the body. Of course, Spinoza does not state in an affirmative way that the baby's body, which has become an adult body, is a body that has met death (*mortem obire*), but he strongly suggests it, notably by using the expression '*naturam diversam*'. In the first half of the Scholium, death is defined as the transformation into a nature totally different from one's own (*a sua prorsus diversam*); it is then said, at the end of Scholium, that the man of advanced age believes the nature of the baby to be so different from his own (*a sua tam diversam*) that he needs the mediation of others in order to persuade himself that he was a baby.

It should be pointed out, however, that this is only a 'belief' (*credit*) and that the adult may be mistaken. The rebuttal could be that the man's nature is not so different from that of the baby and that the baby he was is not necessarily dead. But if we look at the structure of the argumentation of this part of the Scholium, we note that the case of the baby who has become an adult generalizes the case of the poet who has become an amnesiac: Spinoza is telling us that if we consider the rather exceptional case of the Spanish poet incredible (*incredibile*), then we ought to take the far less exceptional, and therefore much more credible, case of the baby — here '*credit*' is the counterpart of '*incredibile*', and shows us that the case of the baby has a stronger experiential value than that of the amnesiac poet. Here again, however, we are dealing with a problem of self-recognition: the man of advanced years finds it very difficult to recognize himself in a past which is, in a sense, his own, and because he is also forgetful of this past, he needs others to persuade him that he was once a baby. The man of advanced age is neither in error nor in rational certainty when he 'believes' the nature of babies very different from his own, nor is he in error or certainty when he allows himself to be persuaded by others that he was once a baby. On the one hand, he can see that there is a form of continuity from baby to adult (in others, and therefore in himself), and that is why it is not irrational for him to form the conjecture that he was once a baby — but it is only a conjecture (*de se conjecturam faceret*). On the other hand, he has great difficulty in believing in this continuity of nature, and this difficulty is the indication that he feels that he is no longer the same, that he has experienced an upheaval and that something of him has died. It may even be the case — but the text does not make it possible to decide this — that what he feels within himself (the absence of community with the baby) may have more truth than what he convinces himself of via others (the continuity between the baby and himself).

This example shows the ways in which Spinoza provides a definition of death that goes beyond the simple framework of becoming a corpse. He suggests that life cannot be reduced to organic life alone or to the mere preservation of physiological functions. We can call this the life of the body, which is not strictly organic, affective life, but also includes how life is constituted by the connection of images, defined by the remembrance in and by the body, and by the body's ability to affect and be affected. The life of the organic body is certainly necessary for the development of its affective life; moreover, there is no affective life that is not inscribed in a life of organs, tissues, skin, and physiological functions; however, if this life of the affective body is not reducible to the life of the organic body, it is because, according to this Scholium, the organic body can conserve itself while, at the same time, the affective or sensitive body can be transformed. To put it another way: the organic body can live while the affective body can die and become another. This seems to be the case with the example of the baby, which lives on as an organic body but 'dies' when it becomes another affective body. It is important to insist on this becoming other of the affective body because, as long as the organic body endures, the death of the affective body is not a simple disappearance but rather the advent of a new life of the affective body.

If the transformation is indeed what necessarily happens to the body of childhood (infantile amnesia, which concerns the first three or four years, and which occurs around the age of seven or eight, is one of the signs of it), then a materialist education must take note of this transformation, and accompany it as well as possible: it must aim at making the transformation take place in such a way that the infant's body, or more generally speaking the child's body, becomes a body with very great sensory and sensitive aptitudes that are connected to a very intelligent and consciously aware mind.[8] If one wanted to say

---

8   See *Ethics* v, 39 Schol.; *CWS* I, p. 614: 'And really, he who, like an infant or a child, has a body capable of very few things, and very heavily dependent on external causes,

things in a provocative way, one could say that materialist education
aims at a form of death for the child related to memory and affect and
not biology. This form of death induced by the materialist education
of the child's body is a way of replacing it with another, stronger body.

However, it should be pointed out here that the aim is to transfer
the body of childhood from its first nature to another nature that is suitable for it, one that is really *different* from the first but not *contrary* to it.
The opposite transformation of the body into a different *and contrary*
nature would be a brutal cadaveric transformation, for example the one
produced by suicide. In such a case, as Spinoza points out, the idea of
the new nature is not reproduced in the mind, and the transformation
amounts to a pure destruction of the one who is transformed.[9] The
whole point of the transformation that accompanies education is to
give birth to a new nature which can be affirmed and desired by the
one who is educated. This new nature preserves traces of the previous
nature as not all memory or all feeling is abolished by it;[10] it necessarily
has properties in common with the previous nature, and there is therefore a degree of continuity, which is why the child can contribute to
this transformation ('as much as its nature allows and assists'). But he
can do so only under the educational impulse, only through collective
striving, since one thing, by itself, strives to persevere in its being, and
not to transform itself into another.

The expression 'as much as its nature allows and assists' indicates
both the dimension of passivity and the dimension of activity that are
specific to the child in changing their body. The nature of the child's
body is acted on through such a change, in the sense that effects will
be produced in its corporeal nature that are only partially explicable

---

has a mind which considered solely in itself is conscious of almost nothing of itself, or
of God, or of things. On the other hand, he who has a body capable of a great many
things, has a mind which considered only in itself is very much conscious of itself, and
of God, and of things'.

9   See *Ethics* IV, 20 Schol.; *CWS* I, p. 557: 'Someone may kill himself [...] because hidden
external causes so dispose his imagination, and so affect his body, that it takes on
another nature, contrary to the former [*aliam naturam priori contrariam*], a nature of
which there cannot be an idea in the mind (by IIIP10). But that a man should, from
the necessity of his own nature, strive not to exist, or to be changed into another form,
is as impossible as that something should come from nothing'.

10   See *Ethics* III, Post. 2; *CWS* I, p. 493: 'The human body can undergo many changes
[*multas pati potest mutationes*], and nevertheless retain impressions, *or* traces, of the
objects (on this see II Post. 5), and consequently, the same images of things'.

through it, for although they can indeed be explained in large part by the desires of the educators, by the (more or less conscious) striving of the social body which determines (at least in part) the change in the child's body, Spinoza does not understand the child's body as a passive, receptive object. He also evokes its activity, or rather, to be more rigorous, something like its activity (because '*ei conducit*' is not '*ad eum conducit*', a syntactic form that would more completely suggest the idea of full participation of the body in this transformation). We see that the child's body does not only undergo this fundamental change, but rather, if the education is successful in terms of not being pure compulsion effecting obedience, then the body in question directly participates in its own transformation. With the expression 'as much as its nature allows and assists' Spinoza suggests that the child stands somehow in-between, that is, between passivity and activity, between a joyful passivity that is not refractory to this useful change, and an inchoate activity that participates in its own transformation, however incompletely. This means that in the 'we' of the *conamur*, in the collective nature of the educational striving, we can also hear the very striving of the child as they gradually become their own educator.

FROM MORAL EDUCATION TO ETHICAL EDUCATION

Rather than being called 'education', it seems to me that materialist education should be characterized as 're-education' or 'counter-education'. This is because usually education is geared towards obedience, and perhaps it is not even possible to escape this moral education when we are dealing with a relationship between beings who are dominated by the imagination — certainly this is true of children, but it can also be said for most adults. For their own sake, should children not be taught to obey the rules set by parents?[11] This moral or moralistic education is even useful, since it teaches individuals to conform to the

---

11   See *TTP* xvi, 35; *CWS* ii, p. 289:'even though children are bound to obey all the commands of their parents, they are still not slaves. For their parents' commands are primarily concerned with the advantage of the children. We recognize a great difference, then, between a slave, a son, and a subject. We define these as follows: a *slave* is someone who is bound to obey the commands of a master, which are concerned only with the advantage of the person issuing the command; a *son* is someone who does what is advantageous for himself, in accordance with a parent's command; and a *subject*,

values of the group to which they belong, and teaches them the principle that recognition from the group is offered to those who recognize
the group. It thus teaches them a form of autonomy which consists of
self-restraint and emotional self-control: in short, ordinary education
constitutes the child as a moral subject who is responsible for his or
her actions; it produces in him or her an '*ingenium*' (a temperament)
of self-discipline so that, thanks to this emotional and reflexive interiority, 'it works on its own'. In this respect, we can say of moral
education what Michel Foucault says of disciplinary power, the objective of which is not a discontinuous grasp on individuals but a perpetual
hold over them, which means that 'one is perpetually in the situation
of being watched' — and we could add, in the case of moral education,
'watched by oneself'. Thus, moral education, like disciplinary power,
'looks to the future, to the moment when it will work on its own and
when surveillance may no longer be anything more than virtual, when
discipline, therefore, will have become a habit'.[12]

Spinozist materialist education consists of the work of self-
transformation, that is, the transformation of a self that is always first
educated for the purposes of obedience: such education is 'counter-
education' or 're-education' in the sense of medical re-education,
which involves recovering a lost, damaged, or calcified capacity,
regaining flexibility, awakening frozen organs, reviving tetanized
muscles, undoing (in short) mechanisms which have become
hardened in order to produce connections that increase the power of
acting. To unbind and to bind again, forming new connection, disturbs
what is fixed or frozen and thus produces a liberating disconnection:
such is the task of a materialist education that can be deduced from
certain passages of the *Ethics* and which makes it possible to lay the
foundations of an education understood as an ethics rather than a
moral one.

---

finally, is someone who does what is advantageous for the collective body — and hence,
also for himself — in accordance with the command of the supreme "power".

12   Michel Foucault, *Psychiatric Power: Lectures at the Collège de France 1973-1974*, trans.
by Graham Burchell (London: Palgrave Macmillan, 2006), p. 47. In the original, '[le
pouvoir disciplinaire] regarde vers l'avenir, vers le moment où ça marchera tout seul
et où la surveillance pourra ne plus être que virtuelle, où la discipline, par conséquent,
sera devenue habitude' (Michel Foucault, *Le Pouvoir psychiatrique. Cours au Collège de
France. 1973-1974* (Paris: Gallimard Seuil, 2003), p. 49).

The first text to be considered from the *Ethics* is one of the few where education is explicitly mentioned.

> [...] it is no wonder Sadness follows absolutely all those acts which from custom are called wrong, and Joy, those which are called right [omnes omnino actus, qui ex consuetudine pravi vocantur, sequatur tristitia, et illos, qui recti dicuntur, lætitia]. For from what has been said above we easily understand that this depends chiefly on education [nam hoc ab educatione potissimum pendere]. Parents — by blaming the former acts, and often scolding their children on account of them, and on the other hand, by recommending and praising the latter acts — have brought it about that emotions of Sadness were joined to the one kind of act, and those of Joy to the other [parentes nimirum, illos exprobanbo, liberosque propter eosdem sæpe objurgando, hos contra suadendo, et laudando, effecerunt, ut tristitiæ commotiones illis, lætitiæ vero his jungerentur].
>
> Experience itself confirms this. For not everyone has the same custom and Religion. On the contrary, what among some is holy, among others is unholy; and what among some is honourable, among others is dishonourable. Hence, according as each one has been educated, so the either repents of a deed or exults at being esteemed for it.[13]

What is ordinary education? It is about valuing some actions and devaluing others. For educators, first and foremost parents, it is a question of associating affects with certain acts (performed by children) so that these acts are perceived — or better said, felt — as positive or negative. Education, in terms of cognitive development and the direction of conduct, is above all an undertaking that produces cognitive-affective connections in the child in order to solicit or prevent certain behaviours: it consists in combining (*jungere*) the representation of certain acts with emotions (*commotions*) of joy or sadness.

How is this junction between representations and emotions achieved? First, through an operation of nomination (*vocantur, dicuntur*) that depends on customs (*ex consuetudine*): based on traditional ways of speaking about the group to which they belong, parents interpret certain acts and use terms charged with positive or negative affects ('wrong', 'right', 'good/bad', 'kind/bad'). At the same

---

13   *Ethics* III, DA xxvII Exp.; *CWS*, I, p. 537.

time, parents repeatedly formulate reproaches or encouragement by blaming, reproving, and reprimanding (*exprobrando, objurgando*), or congratulating, exhorting, and praising (*suadendo, laudando*). In short, it is a question of the parent attaching (*sequatur*) an emotion to the representation of the act the child has committed, which in turn either increases or diminishes the child's power to act. On the basis of this production of an association between representation and emotion more complex affects are then formed, which can be sorted into the two types of love or hatred (love being a 'joy accompanied by the idea of an external cause' and hate a 'sadness accompanied by the idea of an external cause').[14]

The educational operation therefore shows that the very act performed by the child, in itself, can be perfectly 'innocent': it only becomes a moral act through the habit of appointment, and of valuation or devaluation, which is performed by the parents.

Through this activity of cognitive-emotional conjunction, ordinary education — which we would gladly call 'moral education' — consists in producing in the child aspirations towards or repudiations of certain acts, and not only concerning behaviours but also thoughts or feelings. But whether or not these acts have an external expression, or remain within the interiority of the child, the essential thing is that they do not refer to 'external causes' but to 'internal causes' — that is, to the 'interiority' of the child. This psychological interiority is even constituted by the moralistic education of the child, which produces in him what we can call 'self-love' or 'self-loathing', and which Spinoza more readily calls 'self-esteem' or 'repentance', or 'love of esteem' and 'shame', these two affects being the socialized forms of satisfaction and repentance.[15] All education contributes to the activation of this law in the child:

> If someone has done something which he imagines affects others with Joy, he will be affected with Joy accompanied by the idea of himself as cause, or he will regard himself with Joy. If, on the other hand, he has done something which he imagines affects others with Sadness, he will regard himself with Sadness.[16]

---

14   See *Ethics* iii, DA vi and vii; *CWS* i, p. 533.
15   See *Ethics* iii, 30 Schol.; *CWS* i, pp. 511–12, and iv, 52 Schol.; *CWS* i, p. 523.
16   *Ethics* iii, 30; *CWS* i, p. 510.

Education therefore produces in the child a self-awareness which is above all a moral awareness: by producing in the child affects of joy and sadness 'which are accompanied by the idea of an internal thing as cause',[17] ordinary education makes for the child a cause, a moral cause of affects that reward or sanction which is produced through the judgment of others and the good or evil that has been done. The moral educator's challenge is to produce cognitive-emotional sequences in order for the child to form judgements about themself, to rejoice or to feel sad about themself: the child learns to make value judgments not first of all about things or other people but about themself and their own actions — whether of the body, of language, thought, or of desire. In order to behave well, they learn a kind of reflexivity which is first of all an emotional reflexivity: they learn to glorify themself or to repent. They are trained to train themselves, since there is no better government of the other than a government of the affects by which the other governs themselves

Such an education gives rise to an indefinite multiplicity of concrete educational practices, customary forms of moral education, which are often based on religion. However, I would like to distinguish an education that the *Theological-Political Treatise* characterizes as 'good'[18] and that from the *Ethics* we could qualify, precisely, as 'ethical' from these other forms of moral, social, and religious education. Its most significant quality is that it does not submit to a power as soon as it becomes tyrannical.[19] Therefore, good education is characterized by a political virtue, namely resistance to abuse of power; and this resistance itself is characterized by two remarkable properties: its form (speaking out) and its radicality (resistance to the peril of one's life). According to Chapter xx of the *Theological-Political Treatise*, these two characteristics have emotional prerequisites: in a negative way, they imply not being carried away by certain affects, those that lead to submission (greed or sycophancy), but also and especially the fear of death; and, in a positive way, possessing and cultivating a 'moral force' and a love of freedom, above all the 'freedom to speak'.

---

17   See *Ethics* III, DA xxiv Exp.; *CWS* I, p. 536.

18   *TTP* vii [90]; *CWS* ii, p. 206, and xx [28]; *CWS* ii, p. 349: 'good education [*bona educatio*]'.

19   See *TTP* xx (the end).

However, the production of such affects, which run counter to the affects of subjection, requires the defeat of ordinary loves and hatreds and the development of new sequences of affections — those which proposition 10 of *Ethics* v tells us are made 'according to an order for the intellect'. Good education is above all an education in reason: an education in the affected reason, which is at the same time an education in rational affectivity.

Who is such an education for? For children, undoubtedly, since a good education doubles ordinary education and develops in the child (alongside moral affectivity and self-discipline) a desire for rationality and freedom: if such an education does not produce rationality in them, it at least can cultivate the beginnings of adequate thought, which is above all thought aimed at continuous reform. This makes possible, if only at a later time, a re-education of passionate self-satisfaction. This good, rational education is also aimed at adults if they are eager for a new, firmer, and more serene existence. For Spinoza places this task of re-education is very high on the agenda.[20]

While Spinoza did not write the 'science of education' mentioned in the prologue to the *Treatise on the Emendation of the Intellect*, he at least showed in the *Ethics* a real concern for education, so much so that one might wonder whether this treatise on the science of education would not have ended up resembling the *Ethics* or have been somehow a derivative of it. And in more general terms, we should understand Spinoza's ethics as a practical philosophy that consists of a materialist education — of children and of oneself — aimed at transforming the affective sensibility of body and mind.

---

20   See *Ethics* IV, App. IX; *CSW* I, 589: 'because, among singular things, we know nothing more excellent than a man who is guided by reason, we can show best how much our skill and understanding are worth by educating men so that at last they live according to the command of their own reason'.

III. CRITICAL MATERIALITIES IN FEMINISM AND NEW MATERIALISM

Introduction to Part III
ALISON SPERLING

The contributions of this part elucidate the complicated relationship between feminism and New Materialism. The contributors in what follows both highlight the affinities between feminism and New Materialism as well as challenge the multiple intellectual histories out of which 'feminist New Materialism' can be said to have emerged. They also question the ways in which political thought has operated (or has not done so) in various strands of New Materialism.

Cornelia Möser's essay opens the third part of this volume and provides a helpful overview of the ways in which New Materialism has been received and developed, specifically in the French context. She situates New Materialism as originating in STS and in linguistic and structuralist philosophy, and suggests that Stacy Alaimo and Susan Hekman's collection *Material Feminisms* from 2008 might serve as a starting point, as it is certainly a touchstone text, across the essays in the field. Möser describes New Materialism as an intellectual project that interrogates the relation between the linguistic and the material and which addresses things and thing-ness, the nonhuman, the boundaries between subject and object, and questions of agency beyond the human and beyond human perception: a kind of posthumanist ontology. According to Möser (citing Jana Tschurenev), an early critique of New Materialism lies in the fact that much of the scholarship did not pay attention to social structures and institutions. Importantly for Möser,

New Materialism is not substantially connected to socialist feminist traditions, French materialist feminism, or to Marxist feminism. This critique of the lack of certain feminist and political traditions in the various collections Möser analyses is echoed in other essays in the part.

Chiara Bottici's contribution reclaims intersectional feminism through anarchist thought; it re-imagines, via anarchic feminism, political embodiment in the world. Bottici argues that anarchist feminism has not received its due as a foremother of intersectional and inclusive politics, which are as important as ever in the contemporary moment, in part because anarchist thought is not often embraced in academia or in public debates (largely, according to Bottici, because it has been wrongly and universally associated with violent tactics). Anarchafeminism has long argued that the liberation of women must include all women, particularly those whose resistance does not accord to the same subjection of power present in electoral politics or in capitalist, or corporate power. If women do not want to be ruled by men, it does not follow that they want to be ruled by women: in other words, Anarchafeminism does not aim to seize or claim state power, but to dissolve that power altogether. The paper develops an idea of the transindividual (following Spinoza) as an anarchist feminist process of becoming as opposed to individuation-as-event or as becoming-singular. Bottici argues that all bodies are processes, a longstanding notion of Anarchafeminism that has been wrongfully ignored in genealogies of New Materialism.

The third chapter in this part by **Émilie Filion-Donato** has the lofty goal of intervening into one of the most complicated challenges of 'standpoint theory' or situated knowledges — that is, in Filion-Donato's words, 'if everything we do, down to how we perceive, has an impact on the things we measure or want to talk about, how can we ever be sure we are getting the "right" measurements? How can we act collectively without this shared account of the world?'.[1] Filion-Donato responds to this set of questions by mobilizing Evelyn Fox Keller's use of the 'psychodynamism of individuation', which allows for a dynamic autonomy or dynamic objectivity that is crucial for her project because it demands attention for *shared* emotions and experi-

---

1   Filion-Donato, in this volume, p. 242.

ences. Through this allocentric perception, the individual oscillates between self and other, or between individuation and a connectivity with the world. Filion-Donato's exploration of these issues is complexly wedged amongst key figures of the discipline: following Fox Keller, then Ernest Schachtel, and decidedly against Helen Longino's critique of Keller, Filion-Donato attempts to confront the challenge towards New Materialism which was raised in response to Karen Barad's diffractive method. What Filion-Donato termed 'killing the subject' in the conference that inspired this collective volume, and 'decentering of the subject' in her contribution to the volume, is not, for Keller or, I think, for Filion-Donato, the same as imagining, even if momentarily, an erasure of the frontiers between subject and object. In other words, Keller only dissolves the subject temporarily, and importantly (as well as somewhat counter-intuitively), she does so through an expansion of the subject to include the object; in short, she creates a relational ontology.

We stay with Karen Barad's work in **Christoph Holzhey**'s contribution to the section. Holzhey poses crucial challenges to Barad while also introducing the nuances that may be required to think physics and ontology together at dramatically different scales. Holzhey approaches the question of ontology by denying the importance of physics for ontological questions at human scales, a kind of 'cut between politics and ontology'[2] that partly follows from foundational work in gender studies, which distinguished between biological sex and the social construction of gender. He details his suspicion of the allure of the performativity of matter, especially at the scale of particle physics because recent philosophies of physics have claimed matter as fundamentally creative and agential. Holzhey attempts to 'deactivate the performative normativity of ontology by re-doubling reduction', that is, if the atomic level is only demonstrable or 'pragmatic' at higher scales, 'then the same properties can emerge in the same pragmatic sense also from a radically different ontology of continuous matter'.[3] Physics does not offer a foundational understanding of matter but rather the tools which we can use to think the performative — and thus the political — power

---

2   Holzhey, in this volume, p. 256.

3   Ibid, p. 265.

of an ontology of matter that is formulated as what Holzhey calls an 'indeterminacy of ontology'.

Together these four essays provide a thorough sense of some of the key contributions of feminist New Materialism, while also boldly challenging certain assumptions that have undergirded its development. These essays are important to our continued understanding of the relation between feminism and New Materialism as they provide a critical eye toward what has thus far been over-determined, presumed, or omitted from what became a quickly accepted and employed mode of feminist thought operating against the linguistic turn that preceded it. These essays convincingly demonstrate that debates about what New Materialisms are and what they can do are still very much unsettled, and still warrant sustained and critical attention.

Materialism, Matter, Matrix, and Mater
Contesting Notions in Feminist and Gender Studies
CORNELIA MÖSER

INTRODUCTION

Under the label of new materialism (NM), a number of scholars, who mostly come from the United States — specifically, from the University of Chicago — as well as from several Northern and Central European countries, have published and defended a scientific approach that they characterize as new and materialist. This approach is among other fields mostly rooted in science and technology studies (STS) and in philosophy. It grapples with the idea of the existence and potential agency of a material world beyond human perception. This approach reached its peak in the early 2010s and then gradually lost influence, although it should be said that it was a rather marginal phenomenon from the start. Surprisingly, in France, where the strongest scientific branch of feminism is a materialist one, NM is almost unknown. Considering the numerous French references of NM, this absence and non-translation recalls the feminist gender debates in France and Germany. Whereas Judith Butler's *Gender Trouble* was translated into German one year after the publication of the original, it took fifteen years before it was translated into French.[1] Although NM

---

1   Judith Butler, *Gender Trouble: Feminism and the Subversion of Identity* (New York: Routledge, 1990); Judith Butler, *Das Unbehagen der Geschlechter* (Frankfurt a.M.:

claims to be an alternative to post-structuralism, its reception (or lack thereof) in France shows that it cannot be understood as the returning spectre of Marxism or of materialist feminism.

WHAT'S NEW IN NEW MATERIALISM?

A series of publications, books, articles, and conferences introduced and discussed NM around 2008. In a recent publication in France, I presented NM to a French speaking audience and compared it to materialist feminism in France.[2] The books I analysed for that purpose showed that nuances in notions of materialism exist theoretically, politically, and in disciplinary projects, and each of these aspects needs to be considered in order to gain an understanding of the non-reception of NM in France. The first collection I analysed, *Material Feminisms,* which was edited by Susan Hekman and Stacy Alaimo and published in 2008,[3] focuses on ecofeminism and calls for a transvaluation of nature. Criticizing postmodern feminism for having gone too far in rejecting nature in its attempt to also reject biological explanations of male domination, the editors of this volume argued that (feminist) research should concentrate on the natural world and the human body. In their view, postmodernism wrongfully privileged culture over nature, and so they argued for the deconstruction of the opposition between nature and culture and for investigation into what they call, for example, transcorporeality. That term signifies the connection of bodies with each another and with other creatures, types of matter, and landscapes.[4] In her review of the book, the materialist, feminist historian Jana Tschurenev observed a discrepancy between the book's project and the actual research represented in the collection.

Suhrkamp, 1991); Judith Butler, *Trouble dans le genre. Pour un féminisme de la subversion* (Paris: La Découverte, 2005); Cornelia Möser, *Féminismes en traductions. Théories voyageuses et traductions culturelles* (Paris: Éditions des archives contemporaines, 2013).

2   Cornelia Möser, 'Néo-Matérialisme. Un nouveau courant féministe?', in *Matérialismes, cultures et communication,* ed. by Maxime Cervulle, Nelly Quemener, and Florian Vörös (Paris: Presses des Mines, 2016), pp. 227–44.

3   *Material Feminisms,* ed. by Stacy Alaimo and Susan J. Hekman (Bloomington: Indiana University Press, 2008).

4   Stacy Alaimo, *Bodily Natures: Science, Environment, and the Material Self* (Bloomington: Indiana University Press, 2010).

Most of the research, she noted, came from literature studies and not from a greater variety of disciplines. As a result, she thought that the contributions failed to consider social structures, the state, and other social and political institutions, as well as social movements.[5]

The second collective volume I analysed was edited by Diana Coole and Samantha Frost in 2010 under the title *New Materialisms* and shared some concerns with the ethics of science and ecofeminist perspectives.[6] However, the collection reduced feminist perspectives to just one approach among many others. The notion of materialism present in this volume was not linked to historical materialism and instead expressed a strong belief in the ethics of science and, most of all, in the impact the natural sciences should have on social and material change. The authors did not analyse science as a sociopolitical formation, and instead of questioning the division of research into the natural sciences and the humanities, they tried to apply the knowledge of the natural sciences to the humanities. They focused on the agency of matter and affirmed a 'new posthumanist ontology' that should break with neo-Marxist and critical theory. The latter tradition is, in their view, too negative and critical, and so for their more positive project they turned to the writings of Baruch Spinoza, Gilles Deleuze, and Michel Foucault.

The third collection I analysed was edited by Iris van der Tuin and Rick Dolphijn and published in 2012 under the title *New Materialism*.[7] The use of the singular noun as opposed to the plural of *New Materialisms* used in the previous collection marks this project as a conceptual and philosophical one. It gathered texts and interviews with the professed aim of inquiring into the ideal and material constitution of the world. What the authors aimed to understand was the reciprocal production of what is in the world and the things we know about the things in the world. Their epistemological project was presented as a philosophy of difference, which might recall postmod-

---

5   Jana Tschurenev, 'Review of "Material Feminisms" by Susan Hekman and Stacy Alaimo', *Das Argument*, 52.287 (2010), pp. 414–16.

6   *New Materialisms: Ontology, Agency, and Politics*, ed. by Diana Coole and Samantha Frost (Durham, NC: Duke University Press, 2010).

7   Rick Dolphijn and Iris van der Tuin, *New Materialism: Interviews & Cartographies* (Ann Arbor, MI: Open Humanities Press, 2012) <https://doi.org/10.3998/ohp.11515701.0001.001>.

ernism. However, instead of focusing on the construction of difference on a symbolic level, they, too, focused on the agency of matter.

Contrary to the Frost/Coole collection, van der Tuin and Dolphijn very much emphasize their inscription in a feminist project of knowledge, but their feminism concentrates on the works of Rosi Braidotti, Elizabeth Grosz, Luce Irigaray, and Simone de Beauvoir. They, too, do not discuss socialist, materialist, or Marxist feminism. Their 'close reading' of Beauvoir presents her as a French feminist and inscribes Beauvoir into their own project of the philosophy of difference. In doing so, they radically erase Beauvoir's own claim to existentialist philosophy as well as, ironically, her strong opposition to the philosophies of difference in French feminism in the late 1970s and early 1980s.[8] Their motivation for this specific reading lies in Beauvoir's notion of the flesh, which, according to the authors, allows for an ontogenesis which serves as an alternative to the opposition of two competing views on gender: naturalism and constructivism. While in naturalism sex would determine gender, in constructivism it is the other way around: gender would determine sex. Dissatisfied with both, the NM of van der Tuin and Dolphijn refutes feminist oppositions to sexual difference and calls for affirming sexual difference and showing sexual differing. Feminism understood in terms of differing would push sexual differences to the extreme and help transcend the nature/culture binary by opting for a monism. Furthermore, this monism is filled with the hopes of transcending anthropocentrism, which, according to the authors, limits human perception. It remains unclear, though, how exactly they wish to access the non-human world and its agency without relying on their own human point of view.

In spite of their more or less close relationships to feminist science, and in spite of their differing perspectives (STS and epistemological), all of these projects have several points in common:

– their attempt to go beyond postmodernism, which is sometimes almost an attack on postmodernist approaches.

---

8   Simone de Beauvoir was one of the founders of the journal *Questions Féministes*, later *Nouvelles Questions Féministes*, which was the declared counter-part to the Antoinette Fouque style of feminism in the group *Psychanalyse et Politique*.

- their understanding of materialism as the study of the material world, that is, of the relationship between words and things.

- their interest in finding out more about the agency of matter that lies beyond human perception.

- their disregard of earlier feminist engagements with materialism, such as socialist, materialist, or Marxist feminism.

This quite schematic presentation nonetheless gives us some elements that are helpful in understanding why there has been no exchange between French materialist feminism and NM(s). If we look back at the history of feminist theory, at least in France, Germany, and the US, which are the contexts I am most familiar with, we need to clarify a number of terms and explain their historical meaning in order to grasp feminist engagements with materialism in the past.

Most of the first attempts to theorize women's oppression in the 1970s started from a historical materialist background and borrowed from Marxist vocabulary and concepts. Among these, one finds Marxist feminism, socialist feminism, materialist feminism, and radical feminism. Marxist feminism is interested in the gendered patterns of capitalism but views gender oppression and capitalism as one social system. In other words, according to Marxist feminism there cannot be any women's emancipation within capitalism. In order to liberate themselves, women not only have to get rid of the patriarchy but capitalism as well. Socialist feminists like Silvia Federici, Josette Trat, or Frigga Haug[9] also view patriarchy and capitalism as interwoven, but through their focus on how the accumulation process relies on reproductive work, they have also shown capitalisms' dependency on patriarchy. Still, for the socialist feminists as well, there can be no partial liberation because both systems are linked.

In her introduction to feminist theory, Linda Nicholson proposes to differentiate between one-system and two-system models. Marxist

---

9   Silvia Federici, *Revolution at Point Zero: Housework, Reproduction, and Feminist Struggle* (Oakland, CA: PM Press, 2012); Josette Trat, *Les Cahiers du féminisme (1977–1988): Vingt ans dans le tourbillon du féminisme et de la lutte des classes* (Paris: Syllepse, 2011); Frigga Haug and Kornelia Hauser, 'Marxistische Theorien und feministischer Standpunkt', in *Traditionen Brüche. Entwicklungen feministischer Theorie*, ed. by Gudrun-Axeli Knapp and Angelika Wetterer (Freiburg: Kore, 1992), pp. 115–49.

and socialist feminisms are examples of one-system models.[10] Radical feminism and materialist feminism, on the contrary, are two-system models, because they consider that there can be important change in the patriarchal order without overcoming capitalism. It is not so much that they do not want to overcome capitalism, but rather that they refuse to wait on the revolution for significant change to happen in women's lives. Not only have these two-system models criticized persistent male domination in socialist countries, which relativizes the promise that the patriarchy would disappear with the end of capitalism, but they also claim that ending the oppression of women is an aim in itself; it does not need to be ennobled by inscribing it into the struggle against capitalism.

Radical feminism is also clearly inspired by the US Civil Rights Movement, from which it borrowed both terminology (sexism developed as an analogy to racism) and praxis (consciousness-raising groups). Materialist feminism in France is closer to the two-system model of radical feminism than it is to socialist or Marxist feminism. Sociologist Christine Delphy, a key figure of materialist feminism in France, has been strongly criticized for her concept of sex classes[11] that comes from Friedrich Engels[12] and was taken up by Virginia Woolf,[13] Simone de Beauvoir,[14] and, later, by Kate Millett,[15] Ti-Grace Atkinson,[16] Shulamith Firestone,[17] and the Radicalesbians. Engels conceived of women as the proletariat and men as the bourgeois, which proved to be an inspiring formula for early feminist theory. Delphy's and other materialist feminist's notion of materialism insists on the material grounds and effects of women's oppression. They do so in

---

10   *The Second Wave: A Reader in Feminist Theory*, ed. by Linda Nicholson (New York: Routledge, 1997).

11   *Geschlechterverhältnisse und Frauenpolitik*, ed. by Projekt sozialistischer Feminismus (Berlin: Argument, 1984).

12   Friedrich Engels, *Der Ursprung der Familie, des Privateigentums und des Staats: im Anschluß an Lewis H. Morgans Forschungen* (Zürich: Hottingen, 1884).

13   Virginia Woolf, *Three Guineas* (London: Hogarth Press, 1938).

14   Simone de Beauvoir, *Le Deuxième Sexe* (Paris: Gallimard, 1949).

15   Kate Millett, *Sexual Politics* (New York: Doubleday, 1970).

16   Ti Grace Atkinson, *Amazon Odyssey: The First Collection of Writings by the Political Pioneer of the Women's Movement Ti-Grace Atkinson* (New York: Links Books, 1974).

17   Shulamith Firestone, *The Dialectic of Sex: The Case for Feminist Revolution* (New York: Morrow, 1970).

order to oppose feminist approaches that conceive of women's oppression as belonging to only the symbolic order or as only a question of behaviour and traditional roles. For such thinkers it was crucial to show the economic exploitation of women by men.

Socialist feminists like Mary McIntosh and Frigga Haug have pointed out the limits of the sex class concept already in the early 1980s. Elsewhere I argued that the notion of sex classes replaces social classes and that, therefore, materialist feminists see no difference between a working woman and a bourgeois woman. Yet for Delphy, women are always defined by their male partners: women do not belong to social classes, they form a class of their own. For Delphy, bourgeois women are mere luxury prostitutes that stand and fall at the will of their husbands and rarely own anything themselves.[18] Maira Abreu has shown that materialist feminists like Delphy and other authors from the *Questions féministes* journal collective actually called themselves radical feminists up to the late 1970s.[19] This re-labelling has caused a deal of confusion today as some now wrongfully suspect there is a proximity between materialist feminism and socialist or Marxist feminism. While it is true that materialist feminism is interested in exploitation and the material ground of women's oppression, it is also true that this type of feminism marks a point of rupture with the socialist and Marxist left in France, as — contrary to the former group's position —socialist and Marxist feminists have always remained close to an anticapitalistic politics. In like manner, NM creates some confusion because it resembles neither of the two models, as it is neither a one- nor a two-system model. It does not resemble radical nor socialist feminism. In order to understand what is new in NM, we need to take a closer look at their notion of materialism.

---

18   Christine Delphy, 'Nos amis et nous. Les Fondements cachés de quelques discours pseudo-féministes', *Questions féministes*, 1 (1977), pp. 20–49 (p. 41). She is not the only one to observe that heterosexual women's status often depends on their husband's status. Recent sociological studies show that for bourgeois women, this is still very often the case, cf. Le Collectif Onze, *Au tribunal des couples: Enquête sur des affaires familiales* (Paris: Odile Jacob, 2013), p. 312.

19   Maira Abreu, 'De quelle histoire le "féminisme matérialiste" (français) est-il le nom?', in *Matérialismes féministes*, ed. by Maxime Cervulle and Isabelle Clair (= *Comment s'en sortir?*, 4 (2017)), pp. 55–79.

NOTIONS, THEIR MEANINGS, AND THEIR MATERIALITY

The political project of historical Marxism was compelling for many feminists. The materialist, feminist translation of the historical Marxist project was to name the exploitation of women by men and criticize the ideology of bourgeois love that made women consent to their exploitation. Yet, Marxism had its own analysis of women's oppression[20] that converged with feminism in the critique of the bourgeois family. The Frankfurt school took up Wilhelm Reich's Freudian-Marxism and produced a number of theories on women's oppression (Leo Löwenthal on Henrik Ibsen, Max Horkheimer on motherhood, Herbert Marcuse and Erich Fromm on sexuality, and even Theodor Adorno was tempted by an analysis of women as merchandise).[21] While part of feminist research in Germany took up these works and tried to use their less sexist parts for their own theories,[22] large parts of radical feminism in the 1970s struggled to break with the Freudian-Marxist framework, which they found barely sufficient to explain women's oppression, and ended up forming new alliances with post-structuralism. This story has been told by Cornelia Klinger in terms of a 'marriage',[23] but ob-

---

20   August Bebel, *Die Frau und der Sozialismus* (Zürich: Hottingen, 1879); Wilhelm Reich, *Die Sexualität im Kulturkampf* (Copenhagen: Sexpol, 1936).

21   Leo Löwenthal, 'Das Individuum in der individualistischen Gesellschaft. Bemerkungen über Ibsen', *Zeitschrift für Sozialforschung*, 5.3 (1936), pp. 321–63; Eva-Maria Ziege, 'The Fetish-Character of "Woman": On a Letter from Theodor W. Adorno to Erich Fromm Written in 1937', *Logos*, 2.4 (2003) <http://www.logosjournal. com/issue2.4.pdf>; Herbert Marcuse, *Eros and Civilization: A Philosophical Inquiry into Freud* (Boston: Beacon Press, 1955); and Max Horkheimer, 'Egoismus und Freiheitsbewegung: Zur Anthropologie des bürgerlichen Zeitalters', *Zeitschrift für Sozialforschung*, 5.2 (1936), pp. 161–234.

22   See, for example, Ursula Beer, *Klasse. Geschlecht. Feministische Gesellschaftsanalyse und Wissenschaftskritik* (Bielefeld: AJZ Verlag, 1987); or Regina Becker-Schmidt, 'Die doppelte Vergesellschaftung — die doppelte Unterdrückung: Besonderheiten der Frauenforschung in den Sozialwissenschaften', in *Die andere Hälfte der Gesellschaft. Österreichischer Soziologentag 1985. Soziologische Befunde zu geschlechtsspezifischen Formen der Lebensbewältigung*, ed. by Lilo Unterkirchner and Ina Wagner (Vienna: ÖGB Verlag, 1987), pp. 10–25. Much later there was a similar attempt by feminists in France: *Adorno critique de la domination. Une lecture féministe*, ed. by Eleni Varikas, Nicole Gabriel, and Sonia Dayan-Herzbrun (= *Tumultes*, 23 (2004)).

23   See Cornelia Klinger, 'Liberalismus — Marxismus — Postmoderne. Der Feminismus und seine glücklichen oder unglücklichen "Ehen" mit verschiedenen Theorieströmungen im 20. Jahrhundert', in *Kritische Differenzen — geteilte Perspektiven. Zum Verhältnis von Feminismus und Postmoderne*, ed. by Antje Hornscheidt, Gabriele Jähnert, and Annette Schlichter (Wiesbaden: Westdeutscher Verlag, 1998), pp. 18–41. Klinger dis-

viously the marriage metaphor obscures the important ways in which feminists have actually contributed to building what was later called post-structuralism. Nevertheless, feminist postmodern theory had its day from the late 1980s to the early 2000s and the new materialist project is a declared attempt to end what they view as the dominance of postmodern theory in academia.[24] However, as we can understand through the analysis of the different forms of feminism and of materialism, NM is probably closest to the theoretical strand it criticizes: postmodernism.

If you try to understand what this school of 'postmodernism' these thinkers oppose actually is, the only reference you will find is to Butler's work. Had their notions of materialism not been so different, new materialists could have joined materialist feminist's critique of Butler and gender theory. NM criticizes postmodern theory for not reflecting on its own implications in modernism. However, NM does not seem to reflect upon its own postmodernist implications and clearly lacks basic engagement with other forms of feminist materialism. Had NM not been so opposed to Butler, they would have actually noticed that she, too, has been working on the notion of agency in her exchanges with Saba Mahmood and Talal Asad.[25] Nevertheless, these exchanges do not really match those of inquiring into whether fossils can be seen as a proof of the agency of matter.[26]

In her work on NM, Pia Garske has undertaken a comparison between NM and historical materialism. For her, these two schools are similar in their efforts against essentialism, and yet she highlights important differences in their perspectives on social humanity. Garske shows how historical materialism distinguishes between

---

cusses the various unhappy marriages of feminism and concludes that feminism is not an appropriate bride for postmodernism. While this argument certainly hinges on the definition of feminism one employs, Klinger is right that Butler's alliance with postmodern theory was devastating for a certain type of radical feminism.

24   See *Material Feminisms*, ed. by Hekman and Alaimo, pp. 1–5; Coole and Frost, *New Materialisms*, pp. 2 and 6; or Dolphijn and van der Tuin, *New Materialism*, p. 91.

25   See Talal Asad, Wendy Brown, Judith Butler, and Saba Mahmood, *Is Critique Secular? Blasphemy, Injury, and Free Speech* (New York: Fordham University Press, 2013); and Saba Mahmood, *The Politics of Piety: The Islamic Revival and the Feminist Subject* (Princeton, NJ: Princeton University Press, 2005).

26   Dolphijn and van der Tuin, 'Interview with Quentin Meillassoux', in *New Materialism*, pp. 71–84.

agency (*Handlungsfähigkeit*) and efficiency (*Wirkmächtigkeit*), which clearly seem to be one and the same thing for NM.[27] While *Handlungsfähigkeit* asks whether someone has the capacity to act, *Wirkmächtigkeit* asks, on the one hand, whether someone or something has an impact, which introduces the question of power once we discuss this quality in relation with humans (there is *Mächtigkeit* in *Wirkmächtigkeit*, that is the question of *Macht*, of power). The term also includes the impact a thing or a substance can have on its environment. This distinction between *Handlungsfähigkeit* and *Wirkmächtigkeit* also brings up the question of intentionality. A substance does not choose to impact its environment the way a human can choose to go on strike. But these differentiations might explain why new materialists could not take part in ongoing feminist debates on agency, because these debates almost exclusively focus on the *Handlungsfähigkeit*-side of the issue while the interest of the NW(s) is clearly limited to the *Wirkmächtigkeits*-side of agency. Or, to put it more clearly, so far feminist theory has mostly been interested in women's capacity to act in a world that is organized to deny their subjective existence.

CONCLUSION

The new materialist project is mostly interesting for its attempt to renew and challenge feminist understandings of nature. It is true that the necessary rejection of nature in feminism, which arose from the misogynistic practices of relegating women to the nature part of the nature/culture binary, as well as the modernist grounding of women's oppression in their supposedly 'naturally' inferior disposition, has created quite a rift between feminism and nature. A renewed interest in the material world had already been attempted by ecofeminists who were almost exclusively socialist feminists (Maria Mies, Vandana Shiva,[28] Françoise d'Eaubonne.[29] Sadly, the NM(s) have not embraced this legacy. The same is true for the rich and strong tradition of feminist theory of embodiment (Iris Marion Young, Sandra Lee Bartky, Susan Bordo, Ann Cahill). It seems that in the same way that many

---

27   Garske, *What's the Matter*.
28   Maria Mies and Vandana Shiva, *Ecoféminisme* (Paris: L'Harmattan, 1998).
29   Françoise d'Eaubonne, *Le Féminisme ou la mort* (Paris: Pierre Horay, 1974).

feminists needed to break with nature and the body, new materialists somehow needed to break with most feminist materialist theories. Particularly in the 1970s and 1980s those that were later labelled French feminists undertook an inquiry into feminist ways of perceiving the body. In Germany, Barbara Duden, Gerburg Treusch-Dieter, and Gesa Lindemann[30] have pursued an analysis of the body from their own perspectives.[31] Bodily materiality was one of the central questions in the German 'Butler Debates' of the early 1990s.[32]

New materialist's call to take on ecological and bodily issues might also have contributed to their difficulty in being received by feminist research in France, because the majority of that research is working to counter naturalist sexism. And yet, NM's proposition to practically undertake the project of rethinking nature is quite deceptive because they also systematically refuse to see the sociopolitical implications of nature. Frieder Otto Wolf has criticized the nature-culture binary and called for a realistic view of our existence as natural beings[33] which would involve understanding humanity's 'natural' side, our dependence on nature's agency, but also the unintended effects of our own actions. NM's exclusion of all of humanity from 'nature' as well as its refusal to see humans as sociopolitical beings that are involved in creating institutions, ideologies, concepts, and tools has led to new materialists falling back upon the exact same dualism of nature-culture that they claim to transcend. This is also valid for their uncritical reproduction of the division of science into natural science and the humanities. This division is itself the product of sociopolitical struggles and expresses a power relation as much as the criticized humanities' divided world view does. The new materialist's project of understanding the reflexive foundations of the naturalization of social relations is extremely

30   Gesa Lindemann, 'Die leiblich-affektive Konstruktion des Geschlechts. Für eine Mikrosoziologie des Geschlechts unter der Haut', *Zeitschrift für Soziologie*, 21 (1992), pp. 330–46.

31   Barbara Duden, *Geschichte unter der Haut. Ein Eisenacher Arzt und seine Patientinnen um 1730* (Stuttgart: Klett-Cotta, 1987); Gerburg Treusch-Dieter, 'Von der Antinorm zur Norm. Neuere Perspektiven weiblicher Sexualität', in her *Von der sexuellen Rebellion zur Gen- und Reproduktionstechnologie* (Tübingen: Gehrke, 1990), pp. 140–67.

32   Möser, *Féminismes en traduction*, pp. 176–85.

33   Frieder Otto Wolf, 'Wider die Kategorie der gesellschaftlichen Naturverhältnisse', *Das Argument*, 50.279 (2008), pp. 867–72.

important, but, in order to have this project succeed, the social and political relations cannot be ignored.

NM might also be viewed as a clever survival strategy connecting the humanities to the natural sciences, which could save the humanities from being abolished. While this strategy, if it is one, would be understandable, it does bear the risk of reaffirming the problematic division of science into these two parts. One can glean a fetishization of the natural sciences from many new materialist writings in exactly their presentation of the natural sciences as the 'actual' science, with humanities playing the supporting role of commentary.

Feminist research began in the early 1980s as a project to radically change not only the universities and science but society as a whole.[34] The different epistemological attempts to reach that goal included standpoint theory and the notion of strong objectivity from thinkers such as Evelyn Fox Keller, Sandra Harding, and Donna Haraway, among others. Haraway is actually the only socialist feminist to be claimed by the new materialists, but all of the socialist feminist impulses in her work are stripped away in order to make her another humanist observant of science. Confronting NM with a feminist and socialist critique of science would allow for a better understanding of science as a sociopolitical process, which is organized by institutions, and which mediates the knowledge it produces.[35]

---

34 Gisela Bock, 'Frauenbewegung und Frauenuniversität — Zur politischen Bedeutung der Sommeruniversität', in *Frauen und Wissenschaft. Beiträge zur Berliner Sommeruniversität für Frauen, Juli 1976*, ed. by Gruppe Berliner Dozentinnen (Berlin: Courage, 1977), pp. 15–22 (p. 22).

35 Émilie Filion-Donato's contribution to this volume undertook such a promising confrontation.

Anarchafeminism & the Ontology of the Transindividual

CHIARA BOTTICI

It has become something of a commonplace to argue that in order to fight the oppression of women, it is necessary to unpack the ways in which different forms of oppression intersect with one another. No single factor, be it nature or nurture, economic exploitation or cultural domination, can be said to be the *single* cause sufficient to explain the multifaceted sources of patriarchy and sexism. Consequently, intersectionality has become the guiding principle for an increasing number of left-wing feminists from both the global north and south. As a result, most publications in gender theory today have engaged with the concept of intersectionality in one way or another — whether to promote it, to criticize it, or simply to position oneself with regards to it.

Yet, strikingly enough, in all the literature engaging with intersectionality there is barely any mention of the feminist tradition of the past that has argued for exactly the same point for a very long time: anarchist feminism or, as I prefer to call it, 'anarchAfeminism.' This specific term was introduced by social movements who wanted to feminize the concept and, in so doing, provide more visibility to a specifically feminist strand within anarchist theory and practice. This anarchafeminist tradition, which has largely been neglected both in academia and in public debate generally, has a particularly vital contribution to offer today.

To begin, together with queer theory's ground-breaking work aimed at dismantling the gender binary of 'men' and 'women', it is important to vindicate once again the need for a form of feminism that opposes the oppression of people who are *perceived as* women and who are discriminated precisely on that basis. Notice here that I am using the term 'woman' in a way that includes all types of women: AFAB women,[1] AMAB women, feminine women, masculine women, lesbian women, trans women, queer women, and so on and so forth. Despite the alleged equality of formal rights, women are still the object of constant discrimination, and the advancement of queer rights can be accompanied by a retrogression in regard to women's battles. The emergence of right-wing figures such as Milo Yiannopoulos showed that one can support gay and queer rights and still be a misogynist. But the most infamous data about the continued oppression of women, even in a context such as the US where we have come to expect im- provements in queer rights, are the data about violence against women and bodies that are perceived as feminine: there are currently between 126 and 160 million 'missing girls' from the global population.[2] Trans women are more likely to be raped and suffer violence than trans men, so much so that the term 'transmisogyny' has been created in order to point to situations in which transphobia and misogyny meet and mutually reinforce each other.

Therefore, far from viewing feminism as an issue of the past, it has become more imperative than ever to connect this standpoint with

---

1   I am using the terms 'Assigned Female at Birth' (AFAB) and 'Assigned Male at Birth' (AMAB) to signal the fact that by speaking about 'male' and 'female' we implicitly accept the state sanctioned view according to which our gender corresponds to the sex assigned to us at birth. Notice here how the (almost always binary) gender system and the state apparatus are tightly interwoven, since it is through our state IDs and passports that a gender identity is attached to our lives.

2   The 'missing girls' are not counted in the hundreds, or thousands, but in the millions. As of today, there are somewhere between 126 to 160 million girls missing from the global population as a consequence of sex-selective abortion, infanticide, and inequalities of care (see <https://www.unfpa.org/gender-biased-sex-selection> and <https://lozierinstitute.org/sex-selection-abortion-the-real-war-on-women/https: //lozierinstitute.org/sex-selection-abortion-the-real-war-on-women/>   [accessed 13 May 2020].

the oppression of all bodies perceived as 'femina'. However, such a standpoint must be supported by an articulation of women's liberation that does not create further hierarchies, and this is precisely where anarchafeminism is useful. While other feminists from the left have been tempted to explain the oppression of women on the basis of a single factor, anarchists have always been clear in arguing that, in order to overcome the patriarchal order, we have to fight the multifaceted ways in which diverse factors — economic, cultural, racial, political, etc. — converge to uphold it.

The neglect, if not outright historical amnesia, that the important leftist tradition of anarchism has been faced with is certainly the result of this viewpoint being banned in academia and public debates in general, where it has most often been misleadingly portrayed as little more than a call for violence and disorder. This ban has been enacted to the detriment of historical accuracy, global inclusiveness, and political efficacy.

My proposal is to remedy such a gap by formulating a specific anarchafeminist approach adapted to the challenges of our time.[3] My aim is not only to make the anarchafeminist tradition more visible as an important component of past women's struggles, and therefore re-establish a kind of historical continuity which has been missing to date, even though this would certainly be a worthwhile endeavour. Besides historical accuracy, recovering anarchafeminist insights has the crucial function of enlarging feminist strategies precisely in a moment when, as intersectional feminists have argued, different factors increasingly converge to intensify the oppression of women by creating further class, cultural, and racial divisions among them.

---

3   A first version of this essay was presented at the Night of Philosophy in New York City on 26 January 2018 and then at the UNESCO Night of Philosophy on 15 November 2018. An extract of the talk was published in Liberation on 15 November 2018 <https://www.liberation.fr/debats/2018/11/15/nuit-de-la-philo-pour-un-anarcha-feminisme_1692047> [accessed 12 April 2020], whereas a full version appeared on Public Seminar 7 March 2018 <http://www.publicseminar.org/2018/03/anarchafeminism/> [accessed 13 April 2020]. A Spanish translation of the latter by Miguel Ibáñez Aristondo appeared on 12 September 2018 in *ReporteSextoPiso* <http://reportesp.mx/anarcafeminismo-chiara-bottici> [accessed 13 April 2020], a French translation by Jeanne Etelain et Anaïs Nony in the journal *La Deleuziana*, 8 (2018) <http://www.ladeleuziana.org/wp-content/uploads/2019/02/Bottici-1.pdf> [accessed 13 April 2020], and an Italian translation in *Per cosa lottare. Le frontier del progressismo*, edited by Enrico Biale and Corrado Fumagalli (Milano: Fondazione Giacomo Feltrinelli, 2019).

In a time in which feminism is often accused of being mere white privilege, this task is more crucial than ever. The emancipation of women from the global north can indeed happen at the expense of women from the global south, whose reproductive labour within the household is often used to replace the labour previously performed by the now 'emancipated' women. It is precisely through the adoption of such a global perspective, which is all the more necessary today because of the increased mobility of capital and labour forces, that the chain connecting gendered labour across the globe becomes more apparent, and the timeliness of anarchafeminism as an intersectional approach along with it. To put it concisely, we need a more multifaceted approach to domination. In particular, we need an approach that is able to incorporate different factors as well as the different voices coming from all over the globe. As Chinese anarchafeminist He Zhen wrote at the dawn of the twentieth century in her *Problems of Women's Liberation*:

> The majority of women are already oppressed by both the government and by men. The electoral system simply increases their oppression by introducing a third ruling group: elite women. Even if the oppression remains the same, the majority of women are still taken advantage of by the minority of women. [...] When a few women in power dominate the majority of powerless women, unequal class differentiation is brought into existence among women. If the majority of women do not want to be controlled by men, why would they want to be controlled by women? Therefore, instead of competing with men for power, women should strive for overthrowing men's rule. Once men are stripped of their privilege, they will become the equal of women. There will be no submissive women nor submissive men. This is the liberation of women.[4]

These words from 1907 show how prophetic and relevant anarchafeminism is, and they present the answer to our question: why anarchafeminism? They show that anarchafeminism is the best antidote against the possibility of feminism becoming white privilege and thus a tool in the hands of a few women who dominate the vast majority of them.

---

4   He Zhen, 'Women's Liberation', in *Anarchism: A Documentary History of Libertarian Ideas*, ed. by Robert Graham, 3 vols (Montreal: Black Rose Books, 2005), I, pp. 336–41 (p. 341).

In an epoch when the election of a woman president is presented as a liberation for *all* women, or when women such as Ivanka Trump can lay claim to feminist battles of the past by transforming the hashtag *#womenwhowork* into a tool to sell a fashion brand, the fundamental message of the anarchafeminists of the past is more urgent than ever: 'Feminism doesn't mean female corporate power or a woman President; it means no corporate power and no Presidents.'[5]

THE ONTOLOGY OF THE TRANSINDIVIDUAL

At this point, one may object: why insist on the concept of feminism and not just call this anarchism? Why focus on women? If the purpose is to dismantle all types of oppressive hierarchies, should we not also get rid of the gender binary which, by opposing 'women' to 'men,' imprisons us in a heteronormative matrix?

I should make it clear immediately that when I write 'women' I do not mean some supposed object, or eternal essence, or, even less so, a pre-given object. Indeed, to articulate a specifically feminist position while maintaining a multifaceted understanding of domination, we, as feminists, require a more nuanced understanding of 'womanhood'. By drawing upon insights from an ontology of the transindividual, I will argue that bodies in general, and women's bodies in particular, must be considered as processes rather than as objects that are given once and for all. We are not things, we are relations. Women's bodies, like all bodies, are bodies in plural because they are processes, processes that are constituted by mechanisms of affects and associations that occur at the *inter-*, *intra-*, and the *supra*-individual level. To give just a brief example of what I mean here, think of how our bodies come into being through an *inter*-individual encounter, how they are shaped by *supra*-individual forces, such as their geographical location, and how they are made up of *intra*-individual bodies such as the air we breathe, the food we eat, or the hormones we swallow.

There can be different roads to articulate an ontology of the transindividual. In Europe, the term has been at the centre of discussions arising from Étienne Balibar's reading of Baruch Spinoza's

---

5   Peggy Kornegger, 'Anarchism: The Feminist Connection', in *Quiet Rumors: An Anarcha-Feminist Reader*, ed. by Dark Star (Oakland, CA: AK Press, 2012), pp. 25–35 (p. 31).

ontology as well as the result of a resurgence of interest in the philosophy of Gilbert Simondon.[6] These two strands of the debate on the
transindividual have at times unfolded separately, and at times converged, as with Balibar's philosophy, since it is from Simondon that
Balibar derived the notion of transindividuality which he uses to interpret Spinoza's *Ethics*.[7] In this article, I mainly draw inspiration from
Balibar's insight that Spinoza's concept of individuality is best understood as transindividuality (1997), and from Moira Gatens's feminist
readings of such an ontology, according to which the most monist of
all ontologies — Spinoza's — is also the most pluralist.[8]

The starting point for Spinoza's philosophy is that there is being
rather than nothing.[9] Indeed, he writes that not to exist is to lack
power, and to be able to exist is to have power. Thus, if what necessarily
exists are only finite beings, then finite beings are more powerful than
an absolutely infinite being, which is absurd. Therefore, he concludes
that either nothing exists or an absolutely infinite being exists. But we
exist, either in ourselves or in something else, which necessarily exists.
Therefore, an absolutely infinite being necessarily exists.[10] This is, in
my view, the most beautiful lesson of Spinozism: if there are twenty
people in a room, then an absolutely infinite being necessarily exists.[11]

---

6   Besides Étienne Balibar, *Spinoza: From Individuality to Transindividuality* (Delft:
     Eburon, 1997), explored below, more recent influential views include: Balibar and
     Vittorio Morfino, *Il transindividuale: soggetti, relazioni, mutazioni* (Milano: Mimesis,
     2014); Balibar, 'Philosophies of the Transindividual: Spinoza, Marx, Freud', trans.
     by Mark G. E. Kelly, *Australasian Philosophical Review*, 2.1 (2018), pp. 5–25; Jason
     Read, *The Politics of Transindividuality* (Leiden: Brill, 2015); Daniela Voss, 'Disparate
     Politics: Balibar and Simondon', *Australasian Philosophical Review*, 2.1 (2018), pp. 47–
     53 — who expands on Gilbert Simondon's concept of transindividuality, by comparing
     it with Balibar's view — and Muriel Combes, *Gilbert Simondon and the Philosophy of the
     Transindividual*, trans. by Thomas LaMarre (Cambridge, MA: MIT Press, 2013), the
     first monograph fully devoted to Simondon and the philosophy of the transindividual.
7   Spinoza does not explicitly use the term transindividual or transindividuality, so
     for those who like to trace the origins of this ontology of the transindividual, one
     should follow Balibar, *Spinoza: From Individuality to Transindividuality*, which expli-
     citly draws inspiration from Simondon, *L'Individuation psychique et collective* (Paris:
     Aubier, 1989), which, in turn, coined the expression 'transindividuality'.
8   Moira Gatens, *Imaginary Bodies: Ethics, Power, and Corporeality* (London: Routledge,
     1996), pp. 56–57.
9   *Ethics* I, Def. 1; CWS [*The Collected Works of Spinoza*, see abbreviations], I, p. 408.
10   *Ethics* I, 11 Dem.; CWS I, pp. 417–18.
11   The argument of the twenty persons is used in *Ethics* I, 8, Schol. 2, CWS I, p. 415, where
     Spinoza starts adding some a posteriori elements to the a priori proof for the existence
     of an infinite substance developed in Propositions 1 to 7 of Part I.

But this also implies that there is an infinite unique substance that expresses itself through an infinity of 'attributes', where the latter term stands for what the intellect perceives of the substance as constituting its essence.[12] Among the infinity of such attributes, those that are accessible to humans (at least under current conditions) are thought and extension. A single thought is therefore just a mode of the attribute of thought, whereas a single body is a mode of the attribute of extension.

But, in order to avoid any possible misunderstanding, I should clarify that this does not mean that thought and extension, or ideas and things, are separate or even parallel to one another. Spinoza clearly states that '[t]he order and connection of ideas is the same [*idem*] as the order and connection of things';[13] thought and extension are the same (*idem*), not parallel to one another, and it is even less true that they are two different substances. It is important to emphasize this because whenever we speak about mind and body, or ideas and things, our long-inherited dualistic metaphysical framework tends to surreptitiously creep in. The first step in order to get to a truly pluralistic conception of the body is to get rid of this framework, and thus of the idea that a body is something different, parallel, or opposite to a mind. When we say 'a body' we do not mean something separate or even opposed to 'a mind' or 'a soul'. 'Body' and 'mind' are just modes expressing two different attributes of the same substance.

This also leads us to the specific understanding of individuality as transindividuality which one can develop by drawing inspiration from Spinoza, particularly from the sort of compendium of his physics that he put forward in Part II of the *Ethics,* where his eccentric materialism fully emerges.[14] If thought and extension are just two of the infinite attributes of the unique substance, then we cannot speak of a materialist ontology without immediately adding that it is not the brute, inanimate, static matter that is at stake here. Spinoza's materialism is an eccentric form of what we might call a 'spiritual materialism', precisely because extension and thought are just two of the infinite attributes of the same substance.

---

12   *Ethics* I, Def. 4; CWS I, p. 408.
13   *Ethics* II, 7; CWS I, p. 451.
14   *Ethics* II, 13–15; CWS I, pp. 457–63.

Within such an ontology, individual things (*res singulares*) exist only as a consequence of the existence of other individual things[15] with which they participate in an infinite network of connections.[16] Notice here that this view also implies that causality must not be understood in the sense of a linear succession of events, but rather as a multiplicity of connections linking individuals, which are themselves made up of more simple and more complex individuals that are all causally related. As a consequence, every individual is constantly composed and decomposed by other individuals with whom it enters into contact through a process of individuation, which involves *infra*-individual, *inter*-individual, and *supra*-individual levels.[17] In order to render this complexity, Balibar argued, individuality must be understood as transindividuality.

In this understanding, individuals are therefore never atoms, events, let alone subjects that are given once and for all. They are processes, the result of constant movements of association and repulsion that connect more simple individuals with other simple individuals, but also with more complex ones that constantly make and unmake bodies. To get a crude but efficient sense of what I mean here, think of how animal bodies are composed and decomposed by the liquids that traverse them; we drink, but we perspire, we urinate, we are constantly processing liquids by which in turn we are being processed. Similarly, human individuals are constantly composed by the molecules that we breath in and out of our bodies through a transindividual process of association and attraction linking different forms of human, animal, and vegetative life into the same network. Notice that within this monist ontology the same holds true for thoughts; as individuals, bodies are the result of all the modes with the attribute of thought that we constantly encounter, be they the reflections you are reading or the phone conversation you had this morning. To put it even more strongly, the order and connection of ideas is the same as the order and connection of things, because ideas are nothing but affirmations of the body. Again, observe here how easily one escapes the trap of metaphysical dualism. Since the body and the mind are nothing but

---

15   *Ethics* I, 28; *CWS* I, pp. 432–33.
16   Balibar, *Spinoza*, p. 27.
17   Ibid.

modes within different attributes of the unique substance, no radical separation between a subject of knowledge and its object can subsist. In fact, the very notion of a self-enclosed individual, let alone of a subject, of a Cartesian ego, does not make any sense in this ontology. Human beings do not occupy a privileged position within this ontology, being themselves nothing but more complex individuals than, say, a stone or a chair, because they result from more complex movements of attraction and repulsion between more or less complex individuals. In other words, they are not given entities, but rather processes, webs of affective and imaginal relations that are never given once and for all.

As Gatens has emphasized, this also means that in the process of individuation that generates individuals in general, and human beings in particular, complex dynamics of imaginary identification become particularly crucial.[18] We constantly meet and recognize or misrecognize ourselves in certain images of the body, which include images that we have of our bodies and of other bodies, as well as images that others have of them and which become constitutive of our own being. For Gatens, the key term for keeping together the mental and the material side of this process is 'the imaginary' and for Spinoza it is 'imagination'. The latter term, in his theory of knowledge, denotes a set of ideas produced on the basis of present or past bodily affections.[19] Following Gatens and Genevieve Lloyd, we can summarize Spinoza's view of imagination by saying that it is a form of bodily awareness, which means awareness of the perceiving body as well as of the perceived bodies encountered and that, as a consequence, it is always, properly speaking, a form of collective imagining.[20] In order to avoid misunderstandings,

---

18 One of the first commentators to point to this constitutive role of imagination in Spinoza was Antonio Negri. See, in particular, his *The Savage Anomaly: The Power of Spinoza's Metaphysic and Politics* (Minneapolis: University of Minnesota Press, 1991), pp. 86–97. According to Caroline Williams, what is new in this book by Negri, Balibar's *Spinoza and Politics* (London: Verso, 1998), and Moira Gatens and Genevieve Lloyd, *Collective Imaginings: Spinoza, Past and Present* (London: Routledge, 1999) is that they draw attention to Spinoza's novel, materialist rendering of imagination, without simply dismissing it as a source of errors. See Williams, 'Thinking the Political in the Wake of Spinoza: Power, Affect and Imagination in the Ethics', *Contemporary Political Theory*, 6 (2006), pp. 349–69 (p. 350). What I am trying to do here is to combine the merit of Spinoza's ontology with a theory of the imaginal that more clearly distances itself from the modern philosophy of the subject.

19 *Ethics* II, 26 Dem.; *CWS* I, p. 469 and *Ethics* II, 40 Schol. 2; *CWS* I, pp. 477–78.

20 Gatens and Lloyd, *Collective Imaginings*, p. 12.

we should recall that an idea does not only consist of mental content. Imagination has a bodily grounding, because the mind is just the body that is felt and thought. Furthermore, according to Spinoza, an idea is 'a conception of the mind'.[21]

Notice here that while Gatens's feminist interpretation of Spinoza focuses on the specifically human usage of this capacity to imagine, there is nothing within this conception that prevents us from extending Spinoza's understanding of imagination to all other forms of extension, or, in more contemporary terms, of materiality. Despite the different forms that this idea could take, there is no a priori reason in this ontology to assume that thinking and imagining would be a prerogative of the human. I also want to point out that while Spinoza uses the typically modern concept of imagination, which, in the history of western philosophy, is imbued with humanism, we can certainly reformulate his insights in terms of a theory of the imaginal. In particular, it is with regards to what Gatens called 'imaginary bodies', and what I would like to call 'imaginal bodies', that we can understand the psychological side of the process of individuation described above. Whenever a body encounters another body, which can be a simple body, like a glass of water, or a more complex one, like another animal, a change in its own constitution will occur. It is in this sense, and in order to keep together what happens at the *infra*, *inter-*, and *supra*-individual level, that the notion of transindividuality becomes particular helpful. In sum, bodies are always necessarily bodies in plural, both social and individual at the same time, because their individuality is always and inevitably a form of transindividuality. But if bodies are always transindividual processes, then we also need a theory that is able to conceptualize our capacity to imagine without falling into the false alternative between theories of imagination as an individual faculty and theories of the imaginary as a social context. And it is precisely at this point that, as I hope I have shown, the concept of the imaginal becomes particularly useful.[22]

---

21   Ethics II, Def. 3; *CWS* I, p. 447.

22   I have developed the concept of the imaginal as an alternative to theories of imagination understood as an individual faculty and theories of the imaginary understood as a social context, in Chiara Bottici, *Imaginal Politics* (New York: Columbia University Press, 2014).

I would like to list the benefits of such an ontological shift towards transindividuality as the prism through which individuality must be understood. Firstly, instead of elaborating a form of feminism and then having to add ecology as something different from feminism itself, here the two positions are unified from the beginning because, in an ontology of the transindividual, the environment is not something separated from us but, rather, the environment *is* us — literally something constitutive of our individuality. Secondly, imaginal collective formations such as sex, race, and class are from the beginning conceptualized as constitutive of our individuality, and thus as intimately intertwined. Thirdly, when women's bodies are theorized as processes, as sites of a process of becoming that takes place at different levels, we can speak about 'women' without incurring the charge of essentialism or culturalism. There is no place here for the opposition between sex (nature) and gender (culture) because there is no place for body-mind dualism. Lastly, by adopting this transindividual ontology, we can also use the concept of woman outside of any heteronormative framework, and thus use the term such that it includes all types of women: feminine women, masculine women, AFAB women, AMAB women, lesbian women, bisexual women, trans women, cis women, asexual women, queer women, and so on and so forth. In sum, 'women' encompasses all bodies that identify themselves and are identified through the always changing narrative of 'womanhood'.

To conclude this point, a transindividual framework allows us to answer the question 'what is a woman?' in pluralistic terms while also defending a specifically feminist form of anarchism. Developing the concept of women as a series of open processes also means going beyond the dichotomy of the individual *versus* the collective: if it is true that all bodies are transindividual processes, then the assumption that there could be such a thing as a pure individual, separate, or even opposed, to a given collective, is at best a useless abstraction and at worst a deceitful phantasy.

WHICH WOMEN? AND WHICH ANARCHAFEMINISM?

Adopting an anarchafeminist lens entails taking the entire globe as the framework for thinking about the liberation of women. This implies going beyond any form of methodological nationalism, that is, privileging certain women and thus certain national or regional contexts. If fighting the oppression of women means we have to fight all forms of oppression, then statism and nationalism are no exceptions. If one begins by looking at the dynamics of exploitation by taking state boundaries as an unquestionable fact, one ends up reinforcing the very oppression one meant to question in the first place. A slogan for this proposal might look something like: 'the globe first.' Adopting anything less than the entire globe as our framework is at best naive provincialism and at worst obnoxious ethnocentrism.

Whereas several feminist theories produced in the global north have failed to understand the extent to which the emancipation of white, middle-class women happened at the expense of a renewed oppression of working-class racialized bodies, anarchafeminists have traditionally adopted a more inclusive perspective. It is no coincidence that many anarchist theorists, from Pjotr Alexejewitsch Kropotkin to Paul Reclus, have been geographers and/or anthropologists. By exploring the processes of production and reproduction of life independent of state boundaries and on a planetary scale, these authors not only were able to avoid the pitfalls of any form of methodological nationalism, but could also perceive the global interconnectedness of forms of domination, beginning with the intertwinement of capitalist exploitation and colonial domination.

A tangential remark I would like to offer here is that while one can use labels such as Latin American or Chinese anarchafeminism, I believe that those labels must be used as ladders to be abandoned as soon as we have reached the top. The vitality of the anarchafeminist tradition consists precisely in its capacity to transcend state boundaries, methodological nationalism, and even the Eurocentric biases that persist throughout most of the radical theory produced in the global north. It is very revealing, for instance, that most of the feminist tools, whether rooted in Marxist feminism, post-structuralist feminism, or radical feminism, derive from theories produced in a very small number of countries. We can actually name and count them on one hand: France, Germany, the United Kingdom, the United States, and perhaps Italy. To combat this Eurocentric trend, and the subsequent privileging of Western Europe in building frameworks of emancipation, it is pivotal to bring texts produced by anarchists worldwide to the centre of the discussion. This global inclusion is the only way to insure a form of feminism beyond Eurocentrism and beyond ethnocentrism.

THE COLONIALITY OF GENDER: ANOTHER WOMAN IS POSSIBLE

If we take the globe as our framework, the first striking datum to emerge is that people across the globe have not always been *doing* gender, and, moreover, even if they did *do* it, they have *done* it on very different terms depending on where they lived. It is only with the emergence of a worldwide capitalist system that the gender binary of 'men' versus 'women' gained worldwide hegemony. This does not mean that sexual difference did not exist before capitalism, nor does it imply that we should indulge in the nostalgia of a gender fluid past. It simply means taking note of the historically situated nature of the current gender regime, and, in particular, of the fact that binary gender roles were not as universally accepted as the primary criteria through which bodies were classified, as they are today. Modern capitalism made the mononuclear bourgeois family — with its binary gender roles — hegemonic, and the modern sovereign state with its bureaucratic apparatus sealed that gender binary on us through state IDs and passports.

Marxist feminists have long emphasized that capitalism needs a gendered division of labour because, as it is predicated on the endless expansion of profit, it needs both the extraction of surplus value from waged productive labour as well as unpaid reproductive labour, which is still largely performed by gendered bodies. To put it bluntly, capitalism needs 'women'. It relies on the assumption that when women are washing their husband's and children's socks, they are not 'working' but merely performing a function ordained for them by nature.

As Maria Mies, among others, has emphasized, perceiving women's care work as the consequence of their nature, instead of as the actual work it is, is pivotal to maintaining the division between 'waged labour', which is subject to exploitation, and 'unwaged labour', which is subject to what she, along with others, has termed 'superexploitation'.[23] This form of gendered exploitation is 'super' because,

---

23   Maria Mies, *Patriarchy and Accumulation on a World Scale: Women in the International Division of Labour* (London: Zed Books, 1986).

whereas the exploitation of waged labour takes place through the extraction of surplus value, the exploitation of women's domestic labour takes place via denying their work *the very status of* work.

By building on these types of insights, Maria Lugones put forward the very useful concept of the 'coloniality of gender.'[24] She uses this concept to emphasize how the 'male/female' binary and the racial classification of bodies were both systems that Europeans exported through the colonial expansion that accompanied the worldwide spread of capitalism. Within the American context, Lugones shows how gender roles were much more flexible and variegated among Native Americans before the arrival of European settlers. Different indigenous nations possess, for instance, a third gender category to positively recognize intersex and queer subjectivities, whereas others, such as the Yuma, attribute gender roles on the basis of dreams, so that a AFAB woman who dreams of weapons is considered and treated, for all practical purposes, as a man. This shows that there has been a systematic intertwinement between the expansion of the capitalist economy, the racial classification of bodies, and gender oppression.

It is manifestly true, and yet all too often forgotten, that to classify people on the basis of their skin colour or their genitalia is not an a priori of the human mind. Classifying bodies on the basis of their sex, as well as classifying them on the basis of their race, implies, among other things, a primacy of the visual register. According to Oyèrónkẹ́ Oyěwùmí, such a primacy is typical of the West, particularly when looked at from the perspective of the Yoruba pre-colonial cultures. As she points out in her seminal work *The Invention of Women*, the Yoruba cultures, for instance, relied much more on the oral transmission of information than on its visualization, and they valued age over all other criteria for social hegemony.[25] They did not even have a name to oppose men and women before colonialism: to put it bluntly, they simply did not 'do' gender.

---

24   Maria Lugones, 'The Coloniality of Gender', in *The Palgrave Handbook of Gender and Development: Critical Engagements in Feminist Theory and Practice*, ed. by Wendy Harcourt (London: Palgrave Macmillan, 2016), pp. 13–33.

25   Oyèrónkẹ́ Oyěwùmí, *The Invention of Women: Making an African Sense of Western Gender Discourses* (Minneapolis: University of Minnesota Press, 1997).

Therefore, questioning the coloniality of gender also means questioning the primacy of the visual: it is by seeing bodies that we say 'here
is a woman!' or 'that is a man!' But it is also within such a visual register
that we have to operate in order to question hegemonic and heteronormative views of womanhood and thereby open new paths toward
subverting them. To propose another slogan, we could say: 'Another
woman is possible; another woman has always already begun.'

AN ONGOING MANIFESTO

These words, 'another woman is possible; another woman has always
already begun' could indeed be the starting point of a new anarchafeminist manifesto. In contrast to other manifestos, an anarchafeminist one
would inevitably need to be open and as ongoing as the transindividual
ontology upon which it rests.[26] Starting with Errico Malatesta's insight
that anarchism is a *method*, and thus not a *programme*[27] that can be
given once for all, the writing of such a manifesto could begin with the
following points:

FIRST: *At the beginning was movement:* Anarchism does not mean
an absence of order but rather searching for a social order without an
'orderer'. The main 'orderer' of our established ways of thinking about
politics is the state. Because we are so accustomed to living in sovereign
states we tend to perceive the migration of bodies across the globe as a
problem. On the contrary, we should remember that sovereign states
are a relatively recent historical phenomenon (for most of humanity,
peoples have lived under other types of political formations) and that
human beings have been migrating across the Earth since the very appearance of the so-called *Homo sapiens*. *Homo sapiens* is therefore also
a *Femina migrans*, or even better, an *Esse migrans*, hence the need for
an anarchafeminism beyond boundaries and beyond ethnocentrism.

SECOND: *Just do it:*[28] Do not aim to seize state power or wait
for the state to give you power, just start exercising your power right

---

26   In May 2019, a collective writing project called 'Anarchafeminist Manifesto 1.0' began
      on Public Seminar. The readers who are interested are invited to follow at <https:
      //publicseminar.org/2020/05/anarchafeminist-manifesto-1-0/>.

27   Errico Malatesta, *L'Anarchia* [1891] (Rome: Datanews, 2001), p. 39.

28   'Just do it' can also mean to subversively re-appropriate a corporate power logo, and
      thus re-appropriate what capitalism has stolen from us.

now. Aiming to seize state power, or asking for recognition from the state, means reproducing that very same power structure that needs to be questioned in the first place. This means not only 'think globally, and act locally'; it also means that a little bit of freedom is within everybody's reach and can be exercised in a number of ways that are not mutually exclusive. This could include general strikes, grassroots organizing, civil disobedience, and boycotts, but also resisting gender norms, subverting or playing with them, refusing to comply, and so on and so forth. The latter actions are not simply 'individualist strategies,' as some have labelled them; instead, they are political acts as such, which can go hand in hand with larger projects, as can be seen in the increasing number of women's strikes, communal living spaces, and *queered* families proliferating around the globe. To think about bodies as transindividual processes also means that we should escape the false alternative between individual *versus* collective strategies, and work at all different levels simultaneously. The oppression is global, and so the fight has to be global as well.

THIRD: *The end is the means; the means is the end*: There cannot and there should not be any fully-fledged political programme for an anarchafeminist manifesto. This does not mean that there cannot and there should not be any site-specific and time-limited political programme: it simply means that there cannot be a unique one fit for all different possible intersections of axes of oppression. If freedom is the end, freedom must also be the means to reach it. Anarchism is a method for thinking as well as for acting, because acting is thinking and thinking is acting. In the same way in which bodies are plural, their oppression is plural as well, and so the strategies of fighting it must be plural as well. As anarchists have been saying for a long time: 'multiply your associations and be free.' In other words, search for freedom in all of your social relations, not simply in electoral and institutional politics, though the latter may also be one of the levels you operate at. But if freedom is both the means and the end, then one can also envisage a world free from the very notion of gender as well as the oppressive structures it generates. Because gendered bodies are still the worldwide objects of exploitation and domination, we need an anarchafeminist manifesto right here and right now. But such a manifesto should be conceived as a ladder that we may well abandon once we have reached the top. Indeed, it is implicit in the very process of embarking upon such an anarchafeminist project, that we should strive for a world beyond the opposition between men and women and thus, also, in a way, beyond feminism itself.

Psychodynamism of Individuation and New Materialism
Possible Encounters
ÉMILIE FILION-DONATO

Organizing life according to differences, be they sexual (male/female)[1] or otherwise,[2] is a social praxis. Indeed, feminists have long argued that though it may be possible to group humans into two groups based on differences which we call sexual, the meaning we ascribe to these differences and the impact we allow them to have is unequivocally social. In other words, what we make of these differences and the psychological and material consequences they

---

1   It has been suggested that I may mean 'gendered' here. Though I personally believe, with Anne Fausto-Sterling (*Sexing the Body: Gender Politics and the Construction of Sexuality*, rev. edn (New York: Basic Books, 2000)), Thomas Laqueur (*Making Sex: Body and Gender from the Greeks to Freud* (Cambridge, MA: Harvard University Press, 2003)), and others, that sex is a scientific construct, using 'gender' here would be misleading because what I am referring to are the perceived physical differences not the social roles extrapolated from the same. Whether these differences are really relevant for deducing any personality or group traits or whether they have been exacerbated (or even constructed) by the superimposed (cultural) bicategorization are a different set of questions (to which I answer: no and yes.)

2   Though other differences, such as 'racial' differences, those pertaining to neuronal or bodily ability, sexual orientation, or those of socio-economic circumstances, have been of equal importance in this social organization of difference, I focus on gender difference here because the epistemologists I study base their theoretical framework on the construction of this specific difference.

result in arise from socio-cultural interactions, alliances — whether explicit or not — and more or less fixed arrangements. Second, feminists have argued that such practices enable the emergence of two different cultures (men/women)(gender),[3] which, through some combination of feedback loops and confirmation biases, reinforce the significance and importance given to the alleged sexual differences. That is, by rewarding members of an in-group for a certain set of behaviours and punishing or discouraging other behaviours, as well as ascribing the converse undesirable behaviours to the out-group, each culture participates in exacerbating and amplifying intergroup differences.

This dynamic reinforcement of differences has important consequences for epistemology. Indeed, many epistemologists argue that knowledge production is a specifically human endeavour which is inextricable from its historical, local, and social context. As a result, according to this viewpoint, knowledge is permeable to cultural or group biases. Feminist epistemologists combined these two insights — the existence of gendered cultures and the permeability of knowledge to culture — and began to ask in the 1970s whether, and if so, how, male cultural (androcentric) biases have impacted the production of scientific knowledge. In other words, if we accept that the way gender

---

3   When I use men or women, I mean the cultural extrapolations from the bodily characteristics (when I mean those, I use male/female). Nicole Claude Mathieu has suggested that there are three paradigms to think of the relationship between sex and gender. In the first, social sex (gender) is undissociated from biological sex (sex). Under this paradigm, all that we associate with the feminine (gender) is a direct and faithful translation of the (female) biological condition and can only be explained by it (Nicole-Claude Mathieu, *L'Anatomie politique: catégorisations et idéologies du sexe* (Paris: Côté-femmes: 1991)). The second paradigm proposes that the social sex symbolizes the biological sex. That is to say, that the first (gender) refers to the second (sex) and is related to it in some way, without being absolutely determined by it. In this paradigm, if biology is not the only determinant of (gendered) behaviour, it is because there is, according to these theories, a number of codes and norms that are learned by individuals, voluntarily or not. The third conceptualization proposes that the obstinacy to confine the heterogeneity of the biological condition to two categories actually comes from the social system which frames or orients the reading of biological data. This conceptualization proposes that the network of norms and codes that governs bodies and pushes them to conform to one of the two groups has the purpose of simplifying social interactions. Because of this simplification, the social model of bicategorization is preferred to more complex models, such as those in which heterogeneity of sex would be accepted. As a result, the data invalidating the dimorphic model are either ignored or reinterpreted in favour of the coherence of the system.

and gender roles are expressed at any given time is a social praxis, and we also accept that knowledge emerges out of a specific cultural context, then the praxis of gender has to be taken into account as part of the general social context from which this knowledge emerges.

This chapter relies upon my own typology of the strategies put forward by U.S. feminists in response to the problem of androcentrism in the production of knowledge. Briefly put, this typology groups the various feminist strategies into three categories: 'changing the subject', 'multiplying the subject', and 'decentring the subject'.[4]

This chapter has two goals. The first is to challenge the category of strategies Helen Longino, in 'Subjects, Power, and Knowledge', ascribes to biologist and epistemologist Evelyn Fox Keller and her strategy: psychodynamism of individuation.[5] The second goal of this chapter is to underline how psychodynamism of individuation and New Materialism can benefit one another, emphasizing the interrelations between them and discussing their relationship to Spinozist materialism.

In her 1993 essay, Longino places Keller in the category she calls — and which I use with some adjustments — 'changing the subject'. According to Longino, this category contains two different strategies: Keller's psychodynamism of individuation and standpoint theory.[6] Longino groups these two strategies together because she believes that they have similar consequences for rethinking how science should be done. That is, in her opinion they both attempt to change who is doing science (what we could call the epistemic subject). Contra Longino,

---

4   The first two categories are inspired by Helen E. Longino, 'Subjects, Power, and Knowledge: Description and Prescription in Feminist Philosophies of Science', in *Feminist Epistemologies*, ed. and intro. by Linda Alcoff and Elizabeth Potter (New York: Routledge, 1993), pp. 101–20. The last category is my own.

5   Ibid.

6   Very briefly, 'standpoint theory', the genealogy of which can be traced back to Marxism and Black feminism, argues that the subject of knowledge's position (be it their gender, 'race', socio-economic background, sexual orientation, mental and physical ability, etc.) has an influence on the type and quality of knowledge produced. Hence, epistemic authority is given to certain people on specific topics. For example, it will be assumed a black woman has access to specific knowledge about the condition of black women in general, something that cannot be spontaneously known to someone who is not part of this group (see Patricia Hill Collins, 'Learning from the Outsider Within: The Sociological Significance of Black Feminist Thought', *Social Problems*, 33.6 (1986), pp. 14–32). This is not strictly speaking an epistemology based on identity since this position can change during one's lifetime.

I argue that Keller's use of object-relation theory allows ontological insights and consequences that are irreducible to a change of the epistemic subject of the sort proposed by standpoint theory. Instead, I propose that Keller forgoes substantial ontology in favour of relational ontology. To help make this point, I place Keller's psychodynamism of individuation in relation with New Materialism, a strategy found in my third category (decentring the subject) where I also place Keller's psychodynamism of individuation.

This discussion sets the stage for the second goal of this chapter which is to underline how both strategies (New Materialism and psychodynamism of individuation) can benefit one another. Particularly, I endeavour to show how Keller's psychodynamism of individuation can help address some of the most devastating criticisms directed at New Materialism. These criticisms are twofold. First, some have contended that the ontology in New Materialism revives the threat of idealism (understood as anti-realism) because the subject of knowledge is also part of the apparatus and hence can impact the phenomena solely through its presence.[7] Second, others have reproached the ontology of New Materialism for making collective action difficult, and even impossible, given the éclatement of the (human) subject.[8] Indeed, in this multiverse of forces, ascribing responsibility can seem difficult. I shall address these criticisms at the end of this paper.

In brief, this paper aims to encourage reflection on an epistemological project that takes both psychic structures and matter seriously by achieving a cross-pollination of New Materialism and the psychodynamism of individuation. My hope is that this cohabitation can lead to more democratic epistemologies. Before going into the details of this cross-pollination, however, I will first situate myself in the materialist tradition, for it would be remiss of me not to mention the impact of Baruch Spinoza on this project. I have borrowed many ideas from Spinoza but principally his monism and immanent causality. Both

---

7   Andreas Malm, *The Progress of This Storm: Nature and Society in a Warming World* (London: Verso, 2018); Andreas Malm, 'Against Hybridism: Why We Need to Distinguish between Nature and Society, Now More than Ever', *Historical Materialism*, 27.2 (2019), pp. 156–87.

8   Malm, 'Against Hybridism'; Eva Bendix Petersen, '"Data Found Us": A Critique of Some New Materialist Tropes in Educational Research', *Research in Education*, 101.1 (2018), pp. 5–16.

concepts, in my opinion, are remedies to the impasses of teleological thinking, which is the source of most biases or 'ideologies' in Louis Althusser's sense.

MATERIALISM

I understand being a materialist in the sense of being a dedicated monist. This monism is inspired by Spinoza's monism in that it is committed to using the same methodology when considering the causal relationships of the attribute of Thought as much as that of Extension. Indeed, in the *Ethics*, Spinoza writes:

> I shall treat the nature and powers of the Affects, and the power of the Mind over them, by the same Method by which, in the preceding parts, I treated God and the Mind, and I shall consider human actions and appetites just as if it were a Question of lines, planes, and bodies.[9]

As such, this methodology means committing to monism even when it seems not to correspond to traditional notions of materialism: i.e., when thinking about social relations as well as psychological forces and states. Arguing for the contrary — that social relations or psychological states have no impact on a phenomenon — is, in my view, to take a dualist stance and claim that psychic and social formations are somehow supra material.

This monism is also, in my opinion, what connects onto-epistemological materialism, or scientific materialism,[10] and historical materialism, both of which are encountered in this volume. The first is a materialism which can be traced back to Democritus and Epicurus and which we associate with a scientific kind of understanding. According to this type of materialism (and monism), matter is the only thing that exists. This school of thought is also known as

---

9   Spinoza, *Ethics* III, Praef.; *CWS* [*The Collected Works of Spinoza*, see abbreviations], I, p. 492.

10   The use of 'scientific' here may lead to some confusion as Marx has been known to use the term 'scientific socialism' or 'communism' to refer to his ideas in opposition to the 'utopian socialism' of the kind proposed by Fourier and Saint-Simon (see Raymond Aron, *Le Marxisme de Marx* (Paris: Editions de Fallois, 2002), p. 579.). I shall use scientific here only to refer to the contemporary sense of 'natural sciences'.

physicalism. Hence, there is no god-like or soul-like force[11] that can make matter bend the rules of its nature. The second, historical materialism, is a materialism which can be traced back to Marx and has more to do with a socio-history which encourages us to learn more about social determinations in order to enact socio-political change. In this sense, I understand Marx's methodology as monist since social relations are analysed on the same plane as natural phenomena.[12] It is a more complex monism than physicalism, but a monism in its methodology nonetheless.[13]

This 'taking into account' of social relations and psychological states as elements that constitute a phenomenon, however, has often been reduced to radical constructivism or dismissed as such by the first kind of materialism (onto-epistemological).[14] Such a dismissal seems to suggest that taking more 'data' into account when considering a phenomenon is alien to science or the scientific method when, in fact, the contrary should be true. In my opinion, this suggestion is the result of some confusion around the ideas of contingency and necessity. Indeed, to say that psychic and social formations may impact matter and vice versa is understood as suggesting that 'things', meaning matter, could have been different (say, if we hadn't interfered). That is, it is understood as saying that 'things' (or even laws of nature) are contingent because it seems that if social and psychic formations

---

11   Though some New Materialists use the terms 'vitality' and 'material vitalism' (e.g. Jane Bennett), they make a point of distancing themselves from older forms of vitalism (which are closer to the idea of a soul). Bennett writes 'Mine is not a vitalism in the traditional sense; I equate affect with materiality, rather than posit a separate force that can enter and animate a physical body' (Jane Bennett, *Vibrant Matter: A Political Ecology of Things* (Durham, NC: Duke University Press, 2010), p. xiii). So my point here is that the traditional form of vitalism is an error that leads to a dualist and teleologistic mode of thinking (though this is might not be the case with the new uses of 'vitality' and 'vitalism').

12   Marlon Miguel has correctly pointed out that not all scholars of Marx would agree with the presentation of his philosophy as monist. While it is true that the question of monism in Marx is complex, I believe his methodology is more straightforwardly monist. Žižek has argued, for example, that it is a dialectical monism (see citation below).

13   Slavoj Žižek, *Absolute Recoil: Towards a New Foundation of Dialectical Materialism* (London: Verso: 2014), pp. 5–15.

14   Donna J. Haraway, 'Situated Knowledges: The Science Question in Feminism and the Privilege of Partial Perspective', *Feminist Studies*, 14.3 (1988), pp. 575–99; Ian Hacking, *The Social Construction of What?* (Cambridge, MA: Harvard University Press, 1999).

have anything to do with matter, then the latter might be changed at will. As a consequence, this supposed contingency of matter is understood as a kind of anti-realism, in the sense that it seems to suggest that some external (human or god-like) will has more bearing on the way matter behaves than any intrinsic laws of its nature. This is a misunderstanding. Spinoza, through his rejection of the very notions of Beginning and End,[15] shows that social and psychic formations are no more free than gravity is. He writes in a Letter 58:

> [C]onceive now, if you will, that while the stone continues to move, it thinks, and knows that as far as it can, it strives to continue moving. Of course, since the stone is conscious only of its striving, and not at all indifferent, it will believe that it is very free, and that it perseveres in motion for no other cause than because it wills to. This is that famous human freedom everyone brags of having, which consists only in this: that men are conscious of their appetite and ignorant of the causes by which they are determined.[16]

Indeed, Spinoza's ontology alerts us to this misconception and proposes ways out of it.[17] First, his notion of a unique and immanent substance throws off the finalist-bias. Second, he shows that the Scholastic notions of necessity and contingency are errors of the same kind: the result of finite modes investing a teleological quality into Nature.[18] It is this teleological investment, which Spinoza understands as imaginary, that makes us both conceive of a will (ours or God's) that

---

15 Louis Althusser saw this in Spinoza as well as a long tradition of materialist thinkers. He writes in 'The Underground Current of the Materialism of the Encounter', in *Philosophy of the Encounter: Later Writings, 1978–87*, ed. by François Matheron and Oliver Corpet, trans. by Geoffrey M. Goshgarian (London: Verso, 2006), pp. 163–207: 'from Epicurus to Marx [via Spinoza], there had always subsisted — even if it was covered over (by its very discovery, by forgetfulness, and, especially, by denial and repression, when it was not condemnations that cost some their lives) — the "discovery" of a profound tradition that sought its materialist anchorage *in a philosophy of the encounter* (and therefore in a more or less atomistic philosophy, the atom, in its "fall", being the simplest figure of individuality). Whence this tradition's radical rejection of all philosophies of essence (*Ousia, Essentia, Wesen*), that is, of Reason (*Logos, Ratio, Vernunft*), and therefore of Origin and End' (p. 188; emphasis in the original).

16 *Ep.* LVIII [G. H. Schuller]; *CWS* II, p. 428.

17 For more on his ontology and the consequences on the notions of Freedom and Necessity, see Stefano Visentin in this volume.

18 See Ericka Itozaku's paper in this volume for a more in-depth discussion of this issue.

shapes things into what it wants and also imagines things as contingent. However, Spinoza shows that the laws underlying the nature of finite things depend upon other finite modes that constitute and limit it.

Once we get rid of this teleological illusion, the epistemological and ethical tasks before us become, in Spinozist terms, to sit with and consider our power in its finitude, i.e., in how it is limited by other finite modes. Consequently, my argument is that what has been missing from the materialist projects (both onto-epistemological materialism and scientific materialism) is this understanding of our finitude, and consequently Spinoza's ethical project. This finitude, however, is not to be understood as a kind of fatalism, as pointed out in the introduction to this volume. Instead, understanding what has determined our lives is the very thing that sets us free from depleting affects (shame, guilt, anger, etc.), allowing us to persevere in our being more joyously, i.e., powerfully, and, in so doing, change how we relate to other finite beings and our environment. Freedom is, as Engels would later write, the appreciation of necessity.[19] Hence, this change should not be conceived as a freely made decision that can direct the will here or there; instead, it is more like a fine tuning of our response to the finite beings that constitute us and which we constitute in return, and this results in a better agreement with ourselves and those around us (be they human or otherwise). This co-constitution of finite things and the fine tuning to what surrounds us is something we also find in the strategy of New Materialism, which I will now discuss.

---

19   Friedrich Engels, *Anti-Dühring*, in *MECW* [*Marx & Engels Collected Works*, see abbreviations], xxv (1987), pp. 1–309 (p. 105).

FEMINIST STRATEGIES

New Materialism

Though many scholars have written on this topic,[20] I will focus here on Karen Barad's account of New Materialism. Barad's method, which she calls the Diffractive Method, is also a metaphor that was inspired by Haraway and quantum physics. It is used as a critical response to representationalist metaphors of reflection. Haraway writes about such metaphors, saying that 'both are optical phenomena, but whereas reflection evokes themes of mirroring and sameness, diffraction is marked by patterns of difference'.[21] She adds that 'a diffraction pattern does not map where differences appear, but rather maps where the effects of differences appear'.[22] This method, therefore, allegedly helps us to better attend to the relational nature of difference.

Using diffraction as a metaphor can help change the way that we perceive and interpret objects in two important ways. First, it helps shift the focus away from the intrinsic characteristics of 'objects'. That is, we can see that what is expressed and hence measured, i.e. that which emerges as the 'characteristics of the waves', actually emerges from the meetings of a 'prior' set of waves. Because any measured 'crest' does not actually exist before its meeting with the other crest, and/or the meeting with the diffracting apparatus — e.g. an island or a rock — Barad calls this meeting an intra-action in contrast to an inter-action. The

---

20   Rick Dolphijn and Iris van der Tuin, *New Materialism: Interviews & Cartographies* (Ann Arbor, MI: Open Humanities Press, 2012); Birgit Van Puymbroeck and N. Katherine Hayles, '"Enwebbed Complexities": The Posthumanities, Digital Media and New Feminist Materialism', *DiGeSt: Journal of Diversity and Gender Studies*, 2.1–2 (2015), pp. 21–29; Bennett, *Vibrant Matter*; Diana Coole and Samantha Frost, 'Introducing the New Materialisms', in *New Materialisms: Ontology, Agency, and Politics*, ed. by Diana Coole and Samantha Frost (Duke University Press, 2010), pp. 1–43; Rosi Braidotti, *Metamorphoses: Towards a Materialist Theory of Becoming* (Oxford : Blackwell, 2002); Elizabeth A. Grosz, *The Nick of Time: Politics, Evolution, and the Untimely* (Durham, NC: Duke University Press, 2004); Elizabeth A. Grosz, *Volatile Bodies: Toward a Corporeal Feminism* (Bloomington: Indiana University Press, 1994); Mariam Fraser, Sarah Kember, and Celia Lury, 'Inventive Life: Approaches to the New Vitalism', *Theory, Culture & Society*, 22.1 (2005), pp. 1–14.

21   Barad, *Meeting the Universe Halfway: Quantum Physics and the Entanglement of Matter and Meaning* (Durham, NC: Duke University Press, 2007), p. 71.

22   Donna Haraway, 'The Promises of Monsters: A Regenerative Politics for Inappropriate/d Others', in *Cultural Studies*, ed. by Lawrence Grossberg, Cary Nelson, and Paula A. Treichler (New York: Routledge, 1992), pp. 295–337 (p. 300), emphasis removed.

nuance is important because inter-action presupposes the existence of some fully formed 'actants' present 'before the meeting', whereas intra-action stresses the co-constitution of those 'actants'. This move from inter-action to intra-action therefore requires one to shift 'the primary epistemological unit' from 'things' to phenomena, i.e. from an inter-action between pre-existing relata to boundary forming intra-action in phenomena. Shifting our analysis from 'things' to 'phenomena' also underlines the inseparability of 'intra-acting' 'components'. [23]

Second, diffraction is a helpful metaphor because it is, especially in the case of light, hard to observe without some special apparatus. Indeed, without the use of a certain set of tools, it may have always been assumed that light only behaved in a particle-like way, i.e. as matter and not as waves. Two things happen with this metaphor. First, it emphasizes humans' (in)capacity to detect, observe, or fully grasp something without a special set of tools and techniques. Second, it emphasizes the active dynamic role humans take, with or without apparatuses, in '(re)configurings of the world'.[24] Therefore, the metaphor is not only helpful to transition from an ontology of 'objects' towards one of 'phenomena', but it is also useful to understand how specific practices shape 'where the effects of differences appear'.[25] The method/metaphor thus helps us understand how our very measuring practices are neither innocent nor inconsequential.

However, this insight confronts us — perhaps ironically — with some problems reminiscent of those faced by an 'anti-realist' or even radical relativist perspective. Indeed, if everything we do, down to how we perceive, has an impact on the things we measure or want to talk about, how can we ever be sure we are getting the 'right' measurements? Further, without an agreed upon measurement, i.e. a shared account of the world, how can we understand one another, let alone, and more importantly, act collectively? Another problem, which is not an anti-realist one per se but is still relevant to the discussion at hand, is how to make sense of responsibility given this fragmented, or even

---

23   Karen Barad, 'Posthumanist Performativity: Toward an Understanding of How Matter Comes to Matter', *Signs: Journal of Women in Culture and Society*, 28.3 (2003), pp. 801–31 (p. 815).

24   Ibid., pp. 816, 818, 819, 821, 822, and 828.

25   Haraway, 'The Promises of Monsters', p. 300.

erased, subject. I suggest that part of the answer to this can be found in Evelyn Fox Keller's use of the psychodynamism of individuation.

Psychodynamism of Individuation

Keller points out that, as is illustrated by the biblical use of 'knowing', and contrary to Bacon's infamous proposition that 'knowledge is power', knowledge needs not only be about power but can instead also have to do with connection. Keller argues that this second possibility has been largely ignored.[26] Furthermore, she argues that knowledge's relationship to power has been overblown to such an extent that domination metaphors permeate scientific writing and thinking.[27] She stresses that the relationship to nature is all too often expressed in terms of scientists 'attacking' or 'solving' nature, or of 'conquering' her/it — implying that something about nature will, through the attack, conquest, or discovery of a solution, disappear and make way for the scientist's vision and will.

In Keller's opinion, this conception of knowledge resembles a conception of objectivity in which the knowing subject, in order to be objective, has to be detached from her object of study. This (mis)conceptualization of objectivity is due, she argues, to a specific (mis)conception of autonomy wherein there is a 'tacit implication [...] that autonomy can be bought only at the price of unrelatedness'.[28] The shared ideal of un-relatedness in both autonomy and objectivity has persuaded her to explore the interaction between emotional and cognitive experiences and development. Not only does this shared ideal suggest that the two are related, but Keller's hypothesis is that her study could help uncover the idea that they are, in fact, co-constitutive. In order to explore this relation between objectivity and autonomy, Keller turns to the object-relation theory of German psychoanalyst Ernst Schachtel and his take on the 'psychodynamism of individuation'.

---

26 Evelyn Fox Keller, *Reflections on Gender and Science* (New Haven, CT: Yale University Press, 1995), pp. 115–16.

27 Ibid., p. 123.

28 Ibid., p. 72.

In traditional Freudian psychoanalysis, the process of individuation, i.e. ego formation, is thought of as the more or less tragic
consequence of a self-awareness, or the delineation between inner
and outer stimuli, that develops as a result of unfulfilled needs. Freud
writes:

> An infant at the breast does not as yet distinguish his ego from
> the external world as the source of the sensations flowing in
> upon him. He gradually learns to do so, in response to various
> promptings. He must be very strongly impressed by the fact
> that some sources of excitation, which he will later recognize as
> his own bodily organs, can provide him with sensations at any
> moment, whereas other sources evade him from time to time
> — among them what he desires most of all, his mother's breast
> — and only reappear as a result of his screaming for help.[29]

That is, by realizing that her mother cannot and is not fulling her needs,
the child understands that she is not, in fact — and this is contrary to
what she may have initially thought/felt — one with her mother or the
world. This is a traumatic experience for the child who then realizes
that she must turn outward to satisfy unmet needs, and this towards
an external world over which she has little control. This initiation into
self-consciousness is condemned, for Freud, to a separation from the
mother/world because it destroys the symbiotic illusion. This makes
the child's relationship to the world conflictual, but also de facto oriented towards instrumentalization. Though Freud acknowledges that
this feeling of connectedness with the world (or symbiosis) may sub-
side in some adults, something he calls in this context the oceanic
feeling, he claims not to recognize it in himself and proceeds to link it
to some primitive pre-individuated ego.[30] Because of this, the oceanic
feeling speaks to, for him, some (regressive) longing to (re)unite with
the world/mother.

Schachtel has a different understanding of that dynamic of individuation. For the latter, fulfilling unmet needs is one of two types
of interest the child can have for the world. According to Schachtel,

---

29 Sigmund Freud, *Civilization and its Discontents*, in *The Standard Edition of the Complete
    Psychological Works of Sigmund Freud*, ed. by James Strachey, trans. by Angela Richards,
    24 vols (London: Hogarth Press and the Institute of Psycho-Analysis, 1953–74), XXI
    (1961), pp. 57–145 (p. 67).

30 Ibid., pp. 64–65.

the child is first and foremost turned towards the world by a curiosity and pleasure that exceeds biological necessities, i.e. there is an intrinsic and independent joy brought about by merely discovering the world. This joy is explained, in Schachtel's view, by the satisfaction the child experiences when she is connected to others and the world. Further, since Schachtel doesn't think of the dynamic of individuation as traumatic, the kind of uniting effort such as that sought out through Freud's 'oceanic' feeling can be positive and desirable.[31] This is the case so long as the transition from the symbiotic moment to the moment of individuation is dynamic. For this dynamism to be possible at all the child must have a secure sense of self, which Schachtel describes as one that can tolerate both difference and continuity between self and world. This in turn enables an attention for the world and its objects that is not only vested with or contingent upon one's needs and desires.[32] Schachtel calls this attention allocentric perception. He calls the instrumentalizing perception which opposes allocentric perception 'autocentric perception'.

Keller uses Schachtel's developments on perception to discuss what I alluded to earlier: a particular conception of autonomy and its relationship with objectivity. Keller terms the traditional conception of autonomy, i.e. one in which one sees oneself as separated from and impermeable to the world, static autonomy. Keller adds, however, that the allocentric perception that I just mentioned allows for another conception of autonomy, which she calls dynamic autonomy. This autonomy requires that one trust her capacities and abandon the delusion that she is fully self-sufficient, can act independently of the world and others, or can avoid being acted upon. This will allow 'for that vital element of ambiguity at the interface between subject and object'.[33]

The notions of objectivity corresponding to dynamic and static autonomy are dynamic and static objectivity. 'Dynamic objectivity aims at a form of knowledge that grants to the world around us its independent integrity but does so in a way that remains cognizant

---

31   Ernst Schachtel, *Metamorphosis: On the Conflict of Human Development and the Psychology of Creativity* (New York: Routledge, 2001), p. 182.

32   Keller, *Reflections on Gender and Science*, p. 119.

33   Ibid., p. 84, my emphasis.

of, indeed relies on, our connectivity with that world'.[34] Keller compares this sort of objectivity to empathy. Like empathy, then, dynamic objectivity is an objectivity that mobilizes shared experiences and emotions between the subject and object of knowledge.[35] In static objectivity, on the contrary, the understanding of the other can only be attained by separating and fracturing the subject from her object of knowledge, which involves dissociating the object from the subject so that the latter can instrumentalize it. This leads to a type of knowledge where difference is thought of in terms of frontiers and sharp edges. In this paradigm of objectivity, perception becomes an 'act of aggressive violence in which the perceiver, like Procrustes with his hapless victims, cuts off those aspects of the object which he cannot use for his purposes'.[36]

In sum, Keller's vision of the subject is not, strictly speaking, a 'decentring' of the subject in the sense that it makes the subject disappear. In fact, as we have just seen, Keller spends a significant amount of energy describing how a subject is formed, or individuated, and how that impacts her relationship to the world and therefore also to knowledge. My point is, however, that this dynamism of individuation — which at one point accepts a certain degree of separation and at another unites subject and object — forces us to think of the frontiers between subject and object as at least momentarily absent. This 'decentring of the subject' is the key, in my opinion, to answering the criticisms addressed to New Materialism which I have mentioned above.

Longino's Critique of the Psychodynamism of Individuation

Before addressing how the psychodynamism of individuation can help to answer the criticism addressed to New Materialism, let us turn to Longino's own criticism of the psychodynamism of individuation. Longino's characterization of the psychodynamism of individuation focuses on the aspect of the theory that attempts to show that 'cog-

---

34   Ibid., p. 117.
35   Ibid., p. 116.
36   Schachtel, *Metamorphosis*, p. 171, quoted by Keller, *Reflections on Gender and Science*, p. 120.

nitive efforts have an ineluctably affective dimension'.[37] From that reading, therefore, she places Keller's psychodynamism of individuation alongside standpoint theory[38] for both theories, in her opinion, aim to highlight the subjective conditionality of descriptive claims by emphasizing their 'social and historical location'. Her criticism of both theories is, therefore, that they 'fail to explain how we are to decide or to justify decisions between what seem to be conflicting claims'.[39] In other words, if subject X describes 'Phenomenon A' as 'a' and subject Y describes 'Phenomenon A' as 'b', how are we to determine who is right?

Though Longino writes that both theories fail at answering this question, she also proposes that standpoint theory attempts to solve it by ascribing more epistemic authority to one subject based on their social and historical location. It is less clear how she thinks the psychodynamism of individuation ascribes epistemic authority, but she nevertheless criticizes it on the same grounds. For Longino, the 'analytical task is not to determine which is epistemically most adequate. Rather, the task is to understand how these complexly conditioned subjectivities are expressed in action and belief.'[40]

This criticism resembles what we have seen earlier about the 'threat of anti-realism' directed at New Materialism. That is to say, that standpoint theory, the psychodynamism of individuation, and New Materialism all, to use Longino's wording again, 'fail to explain how we are to decide or to justify decisions between what seem to be conflicting claims'. It is indeed conceivable that the accounts of a phenomenon given by New Materialism would lead to different descriptive claims about that phenomenon. These accounts may change according to the apparatus involved. So how can Keller's psychodynamism of individuation help at all with the 'anti-realist' problems New Materialism seems to reiterate?

---

37   Longino, 'Subjects, Power and Knowledge', p. 108.
38   As a reminder, 'standpoint theory' argues that the subject of knowledge's position
      (be it their gender, 'race', socio-economic background, sexual orientation, mental and
      physical ability, etc.) has an influence on the type and quality of knowledge produced.
39   Longino, 'Subjects, Power and Knowledge', p. 109.
40   Ibid.

Relational Ontology

My hope is to have shown above that the psychodynamism of individuation, contrary to what Longino suggests, is not about lending
epistemic superiority to one subject, but instead about redefining the
epistemic subject altogether by redefining what could be called his or
her epistemic virtues — a topic I will discuss in a moment — and by
extending who/what counts as subject. This expansion of the subject
is something this theory shares with New Materialism and what I have
called here relational ontology. As for the redefinition of the subject's
epistemic virtues, New Materialism already hints at the connection
between ontology, epistemology, and ethics, but does not really expand upon the topic of epistemic virtues.

I have already claimed that New Materialism and the psychodynamism of individuation share a common shift in ontological terms.
Indeed, what New Materialism and, I argue, Keller, ask us to do is
to try to think of object and subject in terms of the relationship they
have with one another, and how these relationships are shaped by and
shape these entities, critters, or relata. In Keller, this shift in ontology
is captured by her discussion of the 'vital element of ambiguity'[41] and
of the continuity between the subject and object, which questions the
impermeability of both and highlights their inter/intra-dependence.
Whereas in Haraway and Barad, the subject is 'heterogenous', 'noni-
somorphic', and 'partial',[42] these descriptors all point to an ontology
in which subject-object formation is not only co-constitutive, but in
which the relation and cosmological organization bears more weight
than its 'individual' components. Therefore, the subject is redefined as
an emerging pattern of difference, which 'highlight[s], exhibit[s], and
make[s] evident the entangled structure of the changing and contingent ontology of the world, including the ontology of knowing.'[43]

Furthermore, both, beyond offering a different ontology, propose
in and by this ontology, an ethical framework. The suggestion that the
self cannot be defined or thought of outside of its relationships has two
major ethical consequences. First, it allows for a much more dynamic

---

41   Keller, *Reflections on Gender and Science*, p. 84.
42   Haraway, 'Situated Knowledges', p. 586.
43   Barad, *Meeting the Universe Halfway*, p. 73.

(and emancipating?) self-understanding. That is, one that is not con-
fined to only one or to a cumulative list of identity. This 'departure from
identity' is not, however, reducible to a non-identity, or a point of view
from nowhere, i.e. a detached conception of objectivity which aims to
paradoxically embody the universal. The positionality of every element
in the pattern of diffraction is and has to be taken into account! But that
account, or census of positions, does not determine future outcomes,
nor does it sanction the attribution of blame. The causal chain of the
elements taken into account is neither linear nor monocausal, and it is
therefore neither reproducible nor predictable. Thus, identity is both
constrained by some parameters and, at the same time, understood as
contingent: it is processual.

Processualism and Allocentric Perception

I would now like to discuss processuality and return to the question
of how a reading of the psychodynamism of individuation may answer some criticism addressed to New Materialism. Processuality is
precisely what helps reveal how the 'complexly conditioned subjectivities' Longino worries about 'are expressed in action and belief'. Keller's
understanding of processuality involves 'the growing interest among
physicists in a process description of reality', whereby 'object reality acquires a dynamic character, akin to the more fluid concept of autonomy
emerging from psychoanalysis'.[44] Indeed, where the psychodynamism
of individuation can benefit New Materialism, I argue, is precisely
through these processual, dynamic descriptions of the world that a
'more fluid concept of autonomy' allows for.

Therefore, and as a first response to this anxiety about the spectre
of anti-realism, the psychodynamism of individuation helps us to
understand how the agential cuts into phenomena are made at the human level. That is to say, according to which interests, motivations, and
to what end those cuts are made. It emphasizes that knowledge claims
are not innocent and devoid of emotional or libidinous investments (in
the terms of New Materialism, these emotional-libidinous investments
may be considered part of the apparatus). It does not contend, how-

---

44   Keller, *Reflections on Gender and Science*, p. 94.

ever, that these emotional investments are any ground to reject one claim in favour of another (allegedly less invested) or to hierarchize them into better or lesser claims. Instead, the psychodynamism of individuation calls for an investigation into these emotional-libidinous investments — as real material objects — so that we can share fuller accounts of phenomena.

Second, and while recognizing that this objective may not be achievable (immediately or forever), the psychodynamism of individuation provides us with an insight into the problem of a shared account of the world. Indeed, with allocentric perception and dynamic objectivity, a sketch of what Mirenda Fricker has called epistemic virtues emerges.[45] Though Fricker's theory of epistemic virtues is of inestimable help in the realm of judiciary testimonies as a transitional or intermediate tool in this specific context, my point of departure or premise is that, ultimately, for most knowledge projects, the sort of unbiased judgement she is after is impossible, and may not even be desirable. Therefore, in this quest for epistemic virtues, the orientation would be towards those that result in the questioning of one's own authority and the room that is opened up as a consequence for different and possibly conflicting accounts. These virtues, in common language, might be called generosity, benevolence, patience, and curiosity — though I am hesitant to propose anything that is definitive here, and by giving these examples I only wish to make my meaning as clear as possible. What I can say about these virtues at this point, however, is that in practice they would be of the sort that maximize the possibility for a common ground — even when the language we use seems to lead to deadlocks and contradictions regarding any phenomenon's description.

The examples I have given may seem to put the onus of the epistemological enterprise on the 'listener' rather than the 'speaker' of some information. I want to suggest, however, that the onus is in fact shared between the parties. This is because one finds oneself in either position at different times and also because these virtues, if we come back to the examples of generosity, benevolence, patience, and curi-

---

45   Miranda Fricker, 'The Virtue of Testimonial Justice', in *Epistemic Injustice: Power and the Ethics of Knowing* (Oxford: Oxford University Press, 2007), pp. 86–108.

osity, do not make a demand upon the 'listener' alone. Indeed, in the way she conveys information a speaker can prove to be more or less generous, benevolent, patient, and curious towards her interlocutor. Keller alludes to this when she points to the empathy that dynamic objectivity requires and which consists in finding a common language in shared experiences and emotions.[46] The psychodynamism of individuation therefore suggests that if non-instrumentalized perception is possible, there is finally no such thing as a fully disinvested perception. That is, this non-instrumentalized perception will have to find a common language in shared experiences and emotions which implies an emotional investment. If we accept that perception is always-already oriented and invested, what we need for finding a common ground is a way of accessing multiple grids of analysis. I contend that this is precisely what allocentric perception and dynamic objectivity offer.

Third, this encounter between New Materialism and the psychodynamism of individuation has the advantage of addressing the threat of idealism (understood as anti-realism) by encouraging doubt about the ego's separation from the world and also encouraging processual reflexivity, which forces us to face the ways in which the ego affects objects and how objects, in turn, affect the subject. Indeed, when the subject enters this ambiguous space in which the object affects her completely, there is as little doubt about the object's presence as there is about her own. Keller's psychodynamism of individuation therefore gives us the means to face and negotiate the ambiguity between the inside and the outside without negating our sense of self.

Fourth, and regarding the question of accountability in the face of a dislocated subject, I contend that agenthood, and hence accountability, in this ontological paradigm is not a matter of tracing back intention and therefore responsibility to the original misbehaviour in order to 'punish the mistake' of a 'unified', 'coherent', 'free-acting' subject. Rather, this accountability is one which encourages doubt about one's own presence as a coherent unit,[47] and, by extension, encourages doubt about one's own (epistemological and ethical) omnipotence. This accountability is one which demands that the subject locate her-

---

46   Keller, *Reflections on Gender and Science*, p. 116.
47   Haraway, 'Situated Knowledges', pp. 585–86.

self in the maelstrom of forces pushing her around and thus that she identify where her power lies. Further, this accountability is one that demands 'reponsibility for difference', for where one places the fateful line between self and everything else.[48] This doubt results in what Haraway calls the 'possibility of webs of connections', which are 'called solidarity in politics and shared conversations in epistemology'.[49] This alliance between New Materialism and the psychodynamism of individuation hence shifts the focus from a cartography of matter that demands exhaustive models aimed at predicting future outcomes or at attributing blame to one that dynamically demands responses (personal and collective) to depleting circumstances. In sum, how we arrive where we are does matter (to get out of immobilizing blame and shame), but it matters less than how we can fix/change the depleting circumstances and move forward collectively, whether that be through reparations, mediation, or separation.

---

48   Ibid., p. 585.
49   Ibid., p. 584.

Emergence that Matters and Emergent Irrelevance
On the Political Use of Fundamental Physics
CHRISTOPH F. E. HOLZHEY

Physics was long considered as *the* model science. It arguably lost this role to the life sciences towards the end of the twentieth century, but some strands of new materialism have helped to give it a second wind. How physics theorizes matter seems to matter again, and not only intellectually but politically as well. As an ex-physicist who is semi-converted to the humanities, I am quite interested in the idea of mobilizing the critical potential of physics, but for this very reason I find it important to problematize some of the ways in which this potential tends to be all too quickly either embraced or rejected.

In this chapter, I will need to be quite quick and schematic myself and will only give some indications and elaborations on three points. They are, firstly, my claim that the fundamental ontology of matter has no political relevance; secondly, my position that what is politically relevant is, instead, to devise effective strategies to deactivate the normative power of fundamental ontologies; and thirdly, the proposition that physics can be helpful to address these first two points, that is, to understand its own irrelevance and at the same time inspire strategies to deactivate the normativity of ontologies of matter.

1. THE FUNDAMENTAL ONTOLOGY OF MATTER IS (POLITICALLY) IRRELEVANT

Let me begin with some clarifications of my claim. I speak of the 'fundamental ontology of matter' and take it primarily in the sense that one might associate with physics, that is, in terms of defining elementary material constituents and establishing their laws of interaction, or what is often referred to as the 'theory of everything'.[1] This is what I will primarily mean by the term 'ontology' even when I do not qualify it further; I do not thereby intend to subsume or exclude other dimensions or meanings of ontology, in particular not a 'materialist ontology', which I would consider to have a far broader meaning.

By claiming that the ontology of matter has no relevance, I mean that no difference could be detected on our human scale — or indeed any finite length scale — if the fundamental ontology were quite radically different. I am thinking of alternatives such as discrete particles moving in a vacuum vs a continuum conception of matter; or processes fully determined by laws of motion (which is associated with mechanics) vs allowing for random deviations or something like free will.

My claim, then, is that any of these ontological options are compatible with all that could possibly matter on any specified scale. When it is understood in this way my claim could seem unsurprising. Who would have thought that the ontologies of matter proposed by physics are politically relevant? Wouldn't that imply, among other things, an archaic appeal to nature, falling prey to the naturalistic fallacy of de-

---

1   See, e.g., the glossary of Brian Greene, *The Elegant Universe: Superstrings, Hidden Dimensions, and the Quest for the Ultimate Theory* (New York: Vintage Books, 2000): 'T.O.E. (Theory of Everything). A quantum-mechanical theory that encompasses all forces and all matter' (p. 423). The term became popular in the 1980s in the context of string theory as a promising candidate to address the fundamental incompatibility of highly successful fundamental theories such as quantum mechanics and gravitation. While it seems uncontroversial within physics that a 'theory of everything' in this sense of describing all matter and interactions should be possible, even Greene remarks that there is no agreement on further associations with this 'grandiose descriptive term' (p. 16): for a 'staunch reductionist', such a theory would truly describe everything and effectively represent the end of physics, while others, himself included, would highlight that reduction in principle does not imply reduction in practice; they would consider a T.O.E. as but the beginning, namely as 'the firmest foundation on which to *build* our understanding' (p. 17). Others, still, some of whom I will cite in section three, insist that 'unexpected phenomena' and 'new physical principles' and 'independent laws' would emerge at larger scales (p. 17).

riving an 'ought' from an 'is'? Isn't it uncontroversial that physics only describes but cannot establish political or ethical norms?

Yet, much of what is written under the label of new materialism argues for the political importance of ontology in the sense I outlined earlier. Their proponents tend to agree on insisting that matter is fundamentally active, agential, vibrant, even vital. In this way, they seek to correct what they interpret as the still-dominant ontology of Descartes and its solidification through Newton's mechanics, which through its success established the paradigm for all modern scientific knowledge. This ontology is dualistic, conceiving matter as passive and inert, and as animated and activated by human subjects — be it directly or in a more complex cultural and linguistic way.[2] In like manner, the tradition of historical materialism also gets targeted as presupposing the passivity of matter.[3]

Why is it so important for new materialism to overcome this ontology by insisting on the activity of matter? In what sense is it political? To put it very briefly and roughly, the argument is that the dualism of active subject vs passive matter lies at the heart of a host of hierarchical binaries in which one side masters and dominates the other, which has led to the violence of sexism, classism, racism, and the exploitation of nature.

This understanding of the political and its criteria are certainly not new: there is a long tradition of tracing fundamental, political issues to the persistence of hierarchical binaries, and of adopting different positions and strategies in response that seek to overcome the violent consequences of these binaries. Most feminist traditions could be mentioned here, especially ecofeminism, as well as queer theory with its

---

2   See, e.g., Stacy Alaimo and Susan Hekman, 'Introduction: Emerging Models of Materiality in Feminist Theory', in their co-edited *Material Feminisms* (Bloomington: Indiana University Press, 2008), pp. 1–19; Diana Coole and Samantha Frost, 'Introducing the New Materialisms', in *New Materialisms: Ontology, Agency, and Politics*, ed. by Diana Coole and Samantha Frost (Durham, NC: Duke University Press, 2010), pp. 1–43; Jane Bennett, *Vibrant Matter: A Political Ecology of Things* (Durham, NC: Duke University Press, 2010).

3   See, e.g., Samantha Frost, 'The Implications of the New Materialisms for Feminist Epistemology', in *Feminist Epistemology and Philosophy of Science*, ed. by Heidi E. Grasswick (Dordrecht: Springer Netherlands, 2011), pp. 69–83 and Simon Choat, 'Science, Agency and Ontology: A Historical-Materialist Response to New Materialism', *Political Studies*, 66.4 (2018), 1027–42 <https://doi.org/10.1177/0032321717731926>.

critique of heteronormativity. To use an intellectual shortcut, one can say that what unites otherwise quite diverse positions and problematizes the naturalistic-fallacy argument is the notion of performativity, which undermines the systematic separation of registers: no description or representation of what *is* is ever neutral. Instead, it is always also performative, productive, and normative.

2. THE RELEVANCE OF DEACTIVATING THE NORMATIVE POWER OF FUNDAMENTAL ONTOLOGIES

While I agree that it is important to acknowledge the performative power of ontology, I also think it is important to distinguish different political strategies relating to it. I am thinking, in particular, of different feminist and queer strategies that oppose gender essentialism, that is to say, the dispositive that turns nature into destiny. One primary and influential strategy in these traditions is to distinguish between biological sex and socially constructed gender, and to insist that the norms and categories of gender are contingent and do not result from biology. This strategy could also be described as insisting on a break or cut between ontology and politics, or between what is and what could be — and arguably ought to be — otherwise, and it seems very similar to what I am proposing.

However, there is also the important counter-argument that such a division only serves to veil the social construction of sexual difference and its function of founding and stabilizing a hierarchical gender binary. According to this view — and I am thinking especially of Judith Butler's *Gender Trouble* and her theory of gender performativity — all reference to a pre-discursive ontology is politically suspect. This position abolishes the distinctions between sex and gender, ontology and politics, and the descriptive and the normative,[4] and replaces them with a continuity. As Butler writes in reference to Monique Wittig: 'sex proves to have been gender from the start.'[5] In other words, ontology is always already politics; 'Ontology is, thus, not a foundation, but a

---

4   Cf. Butler's reflection on the temptation to distinguish between a descriptive and a normative account of gender in her 1999 preface to *Gender Trouble: Feminism and the Subversion of Identity* (New York: Routledge, 1999), p. xxi.

5   Ibid., p. 189.

normative injunction that operates insidiously by installing itself into political discourse as its necessary ground'.[6]

In many circles, this kind of argument has made it quasi-taboo to invoke ontology, 'nature', 'being', etc., at least without using inverted commas. And this development is precisely what new materialisms have reacted to. In my reading, these various thinkers share the intuition that refraining from ontological references may only disavow an ontology of inert, passive matter and unwittingly re-enforce it.[7] They insist on taking matter more seriously and engaging in ontological speculations, asking such questions as, for example, 'What if Culture Was Really Nature All Along?'.[8] Of course, with this reversal of Butler's 'sex has been gender from the start', the question becomes how anything can be said or thought about matter without employing discourse. The new materialist move could perhaps be described as follows: Firstly, to highlight the importance of implicit ontological assumptions — in particular, of the opposition between active discourse and passive matter — and the difficulty of avoiding them.[9] Secondly, to engage with and rework ontology, rather than disavowing it, and thereby seek to improve its politics.

It should be noted that a great deal of the work produced under the banner of the ontological turn — initiated through related but different traditions, especially in science studies and anthropology — is not interested in asserting an ontology that would lie beyond cultural or linguistic construction. Instead, the aim in such work generally seems to be a radicalization of the constructivist impulse and a deflation of

---

6   Ibid.

7   The mechanism of disavowal that I am invoking here is modelled upon Sigmund Freud's account of fetishism as a disavowal of sexual difference, which involves both a denial of the 'reality' of castration and its acknowledgment through anxiety and the defensive creation of fetishes. Disavowal here produces precisely what it was supposed to avert, namely a split (and in that sense castrated) subject. See the entry 'Disavowal' in Jean Laplanche and Jean-Bertrand Pontalis, *The Language of Psycho-Analysis* (London: Hogarth Press, 1973), pp. 118–21. From a feminist perspective, a fetishization of women is just as problematic as their identification with an essential lack.

8   Vicki Kirby, 'Natural Convers(at)ions: Or, What If Culture Was Really Nature All Along?', in *Material Feminisms*, ed. by Alaimo and Hekman, pp. 214–36.

9   Indeed, one might consider it impossible to avoid ontological assumptions, though I wonder whether such a claim would have to be based in pragmatics, anthropology, psychology, or aesthetics rather than logic.

the normative effect of ontology. This is to be achieved through the identification of a multiplicity of different — that is to say, incompatible but individually equally viable — ontologies, and not merely in philosophical or spiritual belief systems but also in social practices.[10]

I find this strategy promising, and while what I will propose resembles it, I also want to note that it is highly ambiguous. Indeed, proliferating ontological discourses rather than renouncing them increases the risk of unwittingly re-enforcing ontological assumptions through disavowal:[11] In particular, the view that all ontologies are constructed and mediated by discourse seems to fit well with an ontology of passive matter and active discourse. This is not to say that a pluralization of 'ontologies' — and what has been called 'ontological politics'[12] — necessarily implies such an underlying ontology of matter and discourse, but its redefinition of ontology forecloses the possibility of critically addressing the effect of underlying ontologies — something that was still possible within the strategy of refraining from positive ontological references.[13]

---

10   Cf. Steve Woolgar and Javier Lezaun, 'The Wrong Bin Bag: A Turn to Ontology in Science and Technology Studies?', *Social Studies of Science*, 43.3 (2013), pp. 321–40 <https://doi.org/10.1177/0306312713488820>; Martin Holbraad, Morten Axel Pedersen, and Eduardo Viveiros de Castro, 'The Politics of Ontology: Anthropological Positions', 2014 <https://culanth.org/fieldsights/the-politics-of-ontology-anthropological-positions> [accessed 26 March 2019]; Christopher Gad, Casper Bruun Jensen, and Brit Ross Winthereik, 'Practical Ontology: Worlds in STS and Anthropology', *NatureCulture*, 3 (2015), pp. 67–86.

11   Cf. Woolgar and Lezaun's worry that the notion of 'ontological politics' may 'entail commitments that take us beyond the long established deflationary stances of sceptical STS' (p. 336).

12   Cf. Annemarie Mol, 'Ontological Politics. A Word and Some Questions', *The Sociological Review*, 47.1_suppl (1999), pp. 74–89 <https://doi.org/10.1111/j.1467-954X.1999.tb03483.x>, referring to John Law.

13   See, e.g., Astrid Deuber-Mankowsky, 'Das ontologische Debakel oder was heißt: Es gibt Medien?', *ZMK Zeitschrift Medien- und Kulturforschung*, 8.2 (2017), pp. 157–68, who observes critically that computer-science discourses of 'operational ontologies' avoid and disavow the philosophical question of ontology — what is being? — with the effect that everything, including human beings, is objectified and treated as given data and 'stock' (Bestand). Giorgio Agamben's book *What Is Real?* (Stanford, CA: Stanford University Press, 2018) is animated by a similar worry, namely that abandoning the properly philosophical question of being means forsaking valuable resources for resisting (neo-)liberal, biopolitical modes of governmentality. But these two thinkers do not employ similar strategies to counter a pluralization of ontologies. While Agamben pushes towards a more properly ontological inquiry, I interpret Deuber-Mankowsky as following the strategy of 'refraining from ontological references' in order to keep the question of ontology open.

By contrast, the new materialist positions that I focus upon target the ontological level underlying discursive practices. Instead of being interested in deflating ontologies by multiplying them, they propose an alternative ontology: one that conceives of matter as active, vibrant, and even alive, rather than as passive, inert, and dualistically opposed to the activity and agency of human discourse and culture. I am especially interested in the influential argument by Karen Barad, who mobilizes theoretical physics to develop what she calls an 'agential realist ontology'.[14]

Although Barad criticizes the excessive power granted to language, she takes no issue with the notion of performativity that, according to Butler, accounts for that power. On the contrary, she extends performativity from language to matter itself. Her neologism 'intra-action' encapsulates much of her argument: this term goes beyond the 'usual "interaction," which *presumes* the prior existence of independent entities/relata',[15] and instead allows for the *emergence* of separate entities. According to Butler, the fact '[t]hat the gendered body is performative suggests that it has no ontological status apart from the various acts which constitute its reality'.[16] While one might limit this argument to manifestly social categories such as gender, Barad emphasizes than in quantum mechanics the ontological status of elementary entities, such as light or electrons, depends on how their reality is constituted in experimental acts: for instance, depending on the apparatus with which they are observed, they materialize as particles or waves.

The parallels Barad draws between discursive and quantum performativity are striking, compelling, and suggestive. However, they also run the risk of short-circuiting different levels, registers, and scales, thereby creating profound ambiguities and losing a sense of what, in her own account, emerges and comes to matter in between.

On the one hand, expanding performativity extends what I would characterize as top-down constructions, from social discourse all the way down to the sub-atomic scale, while, on the other, it also ends

---

14   Karen Barad, 'Posthumanist Performativity: Toward an Understanding of How Matter Comes to Matter', *Signs: Journal of Women in Culture and Society*, 28.3 (2003), pp. 801–31 (p. 811).

15   Barad, 'Posthumanist Performativity', p. 815, emphasis added.

16   Butler, *Gender Trouble*, p. 173.

up flipping to its reverse: Rather than *refraining* from ontological discourse Barad often *affirms* a particular ontology. Asserting a 'relational ontology', insisting on 'nature's queerness', and affirming an ontology of 'indeterminacy', as she does, certainly avoids many problem associated with essentialism and helps to counteract them.[17] Still, I would maintain that any ontology, however indeterminate, relational, or processual, becomes problematically normative when one forgets its speculative, constructed, and strategic character and instead just embraces its performativity, which is seen as operating across all scales from the bottom-up, as it were. Among other things that I cannot unfold here,[18] there is the risk that such an ontology would become unduly extrapolated to suggest that everything *is* indeterminate and queer, and *should* and can be recognized and destabilized as such.[19]

Indeed, Barad insists quite emphatically that her account holds for all scales, from the microscopic to the macroscopic and in a precise and literal — rather than merely analogical way — for discourses as much as for matter.[20] According to my reading, this claim ends up

---

17   Barad, 'Posthumanist Performativity', pp. 812, 816 and Karen Barad, 'Nature's Queer Performativity', *Qui Parle: Literature, Philosophy, Visual Arts, History*, 19.2 (2011), pp. 121–58 (pp. 125, 147).

18   See e.g. the contributions by Cornelia Möser and Marianna Poyares in this volume.

19   Such questions of (post)foundationalism in new feminist materialisms are addressed by Katharina Hoppe, 'Eine neue Ontologie des Materiellen? Probleme und Perspektiven neomaterialistischer Feminismen', in *Material turn: Feministische Perspektiven auf Materialität und Materialismus*, ed. by Christine Löw and others (Leverkusen: Barbara Budrich, 2017). While Hoppe suggests that a 'relational ontology' like Barad's can escape the problem of a normative essentialism, Timothy Morton and Graham Harman warn against over-investing in the political benefits of relational ontologies. See Timothy Morton, 'Treating Objects Like Women: Feminist Ontology and the Question of Essence', in *International Perspectives in Feminist Ecocriticism*, ed. by Greta Gaard, Simon C. Estok, and Serpil Oppermann (New York: Routledge, 2013), pp. 56–69. Heeding this warning does not imply endorsing Harman's 'speculative realist' alternative, his 'Object Oriented Ontology' (OOO). Rather, I find its critique by Thomas Lemke not only compelling, but — for very similar reasons — also applicable to Barad's Agential Realism, including his argument that 'OOO's promise to break once and for all with subject–object dualism results in a revived form of subjectivism'. See Thomas Lemke, 'Materialism without Matter: The Recurrence of Subjectivism in Object-Oriented Ontology', *Distinktion: Journal of Social Theory*, 18.2 (2017), pp. 133–52 (p. 134) <https://doi.org/10.1080/1600910X.2017.1373686>. In other words, while I argue for the strategic value of speculative ontologies, I also see a need for a critical corrective to their proclaimed realism.

20   Karen Barad, *Meeting the Universe Halfway: Quantum Physics and the Entanglement of Matter and Meaning* (Durham, NC: Duke University Press, 2007), pp. 24, 86, 110; 'Nature's Queer Performativity', p. 147. See also Elizabeth Stephens, 'Feminism and

undermining her own sense of 'how matter comes to matter', which requires emergent discontinuities or what she calls 'agential cuts' enacted through intra-action.[21]

I agree that the notion of emergence is key for understanding how matter comes to matter, and also that a cut or discontinuity is important. However, the crucial question is how to relate discontinuity to the notion of emergence, which has gained much currency in recent years but still remains thoroughly ambiguous.[22] Indeed, the notion of a continuously emerging discontinuity seems inherently contradictory, and requiring it as a condition for something coming to matter risks implying that nothing can actually *come* to matter and everything is already determined 'from the start' and 'all along', whether through discourse or nature.

Instead, what I would like to suggest is that matter properly *comes* to matter at any relevant scale to the extent that other scales *cease* to matter. There is no need to claim any discontinuity here, only a

---

New Materialism: The Matter of Fluidity', *Interalia: A Journal of Queer Studies*, 9 (2014), pp. 186–202. I should highlight that Barad's point that quantum phenomena are not necessarily restricted to microscopic scales is well taken if one takes 'scale' only in terms of length scales. Nevertheless, in most interpretations of quantum mechanics (in particular Bohr's), the possibility of describing experiment and its results as classical (rather than quantum) objects is crucial and this requires a large number of accessible degrees of freedom (as can usually be found in macroscopic objects).

21 Cf. Barad, *Meeting the Universe Halfway*, esp. pp. 175–79. For a critique of Barad's denial of 'scale variance', see Derek Woods, 'Scale Variance and the Concept of Matter', in *The New Politics of Materialism: History, Philosophy, Science*, ed. by Sarah Ellenzweig and John H. Zammito (Abingdon: Routledge, 2017), pp. 200–24. While I largely agree with his critique, I am sceptical about his insistence of linking 'scale variance' to the emergence of 'jumps and discontinuities' (p. 201) across scales and maintain that physics can only account for a pragmatic sense of emergence. For a helpful and nuanced assessment of Barad's agential realism, stressing the importance of emergent discontinuities as well as exclusions, see Gregory Hollin and others, '(Dis)Entangling Barad: Materialisms and Ethics', *Social Studies of Science*, 47.6 (2017), pp. 918–41 <https://doi.org/10.1177/0306312717728344>.

22 For entry points into the vast literature on emergence as notion that appeared in late-nineteenth biological and evolutionary theories and 're-emerged' in the last quarter of the twentieth century as a 'legitimate' and widely popularized scientific concept in theories of complexity, self-organization, and chaos, see, for example, Peter A. Corning, 'The Re-Emergence of "Emergence": A Venerable Concept in Search of a Theory', *Complexity*, 7.6 (2002), pp. 18–30 <https://doi.org/10.1002/cplx.10043> and the very helpful reader *Emergence: Contemporary Readings in Philosophy and Science*, ed. by Mark A. Bedau and Paul Humphreys (Cambridge, MA: MIT Press, 2008).

coming to matter and ceasing to matter, which in turn relies on the possibility of material properties changing with scale. One could speak here of a scale-dependent ontology, as some indeed do,[23] but as long as the multiple ontologies at different scales remain reducible to an underlying ontology, the normative power of that ontology is bound to remain irresistible.

While breaking with physics in favour of another, more properly philosophical understanding of ontology is always an option, I argue that the desired discontinuity can also be addressed more immanently within physics by considering the limit of infinitely small or infinitely large scales and seeing how incompatible, discontinuously related fundamental ontologies can account for the same finite-scale properties. In the next section, I will give some indications on how thinking with physics in this manner may be helpful in devising strategies to deactivate the normativity of fundamental ontologies, including those of physics itself.

3. PROPOSITION: A PHYSICS OF EMERGENCE CAN HELP IN DEACTIVATING ONTOLOGICAL NORMATIVITY

There is something to be learned, I suggest, from the ways in which physics routinely combines and mixes incompatible, discontinuously related ontologies when modelling phenomena emerging at some particular scale, such as the crystallization of liquids, the condensation of vapour into droplets, or other so-called phase transitions. With the phrase 'mixing ontologies' I mean describing matter both in terms of discrete particles moving in a vacuum and in terms of continua of energy, temperature, or some other fluid or field that can flow and propagate waves.

In the late nineteenth century these ontological alternatives were hotly debated and ultimately decided upon in favour of atomism.[24]

---

23   In addition to Woods, see, for instance, Robert W. Batterman, 'Autonomy and Scales', in *Why More Is Different: Philosophical Issues in Condensed Matter Physics and Complex Systems*, ed. by Brigitte Falkenburg and Margaret Morrison (Heidelberg: Springer, 2015), pp. 115–35 (p. 133).

24   Debates on atomism, which entangle metaphysics and physics, seem to keep recurring on different time scales even after Immanuel Kant's critical philosophy posits irresolvable antinomies of pure reason. See, for example, Alan Chalmers, 'Atomism from the

Nonetheless, continuum models, which imply an ontology of continuous, indefinitely divisible fluids rather than discrete atoms, are still in use today and indeed continue to be omnipresent when physics models emergent phenomena such as phase transitions. Of course, the common view is that continuum descriptions are only pragmatic approximations and that continuum properties of matter emerge only in a pragmatic sense at large scales, and are, in principle, reducible to the properties of atoms and their interactions. However, it turns out that simple everyday experiences such as the qualitative difference between phases, the transitions between them, and other thermodynamic phenomena are remarkably hard to grasp or even define without relying on continuum descriptions.

In the late nineteenth century, statistical mechanics was developed to make the reduction of everyday phenomena to an atomistic ontology plausible and to understand how the thermodynamic properties of matter can emerge from mechanics. Perhaps the most important and basic issue at stake here is the so-called second law of thermodynamics, the law of irreversibly increasing entropy, which has been interpreted as defining an arrow of time. The challenge is that the laws of mechanics are reversible — any process going in one direction can also go in the opposite direction — and it would seem logically impossible to derive a directed process, such as a tendency towards equilibrium, from reversible laws. Yet, statistical mechanics shows that if you have enough particles there is an overwhelming probability that the complicated and therefore effectively random movement of microscopic particles will behave as described by thermodynamics and approach equilibrium.

Most physicists are quite satisfied with such an account, which considers all material processes to be reducible in principle but allows for the emergence of new properties — such as irreversibility — in

---

17th to the 20th Century', in *Stanford Encyclopedia of Philosophy*, ed. by Edward N. Zalta (Spring 2019 Edition) <https://plato.stanford.edu/archives/spr2019/entries/atomism-modern/> [accessed 5 May 2020] and Torsten Wilholt, 'When Realism Made a Difference: The Constitution of Matter and Its Conceptual Enigmas in Late 19th Century Physics', *Studies in History and Philosophy of Science Part B: Studies in History and Philosophy of Modern Physics*, 39.1 (2008), pp. 1–16 <https://doi.org/10.1016/j.shpsb.2007.04.003>. While physicists may no longer question the reality of atoms, they have also ceased to consider them as elementary and tend rather towards ontologies of continuous fields, strings, or membranes.

practice. Such a pragmatic sense of emergence is sufficient to justify the use of thermodynamics, and more generally, the relative autonomy of phenomena at higher levels and the respective disciplines studying them, such as chemistry and biology.

However, others observe that this view of 'reducible in principle, but emergent in practice' privileges fundamental physics and undermines other sciences and their objects. In other words, critics have highlighted how a pragmatic sense of emergence introduces no discontinuity or cut, and they worry that the fundamental ontology and its laws continue to dominate everything across all scales.

I take this worry seriously. It corresponds, in effect, to what I have called the normative performativity of ontology, which here takes the form of extending reversibility from the fundamental level to all scales and disregarding a pragmatic emergence of irreversibility. When viewed from a certain perspective, such normativity is irresistible as it seems logically impossible to shift continuously between opposite properties.

In the final quarter of the last century, Ilya Prigogine and Isabelle Stengers were particularly vocal in insisting that thermodynamics should be taken more seriously than a pragmatic approximation of particle mechanics. They argued that change is fundamentally impossible in an ontology of particles obeying deterministic, reversible laws, and time is just an illusion, insofar as the past and future are, in principle, fully determined by the present state.[25] Within the paradigm

---

25 To be a little more precise, Prigogine and Stengers highlight in *Order Out of Chaos: Man's New Dialogue with Nature* (London: Heinemann, 1984) that classical mechanics expresses a 'static view of nature' (p. 11). Seeing that mechanics is all about particles moving in space and time, this claim is counter-intuitive, but their point is that with laws of motion that are both deterministic and reversible, a system's state at any given moment fully determines all states in the future and the past. As Alvin Toffler writes in his foreword, 'there is no evolution, neither to order nor to disorder, the "information" [...] remains constant in time' (p. xxix). The problem with classical physics is, for Prigogine and Stengers, therefore not that it implies or may inspire fatalism — though it certainly does — but rather that it does not allow for any real sense of process, transformation, or becoming. It means ultimately, as they say in reference to Einstein, to 'deny the reality of time as irreversibility, as evolution' (p. 293). Such a sense of time is enabled through irreversible laws of transformation, even if they remain deterministic and involve, for instance, a constant loss of information. In any case, Prigogine and Stengers's insistence on irreversibility through the second law of thermodynamics seems only to further fatalism, which implies neither determinism nor reversibility, but is consistent with the presence of randomness (on which Prigogine and Stengers insist) and even free will. Indeed, the second law is usually associated with entropic

of particle mechanics, everyday experiences of change, evolution, decay, or anything else that could matter would only be due to our subjective perception, our ignorance of the fundamental details, and to the way we construct the world at our scale. Prigogine and Stengers therefore stress the importance of finding an alternative ontology in which irreversibility and randomness are fundamental. Even if their context is different and their project more thorough, their insistence on acknowledging the fundamental activity and creativity of matter, and their arguments about the far-reaching political and cultural implications of a post-Newtonian ontology, are strikingly similar to new-materialist arguments of this century.

Again, I am suspicious of the foundationalist gesture that insists on the relevance of matter's fundamental ontology and embraces its performative normativity. As an alternative to either refraining from ontology or developing a less damaging one, I propose to deactivate the performative normativity of ontology by redoubling reduction, that is, by showing how the same properties can, as a matter of principle, be reduced to, and therefore also be considered to emerge pragmatically from, radically different ontologies with conflicting performative normativities. In other words, I propose, on the one hand, to accept physics' weak, merely pragmatic sense of emergence, embracing it as the only thing mattering at any given scale; and, on the other hand, I propose to deactivate the normativity conveyed by the claim that emergent properties remain, in principle, reducible through a strategic redoubling: if atoms could only become plausible by demonstrating how observed properties can pragmatically emerge from them at higher scales, then I maintain that, as a matter of principle, the same properties can also emerge in the same pragmatic sense from a radically different ontology of continuous matter.

---

processes inevitably leading to death, disorder, and decay, and ultimately with the so-called 'heat death of the universe'. However, if fatalism tends to focus on some future event and its imperviousness to whatever happens before, and if standard thermodynamics focuses on describing equilibrium states no matter how they are produced by irreversible processes, the interim is all that matters to Prigogine. In *The End of Certainty: Time, Chaos and the New Laws of Nature* (New York, NY: Free P, 1996), he recalls the anecdote of a 1946 meeting, in which his interest in nonequilibrium physics was received by a hostile comment that highlighted the transient character of irreversible processes and for which he now would have the repartee: 'But we are all transient. Is it not natural to be interested in our common human condition?' (p. 62).

Without going into details, let me just highlight that this is not to deny the reality of atoms, but to insist that one can always go to smaller scales and establish well-defined procedures for re-describing atoms as pragmatically emerging from continuum fields. Here discontinuity is neither in emergence or scale but rather between the contrary ontologies that one can posit speculatively, and the point is that this discontinuity becomes increasingly irrelevant as the scale of the fundamental ontology decreases with respect to ours.

Of course, the very notion of a fundamental ontology becomes problematic in this infinite regress to smaller scales, but whereas relational ontologies tend to invoke such a regress — often through the image of 'turtles all the way down'[26] — in order to stress a lack of foundation that renders everything unstable, my emphasis lies on the emergence of a remarkable stability and consistency at higher scales. Indeed, the higher scales — which is where matter comes to matter — can be considered autonomous or 'protected' from lower scales.[27] Conversely, the fundamental ontology becomes increasingly uncertain because nothing can possibly be experienced that would allow for a decision between different ontological options, and therefore the fundamental ontology becomes utterly irrelevant. Rather than an ontology of indeterminacy, I would prefer to speak of an utter indeterminacy of ontology; of an undecidability of ontology rather than an ontology of undecidability.

Fundamental, so-called high-energy physics seems close to the point of showing its own irrelevance, even if it is no doubt premature to speculate over whether the Higgs Boson is the last evidence that can be of some guidance or whether astronomical observations can give some clues. More interesting and certainly more relevant for most of us is what emerges on intermediate scales, from condensed matter physics to chemistry, biology, and geology (to speak only of the natural sciences).

---

26   See Isabelle Stengers, 'Turtles All the Way Down', in *Power and Invention: Situating Science* (Minneapolis: University of Minnesota Press, 1997); Donna J. Haraway, *When Species Meet* (Minneapolis: University of Minnesota Press, 2008), pp. 32–33 and 287.

27   Important references within physics for the kind of argument to which I am alluding here are Philip W. Anderson, 'More Is Different: Broken Symmetry and the Nature of the Hierarchical Structure of Science', Science, 177 (1972), pp. 393–96 and Robert B. Laughlin and David Pines, 'The Theory of Everything', PNAS, 97.1 (2000), pp 28–31.

If, as I am insisting, the ontologies envisaged by fundamental physics are irrelevant at this scale, my argument that a particle ontology can, in principle, always be re-described in terms of continua (and vice versa) could seem equally irrelevant. My claim is certainly not one in which those working in statistical mechanics, for instance, would be interested, as it would only make the dynamics much more complicated and unmanageable without having any practical advantages.[28]

Conceptually, however, the possibility of such a re-description is significant insofar as large-scale properties, such as the irreversible tendency towards equilibrium, can then be seen as a strict rather than an approximate consequence of the fundamental ontology (which is, as always, only ever posited speculatively). As a consequence, physics' practice of combining descriptions corresponding to incompatible ontologies appears in a different light. Indeed, I would like to point out that the very theory that convinced physicists of the 'reality of atoms' — Einstein's theory of Brownian motion — crucially depends just as much on an atomic description as on a continuum description.[29] While there is an ingrained habit in physics of considering the continuum as but a large-scale approximation of a more fundamental atomic description, my argument on the double reducibility of all phenomena makes it possible to take the continuum just as seriously and consider atoms as but a way of approximating continuous matter.

I suggest that methodically oscillating between such contrary ontologies and combining them on an equal footing helps to deactivate their normative power and to recognize scale-specific phenomena like Brownian motion as mattering in their own right, that is, not just as proof of atomism but equally as proof of the reality of a continuum, and ultimately also as something 'more' — namely, as something coming

---

28 Such pragmatic considerations — rather than an obstinate adherence to classical physics — are the main reason that Prigogine's ambitious project of establishing a 'new physics' with an alternative fundamental description (appropriate for phenomena in far-from-equilibrium thermodynamics) remains popular only outside of physics and must be considered a failure within physics, as Stengers also ended up conceding. See Isabelle Stengers, *Cosmopolitics*, 2 vols (Minneapolis: University of Minnesota Press, 2010–11), II (2011), 'Book v. In the Name of the Arrow of Time: Prigogine's Challenge', pp. 103–204 (pp. 121–22).

29 Cf. Sergio Chibbaro, Lamberto Rondoni, and Angelo Vulpiani, *Reductionism, Emergence and Levels of Reality: The Importance of Being Borderline* (Cham: Springer, 2014), especially section '3.3 The Paradigmatic Brownian Motion' (pp. 57–62).

to matter at a specific scale, requiring physics to work through specific combinations of mutually incompatible ontologies.[30]

CONCLUSION

To conclude, I have argued that the fundamental ontology of matter as theorized by physics is irrelevant at human scales, but that it is politically relevant to address its performative power. I have suggested that this power is due to a seemingly irresistible reductionist attitude that sees in pragmatically emergent properties only the properties of the underlying ontology and not their novel character. In order to deactivate the misleading normativity of ontology, it seems insufficient to highlight that the whole point of physics' reductionist theorizing is to understand how novel properties can emerge from a simple ontology; nor is it effective to refrain from all ontological references or posit an ontology of indeterminacy. Instead, the best political strategy may be to insist on an indeterminacy of ontology, that is, to posit methodically and speculatively mutually incompatible ontologies and work through their consequences in alternation or even conjunction. I suggest that understanding and probing such a methodology in physics may provide helpful models to think with in other domains, even if the relevant ontological questions are quite different, involving not particles and continua, but oppositions such as activity and passivity, matter and language, nature and culture.

According to this view, physics can offer to critical thought not a solid foundation of matter and the world, but rather tools for critique that seem to defy logic and challenge deeply ingrained habits of thought. The political relevance of physics lies in not only showing the irrelevance of its fundamental ontologies, but also in indicating strategies to deactivate their normative ontologies and thereby open spaces for political negotiations.

---

30   Alluding here to Harman's critique of 'duomining', I suggest to take objects seriously precisely insofar as their modelling within physics requires a double undermining (which is effectively an undermining and an 'overmining'). Cf. Graham Harman, 'Stengers on Emergence', *BioSocieties*, 9.1 (2014), pp. 99–104 <https://doi.org/10.1057/biosoc.2013.43> and Graham Harman, 'Agential and Speculative Realism: Remarks on Barad's Ontology', *Rhizomes: Cultural Studies in Emerging Knowledge*, 30, 2016 <https://doi.org/10.20415/rhiz/030.e10>.

IV. TOWARDS A RENEWED
HISTORICAL MATERIALISM

Introduction to Part IV

DANIEL LIU

The following five chapters are varying attempts to reassemble the 'historical' and the 'materialist' constituents of the history of materialism on terms which are not those of the 'historical materialism' that was mandated by Marxist and Leninist orthodoxy for much of the twentieth century.[1] This part begins with **Frieder Otto Wolf**'s call to pay closer attention to what Karl Marx (1818–1883) was trying to articulate under the heading 'the materialist conception of history', in order to dissolve a calcified version of historical materialism from the twentieth century. Wolf emphasizes that Marx's project was one of theory *building,* and calls attention to Raúl Rojas' argument that Marx's so called 'historical materialism' was an 'unfinished project' and should not, therefore, be read as scripture or commandment.[2] In place of an overarching theory of a law-like succession of social orders of production, Wolf argues that a methodological 'finite Marxism' should focus on the specific details of how contemporary capitalism actually operates, and how it produces its unique patterns of power and domination.

The part then moves on to the contributions by **Ayşe Yuva** and **Alex Demirović**, which provide distinctly opposing claims about the

---

1   Tony Judt, 'Goodbye to All That?', *New York Review of Books*, 1111.14 (21 September 2006).

2   Raúl Rojas, *Das unvollendete Projekt: Zur Entstehungsgeschichte von Marx' Kapital,* Philosophie und Sozialwissenschaften, 14 (Berlin: Argument, 1989).

relationship between materialist philosophy and political philosophy. **Yuva**'s chapter returns to the eighteenth century to provide broader historical and geographical contexts for the history of materialist philosophy, paying particular attention to the ways in which materialism has been attacked for being 'reductionist', 'vulgar', or too 'mechanical'. Yuva argues that this blanket critique needs to be counterbalanced with the actual historical contexts in which materialism was adopted in the eighteenth and nineteenth centuries: namely, that materialism was explicitly articulated as alternatives to philosophies based on incorporeal ideals or 'spirit', and in opposition to the theologies and theocracies that used to dominate the world's major political orders. In particular, Yuva explores Germaine de Staël's (1766–1817) influential argument about the opposing tendencies of English materialism vs German idealism, and largely maps this binary opposition to the Ottoman political reformer Beşir Fuad (1852–1887), who adopted the mantle of scientific materialism in order carve out a philosophical space independent of conservative Islamic orthodoxy. On the other hand, **Demirović** marshals two of the dominant French philosophers of the twentieth century, Michel Foucault (1926–1984) and Louis Althusser (1918–1990), to augment Marx and to argue that 'politics is really a kind of spiritualism and it is illusory'.[3] In this way, Demirović can argue that his own so-called 'critical materialism' is 'concerned with the reality of ghosts and the undead precisely because the political mind is spiritual, and because the economy is theological and metaphysical'.[4] It is unclear if there is any middle ground between Demirović's conclusion and Yuva's appeal that we 'not fall back into a dogmatic materialism, unconscious of the ideological parts it inherited from its history'.

The last two chapters in the section elaborate some of the essential ground for Demirović's claims. The contribution by **Facundo Vega** is a close reading and critique of the oeuvre of the leftist political philosopher Ernesto Laclau (1935–2014), in particular Laclau's attempt to juggle the political importance of Marxist historical materialism in the mid-twentieth century with a Heidegger-inflected, post-structuralist

---

3   Demirović, in this volume, p. 323.
4   Ibid., p. 325.

anti-foundationalism. Vega tracks the development of Laclau's thought from the late-1970s to his death in 2014, showing how Laclau's earlier, Marxist arguments about class conflict and modes of production in the 1980s gave way to meditations on the ontological foundation of 'the political' in the 1990s. The end result of Laclau's recourse to 'the political' in the metaphysical sense is, according to Vega, a totalizing conception of political difference, one that elides into populism and proto-fascism.

Vega's critique of Laclau's attempt to cast politics in purely metaphysical terms is complemented by **Marianna Poyares**'s chapter on the salutary uses of ethnography in critical social theory. Poyares argues that the ethnographic method itself calls attention to positionality, difference, and plurality, starting with the explicit need to clarify the relationship between actors' and analysts' categories. For Poyares this self-reflection itself constitutes 'bringing the theorist closer to "matter itself"',[5] primarily by forcing the theorist to question and re-examine the hegemony of her prior theoretical categories.

To round out this introduction, I would like to call attention to a dual use of 'materialism' in these five contributions.

1. The first is the problem of which philosophers or what kinds of philosophy are considered to be 'materialist', either by their contemporaries at the time or by later philosophers in retrospect. This is essentially a problem of distinguishing materialist philosophy from other, presumably non-materialist philosophies. For the moment, let us call this 'materialism$_1$'.

2. The second is the problem of *what kinds of materials or things* such materialist philosophers hold as central or prototypical to their understanding of why materialism, as a general set of philosophical positions, ought to be taken more seriously than other, non-materialist philosophies. Let's call this 'materialism$_2$'.

We might initially construe materialism$_2$ ('What materials are materialists concerned with?') to be a subset of materialism$_1$ ('What is materialism?'), therefore making materialism$_1$ the bigger and more important problem area to address. However, **Yuva**'s chapter in particular

---

5   Poyares, in this volume, p. 346.

calls attention to the fact that the moniker 'materialism' in its various guises was also a way to harness growing natural and social 'scientific' knowledge of materials and material relations in order to challenge the theologies and theocracies that used to dominate the world's major political orders. Materialism, so its protagonists claimed, insisted upon the primary importance of the material, the substantive, and ultimately secular world, over and against the ideal and the spiritual.[6] Another way to put it: a key hallmark of materialist philosophy is that it insists that materialism$_2$ is more important than materialism$_1$, because materialists argue that the totality and variety of material relations supersedes idealist or metaphysical presumptions.

Notice the repeated invocations of the *particular* and the *specific* against the *general* and the *abstract* in these five chapters on historical materialism. In **Wolf**'s chapter, we see (emphases mine):

> According to this analysis, finite Marxism combines a *specific* analysis and reconstruction of the domination of the capitalist mode of production [...][7]
>
> The project of laying bare the *inner workings, structures, mechanisms, and tendencies* of the domination of the capitalist mode of production in modern bourgeois societies, and at least to begin to understand how they present themselves in actual lived experience, has not been entirely lost, in spite of many simplifications and reductionist tendencies [...][8] this field of scientific research [...] insights into the *actual workings* of the historical domination of the capitalist mode of production.[9]
>
> Finite Marxism [...] is uniquely capable of understanding the '*specific* materiality and the characteristic conditions' of other fields of domination.[10]
>
> not [...] by offering 'Marxism' as an overarching theory, but by emphasizing its own *specific* contribution [...][11]
>
> [...] without attempting to subsume them to Marxist *generalities* [...][12]

---

6   Margaret C. Jacob, *The Secular Enlightenment* (Princeton, NJ: Princeton University Press, 2019).

7   Wolf, in this volume, p. 280.

8   Ibid., p. 285.

9   Ibid., p. 286.

10 Ibid., p. 289.

11 Ibid., p. 290.

12 Ibid.

In **Poyares**'s argument for the uses of ethnography (again, emphases mine) via Robin Celikates:

> Critique has to be based on the analysis of social *reality* and its contradictions, and [...] can only find its criteria in the social *practices, struggles, experiences,* and self-understandings to which critique is connected.[13]
> [...] empirical research without the reduction of the object of analysis to the mere instantiation of theory [...][14]

And in his critique of Ernesto Laclau's latter-day populism, **Vega** argues that Laclau's 'operation of de-substantializing and re-substantializing "the people" leads to a disdain for the autonomy of "the *many*"' (again, emphasis mine).[15] Notice that, time and again in all but one of these chapters, the philosophers being studied and the authors of the essays themselves align 'materialism' with specificities, and hold 'reality', 'objects', 'inner workings', 'the many', and the manifold lived experiences against theory and generalities. If Platonism and Heideggerian ontology progressively abstract their way towards the Good, or the One, or to God, or Being itself,[16] then materialism moves in the opposite direction.[17] It should therefore not be a surprise that, since the eighteenth century, the natural sciences provided the empirical foundation of and inspiration for modern materialist philosophy against both theology and metaphysical speculation. Additionally, it must be observed that

---

13   Poyares, in this volume, p. 347.

14   Ibid., p. 350.

15   Vega, in this volume, p. 339.

16   That is to say, the operation Heidegger is engaged in is not so dissimilar to Plato and Plotinus. See Benjamin Crowe, *Heidegger's Religious Origins: Destruction and Authenticity* (Bloomington: Indiana University Press, 2006); Hans Jonas, 'Gnosticism and Modern Nihilism', *Social Research*, 19.4 (December 1952), pp. 430–52; Benjamin Lazier, *God Interrupted: Heresy and the European Imagination Between the World Wars* (Princeton, NJ: Princeton University Press, 2009); Karl Löwith, 'Knowledge and Faith: From the Pre-Socratics to Heidegger', in *Religion and Culture: Essays in Honor of Paul Tillich*, ed. by Walter Liebrecht (New York: Harper, 1959), pp. 196–210. In George Steiner's introductory text *Martin Heidegger* (Chicago: University of Chicago Press, 1991), Steiner objects that, although one could interpret Heidegger as a crypto-Platonist, Heidegger himself rejects this (pp. 60–61). However, one should actually examine how Heidegger does this, rather than simply accept his own interpretation as doctrine.

17   Hans Blumenberg makes a parallel argument about the history of creativity in '"Imitation of Nature": Toward a Prehistory of the Idea of the Creative Being', trans. by Anna Wertz, *Qui Parle*, 12.1 (2000), pp. 17–54.

debates about the relationship between the general and the particular were most robustly *practiced* in the natural and social sciences.[18]

This vast diversity in our material environments is precisely why so many of the 'New Materialists' from the early-2000s found references to the natural sciences so valuable, if fraught. But, as **Poyares** argues quite forcefully, one need not go all the way to the natural sciences to find challenging materials in their particularities: the social and political sciences, which are the home of the ethnographic method, give plenty of examples.

---

18   Lynn K. Nyhart, '*Wissenschaft* and *Kunde*: The General and the Special in Modern Science', *Osiris*, 27.1 (2012), pp. 250–75 <https://doi.org/10.1086/667830>; Lynn K. Nyhart, 'The Political Organism: Carl Vogt on Animals and States in the 1840s and '50s', *Historical Studies in the Natural Sciences*, 47.5 (November 2017), pp. 602–28 <https://doi.org/10.1525/hsns.2017.47.5.602>; Sander Gliboff, *H. G. Bronn, Ernst Haeckel, and the Origins of German Darwinism: A Study in Translation and Transformation* (Cambridge, MA: MIT Press, 2008); Sabina Leonelli, *Data-Centric Biology: A Philosophical Study* (Chicago: University of Chicago Press, 2016); Horst W. J. Rittel and Melvin M. Webber, 'Dilemmas in a General Theory of Planning', *Policy Sciences*, 4.2 (June 1973), pp. 155–69; Charles H. Pence, '"Describing Our Whole Experience": The Statistical Philosophies of W. F. R. Weldon and Karl Pearson', *Studies in History and Philosophy of Biological and Biomedical Sciences*, 42.4 (2011), pp. 475–85 <https://doi.org/10.1016/j.shpsc.2011.07.011>; Theodore M. Porter, *Genetics in the Madhouse: The Unknown History of Human Heredity* (Princeton, NJ: Princeton University Press, 2018). See also Wilhelm Windelband, 'Rectoral Address, Strasbourg, 1894', *History and Theory*, 19.2 (February 1980), pp. 169–85 <https://doi.org/10.2307/2504798>.

Materialism against Materialism
Taking up Marx's Break with Reductionism
FRIEDER OTTO WOLF

INTRODUCTION

There is a problem in the air. On the one hand, after many post-modern criticisms, nobody (or very few people) want to rehabilitate traditional modern materialism in the vein of Julien Offray de La Mettrie or Georgi Plekhanov, to provide just two examples. Its strong tendencies towards simplification and reductionism seem to forbid any further engagement with the theory.[1] On the other hand, the post-modern variant of pluralism seems to have stifled the will to explore, know, or explain what is really going on, in contrast to mere 'outward appearances', as a necessary starting point for a perspective of active political intervention. In particular, any political practice committed to at least creating possibilities of liberating initiatives, which will be or will become capable of overcoming the very material structures of domination in place, will have to lift the veil of superficial 'illusion'.

---

1   Maurice Godelier has classically summarized the underlying criticism of 'false materialisms' in his debate with Lucien Sève. See Maurice Godelier, 'Dialectical Logic and the Analysis of Structures: A Reply to Lucien Sève', *International Journal of Sociology*, 2.2–3 (1972), pp. 241–80 (p. 253).

The perspective of 'finite Marxism', as I defend it,[2] opens the way to simultaneously address the plurality of the structures of domination in place while also maintaining the need to analyse their underlying structural dynamics, particularly including an analysis of the domination of modern bourgeois societies by the capitalist mode of production.[3]

In my opinion, the structures of domination in place today have been (more or less) adequately described by the 'triple oppression' formulated by activists of the 1990s. However, I would argue for replacing the triplet of 'Class, Sex, and Race' with the somewhat more refined and extended quadruplet of structural forms of domination — class, gender, (especially international) dependency, and 'ecological overexploitation' —,[4] and not leaving out the elementary ideological dimensions of, for example, racism, antisemitism, homophobia, and comparable forms of discrimination.[5] And yet I propose to accept the broader underlying claim of aiming at and hitting something real, namely a level of historical reality, as it has been (and still is) defended by the respective historical social and political movements. By so doing, I would claim that it is both possible and feasible to overcome the traditional notions of an essentialist and reductionist materialism. This reductionist approach to reality — which does not accept the complex reality of the given and considers the most immediate realities to be mere appearances (at the very least) — tends to be incapable of providing a realistic orientation for political practice, which has to deal with given socio-historical realities as they effectively present themselves.

---

2   See my attempt in 'Die unabschließbare Aufgabe des endlichen Marxismus: Eine materiell verankerte Arbeit des Begriffs ohne Essentialismus oder Reduktionismus', *Con-Textos Kantianos: International Journal of Philosophy*, 2018.5 (2018), pp. 200–17.

3   My thinking in this respect has certainly been influenced in important ways by Félix Guattari's work since the 1970s, with whom I have had occasion to discuss problems of eco-socialist strategy building. A central role has certainly been played by his essay in *Three Ecologies* (London: Athlone, 2000) — but I am unable to reconstruct how it has impacted my own contributions to eco-socialist strategies.

4   Because they have been relatively focused upon by Marxist, feminist, ecological, and dependency theories. I do not see any possibility of integrating these disparate theories into one overarching theory, as some exponents of these theories have attempted.

5   By concentrating explicitly on this ideological dimension of intersectionality, Karin Stögner makes it salient that critics must also bring out the plurality of the structures of domination overdetermining this ideological dimension. See her article 'Intersektionalität von Ideologien — Antisemitismus, Sexismus und das Verhältnis von Gesellschaft und Natur', *Psychologie & Gesellschaftskritik*, 41.162 (2017), pp. 25–45.

Instead, I want to propose a 'materialism of materialities'[6] —
which would include a 'materialism of emergence', as has been pro-
grammatically formulated by Roy Bhaskar and Mario Bunge.[7] In this
chapter, I shall try to argue that re-reading Karl Marx may help us to
overcome and change the traditional fixation of left-wing debates on
the still-pervasive idea of a need for a materialist reductionism.[8] This
begins with Marx's own breaking away from traditional 'materialism',
which he found so decisively wanting that some have misinterpreted
his rejection of 'all hitherto existing materialism' as a farewell to 'materialism' as such.

MATERIALISM OF MATERIALITIES, OR A NON-REDUCTIONIST
MATERIALISM

One of the points Marx forcefully made in his private notes on
Feuerbach[9] concerned taking his distance from this 'hitherto existing materialism (the one of Ludwig Feuerbach included)'.[10] I want
to argue for a re-reading of Marx which sees him (accompanied by
Friedrich Engels) philosophically on the way towards a new, non-
reductionist kind of materialism, i.e. a 'materialism of materialities'.[11]
Such a 'materialism of materialities' should be understood as fully ex-

---

6   See my 'Ein Materialismus für das 21. Jahrhundert', in *Kritik und Materialität: im
     Auftrag der Assoziation für kritische Gesellschaftsforschung*, ed. by Alex Demirović
     (Münster: Westfälisches Dampfboot, 2008), pp. 41–59.

7   See Roy Bhaskar's *A Realist Theory of Science* (London: Verso, 2007), as well as his *The
     Possibility of Naturalism* (London: Routledge, 1979), and Mario Bunge's *Emergence
     and Convergence: Qualitative Novelty and the Unity of Knowledge* (Toronto: University
     of Toronto Press, 2003). See also Tuukka Kaidesoja, 'Bhaskar and Bunge on Social
     Emergence', *Journal for the Theory of Social Behaviour*, 39.3 (2009), pp. 300–22.

8   Which has taken a new (and regrettable) form in the more or less openly 'vitalist' turn
     taken by many defenders of 'new materialisms'. See the critique formulated by Paul
     Rekret, 'A Critique of New Materialism: Ethics and Ontology', *Subjectivity*, 9.3 (2016),
     pp. 225–45.

9   The obvious question of what may have been in his mind as '2)' seems to remain
     unanswerable, and is, therefore, ordinarily avoided.

10   Karl Marx, 'Thesen über Feuerbach', in *MEW* [*Marx-Engels-Werke*, see abbreviations],
     III (1958), pp. 5–7 (p. 5; my translation).

11   As Louis Althusser has formulated it, influenced by Sigmund Freud's discovery of the
     irreducible unconscious in modern subjectivity in parallel with Marx's discovery of
     class-struggle as the material process underlying the reproduction of modern societies.
     See especially Althusser, 'On Marx and Freud', trans. by Warren Montag, *Rethinking
     Marxism*, 4.1 (1991), pp. 17–30.

tending to the worlds of feelings, practices, organizations, institutions, and even ideas.

This new materialist perspective of Marx was explicitly articulated (and partially worked out) by Louis Althusser in his struggle to overcome the historical crisis of Marxism as it had been constituted by Engels in its 'classical' form. I think it is time, after a long *traversée du désert* (crossing the desert), to reopen the question of Marxism, i.e. of a conscious development of Marx's theoretical critiques,[12] as well as the question regarding the corresponding, but clearly distinct, practical perspective of radical Marxist politics, as well as the articulation of both of these problematics in a philosophical materialism of materialities which can situate finite Marxism. According to this analysis, finite Marxism combines a specific scientific analysis and reconstruction of the domination of the capitalist mode of production over modern bourgeois societies, and of the ways in which modern states reproduce capitalist class domination, with the openness to learning from the theoretical breakthroughs arising from the other struggles of liberation which necessarily arise in modern bourgeois societies. Using this foundation, finite Marxism is aware of its own specificity as a limitation — and it rejects any temptations to 'overarch' or 'hegemonize' feminist theories, de-colonialism, or ecological critical theory. Instead, it recognizes and learns from the ways in which these theories understand specific structures and the internal 'contradictions' that are constitutive for these structures of domination in the historical reality of modern societies. On the other hand, finite Marxism also strives to deserve an equal treatment from these 'other sides'.

While it is true that Marx left his theoretical work to us as an 'unfinished project' (Raúl Rojas),[13] he also opened up a field of real and effective scientific research which has found important continuation in the work of Marxists since the 1890s. This scientific work has been continued with considerable success — in spite of the relative blockade of the philosophical and political reflection of its presuppositions

---

12   In order to justify this plural I shall elaborate on the distinction between his critique of political economy and his critique of politics (cf. below, next paragraph).

13   See his pioneering study of Marx: Raúl Rojas, *Das unvollendete Projekt. Zur Entstehungsgeschichte von Marx' Kapital* (Berlin: Argument, 1989), which has not had the reception it still deserves.

and implications which seems to have started with Engels's redaction of the notes on Feuerbach where he eliminated some reflexive turns as being 'too difficult', and then has been finalized by Plekhanov's attempt to reinsert Marxism into the tradition of modern 'materialism'. Indeed, this historical blocking, very probably, has been the unavoidable side effect of academic exclusion of Marxist theory building and historico-empirical analysis, while, in the political sphere, Stalinism distorted the forms of Marxism within institutionalized science regarding 'real socialism'. The historical development of the political practices which have effectively emerged in Marxist politics have been decisively blunted and perverted by reformist or Stalinist practices. Accordingly, the second breakthrough realized by the late Marx has had a still more complicated fate. His radical and innovative 'critique of politics'[14] has remained in the draft stages of his own analytical sketches, and has been generally misread as a mere application of the insights of the critique of political economy.[15] Therefore, Marx's original critique of politics has found little direct continuation — although its problems have unavoidably imposed themselves upon Marxist political leaders — from Karl Kautsky and Eduard Bernstein, via Lenin, Leon Trotsky, and Rosa Luxemburg, to José Carlos Mariátegui, Antonio Gramsci, and Mao Zedong.

In this regard, one of the decisive blockades which have remained dominant in mainstream Marxism has been due to a notion of materialism that has ignored the insights of Marx on the need to overcome the reductionism characteristic of the radical French enlightenment. Engels did not follow Marx on this issue,[16] as he repeatedly flirted with the French materialist tradition. Meanwhile, Plekhanov later conceived of Marxism as essentially building upon that French tradition,

---

14 As reconstructed in Étienne Balibar, Cesare Luporini, and André Tosel, *Marx et sa critique de la politique* (Paris: Maspéro, 1979), which is still in need of a proper sequel, and requires only some revision in view of the accessibility of further writings of Marx due to the progress of the MEGA.

15 Which has been doubly misleading, as it seems to imply the very idea of 'economicism' and class reductionism.

16 Although Engels first followed Marx in this, he then contributed to obscuring the issue of Marx's new materialism in his redaction of the first publication of Marx's notes *ad* Feuerbach as 'Theses on Feuerbach', or by his masking of the decisive breaks which separated their manuscripts for the *German Ideology* from their earlier publication of the *Holy Family*.

thereby obscuring Marx's explicit distance from what he called the 'old materialism'. Marx, instead, took up a non-reductionist perspective on the materiality of history, as it had been sketched out by Montes-quieu[17] and elaborated by Adam Ferguson.[18]

In order to make it possible to overcome this blockade upon scientific analysis and philosophical reflection, as well as political de-liberation, we need to understand the decisive difference between the traditional, reductionist materialism of emerging bourgeois pro-gressivism[19] (which had the historical function of getting rid of pre-modern political and religious ideas) and the non-reductionist mater-ialism of materialities Marx followed in his research practices (as well as in his organized political work). In this way, we should overcome and account for the 'real illusions' of modern bourgeois practice.

THE 'MATERIALIST ILLUSION' OF THE EARLY MARX

Even in his last-minute contributions to the *Holy Family* Marx still imagined a continuity between his own position and French materi-alism as it had been continued and radicalized by Jeremy Bentham.[20] Therefore, Marx still participated in the exercise of a reductionist materialism which, notably, provided the foundations for modern utilitarianism.[21] This simplifying and strongly reductionist current of radical thought corresponded to the perspective of the radically indi-

---

17   And rediscovered by Althusser in his *Montesquieu. La Politique et l'histoire* (Paris: PUF, 1959).

18   See the analyses presented by Danga Vileisis in her 'Der unbekannte Beitrag Adam Fergusons zum Geschichtsverständnis von Karl Marx', in *Quellen- und Kapital-Interpretation. Manifest-Rezeption. Erinnerungen (Marx-Engels-Jahrbuch. Neue Folge, 2009)*, ed. by Carl-Erich Vollgraf, Richard Sperl, and Rolf Hecker (Hamburg: Argu-ment, 2010), pp. 7–60.

19   Of which La Mettrie presented an advanced form. See the still classical reading by Friedrich Albert Lange, in the chapter on La Mettrie in his *The History of Materialism and Criticism of its Present Importance*, 3 parts (London: Kegan Paul, Trench, Trubner, 1925), ii, pp. 49–91.

20   The new turn taken by Marx in these texts has been convincingly analysed in Danga Vileisis, 'Marx' frühe, utilitaristische Auffassung des Kommunismus', in *Marx, Engels und utopische Sozialisten (Marx-Engels-Jahrbuch. Neue Folge, 2016/17)*, ed. by Carl-Erich Vollgraf, Richard Sperl, and Rolf Hecker (Hamburg: Argument, 2010), pp. 9–38.

21   In spite of his earlier sympathy towards Bentham, Marx later attacked him as the philosopher giving voice to the 'appearing surface' of modern bourgeois societies, and thereby blocking scientific inquiry: 'It is the exclusive realm of Freedom, Equality,

vidualized private subjectivity of the owner of commodities.[22] Due to having to consider his or her own labour power as a commodity to offer on the market, the perspective of the private individual reduced everything to its market price. This, evidently, implied an attitude and a practice of more or less violently 'abstracting' from all specific 'use values', while in actual practice referring exclusively to the acquisition of exchange value and the embodiment of the same in the form of money.

Later on, in the *German Ideology* manuscripts, Marx explicitly articulated his break from this kind of 'old' materialist reduction-ism, which is evident in the original version of Marx's theses on Feuerbach.[23] As becomes clear in the manuscripts produced for a pro-jected journal under the title of 'German Ideology', Marx was quite firm — especially in his critique of Stirner — that his project was not to anchor modern society in a reductionist view of 'human nature'.[24] In this critique, Marx, later followed by Engels, began to address the underlying logic of domination of the capitalist mode of production in modern bourgeois societies. He still had a long way to go in articulating this critique as a scientific alternative to Hegel's philosophical repro-duction of the structures of domination in place in modern bourgeois societies. Initially, Marx formed his critique on the basis of an alterna-tive Feuerbachian philosophy that attempted to replace Hegel's central category of 'spirit' with Feuerbach's idea of the 'human' (*Mensch*).

Property, and Bentham' (Karl Marx, *Capital*, 3 vols (London: Penguin, 1976), I, trans. by Ben Fowkes, p. 280).

22   For a critique, see my *Radikale Philosophie. Aufklärung und Befreiung in der neuen Zeit* (Münster: Westfälisches Dampfboot, 2002), p. 17.

23   Much less so in the *Theses on Feuerbach* after Engels's editorial revamp, see George Labica, *Karl Marx. Les thèses sur Feuerbach* (Paris: PUF, 1987).

24   Marx has fallen into other kinds of reductionism in his manuscripts for the so-called 'Feuerbach-chapter' in the *German Ideology* manuscripts, as Danga Vileisis and myself will show in our forthcoming book *Deconstructing Historical Materialism*. To disen-tangle his search with its advances and setbacks is a main task of contemporary Marx research, which clearly goes beyond mere philology.

MARX'S CRITIQUE OF POLITICAL ECONOMY AS AN EMERGING
SCIENCE ON 'PROPER FOUNDATIONS'

Marx used a number of steps to continuously work out his critical
struggle concerning the illusions shaping the 'surface' of the domination of the capitalist mode of production in modern bourgeois
societies. He pursued this project in his critique of Proudhon, the
Communist Manifesto, the immediate pre-history of *Capital* (especially
in the *Grundrisse*), and in the elaboration of the manuscripts for *Capital* itself. By so doing, he achieved a decisive breakthrough towards
real scientific analysis by unveiling the secret of how capital achieved
the production (and realization) of surplus value within a framework
of an exchange of equivalent values. Although, in the final analysis,
he still had to leave the production of a definitive text of his mag-
num opus to his friend. Indeed, Engels was the only one capable of
presenting Marx's scientific breakthrough in its entirety and full importance.[25] Even volume I of *Capital*, when read from a perspective
of the enlarged reproduction of the domination of the capitalist mode
of production, succeeds in conveying this radically new scientific perspective. However, Engels had to admit that it remained impossible
for him to reconstitute the 'aesthetic unity' of this work as Marx had
planned to realize it. Or, in other words, we can say that the closing of
the dialectical circle from the wealth of nations constituted by many
commodities at the beginning of *Capital*, and the different 'forms of
revenue' of the different categories of commodity owners outlined at
the end of *Capital* volume III, turned out to be far less significant than
Marx himself had anticipated.

This situation leads to interesting questions regarding the reasons
for this impossibility. Was it a contingent failing due to Marx's early
death and Engels's admitted lack of theoretical capability? Or was it
somehow implied by some elements of philosophico-political prejudice that were still inherent to Marx's argument? Asking such explicit
questions opens up the perspective of looking at the traditional issue
of the '*Abschluss*' (closure/finalization) of 'Marx's system', as it was

---

25   See Michael R. Krätke, *Kritik der politischen Ökonomie heute. Zeitgenosse Marx* (Hamburg: VSA, 2017), pp. 211–43.

introduced by Eugen von Böhm-Bawerk in 1898, in a different light.[26] Accordingly, in this perspective, the non-closure of Marx's systematic presentation follows necessarily from its very structure as a materialist dialectic which consciously and methodically respects the 'limitations of the dialectical mode of presentation', as Marx himself underlined. This not only opens up the possibility of looking at Marx's apparent unwillingness to return to his previous elaborations for volume II and III of *Capital*, but, much more importantly, it also makes it possible for us to understand the limitations of *any* possible closure of his theoretical reconstruction of the system of capitalism domination — which is not a way of producing another blockade, but rather encouraging further systematic elaboration concerning the specific field of the ongoing reproduction of the domination of the capitalist mode of production in modern bourgeois societies — as the relation of Marx's 'general theory' to the historical plurality of modern bourgeois societies should be understood.

It is true to say that Marx actually intended for considerable future research to be carried out in the field of the critique of political economy, as he had opened it by his epistemic breakthroughs. In the new MEGA the real state of his work in this field was made accessible as such,[27] which also made it possible to fully appreciate Engels's disparate work to finish and complete this unfinished work.[28] More importantly, Marx's and Engels's selective publications have been historically sufficient to open up a field of effective scientific inquiry that has been taken up and continued by others. The project of laying bare the inner workings, structures, mechanisms, and tendencies of the domination of the capitalist mode of production in modern bourgeois societies, and at least to begin to understand how they present themselves in actual lived experience, has not been entirely lost, in spite of

---

26 See classically, Eugen von Böhm-Bawerk, *Karl Marx and the Close of his System: A Criticism* (London: T. Fisher Unwin, 1898), as well as the retrospective presentation of the ensuing debate in Hans G. Nutzinger and Elmar Wolfstetter, *Die Marxsche Theorie und ihre Kritik: Eine Textsammlung zur Kritik der politischen Ökonomie* (Marburg: Metropolis, 2008).

27 I am referring to the latest complete edition of the works by Marx and Engels in German: 'Marx Engels Gesamtausgabe' (MEGA^2). This new edition has replaced the first MEGA, which had been discontinued under Stalinism.

28 See Michael R. Krätke, *Friedrich Engels oder: Wie ein Cotton-Lord den Marxismus erfand* (Berlin: Dietz, 2020).

many simplifications and strong reductionist tendencies as they have dominated large parts of the history of 'official Marxism'.

In this way, Marx also decisively contributed to the opening up of a field for further research concerning major politico-economic developments, such as credit, monopolization tendencies, or the role of politics and the state within the capitalist mode of production. Despite many impediments and obstructions, this field of scientific research has developed and produced an important body of relevant insights into the actual workings of the historical domination of the capitalist mode of production in modern bourgeois societies. However, neither a first wave of popular rebellions like the Paris Commune, which Marx analysed, nor the socialist revolutions and radical reform initiatives of the twentieth century, which were discussed in 'classical Marxism', were capable of permanently overcoming the 'really existing' domination of the capitalist mode of production.[29] On the other hand, the merely scientific concretization of Marxist theory in terms of the 'concrete analysis of the concrete situation' (Lenin) has turned out to be unfeasible if not downright impossible — and had to be reformulated as the central task of political deliberation.[30]

The resulting deep 'crisis of Marxism', which broke out in the sixties and seventies,[31] finally produced the insight into the finite character of the Marxist theorization of the domination of the capitalist mode of production in modern bourgeois societies. It was only in the 1960s, against the background of a world-wide movement of reading

---

29   This does not justify the retreat from this historical task as pursued by leading exponents of 'neomarxism' in the 1950s and 1960s, as e.g., in a reflective perspective, in Lucien Goldmann, *Recherches dialectiques* (Paris: Gallimard, 1959) or in a new, activist vein in Paul Mason, *Clear Bright Future: A Radical Defence of the Human Being* (London: Allen Lane, 2019).

30   See Georg Lukács's 'Postscript 1967' [1967], in his *Lenin: A Study on the Unity of his Thought*, trans. by Nicholas Jacobs (London: Verso, 2009), pp. 86–97, where Lukács argues that the position taken by Lenin in referring to 'the concrete analysis of the concrete situation' is not an opposite of 'pure' theory, but — on the contrary — it is the culmination of genuine theory, its consummation, the point where 'it breaks into practice', which I take as an implicit recognition that it is logically impossible for scientific analysis ever to fully arrive at this starting point of any meaningful political deliberation.

31   In 1978 a German collection of Althusser's essays from the 1970s was published under the title *Die Krise des Marxismus* (Hamburg: VSA, 1978).

Capital,[32] that new attempts at understanding the epistemological perspectives opened by Marx's scientific breakthrough were made.[33] In this period, the philological reconstruction of Marx's scientific development from the available manuscripts finally began to be employed for a better understanding of key scientific and political problems.

REDUCTIONIST TEMPTATIONS WITHIN HISTORICAL MARXISM

Generally speaking, Marx's break with reductionism in history — and, accordingly, with reductionist illusions in political practice — was not followed in the dominant 'Marxist' line of thought as it emerged with Kautsky, Bernstein, and their followers. Their attempts at 'popularizing' Marxism in the labour movement avoided or even concealed Marx's philosophical and political insistence on a materialism of materialities, with its implicit break with materialist reductionism, and, instead, these thinkers created a line of continuity between Marx and reductionism.

Early creative contributions to advancing scientific knowledge in the fields of inquiry opened up by Marx's two major breakthroughs (in his critique of political economy and his critique of politics) range from applications to historical (or contemporary) analysis of real societal processes and struggles. Examples include Kautsky's discussion of the 'agrarian question' (1988),[34] Lenin's analysis of the impact of the capitalist mode of production on contemporary Russian society (1964),[35] and theoretical constructions addressing central aspects of

---

32 Which I know from personal experience to have reached Paris in at least the end of 1963 — and to which Althusser formulated a first philosophical response by means of his famous seminar of 1964, resulting in Louis Althusser, Étienne Balibar, Roger Establet, Pierre Macherey, and Jacques Rancière, *Lire le Capital* (Paris: Maspéro, 1965).

33 The breakthrough was articulated as an 'epistemological cut' by Althusser or as 'reconstructed' as a 'systematic science' in the Frankfurt variant of a 'new reading of Capital'. See Ingo Elbe, *Marx im Westen. Die neue Marx-Lektüre in der Bundesrepublik seit 1965* (Berlin: Akademie, 2008), pp. 30–87.

34 For a careful and (exceptionally) non-dismissive recent discussion of this question, see Jairus Banaji, 'Illusions about the Peasantry: Karl Kautsky and the Agrarian Question', *The Journal of Peasant Studies*, 17.2 (1990), pp. 288–307.

35 For an exhaustive reconstruction and critical analysis of this question, see Projekt Klassenanalyse, *Neue Stufe des Wissenschaftlichen Sozialismus? Zum Verhältnis von Marxscher Theorie, Klassenanalyse und revolutionärer Taktik bei W. I. Lenin* (Berlin: Verlag für das Studium der Arbeiterbewegung, 1972).

the full development of the capitalist mode of production Marx had not yet been able to fully work out (like credit, state intervention, and international exchange). These aspects were specifically addressed in pioneering research by, for example, Luxemburg, Rudolf Hilferding, and Eugen Varga — even if these texts were often in need of broader clarification regarding their actual presuppositions and implications. In contrast to these developments, and, in parallel, addressing a problematic debate on 'revisionism' vs 'orthodoxy', an effectively 'conservative' philosophical operation has attempted to stop these dynamic developments of Marxist theory: Kautskyanism — and, in a hidden and much more decisive, later parallel, Stalinism — have not only worked upon 'philosophically' reintegrating Marx's science into the 'old materialism', with the central effect of replacing a rationally grounded practice of open political philosophical debate by traditional forms of a linear historical and dogmatic determinism. Much more importantly, both vulgarized Marx's theory of the domination of the capitalist mode of production in modern bourgeois societies by reducing it to a schematic theory of historical 'capitalism' which was neither clearly systematic nor specifically historical, thereby missing the specific reality of the capitalist mode of production as an 'ideal average' (*idealer Durchschnitt*).[36]

Taking Marx's explicit reference to the 'ideal average' as the decisive indication for a materialist theoretical reconstruction — which, in his opinion, should take place in the 'real sciences'[37] — has important implications. Firstly, it assists to overcome the illusions of 'theoreticism' which view concrete, practical reality as a mere 'emanation' of the level discussed in theory building. Secondly, it reveals the assumptions behind 'empiricism'[38] and 'practicism' (*Praktizismus*)[39] that put aside the requirements of theory building and only address practical

---

36   In German, this has been exposed in an exemplary fashion by Michael Heinrich in 'Geld und Kredit in der Kritik der politischen Ökonomie', *Das Argument — Zeitschrift für Philosophie und Sozialwissenschaften*, 45.251 (2003), pp. 397–409.

37   Marx's changing ways of referring to '*wirkliche Wissenschaft*' — which understandably have made many Marx scholars diffident about his claims to scientificity — finally seem to come down to this.

38   Which has been one of the main tendencies of the dominant bourgeois thinking about science.

39   As it has been philosophically elaborated by pragmatism.

singularities. The level of reality which is reconstructed by the theoretical operations of constructing concepts and statistically describing averages is neither to be confused with the concrete historical realities of particular modern societies (and their states) nor relegated to the status of a mere theoretical fiction. It is a decisive level of historical reality that constitutes a specific characteristic of all modern societies. Sometimes this has led to the illusion of distinguishing and opposing this level of theory (e.g., under the name of a 'theory of value') from or to a real understanding of class struggle, whereas, in actual fact, this level of theory only implies the search for a clear understanding of how class struggle lies under and structures the whole process of the reproduction of the very forms of capitalist domination.

A renewal of Marx's radically innovative perspective on a non-reductionist kind of materialism can make use of two contemporary sets of information. Firstly, a more complete understanding of the complex reality of the domination of the capitalist mode of production in the plurality of modern bourgeois societies, as they are over-determined by other structures of domination (especially gendered, transnational, ecological). Secondly, a renewal of the philosophical debate about the meaning of materialism today.

Accordingly, 'finite Marxism' does not have to relinquish the scientific or political claims characteristic of the 'critique of political economy' as Marx initiated it — and yet, it is also uniquely capable of understanding the 'specific materiality and the characteristic contradictions' of other fields of domination. In particular, finite Marxism will be able to make a significant contribution to concretizing a new kind of radical politics by combining alliance building and mutual respect for the different kinds of liberation struggles with an effective deepening of class struggle. It will do this by seriously taking up Marx's work that has hitherto remained in the form of initial exemplary analyses and general argumentative sketches, especially in his later critique of politics. In doing so, it will decisively advance Marx's 'originary' project of a politics of liberation by not restricting its perspective solely to the politics of class struggle, but fully taking on board the political implications and objects of 'gender trouble', anti-racism (and its correlates), ecological conservation needs, and international co-ordination requirements as they are elaborated by feminist, anti-racist, and ecological theory and research. Again, this will not be achieved by offering 'Marxism' as an overarching theory, but by emphasizing its own specific contribution to understanding the domination of the capitalist mode of production and the structure of the modern state as an agency of domination.

Thereby, finite Marxism will show itself capable of taking up the relative findings of the other fields of scientific research pertinent for modern bourgeois societies in its own research, as well as to conclude non-instrumentalist alliances with other struggles for effective liberation, based on their potential for a mutual understanding of the structures of domination each one is struggling against and for a broad solidarity against all attempts to curtail their liberty. Opening Marxist debates to the findings of feminist, anti-racist, ecological, and 'dependency' theory — without attempting to subsume them to Marxist generalities — will help to revitalize finite Marxism in its 'own field' of class struggle. And a new philosophy, a non-reductionist 'materialism of materialities' will, accordingly, become capable of making decisive contributions to the bringing under way of a process of constituting a real historical alternative — scientifically, as well as politically.

RETURNING TO MARX AND DEFENDING 'FINITE MARXISM'

When he sketched his notes on Feuerbach, Marx still had a long way to go towards his definitive scientific break-through in *Capital*. Step by step, in a journey that was certainly not linear, he discovered the road towards a non-reductionist kind of materialist analysis of the capitalist mode of production, as it is, indeed, dominating modern bourgeois societies. In so doing, he learned to respect the specific kinds of material reality of the many different dimensions of historical and present societies. This is what made it possible for him to actually think of class struggle in its effective historical reality: not as a confrontation of pre-existing subjectivities, but as the emergence of distinct and, eventually, antagonistic subjectivities within the very processes of societal reproduction and historical change.[40]

---

40   In the mainstream of Marxist theory, however, as exemplified by Kautsky and Stalin, this was schematized into assuming the pre-existence of 'class subjectivities'.

In *Capital*, Marx succeeded in radically freeing himself (almost completely) from his previous reductionist illusions in order to completely focus his research on the historical structure of the domination of the capitalist mode of production in modern bourgeois societies. Therefore, he constructed a 'missile' and threw it against the dominating global bourgeoisie(s) and their allies, which led them to discredit his scientific insights and politically obstruct his theoretical insights from spreading into the established institutions of the economic, social, and political sciences.

However, and in spite of an impressive record of struggles aiming at overcoming the domination of the capitalist mode of production in modern bourgeois societies, there still is a tendency in the Marxist tradition to overlook an important caveat that Marx already clearly articulated. This involves the need to observe the difference between the general theory reconstructing the general structures and mechanisms of the capitalist mode of production and an analysis of its specific functioning within a given socio-historical situation, for which the general theory may only serve as a 'guiding thread'.[41] This caveat should be sufficient to overcome a tendency, still frequent among Marxists, of simplifying socio-historical analysis itself down to a deductive application of a general theory of 'capitalism'.[42] What is more — and this is a graver political consequence — is the tendency towards 'class reductionism', as it has spread in historical Marxism, whereas, in practical terms,[43] Marx, at the first Workers' International, clearly addressed the issues of women's liberation or of colonialism in their specificity and on an equal footing.

The renewal of Marxist analysis, needed today, will be capable of combining a critical defence of the actual achievements of Marxist

---

41   This is because critical theory can only establish the general laws of motion of the 'ideal average' (cf. above), and not be prolonged into the 'concrete analysis of the concrete case' without further empirical (or historical) research.

42   See my critique of this simplifying notion in Frieder Otto Wolf, 'Karl Marx und die Globalisierung. Die Problematik des "Kommunistischen Manifests" und ihre Perspektiven', *SoWi — das Journal für Geschichte, Politik, Wirtschaft und Kultur*, 28 (1999), pp. 190–98.

43   Marx's correspondence with Vera Zasulich (especially in his unsent drafts) also makes it clear that in his analysis there is no space for a class-reductionist and teleological or stage-based perspective on the transformation of societies.

science[44] with a renewed radical philosophy. A new openness to the contributions of feminism, dependency theory, and political ecology will help us to find new perspectives for a radical practice of Marxism and a renewal of liberation struggles today. In this way, it will overcome the historical 'crisis of Marxism': not by returning to the kind of Marxism constituted by Engels for the rising workers movement,[45] nor by retreating to a mere 'Marxianism' within scientific research,[46] but by beginning to define an adequate, and of course, unmistakably non-idealist, unequivocally dialectical, 'unity of theory and practice' for the twenty-first century.

In this way, finite Marxism will be capable of contributing to the elaboration of new comprehensive perspectives, developed conjointly with converging movements, which will work against the different structures of domination and the ways they function within given societies. It will also facilitate the politics of building 'new alliances' that will finally be capable of challenging and overcoming the combined structures of domination as they have re-emerged out of the 'night of the 20th century' (roughly from 1914 to 1946). Last but not least, it will assist us not to forget about the 'real elephant in the room', and to understand the specific requirements of organized political struggles and struggles within or about the modern state (in its more or less democratic forms) in the beginning of the twenty-first century.[47]

---

44   See the exemplary analysis in Stefano Breda's *Kredit und Kapital. Kreditsystem und Reproduktion der kapitalistischen Vergesellschaftungsweise in der dialektischen Darstellung des Marxschen 'Kapital'* (Würzburg: Königshausen&Neumann, 2019).

45   This seems to be the underlying project in Krätke, *Kritik der politischen Ökonomie heute: Zeitgenosse Marx*, which I find, indisputably, attractive, but far too limited, with regard to the tasks of analysis that lie ahead.

46   See e.g. Riccardo Bellofiore, 'Taking Up the Challenge of Living Labour: A "Backwards-Looking Reconstruction" of Recent Italian Debates on Marx's Theory of the Capitalist Mode of Production', in *The Unfinished System of Karl Marx: Critically Reading Capital as a Challenge for our Times*, ed. by Judith Dellheim and Frieder Otto Wolf (Cham: Palgrave Macmillan, 2018), pp. 31–89.

47   Decisive parts of the research underlying this essay were realized in cooperation with Danga Vileisis, to whom I am grateful for many insights. And the critical remarks to earlier versions of this essay provided by the editors have certainly helped me to find a clearer expression of my thinking, for which I am grateful.

Materialism, Politics, and the History of Philosophy
French, German, and Turkish Materialist Authors in the Nineteenth Century

AYŞE YUVA

In contemporary materialist traditions such as Marxism or neo-materialism, reference to pre-nineteenth century philosophers is often limited to a small number of authors: Spinoza, sometimes Democritus, Epicurus, and Lucretius. It is striking that other traditions, such as eighteenth-century materialism, when the very category of 'materialism' was forged, or late nineteenth-century scientist materialism, which loudly proclaimed this label, are generally put aside or deemed obsolete. The terms of the accusation are well known: these materialisms are, according to many Marxist materialists, too mechanistic, reductionist, insufficiently emancipatory and subversive, and even judged 'ideological' for having justified the capitalist order that was being established at the time. But if we want to understand the philosophical and political reasons for these judgments, it is necessary to take the 'materialist' categorization of these doctrines seriously, not to judge them as more or less materialist according to their approximation to a current model. My methodology is, in some way, a nominalist one, since my point of departure is not the universal idea of 'materialism' but what has actually been categorized as such. I will take both a historical and a transnational perspective, briefly analysing some of the alliances of materialism and politics since the eighteenth century in France, Germany — in Karl Marx, Friedrich Engels, and Ludwig Büchner — and in some Turkish Ottoman authors. This broader view is important so as to not remain stuck in the identification, which has become commonplace, of an eighteenth-century mechanistic and reductionist materialism as a solely European endeavour. More specifically, my aim is to analyse the political uses of the categorization of materialism as mechanistic and reductionist. I would like to show how, regardless of the current or outdated character of these materialisms, their rejection has often also had an ideological character, as has the narratives that have endorsed these judgments of reductionism and mechanism. To understand how this can be the case, one should bear in mind that materialism is not only about ontological questions relating to the relationship between matter and spirit, but it has also been radically critical of religion, which has led, among other things, to Marx's and Engels' critique of ideology as the dominant form of thought. This point also concerns the teaching of philosophy: materialism has been significantly marginalized in universities and in the history of philosophy until the middle of the nineteenth century at least, and arguably later as well. In return, materialist authors have not spared universities and the specific history of philosophy that they teach from a major critique regarding the separation of this teaching from reality. Thus, the erasure of certain materialist traditions is a question that concerns both politics and the history of philosophy. Following authors such as Louis Althusser and Pierre Macherey,[1] one may wonder to what extent it is possible to adopt a materialist perspective while being a scholar of the history of philosophy, i.e. studying ancient texts, which cannot be transposed as such to the present day — which does not mean that materialism was not somehow efficacious in this time, or that the texts are no longer relevant for us. My own approach is, therefore, to critique the ideology that permeates the practices of the history of philosophy. This is, incidentally, a materialist approach.

---

1   Cf. Pierre Macherey, *Histoires de dinosaure: Faire de la philosophie (1965–1997)* (Paris: PUF, 1999).

EIGHTEENTH-CENTURY FRENCH MATERIALISM AND THE
CRITIQUE OF ORTHODOXY

The Connection between Ontology and Politics

'Materialism', a term which in French dates back to the early eighteenth century in a text Gottfried Wilhelm Leibniz wrote against Pierre Bayle from 1702,[2] was then applied retrospectively to a number of doctrines that emerged since Democritus and Epicurus. In the eighteenth century, the polemical and politically subversive meaning of the term 'materialism' could hardly be separated from its ontological meaning.[3] In France, materialism only came out of hiding, and still only partially, in Julien Offray de La Mettrie's books *L'Histoire naturelle de l'âme* (1745) and *L'Homme-machine* (1747).[4] The association of 'materialism' with 'fatalism' and 'atheism', for example in the thought of Paul Thiry, baron d'Holbach, was at least as subversive as monism.[5] This is not the place to discuss the association, which was made as early as the eighteenth century, between Spinozism and materialism, or the distinctions often made by some materialist authors between Spinoza and their own doctrines. Rather, I would like to point out that the definition of eighteenth-century materialism in terms of mechanism, reductionism,[6] and utilitarianism does not do justice to the complexity

---

2   According to the etymological dictionary, it is necessary to go back in French to
    Leibniz's text of 1702 *Réplique aux réflexions de Bayle* to find the word 'matérialisme',
    which was then translated into English. The adjective 'materialist/matérialiste' is a
    little older and appeared in English around 1660 (in Ralph Cudworth, Henry More
    and Robert Boyle), in French in 1698 (in Bonaventure de Fourcroy) and in 1700 in
    the first French translation of John Locke's *Essay Concerning Human Understanding*
    by Coste. Cf. <http://www.cnrtl.fr/etymologie/matérialisme> and <https://www.
    cnrtl.fr/etymologie/matérialiste> [accessed 1 November 2020].

3   Cf. Franck Salaün, *L'Affreuse Doctrine: Matérialisme et crise des mœurs au temps de Di-
    derot* (Paris: Kimé, 2014); the classic work of Daniel Mornet, *Les Origines intellectuelles
    de la Révolution française* (Paris: Armand Colin, 1933) should be mentioned as well.

4   Jean-Claude Bourdin, *Hegel et les matérialistes français du XVIIIᵉ siècle* (Paris: Klinck-
    sieck, 1992), p. 23.

5   This term was used only from the end of the nineteenth century, based on the work of
    Ernst Haeckel.

6   Even in the work of Julien Offray de La Mettrie, the very complex mechanism cannot
    be reduced to the model of shocks and to one simple explanation. Cf. La Mettrie,
    L'Homme-machine (Paris: Fayard, 2000 [1747]), p. 49, translated in *The Monist*, 3.2
    (April 1913), p. 300: 'Man is so complicated a machine that it is impossible to get
    a clear idea of the machine beforehand, and hence impossible to define it. For this
    reason, all the investigations have been vain, which the greatest philosophers have
    made *a priori*, that is to say, in so far as they use, as it were, the wings of the spirit.'

of materialist texts from the eighteenth century. In these texts the living character,[7] not the inert character,[8] of matter[9] is often discussed; far from referring only to Newtonian physics,[10] these texts also use the model of chemistry and the natural sciences to oppose any kind of teleology in living beings. While d'Holbach did write a *Système de la Nature*, the materialisms of this time are far from always being in a systematic, even dogmatic form. For example, Denis Diderot's conjecture that matter could be endowed with sensibility is sometimes presented using a literary model, notably in the form of fiction and dream, and not that of a first principle from which everything else could be deduced.[11] According to many commentators, Diderot's ontology also has a plural character, which precisely derived from the plurality of possible approaches to matter using different sciences.[12]

Thus it is only *a posteriori* or by trying to disentangle the soul from the organs of the body, so to speak, that one can reach the highest probability concerning man's own nature, even though one cannot discover with certainty what his nature is.'

7   Cf. Denis Diderot, Letter to Sophie Volland, 15 October 1759, in *Œuvres complètes de Diderot*, 20 vols (Paris: Garnier, 1876), xviii, pp. 408–09. This is the famous letter where Diderot dreams that his ashes will mingle with those of his lover, suggesting they might still have 'a remnant of warmth and life'.

8   Cf. Paul Thiry, baron d'Holbach, *The System of Nature*, 2 vols (Kitchener: Batoche Books, 2001), i, p. 20: 'If they [natural philosophers] had viewed Nature uninfluenced by prejudice, they must have been long since convinced, that matter acts by its own peculiar energy, and needs not any exterior impulse to set it in motion.'

9   Cf. Claude A. Helvétius, *De L'Esprit; or, Essays on the Mind, and its Several Faculties* (London: Albion, 1810), p. 27: 'all that remained was to know [...] whether the discovery of a power, such for instance as attraction, might not give rise to a conjecture that bodies still had some properties hitherto unknown, such as that of sensation, which though evident only in the organized members of animals, might yet be common to all individuals.'

10   Cf. Jean-Claude Bourdin, *Les Matérialistes au xviiie siècle* (Paris: Payot, 1996), p. 31. On the contrary, Mario Bunge could argue that Kant understood Newtonian physics as saying that matter was inert. Cf. Mario Bunge, *Scientific Materialism*, Episteme, 9 (Dordrecht: Springer Netherlands, 1981), p. 4: 'Kant, who could not read Newton's equations for lack of mathematical knowledge, misunderstood Newtonian physics as asserting that whatever moves does so under the action of some force, be it attractive or repulsive. And Voltaire, who did so much for the popularization of Newtonian physics in his Cartesian country, was struck by the pervasiveness of gravitation but could not understand it adequately because he, too, was unable to read Newton's equations of motion. So neither Voltaire nor Kant realized that the inertia of bodies and light refutes the belief that matter is inert, i.e. incapable of moving by itself.'

11   Cf. Jean-Claude Bourdin, *Diderot et le matérialisme* (Paris: PUF, 1998), pp. 75 and 79; Jean-Louis Labussière, 'Diderot métaphysicien. Prédication, participation et existence', in *Lumières, matérialisme et morale: Autour de Diderot*, ed. by Colas Duflo (Paris: Editions de la Sorbonne, 2016), pp. 21–72 (p. 70).

12   Cf. François Pépin, 'Le Matérialisme pluriel de Diderot', in *Lumières*, ed. by Duflo, pp. 73–95 (pp. 85 and 94).

However, this ontology is connected to a radical critique of spiritual orthodoxy. This connection is not only a contingent historical fact in the history of ideas that could be explained by the censorship of that time, but has a philosophical basis. In eighteenth-century France, materialism was both a dangerous theory to defend publicly (and therefore marginalized by the official authorities) and a theme that occupied the public space since at least 1751. We must add, however, that this polemical dimension is present in the texts themselves, and their radical critique of spiritual orthodoxy is what makes these theories immediately political. As Bertrand Binoche has underlined, they are political not in the sense that their authors would have held a revolutionary or even reformist political position, or acted in such a way, but in the sense that their materialist critique immediately placed them in a combative and destructive position both in the Republic of Letters and in society.[13] The ontological thesis of materialism concerning the relationship between body and mind can be said to be particularly important at that time precisely because of its subversive charge against religion and the immortality of the soul, and because it was associated with atheism and held a controversial position on the question of free will. The power to overturn dogmas — upon which a state's false spiritual social harmony is based — is an integral part of these materialisms.

This first detour through the history of materialism allows us to reaffirm something that is perhaps self-evident: the polemical dimension of materialism is an integral part of it. Certainly, all philosophical systems are engaged in theoretical conflicts; as early as the eighteenth century, even before Immanuel Kant's *Critique of Pure Reason*, the incessant 'struggles' between systems became a philosophical problem. But materialism is distinctive because it not only presents itself as a generator of conflict in the philosophical field, but is also at risk of spreading this conflict into the political and social fields, as Kant himself asserted:

> Through criticism alone can we sever the very root of *material-ism, fatalism, atheism,* of *freethinking unbelief,* of *enthusiasm* and

---

13   Bertrand Binoche, *'Ecrasez l'Infâme!'. Philosopher à l'âge des Lumières* (Paris: La Fabrique, 2018), p. 23.

> *superstition,* which can become generally injurious, and finally
> also of *idealism* and *skepticism,* which are more dangerous to
> the schools and can hardly be transmitted to the public.[14]

The reason why the ontological theses of materialism concerning the relationship between body and mind, and between extension and thought, are so important is that they imply atheism and the denial of free will, which in turn calls into question the foundations of (spiritual) harmony in European states.

The Practical Effects Attributed to 'Materialism' after the French Revolution

Concerning the attribution of political subversion and atheism to materialism, the French Revolution and the repercussions it had throughout the nineteenth century radicalized this polemical perspective on materialism and determined how it is still approached today. As early as 1789, a thesis emerged that would go on to become a commonplace, according to which the writings of eighteenth-century philosophers had provoked the French Revolution.[15] This revolution was, according to many contemporaries, unparalleled since it was an example of the application and realization of philosophical principles. The authors mostly targeted here, Voltaire and Jean-Jacques Rousseau, were certainly not explicit materialists,[16] nor were they atheists; yet, quite quickly, and particularly after the Terror, an argumentative strategy emerged which consisted in making 'materialism' the quintessence of French philosophy in the eighteenth century. This was the means whereby authors could then make these 'materialist' doctrines responsible for the wrong-doings of the French Revolution, and even later for the Empire's.

---

14   Immanuel Kant, *Critique of Pure Reason,* trans. by Paul Guyer and Allen W. Wood (Cambridge: Cambridge University Press, 1998), Bxxxiv, p. 119.

15   One of the first to evoke the responsibility of 'philosophism' was Abbé Barruel, as early as the summer of 1789, in *Le Patriote véridique* (The True Patriot); he would later become a follower of the theory of the 'conspiracy of the philosophers' that provoked the French Revolution.

16   Although Rousseau's position on materialism may have been judged ambiguous, he at least affirms his willingness to refute it. Cf. Franck Salaün, 'Les Larmes de Wolmar. Rousseau et le problème du matérialisme', in *Rousseau et la philosophie*, ed. by Jean Salem and André Charrak (Paris: Editions de la Sorbonne, 2004), pp. 71–86.

This is not an anecdotal fact that is only of interest for the history of ideas, but a vision that has influenced the image we still have today of French materialist philosophies in the eighteenth century. It consists of applying the label 'materialist' to authors who have sometimes not claimed this term for themselves systematically, as well as in diluting their theses into a form of mechanism and reductionism, as well as fatalism and atheism. Moreover, it consists in judging the entire French 'materialist' philosophy of the eighteenth century through the light of its supposed revolutionary consequences (and failures).

This criticism is not only to be found among some counter-revolutionary or reactionary authors. For instance, during the first Republic Germaine de Staël wrote a moderate criticism of the philosophers of the Enlightenment, praising their combativeness but deploring their irreligion. However, in that time she nevertheless established (this is around 1796–1800) a continuity between certain eighteenth-century doctrines and the one she believed would be appropriate for the Republic in France.[17] But things changed with Napoleon Bonaparte's founding of the Empire: Staël attributed the submission of the French to despotism, to a selfish, utilitarian state of mind, the roots of which she found in the eighteenth century. Under the term 'materialism', she combined ontological theses on the nature of substance, epistemological empiricism, and a moral approach based on self-interest and the satisfaction of needs. According to Staël, this materialism had its roots in English philosophy, particularly John Locke, but it had only showed its full destructive effects in the institutional and intellectual context specific to France.[18] She wrote her book *On Germany* partly because she saw in German 'idealism' a spiritual remedy to this Anglo-French 'materialism'. Idealism could provide the courage needed to sacrifice oneself to justice, while materialism encouraged careerism, petty calculations of interest, and submission to force.[19] The current, non-philosophical use of the terms 'materialism', 'materialist', and 'materialistic' is certainly still affected by this association, according to which theoretical 'materialism' is linked to a 'materialistic' attitude.

---

17 Cf. Germaine de Staël, *De la littérature* (Paris: Garnier-Flammarion, 1991), p. 287.

18 Cf. Germaine de Staël, *De l'Allemagne*, 2 vols (Paris: Garnier-Flammarion, 1968), II, p. 110.

19 Cf. Bertrand Binoche, 'La Faute à Helvétius ou le matérialisme après-coup', in *Lumières*, ed. by Duflo, pp. 173–84 (p. 179).

THE DANGERS OF MATERIALISM AND THE PLACE GIVEN TO IT IN
THE HISTORIES OF PHILOSOPHY IN THE FIRST HALF OF THE
NINETEENTH CENTURY

The Marginalization of Materialism by Victor Cousin

The reading of eighteenth-century materialism which Staël constructed along with other theorists spread widely in the nineteenth century
and still influences our vision of how eighteenth-century materialism
inspired the French Revolution, with its various achievements and limitations. The writing of the history of philosophy, in particular, played
a crucial role in this marginalization.

For example, such a reading was conveyed by Victor Cousin in the
French university culture in the nineteenth century. Cousin (1792–
1867), who had a great influence on the teaching of philosophy in
France in the first half of the nineteenth century, gave a major role to
the history of philosophy. After Joseph Marie Degérando, who was the
author of the first modern history of philosophy in French in 1804,
he encouraged a reading of the history of philosophy which aimed
to refute materialism and, in general, any philosophy which would
claim to have revolutionary consequences.[20] As Pierre F. Daled noted,
Cousin undermined the importance of materialist authors, practically
silenced the names of d'Holbach and La Mettrie, or made Claude-
Adrien Helvétius a disciple and successor of Étienne Bonnot de Con-
dillac, which is historically and philosophically untrue.[21] Cousin made
'materialism' a subcategory of 'sensualism', that is, a doctrine according
to which all ideas come to us from the senses. He believed that this
doctrine dominated the eighteenth century, first in England and then

---

20 Cf. Victor Cousin, *Manuel de l'histoire de la philosophie. Traduit de l'allemand de
    Tennemann* (Paris: Sautelet, 1829), preface, pp. v–vi: The history of philosophy is a
    way of exposing the 'terrible consequences' of Condillac's sensualism and of Locke's
    philosophy, which at the end would lead to 'Holbach and La Métrie [*sic*] and all the
    saturnals of materialism and atheism'.

21 Cf. Pierre-Frédéric Daled, *Le Matérialisme occulté et la genèse du 'sensualisme'. Ecrire
    l'histoire de la philosophie en France* (Paris: Vrin, 2005), p. 237. See also the founding
    work of Olivier Bloch, 'Sur l'image du matérialisme français du XVIIIᵉ siècle dans
    l'historiographie philosophique du XIXᵉ siècle: Autour de Victor Cousin', in *Images au
    XIXᵉ siècle du matérialisme du XVIIIᵉ siècle*, ed. by Olivier Bloch (Paris: Desclée, 1979),
    pp. 39–54.

in France through Locke's reception in that country.[22] However, to make materialism a subcategory of sensualism is to think of it through an epistemological criterion rather than a practical one. Ultimately, Cousin presented sensualism as a timeless trend of the human mind and one of the four doctrines (beside 'dogmatism' divided between 'idealism' and 'realism', 'scepticism' and 'mysticism') that regularly appeared in the history of philosophy.[23] Cousin's goal, which we can date to around 1829, was then to present his own doctrine as a 'middle ground', both philosophically and politically, between Republicans and Catholics, and between the French philosophy of the eighteenth century and German metaphysics. His strategy consisted in placing his philosophy on the seemingly depoliticized ground of the history of philosophy, something which would in fact lay the foundations for a new spiritual harmony that would destroy the danger represented by materialism (and, on the other side, by ultra-conservative Catholics). Finally, we can see that this discrediting of the eighteenth-century 'materialists' lives on in today's academic institutions, in a way, without any explicit awareness of its political origins, which in the French case emerged, as we have seen, in the post-revolutionary context.[24]

The Revival of a Certain Image of Eighteenth-Century French Materialism by Marx and Engels

As paradoxical as it may seem, it appears that the authors of the *Vormärz*, some of whom emigrated to France — including the young Marx and Engels, but also, for example, Heinrich Heine — were not entirely detached from these patterns of interpretation of eighteenth-century materialism. A recurrent question in the materialist texts of the nineteenth century is to know which relationship — whether of continuity or rupture — must be established between eighteenth-century

---

22   Of course, the importance to materialism of English authors such as David Hartley and Joseph Priestley cannot be denied. However, retrospectively, in the nineteenth century, the rise of materialism in France in the eighteenth century was linked to the reception of Locke's work, rather than that of other authors.

23   Cf. Victor Cousin, *Cours de l'histoire de la philosophie. Histoire de la philosophie du XVIIIe siècle*, 2 vols (Paris: Pichon et Didier, 1829), I, p. 178.

24   Cf. *Une arme philosophique. L'éclectisme de Victor Cousin*, ed. by Delphine Antoine-Mahut and Daniel Whistler (Paris: Éditions des Archives contemporaines, 2019).

materialism and the theory that would be appropriate for a nineteenth-century revolution. For example, Heine, in his book *On the History of Religion and Philosophy in Germany*, which was written in response to Staël's book on the same topic and with the same title in French (*De l'Allemagne*), states that Spinoza's pantheism should inspire the revolution in Germany, unlike the 'materialism' which was the doctrine of the revolution in France, which could not suit Germany.[25] In Heine's work, materialism was not only defined by atheism (in contrast to Spinoza's pantheism), but by a principle of frugality that Heine considered politically insufficient and unsatisfying.[26]

In *The Holy Family*, on the contrary, Marx and Engels acknowledged the contributions of eighteenth-century French materialism. Against Bruno Bauer, Marx asserted the eighteenth-century source of materialism (inaugurated by Bayle) rather than the Spinozist source of nineteenth-century materialism. According to *The Holy Family*, this eighteenth-century materialism drew upon Cartesian mechanistic physics and Hobbesian nominalism. As with Staël (whose value judgements are, however, reversed in the work of Marx and Engels), seventeenth-century metaphysics (restored by German idealism) is opposed to the subversive materialism of the eighteenth century. Marx and Engels recognized the superiority of eighteenth-century moral theories based on the particular interest of individuals over those theories which were based on an abstract general political interest. However, Olivier Bloch has shown that the categories included in this text by Marx and Engels come from the history of Charles Renouvier's spiritualist philosophy, parts of which they copied.[27] Admittedly, invoking paradoxical sources is not enough to criticize a text or deem it inconsistent, but it should be said that the positions proposed by Marx and Engels in the *Holy Family* were quickly overtaken by *The*

---

25   Cf. Heinrich Heine, *De l'Allemagne* (Paris: Gallimard, 1998 [1855]), pp. 81 and 83.

26   Ibid., p. 93, translated in *The London and Paris Observer*, 12 (Paris: Galignani, 1836), p. 84: 'We want neither *sans-culottes*, nor frugal citizens, nor parsimonious presidents; we desire to found a democracy of terrestrial gods, all equals in happiness and *holiness*. You ask simple raiment, austere manners, and cheap pleasures — we, on the contrary, wish for nectar and ambrosia, mantles of purple, the voluptuousness of perfumes, the dancing of nymphs, music and comedies.'

27   Olivier Bloch, 'Marx, Renouvier et l'histoire du matérialisme', *La Pensée*, 191 (February 1977), pp. 3–42.

German Ideology, where they claimed the character of French materialism in the eighteenth century was insufficient. La Mettrie and Cabanis, for example, were now seen as shifting to the side of 'ideology', but in the new sense of a doctrine that forgets the material anchoring of ideas and the relationships of social domination.[28] Marx and Engels considered the materialist doctrines of the eighteenth century insufficiently transformative. However, in *The Holy Family*, they saw Helvétius as a 'materialist' because of the weight he gave to external circumstances in education.[29] Later Marx judged such a position to be insufficient in the third thesis on Feuerbach, written shortly before *The German Ideology*.[30]

To interpret the materialist philosophies of the eighteenth century as 'ideologies' is certainly profoundly innovative. The political effects attributed to these doctrines are thus almost reversed: from being seen as destructive and revolutionary, they now appear to be vectors for the promotion, or even justification, of a new bourgeois order. During the quarrel of materialism that shook Germany from 1847 onwards, Marx and Engels stood aside and criticized authors such as Büchner, Carl Vogt, and others who themselves stood on the side of materialism, but whom Marx criticized harshly in letters[31] and whom Engels described as 'vulgar materialists'.[32] Engels also somehow associated these thinkers with the materialists of the eighteenth century. What these old and new materialists had in common, according to Marx and Engels, was that they did not measure the importance

---

28 Cf. Pierre Macherey, *Études de philosophie 'française'. De Sieyès à Barni* (Paris: Publications de la Sorbonne, 2016), pp. 87–109.

29 See also Claude A. Helvétius, *Œuvres complètes d'Helvétius*, 3 vols (Paris: Lepetit, 1818), II: *De l'homme*, p. 3, where he claims that the humans are the result of their education, and that improving the science of education is therefore an important means of happiness for the nations.

30 About the materialist use of this thesis, see Marlon Miguel's contribution in this volume.

31 Cf. Marx to Engels, 14 November 1868, in *MEW* [*Marx-Engels-Werke*, see abbreviations], XXXII (1974), pp. 202–03 (p. 203) and Marx to Kugelmann, 5 December 1868, in *MECW* [*Marx & Engels Collected Works*, see abbreviations], XLIII (1988), pp. 173–75 (p. 173).

32 Cf. Friedrich Engels, 'Ludwig Feuerbach and the End of Classical German Philosophy', in *MECW*, XXVI (1990), pp. 353–98 (p. 369): Engels associates Feuerbach with 'the shallow, vulgarised form in which the materialism of the eighteenth century continues to exist today in the heads of naturalists and doctors, the form in which it was preached on their tours in the fifties by Büchner, Vogt and Moleschott'.

of social relations — or, in the case of their contemporaries, misapplied Darwinism to social relations — and therefore remained within an ahistoric materialism based solely on the natural sciences. In this way the dichotomy between scientist materialism, based on the natural sciences, and Marx and Engels's materialism, which was later given the general label of 'Marxist materialism' in the twentieth century and was generally coupled with the economic and social sciences, was constituted. However, Engels, who was more interested in these questions than Marx, reinforced the image of a mechanistic eighteenth-century materialism. His article 'Ludwig Feuerbach and the End of German Philosophy' illustrates this view well.[33] Engels did not forget or erase the theses of The Holy Family: his book is even closer to this text than any work by Marx himself. For instance, a certain cultural and national affiliation of materialism remains; in his 1880 text Socialism: Utopian and Scientific, and more precisely in the introduction to its first English edition, Engels reproduced some passages from The Holy Family and was amused that the English people of his time were still horrified by the thesis that modern materialism had its roots in their country. According to Engels, Bacon, Hobbes, and Locke were the founders of English materialism and the ancestors of the eighteenth-century French materialists.[34]

---

33 Cf. ibid., p. 370: 'The materialism of the last century was predominantly mechanical, because at that time, of all natural sciences, only mechanics, and indeed only the mechanics of solid bodies — celestial and terrestrial — in short, the mechanics of gravity, had come to any certain conclusion. Chemistry at that time existed only in its infantile, phlogistic form. Biology still lay in swaddling clothes; plant and animal organisms had been only crudely examined and were explained as the result of purely mechanical causes. What the animal was to Descartes, man was to the materialists of the eighteenth century — a machine. This application exclusively of the standards of mechanics to processes of a chemical and organic nature — in which processes the laws of mechanics are, indeed, also valid, but are pushed into the backgrounds by other, higher laws — constitutes one specific but at that time inevitable limitation of classical French materialism. | The other specific limitation of this materialism lay in its inability to comprehend the world as a process, as matter undergoing uninterrupted historical development. This accorded with the state of the natural science of that time, and with the metaphysical, that is, anti-dialectical manner of philosophising connected with it. Nature, so much was known, was in eternal motion. But according to the ideas, this motion turned just as eternally in a circle and therefore never moved from the spot; it produced the same results over and over again.'

34 Friedrich Engels, Socialism: Utopian and Scientific (London: Swan Sonnenschein, 1892), p. xiii.

My aim here is not to dwell on the current understanding of eighteenth-century materialism, but to stress that under different modalities, defining a theory that leads to transformative practice has implied a reconstruction, sometimes partial and lapidary, of the history of materialism. It seems that in this reconstruction the image of eighteenth-century materialism has become fixed, even in Marx and Engels, into categories inherited from a polemical and post-revolutionary interpretation of the subject. A certain number of commonplaces have therefore emerged about it and been expanded beyond the original context that gave rise to them. The history of philosophy has been one of the main instruments of this marginalization, even in authors such as Marx and Engels, who were most critical of the classical history of philosophy.

This insight leads me to deepen, in the following section, the problem of the relationship between the history of philosophy and the materialism of the nineteenth century, and to sketch how materialism has both criticized and used the history of philosophy. If this history has been one of the places where a certain ideological or dogmatic reading of eighteenth-century materialism has imposed itself, leading many materialist authors to criticize the history of philosophy for being too idealist and orthodox, it has nevertheless also been taken up in a view that claimed to be a materialist one.

CRITICISM AND MATERIALIST USES OF THE HISTORY OF PHILOSOPHY

The Critique of the Academic History of Philosophy by Marx, Engels, and Büchner

Regarding the relationship between the writing of a history of philosophy and materialism, I can only give a concrete and single answer, which cannot claim to be universal. The fact that Marx and Engels took up certain categories of the French debate does not mean that they were not radically critical of a certain practice in the history of philosophy, notably in *The German Ideology*. Therefore, they considered a history of philosophy that would claim complete autonomy, or would make ideas the driving forces of any history and overestimate the importance of philosophical conflicts in history, to be insufficient. This is, in a way, what Althusser later affirmed by writing that 'the history of philosophy, in the strict sense, *does not exist*'.[35] According to Marx and Engels, one cannot expect the outcome of a philosophical conflict to lead to any real emancipatory effect, since philosophical criticism, which focuses on purely ideal philosophical struggles, blinds itself to the conflicts of civil society. Any criticism of the history of philosophy cannot therefore be separated from the criticism of an 'idealist' philosophy of history, which is itself a prisoner, in the Hegelian sense, of its restoration of the religion it claims to override. What is left, in Marxist terms, is the overcoming of a philosophical history of philosophy in favour of the 'materialist conception of history' and then the 'critique of political economy'.

I would like to note, however, that criticism of the 'pure' history of philosophy is also found among the authors that Marx and Engels classify as reductionist, 'vulgar' materialists. Büchner, for example, overcame the 'pure' philosophy of history, even if he did so in a way that Marx and especially Engels contested. In *Kraft und Stoff* (Force and Matter), Büchner criticized the historical study of materialism, sensualism, and determinism the thinkers of the *Schulphilosophie*.[36] In his opinion, a kind of 'thorough' materialism and good methodology imply, in their own way, the necessity of departing from the history of academic philosophy. Like some eighteenth-century materialists, Büchner aimed to conquer the public space outside of universities rather than the academic institution itself, as well as to subvert orthodoxy.[37] Certainly, the criticism of *Kraft und Stoff* that Marx and Engels noted, which concerned its justification of the organization of the modern world, cannot be denied. In particular, it is evident that Büchner, using a model inspired by Feuerbach, thought that humans had separated themselves from religion in their practices, and had become atheists by enjoying all kinds of material comfort, which is an evolution he praises, even if he remarks how contradictory most of his contemporaries still are. He thought that their practice contradicted

---

35   Louis Althusser, *Pour Marx*, intro. by Étienne Balibar (Paris: La Découverte, 2005), note 48, p. 80.

36   Ludwig Büchner, *Kraft und Stoff. Empirisch-naturphilosophische Studien* (Frankfurt a.M.: Meidinger Sohn, 1855), p. 13.

37   Ibid.

the beliefs they upheld: in spite of claiming to be Christians, they were actually atheists.[38] In my opinion, it is clear that he believed that the good materialist also tends to be materialistic. But in arguing for such things, Büchner still maintained a certain criticism of common beliefs. In saying this, I am not denying the ruptures between the different forms of materialism, but rather examining at which levels the materialist criticisms of spiritual orthodoxy are situated.

The following three levels of criticism should not be confused: First, materialism contributes to criticizing religious harmony or even, more generally, the dogmas that prevail in society. This criticism, as it is outlined by Marx and Engels, loses the central character it had among eighteenth-century materialists, as well as in Feuerbach and among some representatives of the quarrel of materialism. Second, materialist criticism targets certain philosophical systems that support common social and religious beliefs; it is subversively positioned in philosophical conflicts, and often holds a marginal position in relation to academic philosophy, while seeking to engage with other areas of the public sphere. This can be seen in the work of Staël and Cousin, but also in the young Marx and in later texts from Engels. Third, materialist criticism develops, particularly in Marx and Engels, as a critique of philosophical conflicts in terms of viewing them as a new form of orthodoxy or ideology hiding other more significant types of conflicts.

Does this mean that a thorough materialist position must abandon the field of pure philosophy, and *a fortiori* its history, to open itself up to other sciences — whether to the natural sciences or the social sciences? The natural sciences would have the privilege of grasping the ontological foundation on which philosophical materialism is based; and the social sciences would have the privilege of directly addressing social conflicts that are of more direct importance to practice. However, I would like to conclude by showing, through a single historical example, how materialism has viewed both the history of philosophy and materialism in the eighteenth and nineteenth centuries from a non-European lens, namely a Turkish-Ottoman one.

---

38   Ibid., p. 27. Büchner wrote that 'No one crucifies himself anymore; no one seeks to be deprived instead of enjoying/benefiting [*geniessen*]. But each one hastens and hunts with the best forces of his life for the material goods and possessions of the earth, for the joys and pleasures which the material, refined and refined a thousand times over, offers him' (my translation).

The Possible Use of the History of Philosophy in a Materialist Project: The Case of Beşir Fuad

The French philosophy of the eighteenth century, as well as French and German materialism, was received in the Turkish-Ottoman intellectual arena from 1859 on, when Münif Paşa published translations of Fénelon, Fontenelle, and Voltaire. The study of Turkish texts makes it possible to show the subversive charge that many stories of philosophy retain from a 'materialist' point of view. At the end of the nineteenth century, Turkish materialists were not Marxists, due to the relative absence of Marx's and even Hegel's texts in the Turkish speaking world at the time. While Beşir Fuad (1852–1887) associated Büchner with Voltaire, the Encyclopédistes, and La Mettrie in the same scientific programme,[39] Baha Tevfik (1884–1914), a high school teacher and publisher, associated Büchner with Haeckel and even Nietzsche in his materialist project. Abdullah Cevdet (1869–1932), to give one last example, discovered Büchner during his medical studies, translated numerous works, went back to Pierre-Jean-Georges Cabanis to define his own materialism, before finally claiming his intellectual lineage from Gustave Le Bon. Whether it is consistent or logical is of little interest here. What could be considered here as a doctrinal confusion — and will sometimes be criticized as such by later Turkish philosophers, and particularly some Turkish Marxists — is interesting through the very categorization it produces. One hypothesis to be tested would be asking whether the histories of philosophy, which are certainly not only received by 'materialist' authors in the Turkish-Ottoman intellectual sphere,[40] have the advantage of offering a philosophical space that is not subordinate to religious orthodoxy. The study of the Turkish texts makes it possible to understand that the autonomization of philosophy and its history need not only be thought of, as Marx and Marxists have done, as an abstraction of philosophy to be criticized in relation to its historical roots, but can instead also be seen as an opportunity given to philosophy to distinguish itself, in its history, from the spiritual realm defined as religious. The materialist philosophers of the eighteenth

---

39   Cf. Beşir Fuad, *Şiir ve hakikat* (Istanbul: I.k.y., 1999), p. 493.

40   Cf. Ahmed Midhat (1844–1912), who held more conservative positions, translated for instance Alfred Fouillée's history of philosophy which had been translated in a summarized version by Baha Tevfik before.

century may have had a relevance for such a project that cannot be summarized as a desire for Westernization or as a simple promotion of a mechanistic or reductionist philosophy — and even less an alienation of identity.

To illustrate this idea, I will briefly focus on Beşir Fuad (1852–1887). He became famous for his critical monograph *Victor Hugo*, published in 1885, in which he criticized literary Romanticism.[41] After his suicide in 1887,[42] many of his writings were collected under the title *Şiir ve Hakikat* (*Poetry and Reality*). He was neither a scientist nor a philosopher, but rather a translator and mediator who made many French, English, and German theories accessible in Turkish. The concern for the popularization and dissemination of knowledge was essential to his work. For example, he translated popular and didactic works on physiology, such as Emil Otto's German grammar and Jean Macé's *Histoire d'une bouchée de pain*, an educational work, in whose preface Beşir Fuad insisted on the need to have books that everyone can understand.[43] Although he preferred the theses of La Mettrie, he prioritized Voltaire and the Encyclopaedists because of their efforts to popularize science: this didactic dimension was constitutive of his materialism. His first imperative was to enable the acclimatization and appropriation of these theories in the Ottoman Empire.

From an epistemological point of view, Beşir Fuad can be placed with Comte and Émile Littré since he positioned himself as an opponent to all metaphysics and any search for final causes or origins. But he also insisted on the combative dimension of science and the gallery of 'heroes' who fought on the side of scientific truth against the Church. We are certainly dealing here with a commonplace idea, one which is partly inherited from the eighteenth century, but Beşir Fuad gave an original interpretation of it which he hoped would be adapted to

---

41 He was educated as a member of the Ottoman elite. First an officer, he began, in the last three years of his life, prolific activity as a writer, journalist, and translator in fields ranging from physiology to literary theory.

42 Beşir Fuad's suicide is a very important aspect in the reception of his work and reinforced his image as a 'materialist', as he held, until he lost consciousness, notes that were meant to be objective about the sensations he felt after taking drugs and cutting his veins.

43 Cf. Orhan Okay, *Beşir Fuad Ilk türk pozitivisti ve natüralisti* (Istanbul: Dergah yayinlari, 2008 [1969]), p. 99.

the reality of Turkish-Ottoman society of its time. Thus, his 'heroes' of modern Europe who fought against the priests are first of all located in an original history of the Enlightenment which is not reduced to a purely European phenomenon: Beşir Fuad sketched a history of philosophy in which the Arabs, heirs of the Greeks, transmitted knowledge and enlightenment to a Europe that the Church had plunged into darkness. Thus, according to his reading, the encounter of Christianity and Islam in medieval Spain was at the origin of the Renaissance in Europe. In a similar way, Beşir Fuad reinterpreted Voltaire's criticism of the Church and Voltaire's strategic use of Islam in the second part of his work, to turn Voltaire into a defender of Islam.[44] One point where Beşir Fuad's theory would be opposed to Büchner's concerns the Western character of this struggle for truth. Whereas Büchner opposes the calm of the East to the struggle for truth in the West,[45] and thus makes the history of philosophical and scientific conflicts something strictly European, Beşir Fuad presents a completely different thesis. He portrayed the Church's oppression of science in Europe and the transmission of the Enlightenment to Europe through an encounter with Islam. Here Beşir Fuad's strategy is clear but complex: it is by no means a question of putting his own philosophical position under the authority of Muslim sacred texts and one must also, in practice, take into account the censorship imposed on writers of that time. But he wishes to introduce such doctrines cautiously into an Empire where Islam is the dominant religion. The first Turkish materialists (among whom we could include Baha Tevfik, Büchner's translator) were determined to question a certain orthodoxy but without attacking the dominant religion head on. In this regard, the discursive strategies of eighteenth-century European materialists were interesting to them.

With this in mind, we can see how the historical presentation of philosophy, whether in the form of short historical sketches or biographies, held a twofold interest. On the one hand, it made a real appropriation (and not just a reception) of French and German materialist doctrines possible by blurring at least part of the intellectual boundaries between East and West. It also revealed an openness, in

---

44   Beşir Fuad, *Voltaire* (Konya: Çizgi Kitabevi, 2011), p. 170.
45   Büchner, *Kraft und Stoff*, p. 269.

these European theories, to the East or Islam. Beşir Fuad did not wish to alienate his Ottoman political identity and knew the difference between the works published by French and German authors and the imperialist policies of France or Germany in his time. On the other hand, Fuad wished to create, through this historical presentation of philosophy, a space where philosophy can, in the spiritual domain, distinguish itself from religion, and destabilize dominant ways of thinking without having to attack them head-on. Although Beşir Fuad appeared to erase the practical stakes of the historical presentations of philosophy in France, this is in fact what allowed him to move forward with caution. If his definition of materialism as a critique of orthodoxy and his concern for popularization placed him in continuity with a tradition inaugurated in the eighteenth century, his way of blurring borders without situating himself in one cosmopolitical universal space also distinguished him from that tradition. He used the history of philosophy to undermine the subversive charge of his materialist theses by blurring the boundaries between 'European' and 'Eastern' philosophy without making them disappear.

I conclude with some general and methodological remarks. It seems to me that materialism does not necessarily have to be opposed to the history of philosophy. Studying materialist doctrines is not enough to immanently establish the possibility of a materialist history of philosophy. Writing a social history of philosophy, its institutions, and its actors' strategies, as Jean-Louis Fabiani has done following Pierre Bourdieu, is certainly a possible way forward. But a materialist perspective does not necessarily require setting aside the study of concepts and arguments. I remain convinced that the materiality of the history of philosophy also lies in its concepts, which are not merely a simple translation of structures of domination, but attempts to address conceptual problems that have arisen in a social and economic context. It also seems to me that one of the historically foundational elements of materialism, namely the criticism of dogmas and a certain ideological orthodoxy, must also be applied through the history of philosophy. With this thought I do not seek to produce a new great teleologically oriented narrative myself; rather, I mean to study a succession of significant moments which are certainly distinct but which can be articulated around the problem of the relationship between materialism and the history of philosophy. Historical study also seems to be a means of preserving the plurality of the materialisms and materialities in question and of not falling back into a dogmatic materialism that would be unaware of the ideological aspects it has inherited from its history. If one of the challenges of a materialist approach is to blur the boundaries of philosophy, of what lives in it but is also external to it, then the history of philosophy has its part of the work to do here as well.

The Historicity of Materialism and the Critique of Politics

ALEX DEMIROVIĆ

In the first part of this chapter, I argue that materialism is not an alternative form of metaphysics and philosophy, but rather it opens up the space for an analysis of concrete historical contexts. Materialism thus moves in opposition to metaphysics, idealism, or spiritualism. It only becomes necessary under certain historical conditions. The tradition of critical theory aims at a concept of social development that renders the necessity of materialist thinking superfluous. In the second part, based on various authors from Karl Marx to Theodor Adorno and Michel Foucault, I discuss the ways in which politics should become the object of materialist criticism, which not only (with its contradictions) makes freedom possible, but also blocks it.

MATERIALISM

Since Marx's Feuerbach theses, critical theory of society has understood itself as a critical continuation and renewal of the tradition of materialism. This has meant that it criticizes aspects of idealist philosophy including its denial of matter, its claim that matter is unknowable, and the constitutive role of consciousness. Within the context of this tradition, materialism means, first of all, making nature the object

of inquiry. Max Horkheimer emphatically emphasized that materialism is not another type of metaphysics or philosophy. It is always
— and this is my first thesis — a political-strategic intervention that
contests religious and spiritualist explanations of the world because
such explanations have always been closely connected to domination
and exploitation. Materialism does not aim to create a comprehensive philosophical system of thought, nor is it connected to a body
of philosophical texts; instead, it is concerned with *praxis* and tries to
contribute to its further understanding.

However, ever since the sixteenth and seventeenth centuries materialism has been predominantly mechanistic and deterministic, and
for that reason it has been criticized by critical theory. While it was fitting that materialism was mechanistic and deterministic in the Renaissance and afterwards, such definitions have proven inadequate for
more modern phases of social development. Marx criticized the materialist tradition up to the philosophy of Ludwig Feuerbach for tending
to turn materialism into a philosophy. He wrote that sensuousness,
when viewed philosophically, was conceived as the form of the object, or of contemplation, rather than as 'sensuous human activity', as
'objective activity', which is a practice performed by active people.[1] In
opposition to deterministic materialism, Marx argued that this active
side was abstractly developed by idealism. Marx rejected the kind of
naturalism according to which society is constituted as it is because it
is determined by nature, a perspective which included ideas like: tools
as the extension of organs, the genetic determination of individuals,
the existing social division of labour between above and below, women
and men, the powerful and the subaltern, or all such hierarchies that
are given based on the argument that the collective cannot survive
unless the many do not subordinate to the command of the few. As
the contrary of this position, materialism wants to understand natural
and social processes in order to be in a position to push back against
the realm of nature as 'wholly determined', and in this way make room
for freedom.

---

1   This is the first thesis on Feuerbach. Cf. Karl Marx, 'Theses on Feuerbach', ed. by
      Friedrich Engels, in *MECW* [*Marx & Engels Collected Works*, see abbreviations], v
      (1976), pp. 6-8 (p. 6); in German: Karl Marx, 'Thesen über Feuerbach', in *MEW*
      [*Marx-Engels-Werke*, see abbreviations], iii (1975), pp. 5-7 (p. 5).

Against the background of this criticism, materialism — according to Horkheimer and Antonio Gramsci — represents an immanent-philosophical understanding of humans in relation to the world. This means that materialism is not about the reduction of society, of thought and meaning, or of individual or collective action to matter that is 'out there'. What is important about Marx's argument here is that he understands human practice and the external world as a unity, or, to use Gramsci's phrase in the *Prison Notebooks*, as a 'historical block'.

Accordingly, nature is not grasped as an 'object', that is, as an already-and-always-to-be-found object of rule. Individuals are purposively active towards nature, that is, towards the 'outside'. This 'outside' is the concrete outside of a historically specific 'inside' that people appropriate and transform through their terms, theories, technologies, and practices. Indeed, Marx characterizes labour as a 'process between man and nature' in which man 'mediates his metabolism with nature through his own action' (*seinen Stoffwechsel mit der Natur durch seine eigne Tat vermittelt*).[2] Furthermore, through their activity they also change, to various degrees, themselves, their thinking, their sensual experiences, nature, other people, and, finally, the concrete species itself.

Material practices, it is important to note, include thought and discourse as social activities and not only as physical and neurophysiological processes. The senses, perceptions, experiences, and concepts all represent concrete practices; each are connected with specific aesthetic, discursive, or scientific relations, or with conceptual-theoretical-technical means of production. Because material practices intervene in these relationships, they can also be said to shape them.

Materialism opposes the school of thought that subordinates human practices to metaphysical principles, norms, or universals. It views the practices themselves as being historically specific, which includes the metaphysical and idealist practices and habits of thought that people engage in within concrete historical relationships. There is no search for an origin or a primal position, principles from which everything else can be deduced, or norms that can provide a conclusive

---

2   Karl Marx, *Capital: A Critique of Political Economy*, 3 vols (London: Penguin, 1976), I, trans. by Ben Fowkes, p. 283; translation modified.

reason for morally correct action. Contrary to what even critical materialism and its followers often claim, economics is not a primal reason
either. It is itself contingent, something that can appear as conditioned
by specific power relationships. Materialism, I argue, does not deal
with desires, projections, or value judgments that deny or gloss over
reality, but rather with the concrete thinking and acting of concrete
people at a particular historical point in time. This kind of materialist
immanence is often subjectively experienced as unsettling and difficult
to bear because there is no ontological assurance, no foundation, no
bottom line in nature and its supposedly eternal laws, no universal
truth, and no sense to history or even to individual existence.

CRITICAL MATERIALISM

Above all else, materialism is critical and historical — and this, following Horkheimer, is my second thesis — because what is considered
matter changes historically. Materialism refers to the concrete problems and challenges that specific people in specific social relations have
to deal with at a certain point in time. This can include the cosmos,
the body, the economy, modes of communication, gender, or the environment. The appropriation of nature always takes place within a
concrete division of labour among people and the connection of their
actions with tools and nature to form a 'historical block'; one which
is, under the conditions of 'pre-history', not organized rationally but
rather in terms of economic exploitation as well as political or cultural
domination. The decisive materialist-historical question is, therefore,
which of the different materialities is dominant in a given conjuncture
of the circle as a whole: the appropriation of nature, health, science
and technology, state power, culture and consensus, gender relations,
or racism.

To the extent that property relations rule over human beings it is
true to say that they are forced to submit to those who claim ownership
of the means of production and, in the name of the self-maintenance
of the collective, claim that freedom for all is not yet possible and
the majority of people must therefore be led by a minority in order
to guarantee the survival and welfare of all. According to this view,
sacrifices are expected to maintain the collective. The most recent

evidence of this practice can be seen in the appeals from US politicians for workers to return to work even if this poses, in the context of the Sars-CoV-2-pandemic, a threat to their health and life. As President Trump put it, going back to work could hit individuals hard but what mattered was reopening the American economy.

Even under this hegemony of capitalist owners there are elements of freedom in the planning and design of products, in the work process itself, or in the forms of social cooperation. Critical materialism thus raises the question of the order of priority of one practice over another. It criticizes the fact that under conditions of domination the intellectual competencies and practical activities of most people are formed in such a way that enables and sustains the reproduction of domination. Freedom, thought, concepts, and sensory experiences are of secondary importance for many people because they have no control over fundamental relations, and therefore they distance themselves from their own capabilities for critical thinking. Materialism thus criticizes any dependence on the appropriation of nature and argues for an historical change in the order of practices such that people can freely shape the conditions under which they live. Therefore, materialism is transformed into what can be paradoxically called material idealism.

POLITICS

Political philosophy often views politics as the sphere of freedom. Accordingly, politics is not conceived of as a matter of an instrumental disposition over nature, which would involve the creation of objects, but rather a challenging collective discussion of issues concerning living together and the common good. Critical materialism doubts the validity of such an emphatic conception of politics. Horkheimer pointedly formulated an opposing position: politics is the epitome of all the paths that lead to the domination of humans over nature, and of humans over other humans, and the means by which this domination is sustained.[3] Critical materialism opposes Hegel's idea that, at least in the case of the state, there can be an instance of the general and

---

3   Max Horkheimer, 'Anfänge der bürgerlichen Geschichtsphilosophie', in *Gesammelte Schriften*, 19 vols (Frankfurt a.M.: Fischer, 1987), II, pp. 177–268 (p. 183).

an embodiment of a general will, for according to this tradition there is no overall subject of society or united and reconciled humanity. Under conditions of market competition and the private ownership of the means of production, interests are tied together in multiple ways. Individual self-preservation in the face of possible destruction depends on others being materially worse off and dependent, and staying that way. The policies that the state pursues by means of a multitude of apparatuses are only the result of short or medium-term compromises between powerful individuals and groups; therefore, they can be highly diverse and contradictory. Domination prevents questions concerning the public good from being freely discussed and decided for in favour of the good of all. Private actors, pursuing particular interests, make decisions affecting the public good and the development of society as a whole. In a market, economic freedom is limited to those few who have asserted themselves within the struggle over the surplus product and economic competition.

The numerous discussions of this minority, which the bourgeoisie support within an array of organizations within civil society, represent a pursuit in which individuals attempt to position themselves favourably within the struggle over the surplus product and economic competition; that is, they try to avoid mistakes, anticipate future developments, pre-empt competitors, and structure actors' expectations. Private actors — such as corporations or owners of capital — determine the resources available to society (for example, machines or raw materials) according to certain paths of development, and compel others to accept this determination or to assert their private interests. In the event of disappointments, action turns into silence, apathy, and political distance, or takes the form of protest, which in turn can be devalued as isolated, and thus inconsequential, events. If all goes according to plan, government policies accompany and coordinate these investment and structuring processes throughout the different areas of society — that is, industry, finance, development of technology, raw materials, transport, production of knowledge, work skills and a work ethic, nutrition, health, housing, and mobility — in order to avoid too much friction or even setbacks in development (such as when a factory cannot find the necessary qualified workforce, cannot transport products, has no legal certainty, cannot count on credit, or faces bankruptcy). Policies and policy makers must be carefully informed, influenced, monitored, tested, and evaluated by society's dominant actors, because activities within the political sphere are carried out by individuals unilaterally and according to particular interests: income, career, or influence. In such a system, inability, ignorance, inefficiency, corruption, arbitrariness, and conflicts among politicians can affect political decision making and administration.

Marx described the consequences of this chiasma of factors for capitalist-bourgeois society very well: Firstly, at the level of private owners of capital seeking their own benefit, decisions important to society as a whole are constantly being taken at a sub-political level. With the increasing centralization of corporate power, the effects of these decisions constraining the public good continually expand over time: they more greatly affect both nature and people and reach further and further into the future. Secondly, the political community in which man behaves as a communal being in terms of the general public serves only to protect the private interests and needs of citizens as selfish individuals. This also applies to those who act on behalf of the general public. The common good is the subject of private calculations by officials and representatives; it is a practical illusion of the state. In Marx's words, the state can be considered an 'illusory general estate'.[4] For, under the conditions he outlined, what is supposed to be general is not decided upon on the basis of general considerations, but rather represents a compromise between different powerful groups which is formed under the leadership of one of these groups. The state is the particular social practice that enables such compromises between the individual market players.

Politics is thus bound up with something illusory, something fabricated, and with Marx's help I would like to explain this idea further. In his analysis of the French Revolution, Marx argues that in revolutionary processes lower classes become political idealists and feel that they are the representatives of general social needs. Because these classes see themselves as representing the generality of each particular historical moment, they shape, in each historical moment, the formulas

---

4   Karl Marx, *Contribution to the Critique of Hegel's Philosophy of Law*, in *MECW*, III, pp. 3–129 (p. 50).

embodying common goals which mobilize the short-term enthusiasm and agreement of large crowds of people. But the political enthusiasm of the constitutive moment which seizes people, their political slogans and formulas, and their coalitions and alliances immediately disperses in light of the goals and needs of other classes or groups, for whom the common goals turn out, as the political process continues, to be deceptions: women (who do not appear at all), urban workers, the veterans of the revolutionary army, farm workers and small farmers, and colonized people. That is why Marx criticized 'political reason' [*politischer Verstand*, translated by 'political mind'] in principle.[5]

The French revolutionaries of 1789 were paradigmatically tied to such 'political reason'. They believed in political power and political will; therefore, they could not recognize that the source of social deficiencies was to be found in the state, but believed instead that social deficiencies were the source of political evils. They thought they could eliminate these evils through politics by trying to establish equality at the low level and form of a *petit-bourgeois* equality. This led to politics becoming more and more authoritarian, because revolutionary leaders such as Robespierre suspected individuals of deliberately opposing this politics of equality.

Against this viewpoint, Marx argued that no government in the world can eliminate pauperism — and we can say today that Marx was right.[6] And the same can be said for the exploitation of nature: despite many political assurances and treaties, no government in the world will prevent climate change. Therefore, according to Marx, it is wrong to appeal again and again to a political will. Instead, it would be better to analyse the material practices of politics and pursue other practices.

---

5   Karl Marx, 'Critical Marginal Notes on the Article "The King of Prussia and Social Reform. By a Prussian"', in *MECW*, III, pp. 189–206 (p. 199); 'Kritische Randglossen zu dem Artikel "Der König von Preußen und die Sozialreform. Von einem Preußen"', in *MEW*, I (1981), pp. 392–409 (p. 402).

6   China confirms this insight once again: The Communist Party continues the Jacobin tradition. However, invoking Communism proves to be in vain if the private or state disposition over living labour is not eliminated; poverty is renewed and returns at a higher level, as it always will in all capitalist societies.

POLITICS AS ILLUSION

Marx has been critically interpreted in such a way that portrays him as reducing politics to mere appearances and therefore not taking them seriously enough. Along these lines, Slavoj Žižek has accused Marxism of understanding politics merely as shadow theatre, but this kind of criticism is paradoxical and quite contradictory.[7] For, when Marx is properly understood according to a critical materialist theory of society, 'illusions' and 'shadow theatre' must be taken very seriously. They represent their own practices and social realities, which in turn have effects in the real world.

I want to argue that Marx really did condemn politics as an illusion. He thought of 'political reason' ['political understanding'] as 'spiritualist',[8] and he meant that seriously and critically, for politics consumes a lot of time and produces extensive material effects with its own kind of spiritualism. Marx's critical point here is that political reason obscures the roots of social distress and falsifies the insights of those who really want to change social reality, because thinking in terms of politics suggests that all surface phenomena are founded on the will of individuals who do not do what they could or should do. Everything is transformed into a will; objective processes are personalized. The remedy for such a situation seems to be the overthrow of certain forms of the state. As I already explained above, the spiritualism of the political does not only act as an obstacle to knowledge but also represents an additional moment in the reproduction of the separation of the general from the particular, in this case, the community from the unique life of the individual. In other words, the very illusion of politics is a material practice; and it poses a problem in that it impairs emancipatory action because it pursues goals that must remain fruitless.

Although, when speaking of illusion, it would seem to make sense to look for the reality behind it, critical materialism asks a different question; what reality requires these illusions and, *contra* the Enlightenment, always produces them?[9] A basic premise of this question

---

7   Cf. Slavoj Žižek, *The Ticklish Subject: The Absent Centre of Political Ontology* (London: Verso, 1999).

8   Marx, 'Critical Marginal Notes', p. 203.

9   Cf. Karl Marx, *Contribution to the Critique of Hegel's Philosophy of Law. Introduction*, in *MECW*, III, pp. 175–87 (p. 176).

is that a certain reality cannot exist without the illusions also found within it. Marx's own research did not only lead him to hard facts, to economic matters, to nature and work, but instead to another metaphysical, theological, spiritual level of reality: the metaphysics of the value of commodities and money. This is the illusion he was interested in. Marx saw money and value as kinds of religious transubstantiation and also as irrational objects, given his view that human labour has no value and no price. However, it is characteristic of the capitalist appropriation of surplus labour from those subjected to domination that the relations of concrete people — those who perform particular tasks within the division of societal labour as a whole — take the form of value, a created thing, with the expended labour power presenting itself as the value of a commodity. With such a system, people face their own cooperative labour as an objective relation that unfolds following the dynamic of the play of supply and demand of the market. What Marx has discovered has a specific ontological status. For the value of the human capacity for work is something irrational, something nonexistent and fictitious which nevertheless determines the actions of people.

To make this insight even clearer, one can turn to Louis Althusser's explanation of the concept of ideology using the example of religion. If one were to follow the Enlightenment's critique, one would argue that there is no God. In this case, the expectation is that people will no longer believe in Him because, based on scientific, evidence-based knowledge, one can say that there is no such world above the clouds. However, surprisingly, one finds that people continue to believe in God, in the power of the star constellations or in natural forces. Here it is a matter of how religions are criticized, for according to the Enlightenment's understanding, belief in God is described in the psychological and philosophical terms of a philosophy of consciousness: it is understood as something that takes place sensibly in the flow of thought of the individual and that refuses to reason and reflect empirically.

From the perspective of critical materialism, one would speak of a false consciousness that should in fact dissolve. But the deeper question is to ask why the belief in God persists, reproduces, and even spreads. This is the starting point of Althusser's theory of ideology.

Its decisive modification in the conception of materialism consists in precisely the sort of analytical shift I have outlined regarding religion. According to his theory of ideology, religious beliefs and attitudes must be taken seriously: God exists simply because He is a worldly practice of individuals and collectives. Practices take place as though He existed: people kneel, fold their hands, sing hymns, kill others in the name of God, or have their children baptized. Althusser carries out a materialist proof of God by showing how He exists in all these practices, rituals, and discourses. Althusser's theory is useful to show how these processes reproduce certain kinds of subjectivization which, at the same time, subjugate people and make them into the free subjects of their actions, which in turn isolates them from each other and brings them under a collective 'third term', whether it be God or nation or gender.

I think a distinction made by Foucault would be helpful here to understand the peculiar ontological distinction between being and consciousness which is at play here. Foucault argues that one has to leave aside universals such as the people, state, or civil society, and start instead with concrete practices. Pursuing this line of thought, he claims that madness, delinquency, and sexuality do not exist as such [as 'ready-made object'] and yet are nevertheless something.[10] He is gesturing toward those 'interferences', which make 'something non-existent still something while remaining non-existent'. Analogously, he also says that the economy and politics do not exist, as they are not existing things, errors, illusions, or ideologies. They are 'things that do not exist and yet which are inscribed in reality'.[11]

POLITICS AS ILLUSION: TWO MISUNDERSTANDINGS

According to critical materialism's understanding of things, politics is really a kind of spiritualism and it is illusory. It does not exist, but with

---

10   Cf. Michel Foucault, *Security, Territory, Population: Lectures at the Collège de France, 1977–78*, ed. by Arnold I. Davidson (Basingstoke: Palgrave Macmillan, 2007), p. 118; and Michel Foucault, *The Birth of Biopolitics: Lectures at the Collège de France, 1978–79*, ed. by Arnold I. Davidson (Basingstoke: Palgrave Macmillan, 2008), p. 19.

11   Foucault, *The Birth of Biopolitics*, p. 20.

its interferences it is and does something. This point is made with three arguments that I would like now to briefly repeat and expand on.

a) The political community appears as the authority of the general and confirms individuals in their bourgeois, selfish isolation from each other. Individuals experience their social context through money and the state. They only experience their connection — entirely in the religious tradition — through a third, a general, to which they have to submit and over which they have hardly any influence. Individuals always remain particular and face the state as the general, and the state as general confronts them in the form of legal norms or administrative power as a foreign force. This still applies even if you can identify with individual regulations and measures, or if you also enjoy advantages. For just as they can favour an individual or a group in the name of the general public, they can also disadvantage them in the name of the general public.

b) Politics personalizes social processes because everything appears as a result of a will of individuals, their power, their special ability or inability. The general cannot appear directly as a general, but must always take the form of individual actors. This gives the impression that political goals are not being pursued, or are not being pursued adequately, because the wrong person is responsible or is doing the wrong thing and vice versa: if a policy is to be prevented, it appears as if a concrete person is the obstacle and must therefore be pushed out of the political function ('Merkel must go').

c) There can be no collective subject and no collective will under capitalist conditions, the general is illusory. Powerful particular forces agree on a compromise on how to divide and use the power of the state.

I would like to now briefly address two possible misunderstandings. The first misunderstanding is that the state is associated with the claim to generality: it is the means through which generally binding rules are created and enforced. However, these rules, which affect many social contexts, always represent compromises that relevant forces can agree upon at a certain point in time. The struggle for the establishment of general rules and their use is an ongoing one, so they are never, in fact, general. The general is constantly being postponed. For example, bureaucracies can undermine it, powerful social actors can ignore a rule, try to enforce new rules, make use of grey areas of existing rules, or use laws to dominate weaker social agents, who then have to fight for new rules but cannot prevail for years or decades. In this way the generality of the law becomes a powerful force against the subaltern.

The second misunderstanding concerns the illusionary general. When using this term, I do not draw upon the Rousseauian expectation of a real, uniform general public, as if there could be a people's sovereign who was not shaped by many different interests and ways of life. However, I also do not draw on the expectation that discursive decision-making in the public sphere could solve the problem of the illusory character of the general. Rather, from the point of view of critical materialism, we are concerned here with two things. Firstly, new forms of coordination must arise from within the social processes of work, whereby those who do socially performed work also coordinate themselves, and no longer fall under the command and control rights of powerful owners. Secondly, there will be different interests, but these will be coordinated according to the nature of the specific socially performed work to be done by those performing it. Coordination does not take place under the aegis of the (national) state as the general, but is a collective will that is determined by those who take part in decision-making from the perspective of their contribution to overall socially performed work.

THE REALITY OF GHOSTS

Critical materialism can be said to be concerned with the reality of ghosts and the undead precisely because the political mind is spiritual, and because the economy is theological and metaphysical, and therefore involves the rule of the dead over the living. The consequences for a materialist relationship to politics is obvious. It is critical of and dismissively hostile to politics as well as the economy. Marx, as well as Althusser and Foucault, all argue against acting politically, for politics represents an imaginary, that is, a metaphysical form of practice, one which has far-reaching consequences for people, especially in its imaginary, metaphysical form. Since Marx, critical materialism has been concerned with not restricting itself to prehistory, but to give space instead to world-opening practices — that is, to a freedom that is no longer restricted by the 'prehistory' of the preservation interests of the owners of dead capital.

Foucault argues that criticizing the local power of psychiatric practices and institutions of prisons, or blaming reason in general, is not enough. According to him, one must ask how such power relations are rationalized. Asking this question 'is the only way to avoid other institutions, with the same objectives and the same effects, from taking their stead'.[12] Liberation is achieved only by attacking the roots of political rationality itself.

But for the time being, politics cannot be avoided, as Foucault proved beyond measure with his own engagement. In a similar vein, Adorno argued for a dialectical understanding of the nature of the political. Although politics is ideological and an epiphenomenon, it is in fact covering up what is actually going on: it has, in short, real effects. But politics also has the potential to act on the societal substructure and change it.[13] That is why the decisive practice takes the form of politics — but with the aim of abolishing this form.[14] It is a Beckett-like situation: even if you cannot go on, you have to go on; so that, paraphrasing Marx,[15] once humans [the world] awaken from the dream about themselves that they live in, and with their *last* rather than their *first* political act enter into their own, self-created reality, they will become materialists — but this will only be possible if they have moved beyond both idealism and materialism.

TRANSLATED BY RON FAUST

---

12   Michel Foucault '"Omnes et Singulatim": Toward a Critique of Political Reason', in *Essential Works of Foucault 1954–1984: Power*, ed. by Paul Rabinow, James D. Faubion (New York: New Press, 2001), pp. 298–325 (p. 325).

13   Theodor W. Adorno, *Philosophische Elemente einer Theorie der Gesellschaft* (Frankfurt a.M.: Suhrkamp, 2008 [1964]), footnote, p. 67.

14   Letter from Adorno to Horkheimer 11 March 1957, in Adorno, Theodor W., and Max Horkheimer, *Briefwechsel*, 4 vols, in *Theodor W. Adorno. Briefe und Briefwechsel*, 8 vols (Frankfurt a.M.: Suhrkamp, 1994–), IV.4: *1950–1969* (2006), p. 454.

15   Karl Marx, 'Letters from the Deutsch-Französische Jahrbücher', in *MECW*, III, pp. 133–45 (p. 144).

On Populist Illusion
Impasses of Political Ontology, or How the Ordinary Matters
FACUNDO VEGA

The theoretical and political reasons that animate radical thought today are products of a past glory based, to a great extent, on the fascination with 'the extraordinary'. Images of the break, of the act that disturbs regularity, are what mostly draw the attention of those who ascribe to a way of thinking politics that claims to be radical. At the crossroads of our time, however, we find the absence of such images of breaks and *new political beginnings*.

The generalization of this landscape within critical theory is concomitant with the replacement of *faith* in the great political act with *faith* in the power of ontology. The post-Marxist variants that pointed out the closed-mindedness of economism, determinism, and historical materialism in leftist tradition sought to overcome a *new* crisis in Marxism by appealing to the notion of 'the political'. This extrapolation of ontological analysis onto the territory of politics has led to a new exaltation of 'the extraordinary'. The issue is no longer to postulate a beginning as a great political act guided by historical materialist motifs, but, in a Heideggerian fashion, to establish ontological foundation as the abyssal dimension of politics as such. Despite the philosophico-political transformations that derive from this theoretical novelty, what really animates it is the condemnation of what is conceived as 'ordinary'. In sum, 'the political' seems to reinvigorate radical thought after determinism has exhausted the leftist tradition — but at what cost?

This essay will consist of three sections in which I follow the conviction that Ernesto Laclau's discursive materialism and later interventions on 'populism' offer important insights into these topics but that they also catalyse blind spots on the ordinary matter of life in common. First, I show how Laclau's post-Marxist theory is based on the idea that social division is the *ground* of politics and therefore is inscribed within an ontology-oriented (post-)metaphysics. In this context, it makes sense that Laclau operates a Heideggerian rearticulation of the notion of 'the political'. Second, I examine how this philosophico-political move is exasperated by the Laclaudian understanding of populism. In particular, in the terms laid out by the later Laclau, all radical politics requires the figure of the populist leader who points towards the path of emancipation. However, while accepting the productivity of 'political difference' — that is, the binary distinction between 'politics' and 'the political' — under a populist inflection, I argue that Laclau both restrains his previous 'deepening of the materialist project'[1] and consecrates 'political exceptionalism'. Faced with the assumption that the body of the populist leader as the epitome of 'the political' primordially animates political beginnings, the last section of this essay offers, as an alternative, the contours of an ordinary politics of 'the many' as the territory *par excellence* of democratic foundations.

THE 'DISCREET' CHARM OF 'THE POLITICAL'

A number of works in contemporary thought have vindicated the contentious character of politics by pointing out the dangers of con-

1   Ernesto Laclau, 'Political Significance of the Concept of Negativity', *Vestnik*, 1, (1988), pp. 73–78 (p. 76). See also Ernesto Laclau, 'La Politique comme construction de l'impensable', in *Matérialités discursives*, ed. by Bernard Conein, and others (Lille: Presses Universitaires de Lille, 1981), pp. 65–74; 'The Controversy over Materialism', in *Rethinking Marx*, ed. by Sakari Hänninen and Leena Paldán (Berlin: Argument, 1984), pp. 39–43; 'Ideology and Post-Marxism', *Journal of Political Ideologies*, 11.2 (June 2006), pp. 103–14 (p. 104); Ernesto Laclau and Chantal Mouffe, 'Post-Marxism without Apologies', in Laclau, *New Reflections on the Revolution of our Time* (London: Verso, 1990), pp. 97–132 (pp. 105–12).

sensualism.[2] The focus on such notions as 'conflict' and 'contingency' was aimed at shedding light on the mutability of political acts while challenging the analytical stagnation of philosophies of progress and deterministic economism. In other words, the impugnation of a consensus-based theory and the concomitant vindication of social division as the *ground* of politics sought to respond to the barren summaries given by traditional perspectives that rested on invocations of metaphysical foundations and political essentialism. Remarkably, in the case of Laclau, his radical democratic critique of essentialism staged a controversy over materialism. In fact, he claims that 'the only meaning of the term "materialism" which seems valid to me is that which opposes the reduction of the real to the concept; this implies that we must radically abandon the idea of a unifying *essence* of society'.[3] The tone of Laclau's dispute engendered high expectations for his radical democratic project and its extolment of 'the political'. By seeking to supersede all essentialism, that project migrated to the territory of (post-)metaphysics.

One of the most sophisticated attempts to explain how social division is at the basis of politics will illustrate the kind of problems I refer to. In one of the prefaces to *Hegemony and Socialist Strategy*, Laclau and Chantal Mouffe argue that they 'conceive of the political not as a superstructure but as having the status of an *ontology of the social*. From this argument it follows that [...] social division is inherent [...] in the very possibility of a democratic politics'.[4] There can be no radical politics, Laclau and Mouffe add, without the identification of an adversary. Their theory of politics is grounded on the assertion that antagonism is the realization of the indeterminacy of the social. Thus, they characterize radical democracy as a political form 'which is founded [...] on affirmation of the contingency and ambiguity of

---

2   See, among others, Ernesto Laclau and Chantal Mouffe, *Hegemony and Socialist Strategy: Towards a Radical Democratic Politics* (London: Verso, 2001); Alain Badiou, *Peut-on penser la politique?* (Paris: Éditions du Seuil, 1985); Jacques Rancière, *La Mésentente. Politique et Philosophie* (Paris: Éditions Galilée, 1995); Étienne Balibar, *La Crainte des masses. Politique et Philosophie avant et après Marx* (Paris: Éditions Galilée, 1997).

3   Laclau, 'The Controversy over Materialism', p. 43; emphasis in the original. See the important addition to Laclau's rendition of 'materialism' by Frieder Otto Wolf, 'Summary of Discussions', in *Rethinking Marx*, ed. by Hänninen and Paldán, pp. 52–53.

4   Laclau and Mouffe, *Hegemony and Socialist Strategy*, p. xiv. Emphasis in the original.

every "essence", and on the constitutive character of social division and antagonism.[5]

This *sui generis* reinvigoration of the materialist repertoire transformed certain presuppositions of the Marxist debate — the 'ontological' supremacy of the working class, the conception of Revolution as a founding moment, and the prospect of collective will as unitary, to name a few. Such an undertaking demanded new theoretical postulates — among others, the idea that, hegemonically, 'the political' is constitutive of the social. The re-centring of 'the political' in Laclau's work is not a merely disruptive operation, but instead leads him to embrace a singular intellectual perspective: post-structuralist thought. *Hegemony and Socialist Strategy*, in fact, can be characterized as the epitome of the post-structuralist political turn developed by Laclau in his later work, which is crowned with two movements: an attachment to the lack and excess of 'the ontological' and its extrapolation onto the political realm.

'Lack' and 'excess' as two necessary moments of a unique ontological condition are essential to Laclau's understanding of politics. Laclau himself asserts that 'lack and excess enter into the determination of social ontology', operating with respect to a 'failed unicity' or 'absent fullness'. Insofar as, for him, 'every identity is a threatened identity', then 'antagonism is ontologically primary'.[6] The onto-political horizon described by Laclau is animated by the inevitable gap between 'fullness of being' and 'actual being'. He views 'lack' and 'excess' as the *raison d'être* of hegemony, that is, the moment when a particular symbol or actor becomes representative of the universality of the community. Ultimately, 'lack' and 'excess' appear as originating principles of the merger of ontological postulates and socio-political relations.

This ambitious combination, however, necessitates a supplementary mechanism. Laclau's post-structuralism requires constitutive foundations for the *abyssal ground* of politics, and because social relations are in the last instance contingent, 'the political' plays that structuring role. Vis-à-vis historical materialism, and understood as 'radical

---

5   Ibid., 193. On antagonism vis-à-vis class struggle, see Ernesto Laclau, 'Antagonism, Subjectivity and Politics', in his *The Rhetorical Foundations of Society* (London: Verso, 2014), pp. 101–25.

6   Ernesto Laclau, 'The Future of Radical Democracy', in *Radical Democracy: Politics between Abundance and Lack*, ed. by Lars Tønder and Lasse Thomassen (Manchester: Manchester University Press, 2005), pp. 256–62 (p. 257).

relationalism', Laclau's post-Marxist materialism proposes that ideas, including those related to political grounding, 'do not constitute a closed and self-generated world, but are rooted in the ensemble of material conditions of society'.[7] His invocation of 'the political', then, is the backbone of a situation traversed by the impossibility of totalization. The resolution of this stalemate has a precise significance in Laclau's project: 'radical democracy is the first strictly political form of social organisation, because it is the first one in which the posing and the withdrawal of the social ground is entirely dependent on political interventions'.[8] On the one hand, Laclau establishes the impossibility of an ultimate foundation of the social, and does so in a post-structuralist fashion that seeks to avoid the limitations inherent to the contraposition of classical idealism and materialism.[9] On the other, this operation is consolidated by appealing to 'the political' as the moment of institution of the social.

Notably, Laclau's onto-political operations rely on a return to Martin Heidegger's thought. In particular, Heidegger's 'ontological difference' appears profusely in Laclau's work after *Hegemony and Socialist Strategy* to conform what was called 'political difference': while 'politics' refers to the concrete realm of decision making, 'the political' would be the sphere from which politics originates. Laclau — sometimes defined as a 'leftist Heideggerian' — forges a post-foundational theory that seeks to comprehend the ontological 'un-grounding' of political principles.[10] By vindicating the conflictual and contingent character of politics under the aegis of anti-essentialism, Laclau claims that 'since, for essential reasons [...] the fullness of society is unreachable, this split in the identity of political agents is an absolutely constitutive "ontological difference" — *in a sense not entirely unrelated*

---

7   Laclau and Mouffe, 'Post-Marxism without Apologies', p. 110.

8   Laclau, 'The Future of Radical Democracy', p. 261.

9   Neither related to the problem of the external existence of objects, nor to a contraposition of form and matter in which the latter is conceived as the 'individual existent', Laclau is more interested in suggesting that 'a world of fixed forms constituting the *ultimate* reality of the object (idealism) is challenged by the relational, historical and precarious character of the world of forms (materialism)' (Laclau and Mouffe, 'Post-Marxism without Apologies', p. 110; emphasis in the original).

10   See Oliver Marchart, *Post-Foundational Political Thought: Political Difference in Nancy, Lefort, Badiou and Laclau* (Edinburgh: Edinburgh University Press, 2007).

to Heidegger's use of this expression.[11] Laclau's radical-democratic approach relies on stressing the difference between *Sein* and *Seiende*. When 'ontological difference' is extrapolated onto the political realm it becomes a necessary moment of Laclau's 'ontology of the social'.[12]

It is remarkable how Laclau's invocation of democracy as a radical order that resists the imprisonment of essentialist foundations reproduces 'political difference' over and over again. Laclau's onto-political instances are recurrent: '"Politics" is an ontological category: there is politics because there is subversion and dislocation of the social'.[13] Laclau's analysis, to be sure, not only extrapolates 'ontological difference' onto 'political difference' but also, in particular, elevates one of the structuring principles of the former, 'the ontological'. Concerning the allegation that his oeuvre focuses on the ontological dimension of social theory and not on ontic research, Laclau replies that 'this is a charge to which I plead happily guilty, except that I do not see it as a criticism at all. I have located my theoretical intervention at the theoretical and philosophical level and it is at that level that it has to be judged'.[14] Laclau's celebration of ontologism reaches a climax in his later published works — to the extent that, in his own reckoning, they show the 'ontological centrality of the political'.[15] His argument is simply supernumerary insofar as 'the ontological' plays the role of a ubiquitous *Deus ex machina*.

By pointing out these deficits in Laclau's work, I do not mean to minimize his influence over contemporary thought. Some of the interest that Laclau's intervention has aroused derives from his perception that hegemonic politics moves from the struggle against the

---

11   Ernesto Laclau, *Emancipation(s)* (London: Verso, 1996), pp. 60–61. Emphasis added.

12   See, among others, Ernesto Laclau and Lilian Zac, 'Minding the Gap: The Subject of Politics', in *The Making of Political Identities*, ed. by Ernesto Laclau (London: Verso, 1994), pp. 11–39 (p. 30); Laclau, 'Identity and Hegemony: The Role of Universality in the Constitution of Political Logics', in *Contingency, Hegemony, Universality: Contemporary Dialogues on the Left*, ed. by Judith Butler, Ernesto Laclau, and Slavoj Žižek (London: Verso, 2000), pp. 44–89 (pp. 58, 71, and 84–85); Laclau, 'Glimpsing the Future', in *Laclau: A Critical Reader*, ed. by Simon Critchley and Oliver Marchart (London: Routledge, 2004), pp. 279–328 (pp. 307–11 and 323); Laclau, 'Antagonism, Subjectivity and Politics', pp. 112 and 115.

13   Ernesto Laclau, 'New Reflections on the Revolution of our Time', in *New Reflections on the Revolution of our Time*, pp. 3–85 (p. 61).

14   Laclau, 'Glimpsing the Future', p. 321.

15   Laclau, *The Rhetorical Foundations of Society*, p. 8.

rigidities of historical materialism toward the reference to fundamental ontology. 'Like the Heideggerian *Abgrund*', Laclau claims, 'the hege-monic operation consists in a radical investment which, at the same time as it attempts to establish a bridge between the ontic and the ontological, reproduces their impossible convergence.'[16] At this stage, we should note that the invocation of 'political difference' conflates two distinct strands in Laclau's oeuvre: on the one hand, his emphasis on the 'dissolution of the myth of foundations'[17] as a radicalization of emancipatory thought attentive to a post-Marxist 'materialism', and, on the other, the inscription of that *abyssal nature* of political founda-tion on the altar of ontology. Laclau's theory thus leads to a specific impasse, in which a kind of post-structuralism conceived as post-metaphysical is actually erected upon the essentialist coordinates of fundamental ontology.

By examining Laclau's attribution of an ontological character to politics, I intend to note his 'forgetfulness' of the power and action of 'the many'. That 'forgetfulness' is remarkable, especially since, accord-ing to Laclau, his theorizations were in large measure derived from his youthful activism. As Laclau explains:

> when today I read *Of Grammatology*, *S/Z*, or the *Écrits* of Lacan, the examples which always spring to mind are not from philosophical or literary texts; they are from a discussion in an Argentinian trade union, a clash of opposing slogans at a demonstration, or a debate during a party congress. Through-out his life Joyce returned to his native experience in Dublin; for me it is those years of political struggle in Argentina of the 1960s that come to mind as a point of reference and compar-ison.[18]

Rather than reading these recollections as manoeuvres concerning the exoticism of a native land and of youthful political practice, I would rather conceive of them as invectives with respect to a philosophico-political plexus in crisis. Laclau himself notes that 'the loss of collective

16   Laclau, 'Antagonism, Subjectivity and Politics', p. 121.
17   Ernesto Laclau, 'Politics and the Limits of Modernity', in *Universal Abandon? The Politics of Postmodernism*, ed. by Andrew Ross (Minneapolis: University of Minnesota Press, 1988), pp. 63–82 (p. 81).
18   Ernesto Laclau, 'Theory, Democracy and Socialism', in *New Reflections on the Revolu-tion of our Time*, pp. 197–245 (p. 200).

memory is not something to be overjoyed about. It is always an impoverishment and a traumatic fact. One only thinks *from* a tradition'.[19] In the next section, I show that Laclau's defence of the ontological embodiment of the populist leader constitutes a renewed stage of his *Auseinandersetzung* with the Marxist legacy — and that the tradition that Laclau never abandoned is that of 'political exceptionalism', one in which political beginnings are ontologically constituted and extraordinary in nature.

THE LEADER'S NEW ONTOLOGICAL CLOTHES: POPULISM AND THE POLITICAL EXCEPTION

In this section I examine how, in Laclau's theory, the radical-democratic 'praise of the political' takes a populist form. Laclau's considerations on populism are not restricted to his later work. In fact, such reflections began during his political activism in Argentina and coalesced with the publication of *Politics and Ideology in Marxist Theory* in 1977. While there are exceptionalist constants in Laclau's work, his later encomium of 'the political' in a populist sense adds a fundamental ingredient to his theoretical position: the supposed radicalization offered by 'ontological difference' in its political inflection.

According to this later Laclau, populism, understood as a 'way of *constructing the political*'[20] that is clearly different from institutionalism and its emphasis on gradualist administration, remains 'an ontological and not an ontic category'.[21] Étienne Balibar has incisively summarized the spectrum of Laclau's theoretical attempt in the following terms: 'populism, rethought and generalized according to a modality that is no longer normative but ontological, is not a marginal, still less a pathological, phenomenon. It is a presupposition of politics itself'.

19   Ernesto Laclau, 'Building a New Left', in *New Reflections on the Revolution of our Time*, pp. 177–96 (p. 179; emphasis in the original).
20   Ernesto Laclau, *On Populist Reason* (London: Verso, 2005), p. xi; emphasis added.
21   Ernesto Laclau, 'Populism: What's in a Name?', in *Populism and the Mirror of Democracy*, ed. by Francisco Panizza (London: Verso, 2005), pp. 32–49 (p. 34).

Hence, Balibar concludes, 'its denial [...] appears as itself the effect of society's blindness to its own bases'.[22]

For Laclau, undoing this blindness with respect to the constitution of the social involves moving toward a definition of populism as a 'political logic' and a 'performative act endowed with a rationality of its own'.[23] On the one hand, Laclau asserts that the 'dismissal [of populism] has been part of the discursive construction of a certain normality';[24] while, on the other hand, Laclau argues that confronting this situation endows the difference between 'the ontic' and 'the ontological' with a political significance, giving primacy to the second term.[25] In a world in which politics is conceived as mere administration, it is imperative to solve the theoretical impasse around 'the political' in a populist vein. The condition for this solution that is not asserted categorically, however, is that populism must be understood with reference to the command of the leader. According to Laclau, administrative politics, which is opposed to populism, embodies the myth of the '*totally* reconciled society — which invariably presupposes *the absence of leadership, that is, the withering away of the political*'.[26] Inversely, for Laclau leadership is constitutive of 'the political' and expresses the nature of 'political difference' in the highest sense.

Both undertheorized and omnipresent, the populist leader offsets the dispersion of 'the people'. The notion of 'social demand' is essential in this regard, for, according to Laclau, it remains the smallest unit to analyse the constitution of 'the people'. Although 'demand' may equally refer to 'request' as it may to 'claim',[27] it should not be necessarily restricted to the domain of the antagonism of 'the people' against the power bloc. Rather, Laclau himself stresses that 'the people' necessitates a specific 'other' to catalyse *its* demands: the leader. Without the leader's acts, in fact, 'democratic demands', which are of an isolated

---

22   Étienne Balibar, *La Proposition de l'Égaliberté* (Paris: PUF, 2010), p. 232; *Equaliberty: Political Essays*, trans. by James Ingram (Durham, NC: Duke University Press, 2013), pp. 189–90.

23   Laclau, *On Populist Reason*, pp. 117 and 18.

24   Ibid., p. 19.

25   See ibid., pp. 4, 67–68, 71–72, 87–88, 94, 103, 111, 114–16, 127, 132, 160–61, 163, 222, 224–26, 229, and 245–46.

26   Ibid., p. 63; emphasis in the original and added.

27   Ibid., 73.

nature, could never become 'popular demands', which help 'to constitute the "people" as a potential historical actor'.[28]

Laclau is cautious regarding the idea that the love of the leader
might be the only libidinal tie of a group. Nonetheless, he also argues
that the elimination of 'the need for a leader corresponds, almost point
by point, to a society entirely governed by what I have called the logic
of difference'. He then adds that 'such a society is an impossibility'.[29]
The emergence of 'the people', according to Laclau, entails the intervention of something 'qualitatively new'. In this vein, he asserts that
the constitution of popular identity, as a symbol, does not express in
a passive way but actually constitutes what it expresses. Laclau's discursive materialism conveys, in his own words, 'the attempt of showing
how the being of objects, far from being fixed and simply "given" to the
contemplation of human beings, is socially constructed through their
actions'.[30] And yet, the process that he describes cannot establish 'the
many' as protagonists of democratic politics.

The obliteration of the role of 'the many' in populist politics is
even clearer when Laclau decrees that 'an assemblage of heterogeneous
elements kept equivalentially together only by a name is [...] necessarily a *singularity*'. Asserting that individuality is the most extreme form
of singularity, Laclau arrives at a corollary that reveals the 'truth of
populism': 'In this way, almost imperceptibly, the equivalential logic
leads to singularity, and singularity to identification of the unity of
the group with the name of the leader'.[31] In sum, although Laclau's
analysis is sparse on this point, we can infer that the figure of the leader
animates the populist phenomenon — which is remarkable, since,
for him, 'populist reason [...] amounts [...] to *political* reason *tout
court*'.[32] Populism, then, stages the subjection of 'the people' to the
dictates of popular 'authority', forging a unity based on the power of
the 'great man' which vanishes once this figure passes away.

The invocation of the extra-quotidian character of the leader
within Laclau's construct deserves further scrutiny. It is possible to

---

28   Ibid., pp. 74 and 120.
29   Ibid., p. 82.
30   Laclau, 'Political Significance of the Concept of Negativity', p. 76.
31   Laclau, *On Populist Reason*, p. 100.
32   Ibid., p. 225; emphasis in the original.

address this issue by observing that, aside from the notions of 'demands' and 'the name of the leader', the concept of 'representation' is central to Laclau's understanding of populism.[33] Laclau's discussion of representation is primarily aimed at comprehending the leader as a symbol maker. His or her activity, Laclau argues, 'no longer conceived as "acting for" his constituents, becomes identified with effective leadership'.[34] Laclau emphasizes that 'identity' does not precede the 'process of representation' but rather results from it. *Mutatis mutandis*, representation is the premise for the constitution of a 'popular will'. In Laclau's terms, the construction of a 'people' cannot but take place through representation.

Critics have pointed out the fallacy in the assumption that the representative articulation of demands necessarily leads to the emergence of a cohesive political entity. As Slavoj Žižek suggests, 'there is nothing in the heterogeneity of demands that predisposes them to be unified in *people*'.[35] Certainly, Laclau understands representation as having a performative character. Populism, in this sense, becomes a discourse that brings into being what it claims to represent, namely 'the people'. But even considering populism within the domain of political performativity is not a sufficient basis to conclude, as Laclau does, that every will is constituted as such *after* representation. And if representation is by and large equivalent with the expression of the leader's will, then it is restricted to playing the role of a unifying force.

Be that as it may, Laclau's defence of the role of the populist leader is even more questionable given the author's familiarity with Ernst Kantorowicz's theory of the King's two bodies.[36] Though I cannot scrutinize the implications of this debate around political legitimacy and corporality here, I would like to return to Laclau's last dictum: 'the logic of the King's two bodies has not disappeared in democratic society: it is simply not true that pure emptiness has replaced the

---

33   On 'representation' in his work, see, among others, Laclau, 'Power and Representation', in *Emancipation(s)*, pp. 84–104; *On Populist Reason*, pp. 157–71.

34   Laclau, *On Populist Reason*, p. 160.

35   Slavoj Žižek, 'Against the Populist Temptation', *Critical Inquiry*, 32.3 (Spring 2006), pp. 551–74 (p. 564); emphasis in the original.

36   Ernst Kantorowicz, *The King's Two Bodies: A Study in Mediaeval Political Theology* (Princeton, NJ: Princeton University Press, 1957).

immortal body of the King. This immortal body is revived by the hegemonic force'. Laclau adds:

> What has changed in democracy, as compared with the *anciens régimes* [sic], is that in the latter that revival took place in only one body, while today it transmigrates through a variety of bodies. But the logic of embodiment continues to operate under democratic conditions and, under certain circumstances, it can acquire considerable stability.[37]

It is surprising that Laclau, an author who is so prone to conceptual constructs, does not specify the nature of the democratic 'variety of bodies' to which he refers. Whisking this specification away, Laclau neglects a radical materialist consideration of 'the many' — an oversight that leads him to focus on the corporality of leaders. His thesis is that hegemonic force rekindles a sort of immortal 'energy'. Even if we accept this proposition, it seems difficult to see where the limits of that 'extraordinariness' might be — especially when Laclau himself assumes that democratic incarnations are always contingent and that there is no ultimate guarantee or transcendental source of legitimation that might structure life in common.

BETWEEN THE ORDINARY AND THE EXTRAORDINARY: THE
COMBINED POWER OF 'THE MANY'

Beyond the equivalence between populism and politics and its hypostasis in the body of the leader, I want to argue that life in common does not have impregnable origins waiting to be disinterred. Political beginnings are nothing but a complex of intertwined ordinary and non-ordinary moments which evade all confinement in the binary edifice erected between 'politics' and 'the political'. The extolment of 'the political', and particularly the proverbial instantiation of exceptionalism in radical thought, cannot account exhaustively for the emergence of beginnings enacted by the politics of 'the many'.[38]

---

37   Laclau, *On Populist Reason*, p. 170.

38   To avoid the idealization and aestheticization of 'lack', the phrase 'the ordinary' is used in this essay to refer to a realm of action and not to 'the many' themselves. At the same time, 'the many' indicate that democracy is evasive vis-à-vis the sanctification of *the* will of 'the people'. To put it differently, the appeal to 'the many' acknowledges the

In Laclau's later works, this neglect is embodied in his enthroning of the populist leader and is also apparently compensated for by the author's interest in the constitution of a political ontology. While in his early work Laclau focused on the multiplicity of struggles inscribed in the democratic revolution and then confronted the narrative of the great emancipatory act with a variety of emancipatory movements, in his later work he moved away from pluralized radical politics. In fact, for Laclau, the construction of a popular subjectivity 'reaches a point where the homogenising function is carried out by a pure name: *the name of the leader*'.[39] What remains to be understood here is why populist hegemony is the form of expression *par excellence* of an antagonistic excess with respect to the democratic institutions that normally regulate political conflict or why, as Laclau claims, '*radical democracy is always "populist"*'.[40]

Laclau's populism implies de-substantializing 'the people' and then, in a (post-)metaphysical and discursive vein, re-substantializing this collective through the figure of the leader. In such theoretical gestures, we can still detect Laclau's *Auseinandersetzung* with materialism through his invocations of the 'materiality of the signifier' or the 'materiality of language'.[41] However, Laclau's 'rhetorical materialism of the subject' might resemble 'a voluntarism of sorts'.[42] More importantly, his operation of de-substantializing and re-substantializing 'the people' leads to a disdain for the autonomy of 'the many'. It is true that the view of 'the people' as irrational plebs has persisted even after the consolidation of modern and contemporary revolutions. Going against this tendency, Laclau's populist project invokes radical democracy to

---

centrality of political subjectivity without somehow acceding to the idea of 'a good people'.

39   Laclau, 'Populism: What's in a Name?', p. 40; emphasis added.

40   Laclau, 'The Future of Radical Democracy', p. 259; emphasis added.

41   See, among others, Laclau, 'Why do Empty Signifiers Matter to Politics?', in *Emancipation(s)*, pp. 36–46; *The Rhetorical Foundations of Society*.

42   John Kraniauskas, 'Rhetorics of populism', *Radical Philosophy: A Journal of Socialist and Feminist Philosophy*, 186 (July/August 2014), pp. 29–37 (p. 33). On the relation between discourse and materialism in Laclau, see, among others, Rosemary Hennessy, *Materialist Feminism and the Politics of Discourse* (New York: Routledge, 1993), pp. 59–64; Benjamin Glasson, 'Unspeakable Articulations: Steps Towards a Materialist Discourse Theory', in *Material Discourse-Materialist Analysis: Approaches in Discourse Studies*, ed. by Johannes Beetz and Veit Schwab (Lanham, MD: Lexington Books, 2017), pp. 81–94.

revalue the politically marginalized: And yet, rather than considering the underdog as autonomous, he suggests that it is the extra-quotidian nature of the body of the leader which brings the marginalized into actual political existence.

It may be that these elaborations are aimed at extricating 'the people' of populism from the danger of 'homogeneity'. But after the foregoing analysis, we may discern an additional motif of the 'political exceptionalism' that consecrates the disdain for the autonomy of 'the many' in the work of Laclau and other theorists of populism. 'The people', or rather *their* 'people', is not only subordinated to the figure of the leader; *it* is also an intellectual construct. 'A first theoretical decision', Laclau declares, 'is to conceive of the "people" as a *polit-ical* category, not as a *datum* of the social structure.'[43] In this way, 'the people' is not just born from the political will of the populist leader. More fundamentally, this collective originates from the analyt-ical design of the populist intellectual who places his or her principles beyond the immediate historical context and 'mere' empirical reality. Vis-à-vis this triple imprisonment — by the figure of 'the people', the decisions of the populist leader, and the judgments of the populist in-tellectual — 'the many' must return to the central scene of democratic politics.

Thus far, we have seen how Laclau, by adopting 'political differ-ence', endowed the body of the populist leader with an ontological status. But he also goes further than that. His use of ontological jargon to define politics is not merely descriptive but symbolizes his intention to lay out a 'political ontology' and to elaborate a general theory of 'the political'. Laclau's endeavour to address 'the political' is charac-terized by a polarity: Marx (deconstructed) with Heidegger. Within that dichotomy, Laclau seems to privilege Heidegger, which affects his radical materialist project.[44] In his last published work, he asserts that his aim is 'the construction of a *political ontology* which can respond

---

43   Laclau, *On Populist Reason*, p. 224; emphasis in the original.

44   By embracing Heideggerian 'ontological difference', Laclau avoids a thematization of Heidegger's derogatory rendition of materialism. See, among others, Martin Heideg-ger, *Gesamtausgabe*, 102 vols (Frankfurt a.M.: Klostermann, 1975–) VIII, pp. 27, 160, and 208; IX, pp. 268, 340, and 365; X, pp. 131 and 179–80; XV, pp. 352–53 and 387–89, XVI, p. 703; XXXVI/XXXVII, p. 211; XL, p. 50; L, p. 154; LXV, pp. 54 and 148; LXXVIII, pp. 12–14 and 190; LXXIX, pp. 88 and 94–95; LXXXIII, pp. 179, 209, and 508; LXXXIX,

to the challenges presented by the post-Marxist and post-structuralist situation within which we are operating'.[45] For Laclau, returning to the Marxist legacy requires appreciating its inherent plurality. But the trajectory he delineates, from the vindication of 'post-Marxism' — understood by Laclau himself as the reformulation of 'the materialist programme in a much more radical way than was possible for Marx'[46] — to his final encomium of populism, proves to be an attempt to think beyond the 'relationalist' universe.

Having left class struggle far behind, the plot of Laclau's political drama is neither based on the plural struggles of social movements nor on so-called materialist 'democratic radicalization'. Instead, radical thought is enacted on the stage of a ruptured metaphysics. The establishment of a ground as abyss, together with the understanding of representation as a process of de-grounding, are made legitimate through Laclau's recourse to the notion of 'post-foundationalism'. But due to the abyssal conditions being constitutive, this lack requires an excess. Previously, we have examined how, in Laclau's later works, populist leadership necessitates a supernumerary recourse to ontology. We are now ready to assess a crucial addendum: the *essential* contingency of political foundation requires a particular stabilization that, for Laclau, must come from the political ontology that he has forged — a political ontology that claims to univocally identify 'the *political* (in the ontological sense of the term, which has little to do with political organizations and structures)'[47] and might re-stage a *faith* in a totalizing moment with idealist effects.[48]

The transition from Marx (deconstructed) to Heidegger is not restricted to Laclau's work. This is why the present examination of his theoretical edifice has a broader scope. As we problematize the

---

pp. 461–62 and 527; xcIV, pp. 143, 424, and 428; xcv, pp. 40, 129, 149, and 360; xcvi, p. 150; xcvII, pp. 28 and 127; xcvIII, pp. 382 and 398–99.

45   Laclau, *The Rhetorical Foundations of Society*, p. 1; emphasis added.

46   Laclau and Mouffe, 'Post-Marxism without Apologies', p. 112.

47   Laclau, 'Antagonism, Subjectivity and Politics', p. 123; emphasis in the original.

48   This result is at odds with Laclau's previous insistence on moving away from idealist instances, which would consist 'in showing the historical, contingent and constructed character of the *being* of objects; and in showing that this depends on the reinsertion of that being in the ensemble of relational conditions which constitute the life of a society as a whole' (Laclau and Mouffe, 'Post-Marxism without Apologies', p. 111; emphasis in the original).

fascination with 'the extraordinary' inherent in 'political difference', the point is to set out the bases for a renewed reflection on the ordinary irruption of 'the many' in democratic politics.[49] As a propaedeutic for this task, in the preceding pages I have established how Laclau's 'populist illusion' — not meant in terms of a deception but instead as a high aspiration and unreachable dream — is an outstanding example of 'political exceptionalism'. The bases for that exceptionalism are the conception of division and contingency as the ground of politics, the equation of political reason with populist reason, the figuration of the leader as the guarantor of populism vis-à-vis the postulated 'people' as a counterpart with demands, and the invocation of a Heideggerian 'ontological difference' for the elaboration of a political ontology. When we challenge exceptionalism and understand the distinction between the politically normal and exceptional as a matter that is up for debate, we can hardly take the onto-political stabilization offered by Laclau for granted. Beyond this operation, the leader seems to lose his/her 'extraordinariness' and his/her body becomes the very manifestation of human frailty. In turn, 'the many' — those who are presumably *subjected* to authority — no longer merely express demands and gain an 'ordinariness' to shape common beginnings. All in all, this non-exceptionalist reconfiguration shows that the tasks of the materialist programme that Laclau initiated and, unfortunately, interrupted, can and should move forward.

Throughout this essay, it has become clear that Laclau's narration of populism contains an ambivalent gesture. On the one hand, he repudiates all determinism, and especially the dogma of normality in both the liberal and Marxist traditions. On the other hand, he praises the forces of 'the extraordinary' and forges an ontological essentialism which, reversing his previous 'radical materialism', reinvigorates the idea of having control of the totality of reality and its historical

---

49   That irruption does not necessarily amount to political empowerment. Although the jargon of 'the ordinary', and 'the many' can hardly be mobilized to promote the order of rank, the praise of 'the common man' has not always constituted a call to emancipation. From the *Fronte dell'Uomo Qualunque* in Italy to recent populist movements, including the notion that 'everyone' is an entrepreneur of his/her/their own life, the 'common man' may well be the subject invoked by regressive political currents. See, among others, Judith Butler, *Notes Toward a Performative Theory of Assembly* (Cambridge, MA: Harvard University Press, 2015), p. 3.

development. A critical analysis of Laclau's account yields a valuable lesson for contemporary approaches to grounding politics in a way that is animated by 'the extraordinary'.

Let us now return to the question posed at the beginning of this essay regarding which principle can govern radical democratic politics when its old foundations seem to have vanished. Our examination of Laclau's exceptionalism has offered clues that allow us to avoid the impasse that ensues when we totalize 'the political'. One way to eschew this philosophico-political dilemma is to accept that 'the ordinary' is not the negation but the *matter* of the politically extraordinary. In this light, we may understand not only that '"emancipation" is a performance to which we always arrive late and which forces us to guess, painfully, about its mythical or impossible origins',[50] but, especially, that the unfolding of a *new beginning* also depends on the combined power of 'the many'.

---

50   Laclau, *Emancipation(s)*, 82.

Theory's Method?
Ethnography and Critical Theory
MARIANNA POYARES

INTRODUCTION

Methodological debates in political philosophy and political theory have been gaining increasing importance in academic and non-
academic spaces alike.[1] Whether in the ongoing dispute between
moralism and realism or in newer formulations such as avant-garde
political theory,[2] it is true to say that the debate concerning the epistemological and ontological commitments of research methods seems
to be experiencing a renewal after a period of relative paralysis, a
hibernation period arguably stemming from the domination of the
Rawlsian framework over mainstream Anglophone political theory.[3]
One particular topic of interest has been the use of ethnographic
methods, broadly understood, in political theory and political philosophy.[4] A number of articles have been published recently both using

1   I would like to acknowledge the crucial input, critical comments, and encouragement
    provided by Edward Guetti and Tatiana Llaguno Nieves. I am also grateful to Marcos
    Nobre for sending me his paper, and to Robin Celikates for his support and his push
    for fine-tuning. Finally, I would like to thank the blind reviewers for their engagement.
2   Lea Ypi, *Global Justice and Avant-Garde Political Agency* (Oxford: Oxford University
    Press, 2011).
3   On the dominance of Rawlsianism over the political theory and political philosophy,
    see Katrina Forrester, *In the Shadow of Justice* (Princeton, NJ: Princeton University
    Press, 2019).
4   Matthew Longo and Bernardo Zacka, 'Political Theory in an Ethnographic Key', *Amer-
    ican Political Science Review* 1130.4 (2019), pp. 1066–70.

and defending the use of ethnography in political theory and political philosophy: some have adopted a tone like a manifesto while others have made the case for its epistemic advantages. In this paper, I would like to join this emerging trend by establishing a firmer ground that supports the use of ethnographic methods, making clear which normative and epistemic commitments lie in the background of my claim. My goal here is not to formulate a defence of the research method *itself* (which would entail an uncritical understanding of the 'purity' of the method), but a defence of the use of political ethnography by critical social theory. I will contextualize the topic within a longstanding debate in Critical Theory regarding the relationship between theory and practice, a meta-critical stance towards research methods in general, and the issue of emancipation.

I will start by dispersing the aura of novelty or innovation proposed by some supporters of the use of ethnography in political theory and political philosophy. The recovery of certain theoretical tropes has commonly been misidentified as innovation. This has been the case with ethnography in social theory, which has been celebrated by virtue of either its apparent novelty or its attachment to so-called New Materialism. I will show that the use of such a method has been longstanding for feminist and postcolonial theorists, and that it also played a crucial role in the intellectual development of authors associated with the first generation of the Frankfurt School. My goal is to show the longstanding relationship between the use of such methods by theorists that are, in one way or another, associated with the tradition of historical materialism. Secondly, I would like to address and criticize the association, usually attached to the 'novelty' tendency outlined above, that connects the use of ethnography with so-called 'New Materialism'. As 'new materialism' is an incredibly large umbrella term encompassing different positions, my goal here is to oppose the specific claim that ethnography would serve the purpose of bringing the theorist closer to 'matter itself'. I will do this by highlighting what ethnography within a framework of historical materialism looks like, and what its specific epistemic, normative, and, ultimately, (socio-)ontological commitments are. I will primarily outline the commitments of certain strands within the large denomination of New Materialisms in terms of their conceptions of agency, epistemology, and transhumanism. I argue that such commitments are radically different from the ones I am proposing as productive for the use of ethnography within historical materialism as a materialism that, as pointed out by Étienne Balibar, makes no reference to matter itself.[5] Finally, I will show that the notion of social form is pivotal for the tradition of historical materialism, arguing that ethnographic methods, and the use of thick descriptions, can be useful tools for investigating social formations while avoiding certain ideological traps and maintaining emancipation as a goal for theory.

AGAINST NOVELTY

In his famous essay *Critical and Traditional Theory*, Max Horkheimer outlines four elements that differentiate critical theory from other types of social theory: critical theory is self-reflexive, insofar as it takes into account its own history and conditions of theoretical formation; it is interdisciplinary insofar as it integrates social theory, empirical research, and philosophical analysis; it is emancipatory insofar as its goal is the production of theory in the service of social emancipation, stressing the connection between the production of theory and that of liberating social change; and, finally, it is materialist in the sense that 'it is anchored in oppositional experiences and forms of consciousness as well as social and political struggles, from which it takes its cue, but which it does not uncritically follow'.[6]

Instead of focusing on 'simplistic questions of conscience and clichés about justice', taking refuge from history in morality and 'relying on the armoury of its moral indignation', Horkheimer argued that critique has to be based on the analysis of social reality and its contradictions, and that it can only find its research criteria in the social practices, struggles, experiences, and self-understandings to which critique is connected.[7] Discussions over the method or methods of empirical research, resulting from a meta-critical stance on research methods has been a constitutive element of Critical Theory.

---

5   Cf. Étienne Balibar, *The Philosophy of Marx* (London: Verso, 1995).

6   As appears in Robin Celikates, 'Critical Theory and the Unfinished Project of Mediating Theory and Practice', in *The Routledge Companion to the Frankfurt School*, ed. by Espen Hammer and Axel Honneth (London: Routledge, 2019), pp. 206–20 (p. 208).

7   Ibid., p. 206.

> Critical thinking is the function neither of the isolated indi-
> vidual nor of a sum-total of individuals [...]. The subject is no
> mathematical point like the ego of bourgeois philosophy; his
> activity is the construction of the social present. Furthermore,
> the thinking subject is not the place where knowledge and ob-
> ject coincide, nor consequently the starting point for attaining
> absolute knowledge.[8]

Following these guidelines, it is important to note that the relevance
for social theory of conducting ethnographic research should not be
understood as a consequence of the inherent superiority of this research method as such. Rather, the relevance is brought out by the
methodological scepticism towards the purported autonomy of theory
from its social present. Ethnographic research should be understood
here in a broad sense and, while participatory observation still remains
the central element, different attitudes, including (but not limited to)
historical ethnography, the observation of artefacts, or interviews, are
also essential to include when detailing the approach. However, the description of such research strategies, although relevant, does not fully
capture what is specific about ethnographic sensibility when it comes
to the engagement between the theorist and her object. Instead, it is
precisely the constant renegotiation of these stratifications insofar as
the object is not merely passive, but also defines the scope, nature, and
questions pertinent to the research, that is central to establishing this
ethnographic sensibility. Therefore, it is crucial that the relationship
established between the theorist and her 'object' is a dialectical one
and not one based on mere reporting or calculation. As a result, ethnographic methods serve as a strategy for theory to 'enter into a dynamic
unity'[9] with practice, not as a privileged standpoint for the instantiation of theory, but as a starting point for the constitution of theory.
Ethnographic research, in other words, constitutes an opportunity for
developing a relation between theory and practice, between the theorist and the object of study, and 'in so doing, it serves as an antidote to
analytic specialization by alerting us to the remainder — dimensions
of social reality that our existing categories fail to capture'.[10]

---

8   Max Horkheimer, 'Traditional and Critical Theory', in his *Critical Theory: Selected
     Essays* (New York: Continuum, 2002), pp. 188–243 (p. 210).

9   Ibid., p. 215

10   Longo and Zacka, 'Political Theory in an Ethnographic Key', p. 1067.

Thus, despite its announcement by some as a great novelty or a new movement within political theory and political philosophy, the use of ethnographic methods within empirical research is not a novelty within the field. Here we could mention Adorno's use of interviews in *The Authoritarian Personality* and Marcuse's analysis of capitalist consumerism in *One-Dimensional Man* as examples; however, ethnographic forays have not been as present here as within Feminist and Postcolonial theory. Ethnographic approaches have been extensively employed by Feminist and Postcolonial scholars ever since the 70s because they are particularly fruitful when challenging universal normative claims: they can reveal the internal biases of theory and the internal contradictions within praxis itself. Examples from these disciplines include, but are not limited to, the various contributions to critical historiography made by the Subaltern Studies collective, Gloria Anzaldúa's use of autobiography to examine the condition of Chicana women in the United States, Judith Butler's analysis of various media's portrayals of state violence during the War on Terror to establish the notion of grievability as a marker for radical equality, or Banu Bargu's work on Turkish political prisoners' use of death fast struggle as a way of weaponizing one's body in an act of resistance. In spite of adopting radically different methods, these examples coalesce under a broad definition of ethnography. I would like to call attention to works — best exemplified here by Bargu's — that use political ethnography as their main methodological framework.

Political ethnography is based on the contextual immersion of the researcher through a number of strategies founded upon ethnographic sensibility, such as participatory observation, first-hand interaction, and conversational interviewing, with the goal of articulating an interpretative framework for the meaning of specific social and political practices in order to intervene in a broader theoretical debate.[11] This

---

11 Banu Bargu provides an illuminating description of the relationship between political ethnography and critical theory in the context of her book *Starve and Immolate: The Politics of Human Weapons* (New York: Columbia University Press, 2016): 'The contextual immersion, observation and interaction with the participants of the death fast struggle grant us access to highly personal, differentiated, involved narratives, which complicate the conventional approach to human weapons that simply folds them into a fear-mongering discourse of national security and terrorism. But the voices of those near or at the helm of the state also show how the participants of the death fast

kind of research allows critical social theory to 'problemati[ze] re-descriptions',[12] that is, to challenge theoretical presuppositions and vocabularies. Additionally, 'to adopt an ethnographic sensibility is to remain open to the idea that our object of study is not just a "case" to examine in relation to theories we hold independently, but something that tells us more than we knew to ask'.[13] In other words, the use of political ethnography in social theory moves beyond traditional inductive methodological frameworks, where empirical research is structured to respond to a previously assembled set of questions whose 'sources' or points of conflict have been previously diagnosed or predicted and merely await empirical confirmation. On the contrary, the usefulness of ethnography for critical social theory is precisely that it enables a reciprocal relation between theory and practice. When the four distinctive elements of critical social theory mentioned above — interdisciplinarity, materiality, emancipation, and self-reflexivity — are brought into relation with ethnography, three important elements of the latter approach come to light. The first, which I have just mentioned, is empirical research without the reduction of the object of analysis to the mere instantiation of theory, such as in a case study. The second is the insistence on thick, detailed descriptions as a starting point for theoretical inquiry. The third positions the theorist not as a universal subject but as an individual belonging to a specific class, gender, and race while arguably maintaining a speculative vantage point.

Political ethnography is a useful tool for social theory given its insistence on not grounding the field of research upon the primacy of a priori, abstract, notions of justice or equality, for instance, but rather by looking at how such notions are articulated in the social vocabulary, and how they are enacted and performed by different social groups. It does not begin with an abstract concept but with a 'concrete' concept, so to speak, insofar as it relies on thick descriptions of the

---

struggle and their actions were perceived [...] bringing into light the articulation of the historical, structural, ideological and pragmatic reason for the choice of strategies that were deployed by the state to address the struggle. [...] The resulting analysis troubles an easy judgement, I think, and thereby aspires to keep open a space in which critical theory can operate' (pp. xiii and xiv).

12   Longo and Zacka, 'Political Theory in an Ethnographic Key', p. 1066.
13   Ibid., p. 1067.

rsocial and political arena. The starting point here described as 'thick descriptions' should be understood both as a description itself as well as a critical availability to the act of describing on the part of the theorist, which can possibly include the reformulation of her theoretical vocabulary. The availability of such a critical perspective also allows for further possible identification of contingent phenomena within established orders, opening up the space of normative inquiry towards unforeseen circumstances. In other words, it allows for the possible identification of internal contradictions within normalizing structures, whether in the realm of political phenomena, normative vocabulary, or by highlighting the intrinsic forms of violence and exclusion within such structures.

Finally, a distinctive element of political ethnography that is extremely relevant for empirically engaged social theory is the issue of positionality. The position of the social theorist is neither camouflaged in order to endorse a specific or exemplary kind of objectivity nor, by means of its affirmation, is it considered to signify an automatic embrace of relativism — both of which are equally symptomatic of an understanding of theory that stands above and outside relations of power and ideological structures. Therefore, the emphatic inclusion of positionality must entail more than just a mere addition of a few descriptive lines containing the private history of the scholar, or something like a private confession of the individual in question alongside or within their research findings. What positionality 'positions' is not the theorist as an individual but theorizing as a practice. A critically engaged use of positionality serves to dispel the aura of epistemic privilege of the theorist by including her self-understanding as an element of analysis insofar as this understanding constitutes a reflection on the conditions of the actuality of the research itself. It represents a break with the dogmas of objectivism and scientism while, at the same time, avoiding falling into relativism.

Positionality — just like thick descriptions — places the focus on the dialectical and relational aspect of the research. This element is one that has had very little historical resonance amongst philosophers, even those that did engage with empirical research. Adorno and Marcuse, for instance, despite their critical eye towards positivism in the social sciences, and their insistence on the dual character of empirical research (both normative and descriptive), have not included what I am here defining as positionality in the scope of their methodological inquiries. Postcolonial and feminist theorists, on the other hand, have engaged extensively with positionality, showing how supposedly impartial and universal normative standards are biased in relation to, mainly but not exclusively, gender and race.[14]

A RETURN TO MATTER

The concern with providing clarity for the relational constitution of the research itself is particularly relevant when working with social movements and oppressed groups. However, in recent years, many projects within the humanities and the social sciences have developed an increasing interest in non-human objects and nature, advocating a return to materiality in order to provide new interpretative frameworks for the social world. The so-called New Materialism consists of a heterogeneous field and assembles under this umbrella term a number of thinkers and theories that do not necessarily stand in perfect harmony with one another. Given the range of the term, I do not claim that all authors identified as New Materialists strictly follow or would even necessarily agree with the description I offer below, and if I did not properly acknowledge this fact it might render my criticism unfair or irrelevant for some positions. What I offer is a defence of ethnographic methods within critical social theory that stands in contrast to some descriptions that have been offered as paradigmatic in the New Materialist Turn. The reason I bring this dialogue into the debate about the relevance of ethnographic research methods within critical social theory is precisely because this move has, on multiple occasions, been identified as a trend within new materialism, understood as a strategy of approximation between the researcher and 'matter itself'. I would like to mark the difference between this trend and the use of such a method within canonical examples of historical materialism precisely to provide a sharp distinction in what is considered to be the relevance of such a method: while New Materialists claim that ethnographic

---

14   See, for instance, Charles Mills, *The Racial Contract* (Ithaca, NY: Cornell University Press, 1997).

research enables the coming into relation with material agency, the one that I am proposing, associated with historical materialism, claims no reference to matter itself.

The New Materialist Turn is usually associated with two areas 'where there is sufficient overlapping around a distinctive reorientation for these areas to serve as identifying markers of new materialist thinking'.[15] The first is a renewed interest in non-anthropocentric, matter-oriented ontology. This ontological commitment arises out of what is portrayed to be a rupture with the Kantian paradigm that, it is claimed, inaugurated a 'general anti-realist trend' marked by a strong representationalism that emphasizes the mediation of reality by epistemic and linguistic processes. The main charge against representationalism, however, seems to lie not so much on the grounds of this mediation as it does on an unargued (in the case of Kant) yet historically entrenched understanding of matter as, itself, passive. The excessive weight conferred, amongst others by the Kantian tradition, upon a nexus of normative interaction, between what is supposed to be inert matter and the spiritual bestowals that grant matter its proper dynamicity, is identified as a questionable theoretical assumption underpinning the anthropocentric character of Western thought. In an effort to dislocate and challenge this tradition, one of the main arguments of the New Materialists — one that serves to dismantle binary distinctions such as nature/culture and organic/inorganic — is their emphasis on matter's agency. This is the second distinctive area of interest for New Materialists.

New Materialist ontology, also known as vital materialism or material vitalism, does not understand matter as fixed and inert but as a continuous and, more importantly, as a contingent process of materialization. According to Diana Coole:

> Firstly, this is not about Being, but becoming: crucially, what is invoked is a process not a state, a process of materialisation in which matter literally matters itself. Secondly, this is not, then, the dead, inert, passive matter of the mechanist, which relied on an external agent — human or divine — to set it in motion.

---

15   Diana Coole, 'Agentic Capacities and Capacious Historical Materialism: Thinking with New Materialisms in the Political Sciences', *Millennium: Journal of International Studies* 41.3 (2013), pp. 451–69 (p. 452).

> Rather, it is a materialisation that contains its own energies and
> forces of transformation. It is self-organising, *sui generis*.[16]

Therefore, contingent processes of self-constitution are expressions of
the intrinsic constitution and rationality of matter, understood here
not only as sui generis but, more importantly, as causa sui. The argument that matter, itself, is agential and not inert references the philosophy of Gilles Deleuze and Félix Guattari as laying the foundations for
vital materialism. This is seen in the case of Rosi Braidotti's argument
for the intelligent vitality, or self-organizing capacity, of matter, which
leads to a 'zoe-centred egalitarianism' wherein the shift from agency
to agentic capacities stands against a tradition that associates agency
with (human) volition, deliberation, and intellect.[17] By moving from
agency to agentic capacities, new materialists have argued that 'agentic
capacities are diffused across many different types of material entity'
and that this 'decouple[s] agency from humans while raising questions
about the nature of life and of the place or status of the human within
it'.[18] Such capacities are, according to this view, proper to matter itself;
they are contingently revealed in interactions, which, understood here
beyond the anthropocentric fixation on agency, allows for a collapsing
of the traditional dualisms such as nature/culture which I referred to
earlier.

The transhumanist and vitalist focus on agentic capacities arises
out of very different arguments. My concern here is with the so-called
neo-ontological materialisms which draw upon quantum physics or
upon general descriptions of biological processes that understand
vitalism to occur in a spontaneous speculative organization of natural processes. In this perspective matter is conceptualized under the
framework of relational ontology in the sense that being, or matter,
is constituted by dynamic relationships between elements. Susanne
Lettow has argued that this position results in two shortcomings. The
first concerns epistemology, which, in this context, is no longer understood as the critical interrogation of knowledge claims, including the
claim to know matter itself. Lettow takes issue with Karen Barad's

---

16   Ibid., p. 453
17   Rosi Braidotti, *The Posthuman* (Cambridge: Polity Press, 2013), p. 60.
18   Coole, 'Agentic Capacities', p. 457.

important contribution by highlighting how, despite her attention to distinct features of human cognition, she positions intelligibility as an expression of matter's agency. Therefore 'practices of knowing cannot be fully claimed as human practices, not simply because we use non-human elements in our practices but because knowing is a matter of part of the world making itself intelligible to another part'.[19] Life, as matter, is understood here as a cosmological force, as the unfolding of natural processes, as an expressions of the intelligent organization and reorganization of matter, and generically described as a primordial logic of being where 'epistemic practices are articulated as part of a metaphysical, even cosmological logic of anonymous forces that shape the world'.[20] The problem with this kind of approach is that by assuming material agency to be conceptually expressive, it not only rejects the Kantian paradigm under which there is no unmediated knowledge, no knowledge of things in themselves, but actually brings us to a pre-critical standpoint in which the refusal of mediation becomes a totality of theory or, from a different perspective, the intelligible organization of nature.

This epistemic immediacy — one could even say, epistemic transparency — of matter forecloses a deeper engagement with critical epistemology. 'With regard to epistemology, the attempt to conceive of the totality of being, the quest for a direct and immediate access to being or the real rejects the always precarious and partial position of the epistemic subject'.[21] Material vitality does not, per se, entail the dissolution of epistemic questions regarding the production of knowledge, the categorization of phenomena and its social-historical conditions — not unless we also adopt substantive metaphysical or epistemic commitments such as understanding intelligibility as an expression of material vitality. In the same vein, a rejection of the nature/culture division does not entail an adoption of posthumanism in which we erase the very specific relationships at play between human and non-human actors. Donna Haraway, in her essay 'Situated Knowledges', reminds us

---

19   Karen Barad, 'Posthumanist Performativity: Toward an Understanding of How Matter Comes to Matter', *Signs: Journal of Women in Culture and Society*, 28.3 (2003), pp. 801–31 (p. 829).

20   Susanne Lettow, 'Turning the Turn: New Materialism, Historical Materialism and Critical Theory', *Thesis Eleven*, 140.1 (2017), pp. 106–21 (p. 109).

21   Ibid., p. 110.

that 'the world neither speaks itself nor disappears in favour of a master decoder'.[22] The issue of a presumed disappearance is precisely why I call this erasure of epistemology in favour of the intelligible immediacy of matter 'dogmatic' in the Kantian sense of the term.

Furthermore, there is a second problematic element associated with this reading of material vitalism, represented by theories such as Braidotti's zoe-centred egalitarianism. By uncritically adopting a supposedly generic language such as 'flows', 'exchanges', and 'fields of forces' to describe all phenomena, such theories violently flatten radically different phenomena, especially social phenomena. By assuming ontological parity between the vitality of atoms in their exchange of electrons and the vitality of social interactions, equating them under generic descriptions such as 'agential assemblages', one assumes that power relations and physical forces are both epistemically transparent and ontologically analogous. This kind of interpretation blurs the distinction between (socially and historically constituted) human agency and non-human agency, and thereby creates a second foreclosure: that of the normative, political, dimension of human agency.[23] As a result, the normative and emancipatory character of theory are eclipsed.

It is important to note that a critique of discrete matter along the lines of the critique of the Newtonian model doesn't of itself amount to the speculative transparency of material vitality, nor to a description of agency that collapses the structural disparities between human and non-human agency. Such a position is not the first awakening from the

---

22 Donna Haraway, 'Situated Knowledges: The Science Question in Feminism and the Privilege of Partial Perspective', *Feminist Studies* 14.3 (1988), pp. 575–99 (p. 593). I use Haraway here as an example of an author associated with New Materialism who, nonetheless, does not share the view that I am criticizing in this paper. I do this on purpose in order to also illustrate that, despite my criticism, given the comprehensiveness of the term 'new materialist' and the different positions associated with it, there is certainly a good deal of opportunity for approximations and alliances with historical materialism.

23 Lettow, 'Turning the Turn', p. 111: 'The general problem here is that agency is transferred to anonymous, meta-historical forces like matter or life, and this means that social relations and the practices they result from cannot be adequately analyzed. This includes the highly specific and historically contingent forms of human-nature relations and socio-technological regimes that need to be studied with regard to the very specific and highly stratified assemblages of "human" and "nonhuman" agents. To analyze such assemblages would require a differentiated theory of subjectivity which is able to distinguish between the specific forms of dynamics, activity and praxis that characterize the different entities.'

great slumber of hylomorphism because critiques of hylomorphism have been present throughout the history of philosophy. This begs the question — what kind of materialism is historical materialism if it is not one committed to an engagement with matter itself? This is a question surrounded by extensive debate and a longstanding history. Theorists associated with the first generation of the Frankfurt School such as Horkheimer, Marcuse, and Adorno, as well as others who moved away from the scientificism of early historical materialism, sought to emphasize the social and historical aspects of theory as such, and not only of social theory. This does not necessarily imply the denial of material vitality, but it does insist that any understanding of material vitality is socially and historically determined.

A RESEARCH METHOD FOR A THEORY OF SOCIAL FORM

I would like to call attention to a crucially relevant distinction within Marxist theory, namely the focus on the commodity form as a real phantasmagoria.[24] In his writings regarding the current status of idealism and materialism, Marx alluded to the pitfalls of the idealist/materialist debate of his time by stressing the well-known shortcomings of idealism along with those of a materialism that makes direct references to bodies and objects as haunted by an idealist foundation.[25] The famous passage on the fetishism of the commodity, usually read as the intervention of the notion of praxis over idealist structural-

---

24 This specific focus on the commodity, and its concern with labour as the kind of practice that institutes it, has been identified by some, e.g. Bruno Latour, as fundamentally anthropocentric. Judith Butler has recently made the case against this interpretation by recuperating Marx's notions of the organic and the inorganic body stressing how the kind of agency that is actualized in labour is dialectically constituted by non-human agency as well. Cf. Judith Butler, 'The Inorganic Body in the Early Marx: A Concept-Limit in Anthropocentrism', *Radical Philosophy*, 2.6 (Winter 2019), pp. 3–17.

25 'He also saw very clearly that, from this point of view, the "old materialisms" or philosophies of nature, which substitute matter for mind as the organizing principle, contain a strong element of idealism and are, in the end, merely disguised idealisms (whatever their very different political consequences). This enables us to understand why it is so easy for idealism to "comprehend" materialism and therefore to refute it or integrate it (as we see in Hegel, who has no problem with materialisms, except perhaps with that of Spinoza, but Spinoza is a rather atypical materialist ...)' (Balibar, *The Philosophy of Marx*, p. 24).

ism, can also be read as an argument against a reductionist ontological materialism.

> The mysterious character of the commodity-form consists therefore simply in the fact that the commodity reflects the social characteristics of men's own labour as objective characteristics of the products of labour themselves, as the social-natural properties of these things. Hence it also reflects the social relation of the producers to the sum total of labour as social relation between objects, a relation which exists apart from and outside the producers. Through this substitution, the products of labour become commodities, sensuous things which are at the same time supra-sensible or social.[26]

Furthermore, the mystery of the commodity form cannot be solved by redirecting our gaze to the object as 'simple' matter, or to the body as a 'simple' body, precisely because bodies are already constituted by systems of differential categorization, articulation, identification, and hierarchization, and it is not in the 'materiality of the body' that one would find the justification for, or grounding principle of, its commodification.

> [T]he commodity form, and the value relation of the products of labour within which it appears, have absolutely no connection with the physical nature of the commodity and the material [dinglich] relations arising out of this. It is nothing but the definite social relation between men themselves which assumes here, for them, the fantastic form of a relation between things. [...] As the foregoing analysis has already demonstrated, this fetishism of the world of commodities arises from the peculiar social character of the labour which produces them.[27]

The object of critical social theory, therefore, cannot be matter itself, given that the significance of material reality as such is already determined by social and historical relations. The very impetus to find the ground of social formations in 'pure matter' is already a symptom of fetishism. For example, a body that is marked as female 'expresses

---

26   Karl Marx, *Capital: A Critique of Political Economy*, 3 vols (London: Penguin, 1976),
      i, trans. by Ben Fowkes, pp. 164–65.
27   Ibid., p. 165.

female experience at a particular time and place, located within a particular set of social relations'.[28] By understanding the commodity form as a social form and focusing on this 'real abstraction' as one of the central elements of his theory, Marx implodes the old antagonism between idealism and materialism by showing how the two are not mutually exclusive but mutually dependent.

What concerns us here is the objectivity of the 'phantasmagorical' phenomenon of the commodity. By shifting the focus of inquiry from matter 'itself' or reason to social formations, and by understanding social formations not as instantiations of abstract categories but as historically determined, real abstractions, Marx collapses the apparent division of matter/form into the unity of a social form. Additionally, abandoning the paradigm of individual agency as foundational for action and focusing on the conditions of possibility of action means that the urge to liberate agency from the schema of subjective volition and deliberation — which some have associated with the Kantian tradition — appears incredibly superfluous, given that representations, even those of 'matter itself', are already expressions of a collective life. Critical social theory fulfils the dual criteria of being aware that it emerges out of the same object that it enquires into — that is, social form — and it is only by virtue of this that it can satisfy the four elements mentioned earlier: being emancipatory, interdisciplinary, materialist, and self-reflexive.

Historical materialism stands, therefore, as a 'materialism that has nothing to do with a reference to matter'. The term 'materialism

---

28 Nancy Hartsock, 'The Feminist Standpoint: Developing the Ground for a Specifically Feminist Historical Materialism', in *Disovering Reality: Feminist Perspectives on Epistemology, Metaphysics, Methodology, and Philosophy of Science*, ed. by Sandra Harding and Merrill B. Hintikka (New York: Kluwer, 1983), pp. 283–310 (p. 303). On this topic, Joseph Fracchia makes an important argument regarding the contribution of historical materialism: 'Although gender is a cultural construct, if humans reproduced asexually, there would be no foundation for its construction. The problem lies not in the recognition of physiological differences, but in the issuance of hierarchical verdicts on their significance that both produce and support exploitation, oppression and discrimination. The particular content of those semiotic forms cannot be predicted by any general theory. But it can be analysed in a historical-materialist manner and understood as the particular product of people living within a specific set of social relations inscribing particular meanings onto what are constructed as racialised or gendered bodies' (Joseph Fracchia, 'Beyond the Nature-Human Debate: Human Corporeal Organization as First Fact of Historical Materialism', *Historical Materialism*, 13.1 (2005), pp. 33–62 (p. 56)).

without matter', used by Balibar in his *The Philosophy of Marx*, was borrowed from a letter from Jacobi to Fichte. The object of historical materialist critique is a (real) living phantasmagoria created by the inversion between labour and value, where labour seems to have been socialized by the value-form. The reference to 'materialism without matter' contains the need for a profound rethinking of the constitution of (social) objectivity as well as that of subjectivity. These debates about the mutual constitution of objectivity and subjectivity, as well as that of theory and practice, have been longstanding and must be interpreted as developments of the debate concerning form and matter, where the notion of social form, or 'social formations' — to avoid a language that could be interpreted as reificatory — is the object of historical material critique. If the objects of critique are social formations, then such formations are not transparent because their constitutive processes of inversion, such as that of labour and value, are made opaque, among others, by ideological structures. The question here is not one of proceeding by assuming the falsity of social form and searching for its origin or genetic code hidden within the mere illusions of social formations, but rather of analysing its internal contradictions. To put it another way, contradictions are not the expression or the explosion of a hidden, suppressed, raw genetic element, but rather developments which potentially expose the social and historical character of the phantasmagoria at play, potentially leading to change.

The four elements of critical social theory outlined in the first section of this paper (reflexive, interdisciplinary, materialist, and emancipatory) stand not as a mere list of intentions but as a development of this notion of social form as well as what theory, and its relationship to practice, entails. From the elements mentioned, the element concerning the emancipatory character of theory has generally been regarded as aspirational when it is, in fact, structural. As Balibar writes,

> the theme of domination must thus be at the centre of the discussion. Marx does not produce a theory of the constitution of ideologies as discourses, as particular or general systems of representation and then merely retrospectively raises the question of domination: that question is always already included in the elaboration of the concept.[29]

---

29   Balibar, *The Philosophy of Marx*, p. 45.

Moreover, the recent dominance of debates concerning the normative standards of critique has eclipsed the traditional discussion regarding the relationship between theory and practice, which has led to accusations of stagnation within critical theory. The return to such a debate is crucial because of its ability to fulfil the emancipatory potential of theory through simultaneously placing the relationship of theory-making and practice at the centre, avoiding the dogmatic separation between theorist and non-theorist, and denying the premise that the self-understanding of agents is irrelevant, or even detrimental, to empirical research.

> As these challenges and the foundational problems they stem from — that of the methodological status of critical theory, its relation to practice, and the corresponding role of the critical theorist — are still with us today, one hopes they will no longer be pushed into the background by the dominance of the debate on the normative standards of critique but be discussed in their own right. [...] This suggests that the emancipatory orientation of critical theory is internally linked to its double reflexivity: only reflection on the context in which a theory emerged and in which it is used — a twofold dependency of theory on practice — enables an adequate understanding of the practical character of theory itself, and thus a break with the dogma of scientism and objectivism.[30]

The re-awakening of the question of the relationship between theory and practice entails, necessarily, a re-awakening of the discussion regarding methodology. And it is equally interesting to note how the prevalence of debates concerning the normative standards of social theory has also side-lined the discussion regarding empirically engaged research methods. Although social movements and institutions have been a preferential object of research for critical theorists, a number of questions remain regarding the actualization of research: how to proceed, and how to select which social struggles to focus upon, in a world of total administration and totalizing domination? In a world where, in contrast to fifty years ago, 'socialism is no longer the focus of emancipatory hopes; social movements have proliferated in a decentred way;

---

30   Celikates, 'Critical Theory', pp. 217–18.

and value horizons have been pluralized'?[31] How can critical social
theory be pursued in a society where domination is experienced as
freedom? Or should critical theorists, as Nancy Fraser suggests, not
only engage with normative analysis but also with proposing programmatic and institutional solutions?[32] I do not wish to claim that the
adoption of a specific methodology alone would supply an answer to
such questions, although the reflection on the importance of methodology constitutes part of the theorist's commitment to answering such
challenges. Nonetheless, whether or not critical theorists have a normative or more programmatic goal they definitely benefit immensely
from empirically engaged research, maintaining the old 'unity between
practice and theory' as a central concern.

> If critical theory is sequestered from social engagement and
> activism, vacating the very domain from which the political
> problematic emerges, it deprives itself of the capacity to trace
> that very emergence. This important relation between work-
> ing inside and outside of the academy is linked to the further
> problem of the border between the university and its world.
> Such a critical practice neither takes distance from facts nor
> negates their existence or importance; on the contrary, a con-
> stellation of such 'facts' impresses itself upon our thinking, and
> so the world acts on us and exercises a historical demand on
> thought.[33]

By understanding theory as the relation between theorist and object,
and by relying on thick descriptions as the starting point of theoretical
inquiry, political ethnography provides a useful platform for social
theory while having real current struggles as its main focus point.
Moreover, such research disavows any presupposition of 'automatic
translation of social position into epistemic privilege, and of epistemic

---

31   Marcos Nobre, 'How Practical Can Critical Theory Be?', in *Critical Theory and the
     Challenge of Praxis*, ed. by Stefano Giacchetti Ludovisi (New York: Routledge, 2016),
     pp. 159–72 (p. 167).

32   Cf. Nancy Fraser and Axel Honneth, *Redistribution or Recognition? A Political- Philo-
     sophical Exchange* (London: Verso, 2003), pp. 198–99: 'Unlike their predecessors,
     finally, today's critical theorists cannot assume that all normatively justified claims will
     converge on a single programme for institutional change. Rather, they must take on
     the hard cases — those, for example, in which claims for minority cultural recognition
     conflict with claims for gender equality — and tell us how to resolve them'. Also in
     Nobre, 'How Practical Can Critical Theory Be?', p. 167.

33   Butler, 'The Inorganic Body', p. 4.

privilege into political progressiveness',[34] which, alongside the use of naïve and vague descriptions of social movements — either through superficial or instrumental engagement with such movements, when the theorist engages with political practice only to locate his already-tailored research questions — constitute two extremely problematic features of empirically engaged theory. Ethnographic research is particularly attentive to ideological traps that may not only be invisible to the theorist but also to the activist while, arguably, maintaining a specifically emancipatory role for critique. On the other hand, the critical theorist must enter a relation of partnership with those around her, 'a dialogical struggle for appropriate interpretations and the realization of transformative potentials',[35] for which positionality, understood here not as mere subjective expression, but also as attention to unforeseen biases and blockages while also engaging in dialogical interpretations and realizations of emancipatory potentials, is an important element. Finally, it makes the speculative vocabulary available to redescriptions, as well as to the reflections and input made by those engaged with the social struggle. Political ethnography is a fruitful method for transforming the asymmetry between theorist and activist into a dialogical relation, but only if we understand critical social theory as *already* being a social practice.

---

34 Celikates, 'Critical Theory', p. 217.
35 Ibid., p. 218.

References

Abreu, Maira, 'De quelle histoire le "féminisme matérialiste" (français) est-il le nom?', in *Matérialismes féministes*, ed. by Maxime Cervulle and Isabelle Clair (= *Comment s'en sortir?*, 4 (2017)), pp. 55–79

Abreu, Ovídio, 'O procedimento da imanência em Deleuze', *Alceu*, 5.9 (2004), pp. 87–104

Adorno, Theodor W., *Philosophische Elemente einer Theorie der Gesellschaft* (Frankfurt am Main: Suhrkamp, 2008)

—— *Problems of Moral Philosophy* (Stanford, CA: Stanford University Press, 2001)

Adorno, Theodor W., and Max Horkheimer, *Briefwechsel*, 4 vols, in *Theodor W. Adorno. Briefe und Briefwechsel*, 8vols (Frankfurt a.M.: Suhrkamp, 1994–), IV.4: *1950–1969* (2006)

Agamben, Giorgio, *What Is Real?* (Stanford, CA: Stanford University Press, 2018)

Alaimo, Stacy, *Bodily Natures: Science, Environment, and the Material Self* (Bloomington: Indiana University Press, 2010)

Alaimo, Stacy, and Susan J. Hekman, 'Introduction: Emerging Models of Materiality in Feminist Theory', in their co-edited *Material Feminisms* (Bloomington: Indiana University Press, 2008), pp. 1–19

—— eds, *Material Feminisms* (Bloomington: Indiana University Press, 2008)

Alliez, Éric, 'Appendix I: Deleuze's Virtual Philosophy', in *The Signature of the World, Or, What Is Deleuze and Guattari's Philosophy?*, trans. by Eliot Ross Albert and Alberto Toscano (New York: Continuum, 2004), pp. 85–103

Alpatov, Vladimir, *Istoria odnogo mifa: Marr i marrism* [The history of one myth: Marr and marrism] (Moscow: Ed. URSS, 2004)

Althusser, Louis, 'Le Courant souterrain du matérialisme de la rencontre', in *Écrits philosophiques et politiques*, I (1994), pp. 539–79

—— *Cours sur Rousseau*, ed. by Yves Vargas (Paris: Le Temps des cerises, 2012)

—— 'Du matérialisme aléatoire', *Multitude*, 21.2 (2005), pp. 179–94 <https://doi.org/10.3917/mult.021.0179>

—— *Écrits philosophiques et politiques*, ed. by François Matheron, 2 vols (Paris: Stock/IMEC, 1994–95)

—— *Écrits sur l'histoire* (Paris: PUF, 2018)

—— *Écrits sur la psychanalyse* (Paris: Stock/IMEC, 1993)

—— *Être marxiste en philosophie* (Paris: PUF, 2015) <https://doi.org/10.3917/puf.althu.2015.01>

—— *For Marx*, trans. by Ben Brewster (London: Verso, 2005)

—— *The Future Lasts Forever: A Memoire*, trans. by Richard Veasey (New York: New Press, 1993)

—— 'The Humanist Controversy', in *The Humanist Controversy and Other Writings (1966–67)*, trans. by Geoffrey M. Goshgaran (London: Verso, 2003), pp. 221–305

—— 'Ideology and Ideological State Apparatuses (Notes towards an Investigation)', in *'Lenin and Philosophy' and Other Essays* (New York: Monthly Review Press, 1971), pp. 127–86

—— *Die Krise des Marxismus* (Hamburg: VSA, 1978)

—— Letter to Diaktine, 22 August 1966, in Louis Althusser, *Écrits sur la psychanalyse* (Paris: Stock/IMEC, 1993), pp 83–110

—— 'Machiavel', in *L'Unique tradition* matérialiste, ed. by Corpet, pp. 99–119 <https://doi.org/10.3917/lignes0.018.0099>

—— *Machiavelli et nous*, in *Ecrits philosophiques et politiques*, II, pp. 39–167

—— *Montesquieu. La Politique et l'histoire* (Paris: PUF, 1959)

—— 'The Object of *Capital*', trans by Ben Brewster, in Althusser and others, *Reading Capital: The Complete Edition* (London: Verso, 2015), pp. 215–355

—— 'L'objet du *Capital*', in Althusser and others, *Lire le Capital* (Paris: PUF, 1996), pp. 245–418

—— 'On Genesis', in *History and Imperialism: Writings, 1963–1986*, ed. and trans. by Geoffrey M. Goshgarian (Cambridge: Polity, 2020), pp. 33–36

—— 'On Marx and Freud', trans. by Warren Montag, *Rethinking Marxism*, 4.1 (1991), pp. 17–30 <https://doi.org/10.1080/08935699108657950>

—— 'On Spinoza', in *Essays in Self-Criticism*, trans. by Grahame Lock (London: New Left Books, 1976), pp. 132–41

—— 'The Only Materialist Tradition, Part I: Spinoza', in *The New Spinoza*, ed. by Warren Montag and Ted Stolze (Minneapolis: University of Minnesota Press, 1997), pp. 3–19

—— *Philosophy of the Encounter: Later Writings, 1978–87*, ed. by François Matheron and Oliver Corpet, trans. and intro. by Geoffrey M. Goshgarian (London: Verso, 2006)

—— 'Portrait d'un philosophe matérialiste', in *Écrits philosophiques et politiques*, I, pp. 581–82

—— 'Portrait of a Materialist Philosopher', in *Philosophy of the Encounter*, pp. 290–91

—— *Pour Marx*, intro. by Étienne Balibar (Paris: La Découverte, 2005)

—— 'La querelle de l'humanisme', in *Écrits philosophiques et politiques*, II (1995), pp. 433–532

—— 'Spinoza', in *L'Unique tradition* matérialiste, ed. by Corpet, pp. 75–97 <https://doi.org/10.3917/lignes0.018.0075>

—— *Sul materialismo aleatorio*, ed. by Vittorio Morfino and Luca Pinzolo, 1st edn (Milan: Unicopli, 2000); 2nd edn (Milan: Mimesis, 2006)

—— 'Sur la genèse', in *Écrits sur l'histoire*, pp. 81–86

—— 'Sur l'impérialisme', in *Écrits sur l'histoire*, pp. 103–260

—— 'Sur la pensée marxiste', in Althusser and others, *Sur Althusser*, pp. 11–29

—— *Thèse de juin*, IMEC, ALT2. A29.60.04

—— 'Three Notes on the Theory of Discourses', in *The Humanist Controversy and Other Writings*, pp. 33–84

—— 'Trois notes sur la théorie du discours', in *Écrits sur la psychanalyse*, pp. 111–70

—— 'The Underground Current of the Materialism of the Encounter', in *Philosophy of the Encounter*, pp. 163–207

—— *Les Vaches noires. Interview imaginaire* (Paris: PUF, 2016) <https://doi.org/10.3917/puf.althu.2016.01>

—— *Writings on Psychoanalysis: Freud and Lacan*, trans. by Jeffrey Mehlman (New York: Columbia University Press, 1996)

Althusser, Louis, and others, *Lire le Capital* (Paris: Maspéro, 1965)

—— *Reading Capital: The Complete Edition* (London: Verso, 2016)

—— *Sur Althusser. Passages* (Paris: L'Harmattan, 1993)

—— 'Variantes de la première édition', in *Lire le Capital* (Paris: PUF, 1996), pp. 635–61

Anderson, Philip W., 'More Is Different: Broken Symmetry and the Nature of the Hierarchical Structure of Science', *Science*, 177 (1972), pp. 393–96

Antoine-Mahut, Delphine, and Daniel Whistler, eds, *Une arme philosophique. L'éclectisme de Victor Cousin* (Paris: Éditions des Archives contemporaines, 2019)

Antonioli, Manola, *Deleuze et l'histoire de la philosophie* (Paris: Kimé, 1999)

Aron, Raymond, *Le Marxisme de Marx* (Paris: Editions de Fallois, 2002)

Asad, Talal, Wendy Brown, Judith Butler, and Saba Mahmood, *Is Critique Secular? Blasphemy, Injury, and Free Speech* (New York: Fordham University Press, 2013) <https://doi.org/10.5422/fordham/9780823251681.001.0001>

Atkinson, Ti Grace, *Amazon Odyssey: The First Collection of Writings by the Political Pioneer of the Women's Movement Ti-Grace Atkinson* (New York: Links Books, 1974)

Badiou, Alain, *Peut-on penser la politique?* (Paris: Éditions du Seuil, 1985)

Balibar, Étienne, 'Althusser's Object', trans. by Margaret Cohen and Bruce Robbins, *Social Text*, 39 (Summer 1994), pp. 157–88 <https://doi.org/10.2307/466368>

—— *La Crainte des masses. Politique et philosophie avant et après Marx* (Paris: Éditions Galilée, 1997)

—— *Equaliberty: Political Essays*, trans. by James Ingram (Durham, NC: Duke University Press, 2013) <https://doi.org/10.1515/9780822377221>

—— 'L'Objet Althusser', in *Politique et philosophie dans l'œuvre de Louis Althusser*, ed. by Sylvain Lazarus (Paris: PUF, 1993), pp. 81–116 <https://doi.org/10.3917/puf.lazar.1993.01.0081>

—— *La Philosophie de Marx* (Paris: La Découverte, 2014)

—— 'Philosophies of the Transindividual: Spinoza, Marx, Freud', trans. by Mark G. E. Kelly, *Australasian Philosophical Review*, 2.1 (2018), pp. 5–25 <https://doi.org/10.1080/24740500.2018.1514958>

—— *The Philosophy of Marx* (London: Verso, 1995)

—— *La Proposition de l'Égaliberté* (Paris: PUF, 2010) <https://doi.org/10.3917/puf.balib.2010.01>

—— *Spinoza: From Individuality to Transindividuality* (Delft: Eburon, 1997)

—— *Spinoza and Politics* (London: Verso, 1998)

—— 'Spinoza, the Anti-Orwell: The Fear of the Masses', *Rethinking Marxism*, 2.3 (1989), pp. 104–39

—— *Spinoza politique. Le Transindividuel* (Paris: PUF, 2018)

Balibar, Étienne, and Vittorio Morfino, *Il transindividuale: soggetti, relazioni, mutazioni* (Milano: Mimesis, 2014)

Balibar, Étienne, Cesare Luporini, and André Tosel, *Marx et sa critique de la politique* (Paris: Maspéro, 1979)

Ball, Terence, 'The Formation of Character: Mill's "Ethology" Reconsidered', *Polity*, 33.1 (2000), pp. 25–48 <https://doi.org/10.2307/3235459>

Banaji, Jairus, 'Illusions about the Peasantry: Karl Kautsky and the Agrarian Question', *The Journal of Peasant Studies*, 17.2 (1990), pp. 288–307 <https://doi.org/10.1080/03066159008438422>

Barad, Karen, *Meeting the Universe Halfway: Quantum Physics and the Entanglement of Matter and Meaning* (Durham, NC: Duke University Press, 2007) <https://doi.org/10.1215/9780822388128>

—— 'Nature's Queer Performativity', *Qui Parle: Literature, Philosophy, Visual Arts, History*, 19.2 (2011), pp. 121–58 <https://doi.org/10.5250/quiparle.19.2.0121>

—— 'Posthumanist Performativity: Toward an Understanding of How Matter Comes to Matter', *Signs: Journal of Women in Culture and Society*, 28.3 (2003), pp. 801–31 <https://doi.org/10.1086/345321>

Barbaras, Françoise, 'Le Concept de puissance dans l'héritage de la science cartésienne', *Archives de Philosophie*, 64.4 (2001), pp. 721–39 <https://doi.org/10.3917/aphi.644.0721>

Bargu, Banu, *Starve and Immolate: The Politics of Human Weapons* (New York: Columbia University Press, 2016)

Batterman, Robert W., 'Autonomy and Scales', in *Why More Is Different: Philosophical Issues in Condensed Matter Physics and Complex Systems*, ed. by Brigitte Falkenburg and Margaret Morrison (Heidelberg: Springer, 2015), pp. 115–35 <https://doi.org/10.1007/978-3-662-43911-1_7>

Baudrillard, Jean, *Simulacres et Simulation* (Paris: Gallimard, 1981)

—— *Symbolic Exchange and Death* (Thousand Oaks, CA: Sage Publications 1993)

—— *Le Système des objets* (Paris: Gallimard, 1978)

Bauer, Bruno, 'The Jewish Question', in *The Young Hegelians, an Anthology* (Cambridge: Cambridge University Press, 1983), pp. 187–97

Beauvoir, Simone de, *Le Deuxième Sexe* (Paris: Gallimard, 1949)

Bebel, August, *Die Frau und der Sozialismus* (Zürich: Hottingen, 1879)

Becker-Schmidt, Regina, 'Die doppelte Vergesellschaftung — die doppelte Unterdrückung: Besonderheiten der Frauenforschung in den Sozialwissenschaften', in *Die andere Hälfte der Gesellschaft. Österreichischer Soziologentag 1985. Soziologische Befunde zu geschlechtsspezifischen Formen der Lebensbewältigung*, ed. by Lilo Unterkirchner and Ina Wagner (Vienna: ÖGB Verlag, 1987), pp. 10–25

Becker, Rafael, 'Natureza e direito em Deleuze' (doctoral thesis, Pontifícia Universidade Católica do Rio de Janeiro, PUC-Rio, 2018)

Bedau, Mark A., and Paul Humphreys, eds, *Emergence: Contemporary Readings in Philosophy and Science* (Cambridge, MA: MIT Press, 2008) <https://doi.org/10.7551/mitpress/9780262026215.001.0001>

Beer, Ursula, Klasse, *Geschlecht. Feministische Gesellschaftsanalyse und Wissenschaftskritik* (Bielefeld: AJZ Verlag, 1987)

Beşir Fuad, *Voltaire* (Konya: Çizgi Kitabevi, 2011)

—— *Şiir ve hakikat* (Istanbul: I.k.y., 1999)

Bellofiore, Riccardo, 'Taking Up the Challenge of Living Labour: A "Backwards-Looking Reconstruction" of Recent Italian Debates on Marx's Theory of the Capitalist Mode of Production', in *The Unfinished System of Karl Marx: Critically Reading Capital as a Challenge for our Times*, ed. by Judith Dellheim and Frieder Otto Wolf (Cham: Palgrave Macmillan, 2018), pp. 31–89 <https://doi.org/10.1007/978-3-319-70347-3_2>

Benjamin, Walter, 'On the Concept of History', in *Selected Writings*, IV: *1938-1940*, ed. by Howard Eiland and Michael W. Jennings, trans. by Edmund Jephcott, Howard Eiland, and others (2003), pp. 389–400

—— 'Problems in the Sociology of Language: An Overview', in *Selected Writings*, III: *1935-1938*, ed. by Howard Eiland and Michael W. Jennings, trans. by Edmund Jephcott, Howard Eiland, and others (2002), pp. 68–93

—— *Selected Writings*, 4 vols (Cambridge, MA: Harvard University Press, 1996-2003)

Bennett, Jane, 'Introducing the New Materialisms', in *New Materialisms*, ed. by Diana Coole and Samantha Frost (Duke University Press, 2010), pp. 1–43 <https://doi.org/10.1215/9780822391623>

—— *Vibrant Matter: A Political Ecology of Things* (Durham, NC: Duke University Press, 2010) <https://doi.org/10.1215/9780822391623>

Bennett, Jonathan, *A Study of Spinoza's Ethics* (Cambridge: Cambridge University Press, 1984)

Bensussan, Gérard, 'Émancipation', in *Dictionnaire critique du marxisme*, ed. by Gérard Bensussan and Georges Labica (Paris: PUF, 1999), pp. 382–84

—— 'Feuerbach et le "Secret" de Spinoza', in *Spinoza au XIXe siècle*, ed. by André Tosel, Pierre-François Moreau, and Jean Salem (Paris: Publications de la Sorbonne, 2007), pp. 111–23 <https://doi.org/10.4000/books. psorbonne.158>

Bernard, Michel, *Le Corps*, 2nd rev. edn (Paris: Editions Universitaires, 1976)

Bhaskar, Roy, *The Possibility of Naturalism* (London: Routledge, 1979)

—— *A Realist Theory of Science* (London: Verso, 2007)

Binoche, Bertrand, *'Ecrasez l'Infâme!'. Philosopher à l'âge des Lumières* (Paris: La Fabrique, 2018)

—— 'La Faute à Helvétius ou le matérialisme après-coup', in *Lumières*, ed. by Duflo, pp. 173–84

Bloch, Ernst, *The Principle of Hope*, trans. by Neville Plaice, Stephen Plaice, and Paul Knight, 2 vols (Cambridge, MA: MIT Press, 1986), II

Bloch, Olivier, 'Marx, Renouvier et l'histoire du matérialisme', *La Pensée*, 191 (February 1977), pp. 3–42

—— *Matière à Histoires* (Paris: Vrin, 1997)

—— 'Sur l'image du matérialisme français du XVIIIe siècle dans l'historiographie philosophique du XIXe siècle: Autour de Victor Cousin', in *Images au XIXe siècle du matérialisme du XVIIIe siècle*, ed. by Olivier Bloch (Paris: Desclée, 1979), pp. 39–54

Blumenberg, Hans, '"Imitation of Nature": Toward a Prehistory of the Idea of the Creative Being', trans. by Anna Wertz, *Qui Parle*, 12.1 (2000), pp. 17–54

—— *Die Legitimität der Neuzeit* (Frankfurt a.M.: Suhrkamp, 1999)

Bock, Gisela, 'Frauenbewegung und Frauenuniversität — Zur politischen Bedeutung der Sommeruniversität', in *Frauen und Wissenschaft. Beiträge zur Berliner Sommeruniversität für Frauen, Juli 1976*, ed. by Gruppe Berliner Dozentinnen (Berlin: Courage, 1977), pp. 15–22

Bottici, Chiara, *Imaginal Politics: Images Beyond Imagination and the Imaginary* (New York: Columbia University Press, 2014) <https://doi.org/10. 7312/columbia/9780231157780.001.0001>

Bottiglieri, Carla, 'Soigner l'imaginaire du geste: pratiques somatiques du toucher et du mouvement', *Chimères*, 78 (2012/13), pp. 113–28 <https: //doi.org/10.3917/chime.078.0113>

Boucher d'Argis, Antoine-Gaspard, 'Émancipation', in *Encyclopédie ou Dictionnaire raisonné des Sciences, des arts et des métiers*, ed. by Jean Le Rond d'Alembert and Denis Diderot, 17 vols (Paris, 1755), V, pp. 546–49

Bourdin, Jean-Claude, *Diderot et le matérialisme* (Paris: PUF, 1998) <https: //doi.org/10.3917/puf.bourd.1998.01>

—— *Hegel et les matérialistes français du XVIIIe siècle* (Paris: Klincksieck, 1992)

—— *Les Matérialistes au XVIIIe siècle* (Paris: Payot, 1996)

Bove, Laurent, *Affirmation and Resistance in Spinoza: Strategy of the Conatus* (Edinburgh: Edinburgh University Press, 2020)

—— *La Stratégie du conatus. Affirmation et résistance chez Spinoza* (Paris: Vrin, 1996)

Braidotti, Rosi, *Metamorphoses: Towards a Materialist Theory of Becoming* (Oxford: Blackwell, 2002)

—— *The Posthuman* (Cambridge: Polity Press, 2013)

Breda, Stefano, *Kredit und Kapital. Kreditsystem und Reproduktion der kapitalistischen Vergesellschaftungsweise in der dialektischen Darstellung des Marxschen 'Kapital'* (Würzburg: Königshausen&Neumann, 2019)

Brito Vieira, Mónica, *The Elements of Representation in Hobbes: Aesthetics, Theatre, Law, and Theology in the Construction of Hobbes's Theory of the State* (Leiden; Boston: Brill, 2009) <https://doi.org/10.1163/ej.9789004181748.i-286>

Bunge, Mario, *Emergence and Convergence: Qualitative Novelty and the Unity of Knowledge* (Toronto: University of Toronto Press, 2003) <https://doi.org/10.3138/9781442674356>

—— *Scientific Materialism*, Episteme, 9 (Dordrecht: Springer Netherlands, 1981) <https://doi.org/10.1007/978-94-009-8517-9>

Butler, Judith, *Bodies that Matter: On the Discursive Limits of 'Sex'*, Routledge Classics (Abingdon: Routledge, 2011) <https://doi.org/10.4324/9780203828274>

—— *Gender Trouble: Feminism and the Subversion of Identity* (New York: Routledge, 1990)

—— *Gender Trouble: Feminism and the Subversion of Identity*, with a new pref. by Judith Butler (New York: Routledge, 1999)

—— 'The Inorganic Body in the Early Marx: A Concept-Limit in Anthropocentrism', *Radical Philosophy*, 2.6 (Winter 2019), pp. 3–17 <https://www.radicalphilosophy.com/article/the-inorganic-body-in-the-early-marx> [accessed 2 November 2020]

—— *Notes Toward a Performative Theory of Assembly* (Cambridge, MA: Harvard University Press, 2015) <https://doi.org/10.4159/9780674495548>

—— *Trouble dans le genre. Pour un féminisme de la subversion* (Paris: La Découverte, 2005)

—— *Das Unbehagen der Geschlechter* (Frankfurt a.M.: Suhrkamp, 1991)

von Böhm-Bawerk, Eugen, *Karl Marx and the Close of his System: A Criticism* (London: T. Fisher Unwin, 1898)

Büchner, Ludwig, *Kraft und Stoff. Empirisch-naturphilosophische Studien* (Frankfurt a.M.: Meidinger Sohn, 1855)

Caporali, Riccardo, 'La moltitudine e gli esclusi', in *Spinoza: individuo e moltitudine*, ed. by Riccardo Caporali, Vittorio Morfino, and Stefano Visentin (Cesena: Il Ponte Vecchio, 2007), pp. 93–104

Capriles, René, *Makarenko: O Nascimento da Pedagogia Socialista* (São Paulo: Scipione, 1989)

Caro, Elme-Marie, *Problèmes de morale sociale* (Paris: Hachette, 1887)

Celikates, Robin, 'Critical Theory and the Unfinished Project of Mediating Theory and Practice', in *The Routledge Companion to the Frankfurt School*, ed. by Espen Hammer and Axel Honneth (London: Routledge, 2019), pp. 206–20 <https://doi.org/10.4324/9780429443374-15>

Chalmers, Alan, 'Atomism from the 17th to the 20th Century', in *Stanford Enyclopedia of Philosophy*, ed. by Edward N. Zalta (Spring 2019 Edition) <https://plato.stanford.edu/archives/spr2019/entries/atomism-modern/> [accessed 5 May 2020]

Chaui, Marilena, 'Intensivo e extensivo na Ética de Espinosa: a interpretação dos modos finitos por Deleuze', in *Deleuze Hoje*, ed. by Sandro K. Fornazari (São Paulo: Fap-Unifesp, 2014), pp. 21–40

—— *Política em Espinosa* (São Paulo: Companhia das Letras, 2003)

—— 'A questão democrática', in *Cultura e democracia: o discurso competente e outras falas* (São Paulo: Cortez, 2006), pp. 144–69

Chibbaro, Sergio, Lamberto Rondoni, and Angelo Vulpiani, *Reductionism, Emergence and Levels of Reality: The Importance of Being Borderline* (Cham: Springer, 2014) <https://doi.org/10.1007/978-3-319-06361-4>

Choat, Simon, 'Science, Agency and Ontology: A Historical-Materialist Response to New Materialism', *Political Studies*, 66.4 (2018), pp. 1027–42 <https://doi.org/10.1177/0032321717731926>

Colliot-Thélène, Catherine, 'L'Ignorance du peuple', in *L'Ignorance du peuple: Essais sur la démocratie*, ed. by Gérard Duprat (Paris: PUF, 1998), pp. 17–40

Combes, Muriel, *Gilbert Simondon and the Philosophy of the Transindividual*, trans. by Thomas LaMarre (Cambridge, MA: MIT Press, 2013)

Condorcet, Marquis de, *Essai sur la constitution et les fonctions des assemblées provinciales*, in *Œuvres de Condorcet*, ed. by Arthur Condorcet O'Connor and François Arago, 12 vols (Paris: Firmin Didot Frères, 1847), VIII, pp. 115–662

Coole, Diana, 'Agentic Capacities and Capacious Historical Materialism: Thinking with New Materialisms in the Political Sciences', *Millennium: Journal of International Studies*, 41.3 (2013), pp. 451–69 <https://doi.org/10.1177/0305829813481006>

Coole, Diana, and Samantha Frost, 'Introducing the New Materialisms', in *New Materialisms*, ed. by Coole and Frost, pp. 1–43 <https://doi.org/10.1215/9780822392996-001>

—— eds, *New Materialisms: Ontology, Agency, and Politics* (Durham, NC: Duke University Press, 2010) <https://doi.org/10.1215/9780822392996>

Corning, Peter A., 'The Re-Emergence of "Emergence": A Venerable Concept in Search of a Theory', *Complexity*, 7.6 (2002), pp. 18–30 <https://doi.org/10.1002/cplx.10043>

Corpet, Oliver, ed., *L'Unique tradition matérialiste* (=*Lignes*, 18.1 (1993), pp. 71–119) <https://doi.org/10.3917/lignes0.018.0071>

Cousin, Victor, *Cours de l'histoire de la philosophie. Histoire de la philosophie du XVIIIᵉ siècle*, 2 vols (Paris: Pichon et Didier, 1829)

—— *Manuel de l'histoire de la philosophie. Traduit de l'allemand de Tennemann* (Paris: Sautelet, 1829)

Crowe, Benjamin, *Heidegger's Religious Origins: Destruction and Authenticity* (Bloomington: Indiana University Press, 2006)

Daled, Pierre-Frédéric, *Le Matérialisme occulté et la genèse du 'sensualisme'. Ecrire l'histoire de la philosophie en France* (Paris: Vrin, 2005)

Deleuze, Gilles, *Difference and Repetition*, trans. by Paul Patton (London: Athlone, 1994)

—— *Expressionism in Philosophy: Spinoza*, trans. by Martin Joughin (New York: Zone Books, 1992)

—— 'Gueroult's General Method for Spinoza', in *Desert Islands and Other Texts. 1953-1974*, ed. by David Lapoujade, trans. by Michael Taormina (Cambridge, MA: MIT Press, 2004), pp. 146–55

—— *Kafka: Pour une littérature mineure* (Paris: Minuit, 1975)

—— *The Logic of Sense*, trans. by Mark Lester and Charles Stivale (London: Athlone, 1990)

—— 'One Less Manifesto', in *Mimesis, Masochism, & Mime: The Politics of Theatricality in Contemporary French Thought*, ed. by Timothy Murray (Ann Arbor: University of Michigan Press, 1997), pp. 239–58

—— *Spinoza: Practical Philosophy*, trans. by Robert Hurley (San Francisco, CA: City Lights Books, 1988)

—— 'Spinoza and Us', in *Spinoza: Practical Philosophy*, trans. by Robert Hurley (San Francisco, CA: City Lights Books, 1988), pp. 122–30

Deleuze, Gilles, and Claire Parnet, *Dialogues*, trans. by Hugh Tomlinson and Barbara Habberjam (New York: Columbia University Press, 1987)

Deleuze, Gilles, and Félix Guattari, *Rhizome: Introduction* (Paris: Minuit, 1976)

—— *A Thousand Plateaus: Capitalism and Schizophrenia*, trans. by Brian Massumi (Minneapolis: University of Minnesota Press, 1987)

—— *What Is Philosophy?* (New York: Columbia University Press, 1994)

Deligny, Fernand, *Encontro Deligny* Platform, ed. by Marlon Miguel and Mauricio Rocha (Rio de Janeiro: PUC-Rio) <https://deligny.jur.puc-rio.br/> [accessed 12 September 2020]

—— 'Les Vagabonds Efficaces' (1947), in *Œuvres* (Paris: L'Arachnéen, 2017), pp. 161–221

Del Lucchese, Filippo, *Conflict, Power, and Multitude in Machiavelli and Spinoza: Tumult and Indignation* (London: Continuum, 2009)

Delphy, Christine, 'Nos amis et nous. Les Fondements cachés de quelques discours pseudo-féministes', *Questions féministes*, 1 (1977), pp. 20–49

Descartes, René, *Meditations on First Philosophy*, in *The Philosophical Writings of Descartes*, trans. by John Cottingham, Robert Stoothoot, and Dugald Murdoch, 3 vols (New York: Cambridge University Press, 1984–91), II (1985), pp. 1–62 <https://doi.org/10.1017/CBO9780511818998>

Deuber-Mankowsky, Astrid, 'Das ontologische Debakel oder was heißt: Es gibt Medien?', *ZMK Zeitschrift Medien- und Kulturforschung*, 8.2 (2017), pp. 157–68 <https://doi.org/10.28937/1000107979>

Devel, T. M., and T. B. Tomes, 'Sobranie N. Ia. Marra v fotoarchive LOIA AN SSR' [N. Ia. Marr's Collection in the Archive of the Institute for History of Material Culture], *Istoriko-filologicheski zhurnal*, 3 (1971), pp. 289–95

Diderot, Denis, Letter to Sophie Volland, 15 October 1759, in *Œuvres complètes de Diderot*, 20 vols (Paris: Garnier, 1876), XVIII, pp. 408–09

Dolphijn, Rick, and Iris van der Tuin, *New Materialism: Interviews & Cartographies* (Ann Arbor, MI: Open Humanities Press, 2012) <https://doi.org/10.3998/ohp.11515701.0001.001>

Dosse, François, *Gilles Deleuze and Félix Guattari: Intersecting Lives*, trans. by Deborah Glassman (New York: Columbia University Press, 2010)

Duden, Barbara, *Geschichte unter der Haut. Ein Eisenacher Arzt und seine Patientinnen um 1730* (Stuttgart: Klett-Cotta, 1987)

Duflo, Colas, ed., *Lumières, matérialisme et morale: autour de Diderot* (Paris: Editions de la Sorbonne, 2016)

d'Eaubonne, Françoise, *Le Féminisme ou la mort* (Paris: Pierre Horay, 1974)

Elbe, Ingo, *Marx im Westen. Die neue Marx-Lektüre in der Bundesrepublik seit 1965* (Berlin: Akademie, 2008), pp. 30–87

Engels, Friedrich, *Anti-Dühring*, in *MECW*, XXV (1987), pp. 1–309

—— 'Die Entwicklung des Sozialismus von der Utopie zur Wissenschaft', in *MEW*, IXX (1987), pp. 189–228

—— 'Grundsätze des Kommunismus', in *MEW*, IV (1977), pp. 361–80

—— 'Ludwig Feuerbach and the End of Classical German Philosophy', in *MECW*, XXVI (1990), pp. 353–98

—— 'Principles of Communism', in *MECW*, VI (1976), pp. 341–57

—— *Socialism: Utopian and Scientific* (London: Swan Sonnenschein, 1892)

—— *Socialism: Utopian and Scientific*, in *MECW*, XXIV (1989), pp. 281–325

—— *Der Ursprung der Familie, des Privateigentums und des Staats: im Anschluß an Lewis H. Morgans Forschungen* (Zürich: Hottingen, 1884)

Engels, Friedrich, and Karl Marx, *The Holy Family, or Critique of Critical Criticism*, in *MECW*, IV (1975), pp. 3–211

Erhard, Johann Benjamin, *Über das Recht des Volks zu einer Revolution* (Berlin: Syndikat, 1970)

Espinas, Alfred, *Les Origines de la technologie*, Étude Sociologique (Paris: Alcan, 1897); English excerpts as 'The Origins of Technology [excerpts]', trans. by Catherine Schnoor, in *The Roots of Praxiology: French Action Theory from Bourdeau and Espinas to Present Days*, ed. by Victor Alexandre in coop. with Wojciech W. Gasparski (London: Routledge, 1999), pp. 45–91 <https://doi.org/10.4324/9781351289245-2>

Estlund, David, *Democratic Authority: A Philosophical Framework* (Princeton, NJ: Princeton University Press, 2007)

Fausto-Sterling, Anne, *Sexing the Body: Gender Politics and the Construction of Sexuality*, rev. edn (New York: Basic Books, 2000)

Federici, Silvia, *Revolution at Point Zero: Housework, Reproduction, and Feminist Struggle* (Oakland, CA: PM Press, 2012)

Feuerbach, Ludwig, 'Preliminary Theses on the Reform of Philosophy', in *The Fiery Brook* (London: Verso, 2012), pp. 153–73

—— 'Vorläufige Thesen zur Reformation der Philosophie', in *Gesammelte Werke*, 14 vols (Berlin: Akademie, 1970), IX, pp. 243–63

Firestone, Shulamith, *The Dialectic of Sex: The Case for Feminist Revolution* (New York: Morrow, 1970)

Fischbach, Franck, *Philosophies de Marx* (Paris: Vrin, 2015)

—— *La Production des hommes. Marx avec Spinoza* (Paris: Vrin, 2014)

Forrester, Katrina, *In the Shadow of Justice* (Princeton, NJ: Princeton University Press, 2019)

Foucault, Michel, *The Birth of Biopolitics: Lectures at the Collège de France, 1978–79*, ed. by Arnold I. Davidson (Basingstoke: Palgrave Macmillan, 2008)

—— '"Omnes et Singulatim": Toward a Critique of Political Reason', in *Essential Works of Foucault 1954–1984: Power*, ed. by Paul Rabinow, James D. Faubion (New York: New Press, 2001), pp. 298–325

—— 'The Order of Discourse: Inaugural Lecture at the Collège de France, given December 2, 1970)', in *Untying the Text: A Post-Structuralist Reader*, ed. by Robert Young (London, Routledge, 1981), pp. 51–78

—— *Le pouvoir psychiatrique. Cours au Collège de France. 1973–1974* (Paris: Gallimard Seuil, 2003)

—— *Psychiatric Power: Lectures at the Collège de France 1973–1974*, trans. by Graham Burchell (London: Palgrave Macmillan, 2006)

—— *Security, Territory, Population: Lectures at the Collège de France, 1977–78*, ed. by Arnold I. Davidson (Basingstoke: Palgrave Macmillan, 2007)

Fracchia, Joseph, 'Beyond the Nature-Human Debate: Human Corporeal Organization as First Fact of Historical Materialism', *Historical Materialism*, 13.1, pp. 33–62 <https://doi.org/10.1163/1569206053620915>

Fraser, Mariam, Sarah Kember, and Celia Lury, 'Inventive Life: Approaches to the New Vitalism', *Theory, Culture & Society*, 22.1 (2005), pp. 1–14 <https://doi.org/10.1177/0263276405048431>

Fraser, Nancy, and Axel Honneth, *Redistribution or Recognition?: A Political-Philosophical Exchange* (London: Verso, 2003)

Freire, Paulo, *Pedagogy of the Oppressed*, trans. by Myra Bergman Ramos (New York: Continuum, 2005)

Freud, Sigmund, *Civilization and its Discontents*, in *The Standard Edition of the Complete Psychological Works of Sigmund Freud*, ed. by James Strachey, trans. by Angela Richards, 24 vols (London: Hogarth Press and the Institute of Psycho-Analysis, 1953–74), XXI (1961), pp. 57–145

Fricker, Miranda, 'The Virtue of Testimonial Justice', in *Epistemic Injustice: Power and the Ethics of Knowing* (Oxford: Oxford University Press, 2007), pp. 86–108 <https://doi.org/10.1093/acprof:oso/9780198237907.003.0005>

Frost, Samantha, 'The Implications of the New Materialisms for Feminist Epistemology', in *Feminist Epistemology and Philosophy of Science*, ed. by

Heidi E. Grasswick (Dordrecht: Springer Netherlands, 2011), pp. 69–
83 <https://doi.org/10.1007/978-1-4020-6835-5_4>

Furetière, Antoine, 'Émancipation', in *Dictionnaire Universel*, 3 vols (The
Hague and Rotterdam: Arnoud et Reinier Leers, 1701), ΙΙ, pp. 33–34

Gad, Christopher, Casper Bruun Jensen, and Brit Ross Winthereik, 'Practical
Ontology: Worlds in STS and Anthropology', *NatureCulture*, 3 (2015),
pp. 67–86

Garrett, Don, *Nature and Necessity in Spinoza's Philosophy* (New York:
Oxford University Press, 2018) <https://doi.org/10.1093/oso/
9780195307771.001.0001>

Gatens, Moira, *Imaginary Bodies: Ethics, Power, and Corporeality* (London:
Routledge, 1996)

Gatens, Moira, and Genevieve Lloyd, *Collective Imaginings: Spinoza, Past and
Present* (London: Routledge, 1999)

Genel, Katia, 'Jacques Rancière and Axel Honneth: Two Critical Approaches
to the Political', in *Recognition or Disagreement: A Critical Encounter on
the Politics of Freedom, Equality and Identity*, ed. by Katia Genel and Jean-
Philippe Deranty (New York: Columbia University Press), pp. 3–32

Geroulanos, Stefanos, and Jamie Phillips, 'Eurasianism versus IndoGer-
manism: Linguistics and Mmythology in the 1930s' Controversies
over European Prehistory', *History of Science*, 56.3 (2018), pp. 343–78
<https://doi.org/10.1177/0073275318776422>

Glasson, Benjamin, 'Unspeakable Articulations: Steps Towards a Materialist Discourse Theory', in *Material Discourse-Materialist Analysis: Approaches in Discourse Studies*, ed. by Johannes Beetz and Veit Schwab
(Lanham, MD: Lexington Books, 2017), pp. 81–94

Gliboff, Sander, *H. G. Bronn, Ernst Haeckel, and the Origins of German Darwinism: A Study in Translation and Transformation* (Cambridge, MA: MIT
Press, 2008) <https://doi.org/10.7551/mitpress/9780262072939.
001.0001>

Godelier, Maurice, 'Dialectical Logic and the Analysis of Structures: A Reply
to Lucien Sevè', *International Journal of Sociology*, 2.2–3 (1972), pp.
241–80 <https://doi.org/10.1080/15579336.1972.11769551>

Goldmann, Lucien, *Recherches dialectiques* (Paris: Gallimard, 1959)

Goux, Jean-Joseph, *Frivolité de la valeur* (Paris: Blusson, 2000)

Greene, Brian, *The Elegant Universe: Superstrings, Hidden Dimensions, and the
Quest for the Ultimate Theory* (New York: Vintage Books, 2000)

Grosz, Elizabeth A., *The Nick of Time: Politics, Evolution, and the Untimely*
(Durham, NC: Duke University Press, 2004) <https://doi.org/10.
1215/9780822386032>

—— *Volatile Bodies: Toward a Corporeal Feminism* (Bloomington: Indiana
University Press, 1994)

Guattari, Félix, *Three Ecologies* (London: Athlone, 2000)

Gueroult, Martial, *Spinoza*, 2 vols (Paris: Aubier-Montaigne, 1968), Ι: *Dieu
(Éthique, I)* and ΙΙ: *L'âme (Éthique, II)*

Hacking, Ian, *The Social Construction of What?* (Cambridge, MA: Harvard University Press, 1999)

Haraway, Donna J., 'The Promises of Monsters: A Regenerative Politics for Inappropriate/d Others', in *Cultural Studies*, ed. by Lawrence Grossberg, Cary Nelson, and Paula A. Treichler (New York: Routledge, 1992), pp. 295–337

—— 'Situated Knowledges: The Science Question in Feminism and the Privilege of Partial Perspective', *Feminist Studies*, 14.3 (1988), pp. 575–99 <https://doi.org/10.2307/3178066>

—— *When Species Meet* (Minneapolis: University of Minnesota Press, 2008)

Hardt, Michael, and Antonio Negri, *Commonwealth* (Cambridge, MA: Harvard University Press, 2009) <https://doi.org/10.2307/j.ctvjsf48h>

Harman, Graham, 'Agential and Speculative Realism: Remarks on Barad's Ontology', *Rhizomes: Cultural Studies in Emerging Knowledge*, 30, 2016 <https://doi.org/10.20415/rhiz/030.e10>

—— 'Stengers on Emergence', *BioSocieties*, 9.1 (2014), pp. 99–104 <https://doi.org/10.1057/biosoc.2013.43>

Hartsock, Nancy, 'The Feminist Standpoint: Developing the Ground for a Specifically Feminist Historical Materialism', in *Discovering Reality: Feminist Perspectives on Epistemology, Metaphysics, Methodology, and Philosophy of Science*, ed. by Sandra Harding and Merrill B. Hintikka (New York: Kluwer, 1983), pp. 283–310 <https://doi.org/10.1007/978-94-010-0101-4_15>

Haug, Frigga, and Kornelia Hauser, 'Marxistische Theorien und feministischer Standpunkt', in *Traditionen Brüche. Entwicklungen feministischer Theorie*, ed. by Gudrun-Axeli Knapp and Angelika Wetterer (Freiburg: Kore, 1992), pp. 115–49

Heidegger, Martin, *Gesamtausgabe*, 102 vols (Frankfurt a.M.: Klostermann, 1975–) [hereafter *GA*]

—— *GA*, VIII: *Was heißt Denken?*, ed. by Paola-Ludovika Coriando (2002)

—— *GA*, IX: *Wegmarken*, ed. by Friedrich-Wilhelm von Herrmann (1976)

—— *GA*, X: *Der Satz vom Grund*, ed. by Petra Jaeger (1997)

—— *GA*, XV: *Seminare*, ed. by Curd Ochwadt (1986)

—— *GA*, XVI: *Reden und andere Zeugnisse eines Lebensweges*, ed. by Hermann Heidegger (2000)

—— *GA*, XXXVI/XXXVII: *Sein und Wahrheit*, ed. by Hartmut Tietjen (2001)

—— *GA*, XL: *Einführung in die Metaphysik*, ed. by Petra Jaeger (1983)

—— *GA*, L: *Nietzsches Metaphysik. Einleitung in die Philosophie. Denken und Dichten*, ed. by Petra Jaeger (1990)

—— *GA*, LXV: *Beiträge zur Philosophie (Vom Ereignis)*, ed. by Friedrich-Wilhelm von Herrmann (1989)

—— *GA*, LXXVIII: *Der Spruch des Anaximander*, ed. by Ingeborg Schüßler (2010)

—— *GA*, LXXIX: *Bremer und Freiburger Vorträge*, ed. by Petra Jaeger (1994)

—— *GA*, LXXXIII: *Seminare. Platon. Aristoteles. Augustinus*, ed. by Mark Michalski (2012)

—— *GA*, LXXXIX: *Zollikoner Seminare*, ed. by Peter Trawny (2018)

—— *GA*, XCIV: *Überlegungen II–VI (Schwarze Hefte 1931–1938)*, ed. by Peter Trawny (2014)

—— *GA*, XCV: *Überlegungen VII–XI (Schwarze Hefte 1938–1939)*, ed. by Peter Trawny (2014)

—— *GA*, XCVI: *Überlegungen XII–XV (Schwarze Hefte 1939–1941)*, ed. by Peter Trawny (2014)

—— *GA*, XCVII: *Anmerkungen I–V (Schwarze Hefte 1942–1948)*, ed. by Peter Trawny (2015)

—— *GA*, XCVIII: *Anmerkungen VI–IX (Schwarze Hefte 1948–1949)*, ed. by Peter Trawny (2018)

Heine, Heinrich, *De l'Allemagne* (Paris: Gallimard, 1998 [1855])

—— 'Reise von München nach Genua', in *Heinrich-Heine-Säkularausgabe*, 27 vols (Berlin: de Gruyter, 1970–), VI: *Reisebilder II (1828–1831)*(1986), pp. 7–72 <https://doi.org/10.1524/9783050053080.7>

—— *Zur Geschichte der Religion und Philosophie in Deutschland*, in *Heinrich-Heine-Säkularausgabe*, VIII: *Über Deutschland, 1833–1836. Aufsätze über Kunst und Philosophie*(1972), pp. 125–230 <https://doi.org/10.1524/9783050053127.125>

Heinrich, Michael, 'Geld und Kredit in der Kritik der politischen Ökonomie', *Das Argument — Zeitschrift für Philosophie und Sozialwissenschaften*, 45.251 (2003), pp. 397–409

Helvétius, Claude A., *De L'Esprit; or, Essays on the Mind, and its Several Faculties* (London: Albion, 1810)

—— *Œuvres complètes d'Helvétius*, 3 vols (Paris: Lepetit, 1818), I: *De l'homme*

Hennessy, Rosemary, *Materialist Feminism and the Politics of Discourse* (New York: Routledge, 1993)

He Zhen, 'Women's Liberation', in *Anarchism: A Documentary History of Libertarian Ideas*, ed. by Robert Graham, 3 vols (Montreal: Black Rose Books, 2005), I, pp. 336–41

Hill Collins, Patricia, 'Learning from the Outsider Within: The Sociological Significance of Black Feminist Thought', *Social Problems*, 33.6 (1986), pp. 14–32 <https://doi.org/10.1525/sp.1986.33.6.03a00020>

Hobbes, Thomas, *Leviathan or the Matter, Form, and Power of a Commonwealth Ecclesiastical and Civil*, ed. by William Molesworth, in *The English Works of Thomas Hobbes*, 11 vols (London: Bohn, 1839), III

Holanda, Sérgio Buarque de, *História Geral da Civilização Brasileira*, 11 vols (São Paulo: Bertrand Brasil, 2005), VII

d'Holbach, Paul Thiry, *The System of Nature*, 2 vols (Kitchener: Batoche Books, 2001)

Holbraad, Martin, Morten Axel Pedersen, and Eduardo Viveiros de Castro, 'The Politics of Ontology: Anthropological Positions', 2014 <https:

//culanth.org/fieldsights/the-politics-of-ontology-anthropological-positions> [accessed 26 March 2019]

Hollin, Gregory, Isla Forsyth, Eva Giraud, and Tracey Potts, '(Dis)Entangling Barad: Materialisms and Ethics', *Social Studies of Science*, 47.6 (2017), pp. 918–41 <https://doi.org/10.1177/0306312717728344>

Hoppe, Katharina, 'Eine neue Ontologie des Materiellen? Probleme und Perspektiven neomaterialistischer Feminismen', in *Material turn: Feministische Perspektiven auf Materialität und Materialismus*, ed. by Christine Löw, Katharina Volk, Imke Leicht, and Nadja Meisterhans (Leverkusen: Barbara Budrich, 2017), pp. 35–50 <https://doi.org/10.2307/j.ctvddzkq8.6>

Horkheimer, Max, 'Anfänge der bürgerlichen Geschichtsphilosophie', in *Gesammelte Schriften*, 19 vols (Frankfurt a.M.: Fischer, 1987), II, pp. 177–268

—— 'Egoismus und Freiheitsbewegung: Zur Anthropologie des bürgerlichen Zeitalters', *Zeitschrift für Sozialforschung*, 5.2 (1936), pp. 161–234 <https://doi.org/10.5840/zfs19365273>

—— 'Traditional and Critical Theory', in *Critical Theory: Selected Essays* (New York: Continuum, 2002), pp. 188–243

Hulak, Florence, 'Spinoza après Marx, ou le problème de l'ontologie marxienne', *Revue de métaphysique et de morale*, 56.4 (2007), pp. 483–98 <https://doi.org/10.3917/rmm.074.0483>

Israël, Nicolas, *Spinoza. Le temps de la vigilance* (Paris: Payot, 2001)

Itokazu, Ericka, 'Au-delà du temps mesure. La question du temps chez Spinoza' in *Ontologia e temporalità. Spinoza e i suoi lettori moderni*, ed. by Giuseppe D'Anna and Vitorio Morfino (Milano: Mimesis, 2012), pp. 387–98

—— 'Tempo, Duração e Eternidade Na Filosofia de Espinosa' (Universidade de São Paulo (USP), 2008) <https://www.teses.usp.br/teses/disponiveis/8/8133/tde-18032009-110714/pt-br.php> [accessed 02 July 2020]

Jacobi, Friedrich Heinrich, 'Letter from Jacobi to Fichte', in *The Main Philosophical Writings and the Novel Allwill*, ed. by George di Giovanni (Montreal: McGill-Queen's University Press, 1994), pp. 497–536

Jacob, Margaret C., *The Secular Enlightenment* (Princeton, NJ: Princeton University Press, 2019)

Jacques, Vincent, 'De *Différence et répétition* à *Mille plateaux*, métamorphose du système à l'aune de deux lectures de Spinoza', in *Spinoza-Deleuze: Lectures croisés*, ed. by Pascal Sévérac and Anne Sauvagnargues (Lyon: ENS Éditions, 2016), pp. 29–44 <https://doi.org/10.4000/books.enseditions.7082>

Jakobson, Roman, ed., *N. S. Trubetzkoy's Letters and Notes* (The Hague: Mouton, 1975)

Jaquet, Chantal, *Les Expressions de la puissance d'agir chez Spinoza* (Paris: Publications de la Sorbonne, 2005) <https://doi.org/10.4000/books. psorbonne.127>

—— *Sub specie æternitatis. Études des concepts de temps, durée et éternité chez Spinoza* (Paris: Kimé, 1997)

Jonas, Hans, 'Gnosticism and Modern Nihilism', *Social Research*,19.4 (December 1952), pp. 430–52

Judt, Tony, 'Goodbye to All That?', *New York Review of Books*, 1111.14 (21 September 2006)

Kaidesoja, Tuukka, 'Bhaskar and Bunge on Social Emergence', *Journal for the Theory of Social Behaviour*, 39.3 (2009), pp. 300–22 <https://doi.org/ 10.1111/j.1468-5914.2009.00409.x>

Kant, Immanuel, 'An Answer to the Question: What is Enlightenment?' [1784], in *Practical Philosophy*, pp. 15–22

—— *Critique of Pure Reason*, trans. by Paul Guyer and Allen W. Wood (Cambridge: Cambridge University Press, 1998) <https://doi.org/10.1017/ CBO9780511804649>

—— *The Metaphysics of Morals* [1797], in *Practical Philosophy*, pp. 353–603 <https://doi.org/10.1017/CBO9780511813306.013>

—— *Practical Philosophy*, trans. by Mary J. Gregor, The Cambridge Edition of the Works of Immanuel Kant (Cambridge: Cambridge University Press, 1996) <https://doi.org/10.1017/CBO9780511813306>

Kantorowicz, Ernst, *The King's Two Bodies: A Study in Mediaeval Political Theology* (Princeton, NJ: Princeton University Press, 1957)

Keller, Evelyn Fox, *Reflections on Gender and Science* (New Haven, CT: Yale University Press, 1985)

Kirby, Vicki, 'Natural Convers(at)ions: Or, What If Culture Was Really Nature All Along?', in *Material Feminisms*, ed. by Stacy Alaimo and Susan J. Hekman (Bloomington: Indiana University Press, 2008), pp. 214–36

Klinger, Cornelia, 'Liberalismus — Marxismus — Postmoderne. Der Feminismus und seine glücklichen oder unglücklichen "Ehen" mit verschiedenen Theorieströmungen im 20. Jahrhundert', in *Kritische Differenzen — geteilte Perspektiven. Zum Verhältnis von Feminismus und Postmoderne*, ed. by Antje Hornscheidt, Gabriele Jähnert, and Annette Schlichter (Wiesbaden: Westdeutscher Verlag, 1998), pp. 18–41 <https://doi.org/10.1007/978-3-322-89056-6_1>

Kornegger, Peggy, 'Anarchism: The Feminist Connection', in *Quiet Rumors: An Anarcha-Feminist Reader*, ed. by Dark Star (Oakland, CA: AK Press, 2012), pp. 25–35

Koselleck, Reinhardt, and Karl Martin Grass, 'Emanzipation', in *Geschichtliche Grundbegriffe: Historisches Lexikon*, ed. by Reinhardt Koselleck, Otto Brunner, and Werner Conze, 7 vols (Stuttgart: Klett-Cotta, 1972–97), II (1975), pp. 153–97

Kraniauskas, John, 'Rhetorics of Populism', *Radical Philosophy: A Journal of Socialist and Feminist Philosophy*, 186 (July/August 2014), pp. 29–37

Krätke, Michael R., *Friedrich Engels oder: Wie ein Cotton-Lord den Marxismus erfand* (Berlin: Dietz, 2020)

—— *Kritik der politischen Ökonomie heute. Zeitgenosse Marx* (Hamburg: VSA, 2017).

Kurz, Robert, 'The Crisis of Exchange Value: Science as Productive Force; Productive Labour; and Capitalist Reproduction (1986)', in *Dossier: Marxism and the Critique of Value*, ed. by Neil Larsen, Mathias Nilges, Josh Robinson, and Nicholas Brown (=*Mediations: Journal of the Marxist Literary Group*, 27.1–2 (2013–14)) <https://www.mediationsjournal.org/toc/27_1> [accessed: 15 November 2020]

Labica, George, *Karl Marx. Les thèses sur Feuerbach* (Paris: PUF, 1987)

Labussière, Jean-Louis, 'Diderot métaphysicien. Prédication, participation et existence' in *Lumières*, ed. by Duflo, pp. 21–72

Lacan, Jacques, 'Conférence à Genève sur le symptôme', texte établi par Jacques-Allain Miller, *La Cause du Désir*, 95 (2017), pp. 7–24 <https://doi.org/10.3917/lcdd.095.0007>

Laclau, Ernesto, 'Antagonism, Subjectivity and Politics', in *The Rhetorical Foundations of Society*, pp. 101–25

—— 'Building a New Left', in *New Reflections on the Revolution of our Time*, pp. 177–96

—— 'The Controversy over Materialism', in *Rethinking Marx*, ed. by Sakari Hänninen and Leena Paldán (Berlin: Argument, 1984), pp. 39–43

—— *Emancipation(s)* (London: Verso, 1996)

—— 'The Future of Radical Democracy', in *Radical Democracy: Politics between Abundance and Lack*, ed. by Lars Tønder and Lasse Thomassen (Manchester: Manchester University Press, 2005), pp. 256–62

—— 'Glimpsing the Future', in *Laclau: A Critical Reader*, ed. by Simon Critchley and Oliver Marchart (London: Routledge, 2004), pp. 279–328

—— 'Identity and Hegemony: The Role of Universality in the Constitution of Political Logics', in *Contingency, Hegemony, Universality: Contemporary Dialogues on the Left*, ed. by Judith Butler, Ernesto Laclau, and Slavoj Žižek (London: Verso, 2000), pp. 44–89

—— 'Ideology and Post-Marxism', *Journal of Political Ideologies*, 11.2 (June 2006), pp. 103–14 <https://doi.org/10.1080/13569310600687882>

—— *New Reflections on the Revolution of our Time* (London: Verso, 1990)

—— 'New Reflections on the Revolution of our Time', in *New Reflections on the Revolution of our Time*, pp. 3–85

—— *On Populist Reason* (London: Verso, 2005)

—— 'Political Significance of the Concept of Negativity', *Vestnik*, 1 (1988), pp. 73–78

—— 'Politics and the Limits of Modernity', in *Universal Abandon? The Politics of Postmodernism*, ed. by Andrew Ross (Minneapolis: University of Minnesota Press, 1988) (= *Social Text*, 7.3 (1989)), pp. 63–82 <https://doi.org/10.2307/827809>

—— 'La Politique comme construction de l'impensable', in *Matérialités discursives*, ed. by Bernard Conein, and others (Lille: Presses Universitaires de Lille, 1981), pp. 65–74

—— 'Populism: What's in a Name?', in *Populism and the Mirror of Democracy*, ed. by Francisco Panizza (London: Verso, 2005), pp. 32–49

—— 'Power and Representation', in *Emancipation(s)*, pp. 84–104

—— *The Rhetorical Foundations of Society* (London: Verso, 2014)

—— 'Theory, Democracy and Socialism', in *New Reflections on the Revolution of our Time*, pp. 197–245

—— 'Why do Empty Signifiers Matter to Politics?', in *Emancipation(s)*, pp. 36–46

Laclau, Ernesto, and Chantal Mouffe, *Hegemony and Socialist Strategy: Towards a Radical Democratic Politics* (London: Verso, 2001)

—— 'Post-Marxism without Apologies', in Laclau, *New Reflections on the Revolution of our Time*, pp. 97–132

Laclau, Ernesto, and Lilian Zac, 'Minding the Gap: The Subject of Politics', in *The Making of Political Identities*, ed. by Ernesto Laclau (London: Verso, 1994), pp. 11–39

La Mettrie, Julien Offray de, *L'Homme-machine* (Paris: Fayard, 2000 [1747])

Lange, Friedrich Albert, *The History of Materialism and Criticism of its Present Importance*, 3 parts (London: Kegan Paul, Trench, Trubner, 1925)

Languet, Hubert, *Vindiciae Contra Tyrannos, or, Concerning the Legitimate Power of a Prince over the People, and of the People over a Prince* (New York: Cambridge University Press, 1994)

Lapoujade, David, *Aberrant Movements: The Philosophy of Gilles Deleuze*, trans. by Joshua David Jordan (Cambridge, MA: MIT Press, 2017)

Laqueur, Thomas, *Making Sex: Body and Gender from the Greeks to Freud* (Cambridge, MA: Harvard University Press, 2003)

Latour, Bruno, *Reassembling the Social: An Introduction to Actor-Network-Theory*, Clarendon Lectures in Management Studies (Oxford: Oxford University Press, 2005)

Laughlin, Robert B., and David Pines, 'The Theory of Everything', *PNAS*, 97.1 (2000), pp. 28–31 <https://doi.org/10.1073/pnas.97.1.28>

Lazier, Benjamin, *God Interrupted: Heresy and the European Imagination Between the World Wars*(Princeton, NJ: Princeton University Press, 2009) <https://doi.org/10.1515/9781400837656>

Lācis, Asja, 'A Memoir', *South as State of Mind*, 9 [Documenta 14#4] ([2017]) <https://www.documenta14.de/en/south/> [accessed 12 September 2020])

Le Collectif Onze, *Au tribunal des couples: Enquête sur des affaires familiales* (Paris: Odile Jacob, 2013)

Lecourt, Dominique, 'Marx au crible de Darwin', in *De Darwin au darwinisme: science et idéologie*, ed. by Yvette Contry(Paris: Vrin, 1983), pp. 227–49

Lemke, Thomas, 'Materialism without Matter: The Recurrence of Subjectivism in Object-Oriented Ontology', *Distinktion: Journal of Social Theory*,

18.2 (2017), pp. 133–52 <https://doi.org/10.1080/1600910X.2017.1373686>

Leonelli, Sabina, *Data-Centric Biology: A Philosophical Study* (Chicago: University of Chicago Press, 2016) <https://doi.org/10.7208/chicago/9780226416502.001.0001>

Leroi-Gourhan, André, *Le Geste et la Parole*, 2 vols (Paris: Albin Michel, 1964–65), I: *Technique et Langage* (1964); II: *La mémoire et les rythmes* (1965); in English as *Gesture and Speech*, trans. by Anna Bostock Berger (Cambridge, MA: MIT Press, 1993)

Lettow, Susanne, 'Turning the Turn: New Materialism, Historical Materialism and Critical Theory', *Thesis Eleven*, 140.1 (2017), pp. 106–21 <https://doi.org/10.1177/0725513616683853>

Lindemann, Gesa, 'Die leiblich-affektive Konstruktion des Geschlechts. Für eine Mikrosoziologie des Geschlechts unter der Haut', *Zeitschrift für Soziologie*, 21 (1992), pp. 330–46

Locke, John, *The Second Treatise of Government*, in *Locke: Two Treatises of Government* (Cambridge: Cambridge University Press, 2003), pp. 265–428 <https://doi.org/10.1017/CBO9780511810268.011>

—— *Some Thoughts Concerning Education*, in *The Educational Writings of John Locke*, ed. by John William Adamson (Cambridge: Cambridge University Press, 2011), pp. 21–180 <https://doi.org/10.1017/CBO9780511696879.005>

Longino, Helen E., 'Subjects, Power, and Knowledge: Description and Prescription in Feminist Philosophies of Science', in *Feminist Epistemologies*, ed. and intro. by Linda Alcoff and Elizabeth Potter (New York: Routledge, 1993), pp. 101–20

Longo, Matthew, and Bernardo Zacka, 'Political Theory in an Ethnographic Key', *American Political Science Review* 1130.4 (2019), pp. 1066–70 <https://doi.org/10.1017/S0003055419000431>

Lordon, Frédéric, *Capitalisme, désir et servitude. Marx et Spinoza* (Paris: La Fabrique, 2010) <https://doi.org/10.3917/lafab.lordo.2010.01>

—— *Imperium. Structures et affects des corps politiques* (Paris: La fabrique, 2015)

—— *Willing Slaves of Capital: Spinoza and Marx on Desire* (London: Verso Books, 2014)

Lucretius, *On the Nature of Things*, trans. by William Ellery Leonard (New York: Dover, 2008)

Lugones, Maria, 'The Coloniality of Gender', in *The Palgrave Handbook of Gender and Development: Critical Engagements in Feminist Theory and Practice*, ed. by Wendy Harcourt (London: Palgrave Macmillan, 2016), pp. 13–33 <https://doi.org/10.1007/978-1-137-38273-3_2>

Lukács, Georg, 'Postscript 1967' [1967], in *Lenin: A Study on the Unity of his Thought*, trans. by Nicholas Jacobs (London: Verso, 2009), pp. 86–97

Lærke, Mogens, 'Immanence et extériorité absolue. Sur la théorie de la causalité et l'ontologie de la puissance de Spinoza', *Revue philosophique de la*

France et de l'étranger, 134.2 (2009), pp. 169–90 <https://doi.org/10.3917/rphi.092.0169>

Lévy-Bruhl, Lucien, *How Natives Think* (1910), trans. by Lilian A. Clare (New York: Washington Square Press, 1966)

Lézine, Irène, *A. S. Makarenko, Pédagogue soviétique (1888–1939)* (Paris: PUF, 1954)

Löwenthal, Leo, 'Das Individuum in der individualistischen Gesellschaft. Bemerkungen über Ibsen', *Zeitschrift für Sozialforschung*, 5.3 (1936), pp. 321–63 <https://doi.org/10.5840/zfs1936531>

Löwith, Karl, 'Knowledge and Faith: From the Pre-Socratics to Heidegger', in *Religion and Culture: Essays in Honor of Paul Tillich*, ed. by Walter Liebrecht (New York: Harper, 1959), pp. 196–210

Macherey, Pierre, *Avec Spinoza. Études sur la doctrine et l'histoire du spinozisme* (Paris: PUF, 1992)

—— *Études de philosophie 'française'. De Sieyès à Barni* (Paris: Publications de la Sorbonne, 2016)

—— *Histoires de dinosaure: Faire de la philosophie (1965–1997)* (Paris: PUF, 1999) <https://doi.org/10.3917/puf.mache.1999.01>

—— 'Spinoza 1968: Guéroult et/ou Deleuze', in *Le Moment philosophique des années 1960 en France*, ed. by Patrice Maniglier (Paris: PUF, 2011), pp. 293–313

Macherey, Pierre, and Orazio Irrera, 'Michel Foucault et les critiques de l'idéologie. Dialogue avec Pierre Macherey', *Methodos. Savoir et textes*, 16 (2016) <https://doi.org/10.4000/methodos.4667>

Machiavelli, Niccolò, *The Prince* [1513], ed. by William J. Connell (Boston, MA: Bedford, 2005)

Mahmood, Saba, *The Politics of Piety: The Islamic Revival and the Feminist Subject* (Princeton, NJ: Princeton University Press, 2005)

Makarenko, Anton Semyonovich, 'La Colonie de Poltava dite Colonel Gorki (1925)', in *L'Éducation dans les collectivités d'enfants* (Paris: CEMEA, Les Éditions du Scarabée, 1956)

—— *O Poema Pedagógico* (São Paulo: Editora 34, 2012)

—— *Poème Pédagogique. En Trois Parties*, 3 vols (Moscow: Éditions en Langues Étrangères, 1953)

—— *Poema Pedagógico* (Spain: Omegalfa/ Biblioteca Libre, n.d.) <https://www.omegalfa.es/downloadfile.php?file=libros/poema-pedagogico.pdf> [accessed 12 September 2020]

—— *The Road to Life (An Epic of Education) in Three Parts*, 3 vols (Moscow: Foreign Languages Publishing House, 1955)

—— *Педагогическая поэма* [Pedagogical Poem] (2003) <http://makarenko-museum.ru/Classics/Makarenko/Makarenko_A_Pedagogic_Poem/Makarenko_Ped_poema_full_text.pdf> [accessed 12 September 2020]

Malatesta, Errico, *L'Anarchia* [1891] (Rome: Datanews, 2001)

Malm, Andreas, 'Against Hybridism: Why We Need to Distinguish between Nature and Society, Now More than Ever', *Historical Materialism*, 27.2 (2019), pp. 156–87 <https://doi.org/10.1163/1569206X-00001610>

—— *The Progress of This Storm: Nature and Society in a Warming World* (London: Verso, 2018)

Marchart, Oliver, *Post-Foundational Political Thought: Political Difference in Nancy, Lefort, Badiou and Laclau* (Edinburgh: Edinburgh University Press, 2007) <https://doi.org/10.3366/edinburgh/9780748624973.001.0001>

Marcuse, Herbert, *Eros and Civilization: A Philosophical Inquiry into Freud* (Boston: Beacon Press, 1955)

Marr, Nikolai, 'Aktual'nye problemy i ocherednye zadachi iafeticheskoi teorii' [Current Problems and Imminent Tasks of the Japhetic Theory], in *Izbrannye raboty*, III (1936), pp. 61–77

—— *Ani, knizhnaia istoria goroda i raskopki na meste* [Ani, a Written History of the City and the Excavations] (Moscow: OGIZ, 1934)

—— 'Iazyk i myshlenie' [Language and Thought], in *Izbrannye raboty*, III (1936), pp. 90–121

—— *Izbrannye raboty* [Selected Works], 5 vols (Leningrad: Gosudarstvennaia akademia istorii material'noi kul'tury (GAIMK), 1933–37)

—— 'Novyi povorot v rabote iafeticheskoi teorii' [New Turn in the Work of Japhetic Theory], in *Izbrannye raboty*, I (1933), pp. 312–46

—— 'O proischozhdenii iazyka' [On the Origin of Language], in *Izbrannye raboty*, III (1936), pp. 180–215

—— *O raskopkah i rabotah v Ani leta 1906* [On the Excavations and Works in Ani in Summer 1906] (Saint Petersburg: Imp. akad. nauk, 1907)

—— 'Ob iafeticheskoi teorii' [On Japhetic Theory], in *Izbrannye raboty*, III (1936), pp. 1–34

—— 'Sredstva peredvizhenia, orudia samozazhity i proizvodstva v doistorii' [Means of Transportation, Instruments of Self-protection and Production in Prehistory], in *Izbrannye raboty*, III (1936), pp. 123–51

Marx, Karl, *Capital: A Critique of Political Economy*, 3 vols (London: Penguin, 1976), I, trans. by Ben Fowkes

—— *Contribution to the Critique of Hegel's Philosophy of Law*, in *MECW*, III (1975), pp. 3–129

—— *Contribution to the Critique of Hegel's Philosophy of Law. Introduction*, in *MECW*, III (1975), pp. 175–87

—— 'Critical Marginal Notes on the Article "The King of Prussia and Social Reform. By a Prussian"', in *MECW*, III (1975), pp. 189–206

—— 'Hefte zur epikureischen, stoischen und skeptischen Philosophie', in *MEW*, XL (1968), pp. 13–258

—— *The Holy Family, or Critique of Critical Criticism*, in *MECW*, IV (1975), pp. 3–211

—— 'Instructions for the Delegates of the Provisional General Council', in *MECW*, XX (1985), pp. 185–94

—— 'Kritische Randglossen zu dem Artikel "Der König von Preußen und die Sozialreform. Von einem Preußen"', in *MEW*, I (1981), pp. 392–409

—— Letter to Engels, 14 November 1868, in *MEW*, XXXII (1974), pp. 202–03

—— Letter to Kugelmann, 5 December 1868, in *MECW*, XLIII (1988), pp. 173–75

—— 'Letters from the Deutsch-Französische Jahrbücher', in *MECW*, III (1975), pp. 133–45

—— *Outlines of the Critique of Political Economy*, in *MECW*, XXVIII (1986), pp. 49–537

—— 'Thesen über Feuerbach', in *MEW*, III (1958), pp. 5–7

—— 'Theses on Feuerbach', ed. by Friedrich Engels, in *MECW*, V (1976), pp. 6–8

—— 'Theses on Feuerbach', in *MECW*, V (1976), pp. 3–5

Marx, Karl, and Friedrich Engels, *Collected Works*, 50 vols (London: Lawrence and Wishart, 1975–2004) [=*MECW*]

—— 'Manifesto of the Communist Party', in *MECW*, VI (1976), pp. 477–519

—— *Marx-Engels-Werke*, 44 vols (Berlin: Dietz, 1956–2018) [=*MEW*]

Mason, Paul, *Clear Bright Future: A Radical Defence of the Human Being* (London: Allen Lane, 2019)

Matheron, Alexandre, *Individu et communauté chez Spinoza* (Paris: Minuit, 1969)

—— 'A propos de Spinoza', *Multitudes*, 1.3 (2000), pp. 169–200 <https://doi.org/10.3917/mult.003.0169>

—— 'Women and Servants in Spinozist Democracy', in *Politics, Ontology and Knowledge in Spinoza* (Edinburgh: Edinburgh University Press, 2020), pp. 260–79

Matheron, François, and Yoshihiko Ichida, 'Un, deux, trois, quatre, dix mille Althusser. Considérations aléatoires sur le matérialisme aléatoire', *Multitude*, 21.2 (2005), pp. 167–78 <https://doi.org/10.3917/mult.021.0167>

Mathieu, Nicole-Claude, *L'Anatomie politique: catégorisations et idéologies du sexe* (Paris: Côté-femmes, 1991)

Mauss, Marcel, 'Essai sur le don. Forme et raison de l'échange dans les sociétés archaïques', *L'Année sociologique, nouvelle série*, 1 (1923–24), pp. 30–186; in English as 'Essay on the Gift: The Form and Sense of Exchange in Archaic Societies', in his *The Gift*, expanded edition, trans. by Jane I. Guyer (Chicago: University of Chicago Press, 2016)

—— 'Les Techniques du corps', *Journal de psychologie normale et pathologique*, 32 (1935), pp. 271–93; in English as 'Techniques of the Body', *Economy and Society*, 2.1 (1973), pp. 70–88 <https://doi.org/10.1080/03085147300000003>

Mies, Maria, *Patriarchy and Accumulation on a World Scale: Women in the International Division of Labour* (London: Zed Books, 1986)

Mies, Maria, and Vandana Shiva, *Ecoféminisme* (Paris: L'Harmattan, 1998)

Miguel, Marlon, 'Pour une pédagogie de la révolte: Fernand Deligny, de la solidarité avec les marginaux au perspectivisme', in *Cahiers du GRM*, 15 (2019) <https://doi.org/10.4000/grm.1696>

—— *À la marge et hors-champ: l'humain dans la pensée de Fernand Deligny* (doctoral dissertation, Université Paris 8, 2016) <https://www.theses.fr/2016PA080020/document> [accessed 12 September 2020]

Miki, Yuko, *Frontiers of Citizenship: A Black and Indigenous History of Post-colonial Brazil* (Cambridge: Cambridge University Press, 2018) <https://doi.org/10.1017/9781108277778>

Millett, Kate, *Sexual Politics* (New York: Doubleday, 1970)

Mill, John Stuart, *A System of Logic, Ratiocinative and Inductive* (New York: Harper & Brothers, 1882) <https://www.gutenberg.org/files/27942/27942-pdf.pdf> [accessed 12 September 2020]

Mills, Charles, *The Racial Contract* (Ithaca, NY: Cornell University Press, 1997)

Mol, Annemarie, 'Ontological Politics. A Word and Some Questions', *The Sociological Review*, 47.1_suppl (1999), pp. 74–89 <https://doi.org/10.1111/j.1467-954X.1999.tb03483.x>

Montag, Warren, and Ted Stolze, eds, *The New Spinoza* (Minneapolis: University of Minnesota Press, 1997)

Moreau, Pierre-François, *Problèmes du spinozisme* (Paris: Vrin, 2006)

—— *Spinoza. L'expérience et l'éternité* (Paris: PUF, 1994)

Morfino, Vittorio, 'An Althusserian Lexicon', trans. by Jason Smith, *Borderlands*, 4.2 (2005) <http://www.borderlands.net.au/vol4no2_2005/morfino_lexicon.htm> [accessed 15 November 2020]

—— *Genealogia di un pregiudizio. L'immagine di Spinoza in Germania da Leibniz a Marx* (Hildesheim: Olms, 2016)

—— 'Il materialismo della pioggia di Louis Althusser. Un Lessico', *Quaderni materialisti*, 1 (2002), pp. 85–108

—— *Plural Temporality: Transindividuality and the Aleatory between Spinoza and Althusser* (Leiden: Brill, 2014) <https://doi.org/10.1163/9789004270558>

Morfino, Vittorio, and Luca Pinzolo, 'Introduzione', in Althusser, *Sul materialism aleatorio*, pp. 7–12

Morin, Edgar, *On Complexity* (Cresskill, NJ: Hampton Press, 2008)

Mornet, Daniel, *Les Origines intellectuelles de la Révolution française* (Paris: Armand Colin, 1933)

Morton, Timothy, 'Treating Objects Like Women: Feminist Ontology and the Question of Essence', in *International Perspectives in Feminist Ecocriticism*, ed. by Greta Gaard, Simon C. Estok, and Serpil Oppermann (New York: Routledge, 2013), pp. 56–69 <https://doi.org/10.4324/9780203520840-4>

Möser, Cornelia, *Féminismes en traductions. Théories voyageuses et traductions culturelles* (Paris: Éditions des archives contemporaines, 2013)

—— 'Néo-Matérialisme. Un nouveau courant féministe?', in *Matérialismes, cultures et communication*, ed. by Maxime Cervulle, Nelly Quemener, and Florian Vörös (Paris: Presses des Mines, 2016), pp. 227–44

Negri, Antonio, 'Politiche dell'immanenza, politiche della trascendenza. Saggio popolare', in *Storia politica della moltitudine*, ed. by Filippo Del Lucchese (Rome, DeriveApprodi, 2009), pp. 86–96

—— 'Pour Althusser. Notes sur l'évolutions de la pensée du dernier Althusser', in Althusser and others, *Sur Althusser*, pp. 73–96

—— *The Savage Anomaly: The Power of Spinoza's Metaphysic and Politics* (Minneapolis: University of Minnesota Press, 1991)

—— *Spinoza for our Time: Politics and Postmodernity*, trans. by William McCuaig (New York: Columbia University Press, 2013) <https://doi.org/10.7312/columbia/9780231160469.001.0001>

—— *Time for Revolution* (London: Bloomsbury, 2013)

Nicholson, Linda, ed., *The Second Wave: A Reader in Feminist Theory* (New York: Routledge, 1997)

Nicolau, Jairo, *História do Voto no Brasil* (Rio de Janeiro: Zahar, 2002)

Nietzsche, Friedrich, 'To Franz Overbeck [Postmarked Sils Engd., July 30, 1881]', in Christopher Middleton, *Selected Letters of Friedrich Nietzsche* (Chicago: University of Chicago Press, 1996), pp. 176–77

Nobre, Marcos, 'How Practical Can Critical Theory Be?', in *Critical Theory and the Challenge of Praxis*, ed. by Stefano Giacchetti Ludovisi (New York: Routledge, 2016), pp. 159–72

Nutzinger, Hans G., and Elmar Wolfstetter, *Die Marxsche Theorie und ihre Kritik: Eine Textsammlung zur Kritik der politischen Ökonomie* (Marburg: Metropolis, 2008)

Nyhart, Lynn K., 'The Political Organism: Carl Vogt on Animals and States in the 1840s and '50s', *Historical Studies in the Natural Sciences*, 47.5 (November 2017), pp. 602–28 <https://doi.org/10.1525/hsns.2017.47.5.602>

—— 'Wissenschaft and Kunde: The General and the Special in Modern Science', *Osiris*, 27.1 (2012), pp. 250–75 <https://doi.org/10.1086/667830>

Okay, Orhan, *Beşir Fuad Ilk türk pozitivisti ve natüralisti* (Istanbul: Dergah yayinlari, 2008 [1969])

Orlandi, Luiz B. L., 'Linhas de ação da diferença', in *Gilles Deleuze: uma vida filosófica*, ed. by Éric Alliez (São Paulo: Editora 34, 2000), pp. 49–63

Owen, Robert, *A New View of Society or, Essays on the Principle of the Formation of the Human Character, and the Application of the Principle to Practice* (London: Cadell & Davies, 1813) <https://www.marxists.org/reference/subject/economics/owen/index.htm> [accessed 12 September 2020]

Oyěwùmí, Oyèrónk ę́, *The Invention of Women: Making an African Sense of Western Gender Discourses* (Minneapolis: University of Minnesota Press, 1997)

Pence, Charles H., '"Describing Our Whole Experience": The Statistical Philosophies of W. F. R. Weldon and Karl Pearson', *Studies in History and Philosophy of Biological and Biomedical Sciences*, 42.4 (2011), pp. 475–85 <https://doi.org/10.1016/j.shpsc.2011.07.011>

Petersen, Eva Bendix, '"Data Found Us": A Critique of Some New Materialist Tropes in Educational Research', *Research in Education*, 101.1 (2018), pp. 5–16 <https://doi.org/10.1177/0034523718792161>

Pippa, Stefano, *Althusser and Contingency* (Milan: Mimesis International, 2018)

Porter, Theodore M., *Genetics in the Madhouse: The Unknown History of Human Heredity* (Princeton, NJ: Princeton University Press, 2018) <https://doi.org/10.23943/9781400890507>

Prigogine, Ilya, *The End of Certainty: Time, Chaos and the New Laws of Nature* (New York, NY: Free P, 1996)

Prigogine, Ilya, and Isabelle Stengers, *Order Out of Chaos: Man's New Dialogue with Nature* (London: Heinemann, 1984)

Projekt Klassenanalyse, *Neue Stufe des Wissenschaftlichen Sozialismus? Zum Verhältnis von Marxscher Theorie, Klassenanalyse und revolutionärer Taktik bei W. I. Lenin* (Berlin: Verlag für das Studium der Arbeiterbewegung, 1972)

Projekt sozialistischer Feminismus, ed., *Geschlechterverhältnisse und Frauenpolitik* (Berlin: Argument, 1984)

Pépin, François, 'Le Matérialisme pluriel de Diderot', in *Lumières*, ed. by Duflo, pp. 73–95

Rancière, Jacques, *Disagreement: Politics and Philosophy* (Minneapolis: University of Minnesota Press, 2004)

—— *The Ignorant Schoolmaster: Five Lessons in Intellectual Emancipation* (Stanford: Stanford University Press, 1991)

—— *La Mésentente. Politique et Philosophie* (Paris: Éditions Galilée, 1995)

Ravaisson, Félix, *La Philosophie en France au XIXᵉ siècle* (1867) (Paris: Vrin Reprise, 1983)

Read, Jason, *The Politics of Transindividuality* (Leiden: Brill, 2015) <https://doi.org/10.1163/9789004305151>

Reich, Wilhelm, *Die Sexualität im Kulturkampf* (Copenhagen: Sexpol, 1936)

Rekret, Paul, 'A Critique of New Materialism: Ethics and Ontology', *Subjectivity*, 9.3 (2016), pp. 225–45 <https://doi.org/10.1057/s41286-016-0001-y>

Rikowski, Glenn, 'Marx and the Education of the Future', *Policy Futures in Education*, 2.3–4 (2004) <https://doi.org/10.2304/pfie.2004.2.3.10>

Rittel, Horst W. J., and Melvin M. Webber, 'Dilemmas in a General Theory of Planning', *Policy Sciences*, 4.2 (June 1973), pp. 155–69 <https://doi.org/10.1007/BF01405730>

Ritter, Karl, *Prozesse der Befreiung. Marx, Spinoza und die Bedingungen eines freien Gemeinwesens* (Münster: Westfälisches Dampfboot, 2011)

Rojas, Raúl, *Das unvollendete Projekt: Zur Entstehungsgeschichte von Marx'
   Kapital*, Philosophie und Sozialwissenschaften, 14 (Berlin: Argument,
   1989)
Rosanvallon, Pierre, *Le peuple introuvable: histoire de la représentation démo-
   cratique en France* (Paris: Gallimard, 1998)
—— *Le Sacre du citoyen. Histoire du suffrage universel en France* (Paris: Galli-
   mard, 1992)
Rousset, Bernard, *La Perspective finale de l'Éthique* (Paris: Vrin, 1968)
Runciman, David, *Pluralism and the Personality of the State* (Cambridge:
   Cambridge University Press, 1997) <https://doi.org/10.1017/
   CBO9780511582967>
Salaün, Franck, *L'Affreuse Doctrine: Matérialisme et crise des mœurs au temps
   de Diderot* (Paris: Kimé, 2014)
—— 'Les Larmes de Wolmar. Rousseau et le problème du matérialisme', in
   Rousseau et la philosophie, ed. by Jean Salem and André Charrak (Paris:
   Editions de la Sorbonne, 2004), pp. 71–86 <https://doi.org/10.4000/
   books.psorbonne.18698>
Sauvagnarques, Anne, *Deleuze, l'empirisme transcendental* (Paris: PUF, 2009)
Schachtel, Ernst, *Metamorphosis: On the Conflict of Human Development and
   the Psychology of Creativity* (New York: Routledge, 2001)
Scheidler, Hermann, 'Judenemancipation', in *Allgemeine Encyclopädie der
   Wissenschaften und Künste*, ed. by Johann Samuel Ersch and Johann
   Gottfried Gruber, 167 vols (Leipzig: Johann Friedrich Gleditsch,
   1850), xxvii, pp. 253–315
Sibertin-Blanc, Guillaume, 'Politique et clinique, recherche sur la philosophie
   pratique de Deleuze' (doctoral thesis, Charles de Gaulle University –
   Lille iii, 2006)
—— *Politique et état chez Deleuze et Guattari. Essai sur le matérialisme historico-
   machinique*, Actuel Marx confrontation (Paris: PUF, 2013) <https://
   doi.org/10.3917/puf.blanc.2013.01>
Sieyès, Emmanuel-Joseph, *Reconnoissance et exposition raisonnée des droits de
   l'homme et du citoyen* (Paris: Chez Baudouin, 1789)
Simondon, Gilbert, *L'Individu et sa genèse physico-biologique* (Paris: PUF,
   1964)
—— *L'Individuation psychique et collective* (Paris: Aubier, 1989)
Skeaff, Christopher, *Becoming Political: Spinoza's Vital Republicanism and
   the Democratic Power of Judgment* (Chicago: University of Chicago
   Press, 2018) <https://doi.org/10.7208/chicago/9780226555508.
   001.0001>
Spinoza, Benedictus de, *The Collected Works of Spinoza*, ed. and trans. by
   Edwin Curley, 2 vols (Princeton, NJ: Princeton University Press, 1985–
   2016)
—— *Spinoza opera*, ed. by Carl Gebhardt, 4 vols (Heidelberg: Winter, 1925)
Staël, Germaine de, *De l'Allemagne*, 2 vols (Paris: Garnier-Flammarion, 1968)
—— *De la littérature* (Paris: Garnier-Flammarion, 1991)

Stavrinaki, Maria, *Saisis par la préhistoire. Enquête sur l'art et le temps des modernes* (Dijon: Les presses du réel, 2019)

Steiner, George, *Martin Heidegger* (Chicago: University of Chicago Press, 1991)

Stengers, Isabelle, *Cosmopolitics*, 2 vols (Minneapolis: University of Minnesota Press, 2010–11), II (2011), 'Book V. In the Name of the Arrow of Time: Prigogine's Challenge', pp. 103–204

—— 'Turtles All the Way Down', in *Power and Invention: Situating Science* (Minneapolis: University of Minnesota Press, 1997)

Stephens, Elizabeth, 'Feminism and New Materialism: The Matter of Fluidity', *Interalia: A Journal of Queer Studies*, 9 (special issue: bodily fluids) (2014), pp. 186–202

Strätling, Susanne, *Hand am Werk: Poetik der Poiesis in der russischen Avantgarde* (Paderborn: Fink, 2018) <https://doi.org/10.30965/9783846760925>

Stögner, Karin, 'Intersektionalität von Ideologien — Antisemitismus, Sexismus und das Verhältnis von Gesellschaft und Natur', *Psychologie & Gesellschaftskritik*, 41.162 (2017), pp. 25–45

Sévérac, Pascal, *Le Devenir actif chez Spinoza* (Paris: Honoré Champion, 2005)

—— *Qu'y a-t-il de matérialiste chez Spinoza?* (Paris: H Diffusion, 2020)

Tosel, André, *Du matérialisme, de Spinoza* (Paris: Kimé, 1994)

—— 'La Finitude positive', in *Spinoza ou l'autre (in)finitude* (Paris: L'Harmattan, 2008), pp. 157–72

Trat, Josette, *Les Cahiers du féminisme (1977–1988): Vingt ans dans le tourbillon du féminisme et de la lutte des classes* (Paris: Syllepse, 2011)

Treusch-Dieter, Gerburg, 'Von der Antinorm zur Norm. Neuere Perspektiven weiblicher Sexualität', in *Von der sexuellen Rebellion zur Gen- und Reproduktionstechnologie* (Tübingen: Gehrke, 1990), pp. 140–67

Tschurenev, Jana, 'Review of "Material Feminisms" by Susan Hekman and Stacy Alaimo', *Das Argument*, 52.287 (2010), pp. 414–16

Van Puymbroeck, Birgit, and N. Katherine Hayles, '"Enwebbed Complexities": The Posthumanities, Digital Media and New Feminist Materialism', *DiGeSt: Journal of Diversity and Gender Studies*, 2.1–2 (2015), pp. 21–29 <https://doi.org/10.11116/jdivegendstud.2.1-2.0021>

Vardoulakis, Dimitris, *Spinoza, the Epicurean — Authority and Utility in Materialism* (Edinburgh: Edinburgh University Press, 2020)

Varikas, Eleni, Nicole Gabriel, and Sonia Dayan-Herzbrun, eds, *Adorno critique de la domination. Une lecture féministe* (= *Tumultes*, 23 (2004))

Vileisis, Danga, 'Marx' frühe, utilitaristische Auffassung des Kommunismus', in *Marx, Engels und utopische Sozialisten (Marx-Engels-Jahrbuch. Neue Folge, 2016/17)*, ed. by Carl-Erich Vollgraf, Richard Sperl, and Rolf Hecker (Hamburg: Argument, 2010), pp. 9–38

—— 'Der unbekannte Beitrag Adam Fergusons zum Geschichtsverständnis von Karl Marx', in *Quellen- und Kapital-Interpretation. Manifest-*

Rezeption. Erinnerungen (Marx-Engels-Jahrbuch. Neue Folge, 2009), ed. by Carl-Erich Vollgraf, Richard Sperl, and Rolf Hecker (Hamburg: Argument, 2010), pp. 7–60

Vinciguerra, Lorenzo, *Spinoza et le signe. La Genèse de l'imagination* (Paris: Vrin, 2005)

Visentin, Stefano, 'From Security to Peace and Concord: The Building of a Free Commonwealth in Spinoza's Political Treatise', *Theoria*, 66.2 (2019), pp. 71–90

—— 'A ontologia política de Espinosa na leitura de Antonio Negri', *Cadernos Espinosanos*, 38 (2018), pp. 151–70

—— 'La parzialità dell'universale. La moltitudine nell'imperium aristocraticum', in *Spinoza: individuo e moltitudine*, ed. by Riccardo Caporali, Vittorio Morfino, and Stefano Visentin (Cesena: Il Ponte Vecchio, 2007), pp. 373–90

—— 'Paura delle masse e desiderio dell'uno. Considerazioni sull'ambivalenza della *potentia multitudinis*', in *Storia politica della moltitudine*, ed. by Del Lucchese, pp. 181–98

Voss, Daniela, 'Disparate Politics: Balibar and Simondon', *Australasian Philosophical Review*, 2.1 (2018), pp. 47–53 <https://doi.org/10.1080/24740500.2018.1514966>

Wallon, Henri, *De l'acte à la pensée* (Paris: Flammarion, 1942)

Weiss, Ulrich, 'Emanzipation', ed. by Wolfgang Fritz Haug, *Historisch-Kritisches Wörterbuch des Marxismus*, 15 vols (Hamburg: Argument, 1983–), III (1997), pp. 272–89

Wilholt, Torsten, 'When Realism Made a Difference: The Constitution of Matter and Its Conceptual Enigmas in Late 19th Century Physics', *Studies in History and Philosophy of Science Part B: Studies in History and Philosophy of Modern Physics*, 39.1 (2008), pp. 1–16 <https://doi.org/10.1016/j.shpsb.2007.04.003>

Williams, Caroline, 'Thinking the Political in the Wake of Spinoza: Power, Affect and Imagination in the Ethics', *Contemporary Political Theory*, 6 (2006), pp. 349–69 <https://doi.org/10.1057/palgrave.cpt.9300298>

Windelband, Wilhelm, 'Rectoral Address, Strasbourg, 1894', *History and Theory*, 19.2 (February 1980), pp. 169–85 <https://doi.org/10.2307/2504798>

Winnik, H. Z., 'A Long-Lost and Recently Recovered Letter of Freud', *Israel Annals of Psychiatry*, 13 (1975), pp. 1–5

Wolf, Frieder Otto, 'Karl Marx und die Globalisierung. Die Problematik des "Kommunistischen Manifests" und ihre Perspektiven', *SoWi — das Journal für Geschichte, Politik, Wirtschaft und Kultur*, 28 (1999), pp. 190–98

—— 'Ein Materialismus für das 21. Jahrhundert', in *Kritik und Materialität: im Auftrag der Assoziation für kritische Gesellschaftsforschung*, ed. by Alex Demirović (Münster: Westfälisches Dampfboot, 2008), pp. 41–59

—— *Radikale Philosophie. Aufklärung und Befreiung in der neuen Zeit* (Münster: Westfälisches Dampfboot, 2002)

—— 'Summary of Discussions', in *Rethinking Marx*, ed. by Sakari Hänninen and Leena Paldán (Berlin: Argument, 1984), pp. 52–53

—— 'Die unabschließbare Aufgabe des endlichen Marxismus: Eine materiell verankerte Arbeit des Begriffs ohne Essentialismus oder Reduktionismus', *Con-Textos Kantianos: International Journal of Philosophy*, 2018.5 (2018), pp. 200–17

—— 'Wider die Kategorie der gesellschaftlichen Naturverhältnisse', *Das Argument*, 50.279 (2008), pp. 867–72

Woods, Derek, 'Scale Variance and the Concept of Matter', in *The New Politics of Materialism: History, Philosophy, Science*, ed. by Sarah Ellenzweig and John H. Zammito (Abingdon: Routledge, 2017), pp. 200–24

Woolf, Virginia, *Three Guineas* (London: Hogarth Press, 1938)

Woolgar, Steve, and Javier Lezaun, 'The Wrong Bin Bag: A Turn to Ontology in Science and Technology Studies?', *Social Studies of Science*, 43.3 (2013), pp. 321–40 <https://doi.org/10.1177/0306312713488820>

Yovel, Yirmiyahu, *Spinoza and Other Heretics: The Adventures of Immanence* (Princeton, NJ: Princeton University Press, 1989)

Ypi, Lea, *Global Justice and Avant-Garde Political Agency* (Oxford: Oxford University Press, 2011) <https://doi.org/10.1093/acprof:oso/9780199593873.001.0001>

Ziege, Eva-Maria, 'The Fetish-Character of "Woman": On a Letter from Theodor W. Adorno to Erich Fromm Written in 1937', *Logos*, 2.4 (2003) <http://www.logosjournal.com/issue2.4.pdf>

Zourabichvili, François, *Le Conservatisme paradoxal de Spinoza. Enfance et royauté* (Paris: PUF, 2002) <https://doi.org/10.3917/puf.zoura.2002.01>

—— 'Deleuze et Spinoza', in *Spinoza au xxᵉ siècle*, ed. by Olivier Bloch (Paris: PUF, 1993), pp. 237–46

—— *Deleuze, une philosophie de l'événement* (Paris: PUF, 1994)

—— 'L'Énigme de la multitude libre', in *La Multitude libre. Nouvelles lectures du 'Traité Politique'*, ed. by Chantal Jaquet, Pascal Sévérac, and Ariel Suhamy (Paris: Amsterdam, 2008), pp. 69–80

—— *Le Vocabulaire de Deleuze* (Paris: Ellipses, 2003)

Žižek, Slavoj, *Absolute Recoil: Towards a New Foundation of Dialectical Materialism* (London: Verso: 2014)

—— 'Against the Populist Temptation', *Critical Inquiry*, 32.3 (Spring 2006), pp. 551–74 <https://doi.org/10.1086/505378>

—— *The Ticklish Subject: The Absent Centre of Political Ontology* (London: Verso, 1999)

Notes on the Contributors

Bernardo Bianchi is a research associate at the Centre Marc Bloch, Humboldt University of Berlin. Previously, he was a postdoctoral fellow of the Alexander von Humboldt Foundation and the Coordination for the Improvement of Higher Education Personnel of the Brazilian Government (CAPES) at the Freie Universität Berlin and Goethe-Universität Frankfurt am Main. He recently co-edited the volume *Democracy and Brazil: Collapse and Regression* (2020). His main research interests are Political Philosophy, History of Philosophy, and Contemporary Political Theory.

Chiara Bottici is Professor of Philosophy and Director of Gender Studies at The New School for Social Research and Eugene Lang College (New York). Her research interests include early modern European philosophy, imagination, feminism, and contemporary social and political philosophy. She is the author of *Imaginal Politics: Images beyond Imagination and the Imaginary* (2014), *A Philosophy of Political Myth* (2007), and *Men and States* (2009). Her short stories have appeared in *Il Caffe illustrato* and *L'immaginazione*. Her feminist experimental writing *Per tremiti, forse quattro* was published in 2016.

Alex Demirović is a researcher at Rosa Luxemburg Foundation and visiting professor of Critical Social Theory at the Goethe University Frankfurt. He is the author, among other publications, of *Der nonkonformistische Intellektuelle. Die Entwicklung der Kritischen Theorie zur Frankfurter Schule* (1999). His main subjects of research include state theory, theory of democracy, critical political theory, epistemology, and critical theory.

Émilie Filion-Donato is a doctoral student at the University of Montréal and the Centre for Interdisciplinary Women's and Gender Studies (ZIFG) of the Technical University of Berlin. Her areas of specialization are sociology of science and technology, and epistemology. Her current research focuses on the two following processes within scientific work and the impact they have on the production of knowledge: consensus as a (un)necessary precondition for moving forward in research and the use and misuse of metaphors in models of scientific justification.

Mariana Gainza is a researcher at the Argentinean National Scientific and Technical Research Council (CONICET). She has vast knowledge of political and social philosophies, especially those of Spinoza, Hegel, Marx, and

Althusser. She was one of the founders of the Coloquio Internacional Spinoza (Córdoba, Argentina).

Stefan Hagemann is a doctoral student at the Humboldt University of Berlin with a thesis on the conceptions of reason in early German Idealism. His fields of research are the history of metaphysics, the relation between theoretical and practical reason, and Critical Theory. He has published works on Kant, Hegel, and Friedrich Schlegel.

Christoph F. E. Holzhey is the founding director of the ICI Berlin Institute for Cultural Inquiry, which he has led since 2007. He received a PhD in theoretical physics (1993) and another one in German literature (2001). He has run several projects at the ICI Berlin and (co-)edited several volumes, including *Tension/Spannung* (2010), *Multistable Figures* (2014), *De/Constituting Wholes* (2017), *Re-* (2019), and *Weathering* (2020).

Ericka Marie Itokazu is a professor at the University of Brasília (UnB) and one of the founders of the Spinoza Study Group of the University of São Paulo (USP), as well as coordinator of the Spinoza Studies at the University of Brasília. She holds a PhD in Philosophy and her current research on Modern Philosophy and History of Philosophy focuses on the seventeenth century philosophers, metaphysics, and contemporary resonances of Spinoza's thought.

Marlene Kienberger studied Philosophy, Gender Studies, and Slavistics in Berlin, Saint Petersburg, and Vienna. She is currently working as a manuscript editor. Her research interests lie in (feminist) metaphysics, action theory, and philosophy of the mind. Furthermore, she specializes in the philosophy of the early modern period.

Daniel Liu is a historian of modern life and physical sciences. Since receiving his doctorate in the history of science, medicine, and technology from the University of Wisconsin–Madison, he has been an Andrew W. Mellon Postdoctoral Fellow in Biohumanities at the University of Illinois at Urbana-Champaign, as well as fellow at the Max Planck Institute for the History of Science and the ICI Berlin. His recent article 'The Artificial Cell, the Semipermeable Membrane, and the Life That Never Was, 1864–1901' was published in *Historical Studies in the Natural Sciences*, 45.5.

Marlon Miguel is an FCT — Fundação para a Ciência e a Tecnologia researcher at the Centre for Philosophy of Science of the University of Lisbon (CFCUL) and an affiliated fellow of the ICI Berlin. He holds a double doctorate in philosophy (Federal University of Rio de Janeiro) and fine arts (Université Paris 8). His current research focuses on the intersection between art, contemporary philosophy, and psychiatry.

Vittorio Morfino is Professor of History of Philosophy at the University of Milan-Bicocca, director of the master's course in the Critical Theory of Society, and the Programme Director at the Collège international de philosophie. He is the author of *Il tempo e l'occasione. L'incontro Spinoza Machiavelli* (2002), *Incursioni spinoziste* (2002), *Il tempo della moltitudine* (2005), *Plural Temporality. Transindividuality and the Aleatory between Spinoza and Althusser* (2014), and *Genealogia di un pregiudizio. L'immagine di Spinoza in Germania da Leibniz a Marx* (2016).

Cornelia Möser is a researcher in gender and cultural studies at the French National Centre for Scientific Research (CNRS) in the work group Centre for Sociological and Political Research in Paris (CRESPPA), team GTM (Genre, Travail, Mobilités). She is also a research associate at the Centre Marc Bloch. Her doctoral thesis *Féminismes en traductions. Théories voyageuses et traductions culturelles* was published at the Éditions des archives contemporaines in Paris in 2013. Her current research project '*Penser la sexualité*', analyses sexuality in feminist theory in France, Germany, and the US since the 1960s with regard to narratives of sexual modernity.

Bruno Pace has a transdisciplinary research background, connecting fields such as systems engineering, physics, network and information theory, mathematical biology, biosemiotics, and philosophy. His research interests revolve around complex systems, self-organization, information processing, natural and artificial codes, cognition, the origin of life and agency, evolution, and emergence. He holds a doctorate in computer science from the Bioinformatics department of the Leipzig University.

Catherine Perret is Professor of Aesthetics at the University Paris 8 Saint Denis, and the author of several books on the relationship between aesthetics, philosophy, anthropology, and psychoanalysis. Her most recent book was inspired by Jean Amery's reflections on torture and is entitled *L'Enseignement de la torture* (2013).

Marianna Poyares is a Mellon Foundation Fellow and a doctoral candidate in philosophy at The New School for Social Research. Before moving to New York City, she received her MA in Philosophy from the University of São Paulo. She works on political philosophy, political theory, feminist philosophy, and ethics. Her doctoral research concerns the normative and practical commitments of political solidarity.

Mauricio Rocha is a former professor of philosophy at the Colégio Pedro II and FEBF/ UERJ. Since 2010, he has been a Professor at the Law Department of PUC Rio with a research focus on Politics and Law in Spinoza, Deleuze & Guattari. He is the coordinator of the Spinoza & Philosophy Reading Circle (Rio de Janeiro and Niterói).

Pascal Sévérac (Univ Paris Est Creteil, LIS, F-94010 Creteil, France) is a professor at the Université Paris-Est Créteil. He recently defended his habilitation at the ENS-Lyon, which included his forthcoming book *Puissance de l'enfance. Vygotski avec Spinoza* (Power of Childhood: Vygotsky with Spinoza). Between 2007 and 2013, he coordinated the program 'Le corps et ses affects' (The body and its affects) at the Collège International de Philosophie in Paris. In the same period, he was chief editor of the journal *La Vie des idées*, based at the Collège de France.

Alison Sperling currently holds an International Postdoctoral Initiative (IPODI) Research Fellowship at ZIFG and is an affiliated fellow at the ICI Berlin. She studies twentieth and twenty-first century science and weird fiction, contemporary ecological art, feminist and queer theory, and the Anthropocene.

Facundo Vega is an assistant professor of philosophy at the University Adolfo Ibáñez, Chile. He received his PhD from Cornell University in 2018. Vega is currently completing his first book, titled *Extraordinary Matters: The Political after Martin Heidegger*. His articles have appeared or are forthcoming in, among other venues, *Philosophy Today*, *Cahier de L'Herne*, and *diacritics*. Vega has been a Research Fellow at CONICET as well as at the ICI Berlin.

Stefano Visentin is a senior researcher at the University of Urbino. He is an international reference concerning the analysis of the relation between the metaphysical aspects of Spinoza's work and its implications for the political realm. He has also published several essays on early modern republicanism (*in primis* Machiavelli). His recent research interest is oriented, among other issues, to the relationship between populism and democracy.

Elena Vogman is a visiting professor at the New York University Shanghai. She specializes in the history and theory of cinema with a particular emphasis on forms of visual thinking, practices of montage, and the relations between literature, ethnology, art, and science. She has published *Sinnliches Denken: Eisensteins exzentrische Methode* (2018) and *Dance of Values. Sergei Eisenstein's Capital Project* (2019).

Frieder Otto Wolf is a professor of philosophy at the Free University Berlin (FU Berlin). He has taught at the University of Coimbra and actively participated in European politics, from 1994 to 1999, as a Member of the European Parliament. He is the editor of the Collected Works of Althusser in German and author of, among other publications, *Radikale Philosophie. Philosophische Untersuchungen für Aufklärung und Befreiung* (2002). His research focuses on history of philosophy, political philosophy, Marxism, and politics.

Ayşe Yuva is *maîtresse de conferences* in the philosophy of the nineteenth century at the Université Paris 1 Panthéon-Sorbonne, a visiting fellow at the ICI

Berlin, and associate researcher at the Centre Marc Bloch. Her dissertation, *Transformer le monde? L'efficace de la philosophieen temps de Révolution (1794-1815)* (2016), focused on the political effects of Philosophy in France and Germany at the end of the French revolution. Working from a transnational perspective on French, German, and Turkish philosophy, her work is at the crossroads of the history of philosophy and political philosophy.

Index

Cultural Inquiry

EDITED BY CHRISTOPH F. E. HOLZHEY
AND MANUELE GRAGNOLATI

www.ingramcontent.com/pod-product-compliance
Lightning Source LLC
Chambersburg PA
CBHW030351130626
46549CB00004B/1441